T0369902

Uniquely Okinawan

WORLD WAR II: THE GLOBAL, HUMAN, AND ETHICAL DIMENSION

G. Kurt Piehler, series editor

Uniquely Okinawan

Determining Identity During the U.S. Wartime Occupation

Courtney A. Short

Fordham University Press | New York 2020

Library of Congress Control Number:2019920277

Printed in the United States of America

22 21 0 5 4 3 2 1

First edition

Contents

	Introduction	1
1	**Identifying the Enemy: US Army Wartime Occupation Policy**	21
2	**US Marine Discipline: Strict Directives in Wartime Marine Military Government**	32
3	**"Japanese" Warriors? Okinawan Preparation for Battle**	45
4	**The US Fights Overseas: Americans Charge toward the Battlefield**	51
5	**Having a Say: Okinawan Constructions of Identity**	59
6	**Policy into Action: The US Army Hits the Shore**	74
7	**Benevolent Captors? Okinawans Encounter the Americans**	90
8	**No Initiative: Unbending Policy, Rigid US Marine Action**	102
9	**The US Navy Period: Navigating the Transition to Peace**	124
10	**New Visions, New Interpretations of Identity: The Expansion of US Navy Military Government**	140
	Conclusion	155
	Acknowledgments	163
	Notes	167
	Bibliography	223
	Index	237

Photographs follow page 58

Uniquely Okinawan

Introduction

The bar, Porky's III, occupied the lower level of a high-rise building located at the end of a sloping multilane road in an urban neighborhood on Okinawa. Despite the buzz of daytime traffic in the area, the street lay dormant and unwelcoming in the dark. No cars. No people. No lights. Only the bar's neon sign, with its English words, cast a soft pink glow around its door.

In 2006, my husband and I lived in an apartment at the top of that sloped road. The night we discovered Porky's III, we had intended to explore some local restaurants and bars within walking distance of our home. Some places, like The Alligator, decorated with military patches on the walls and with an English-speaking owner, catered to a crowd that looked American like us. Others, like a second-floor local karaoke bar, gave us a cool greeting and made it known through searing glances and curt service that we did not belong. We left both bars and found ourselves walking down that sloped road, away from the island's shore and into a darker and more desolate part of the city.

For some time, we stood in front of the door to Porky's III debating what to do. Made conscious of our status as strangers on this island by the patrons of the karaoke bar, we had become wary of imposing on any experience strictly reserved for the Okinawans. Our apartment was located quite some distance away from any US military installation, and we had now roamed even farther into neighborhoods on the island that seldom saw American faces.

The street we were now on, though, offered no other nighttime entertainment options. We had already walked that far, we reasoned, and we had wanted our evening to involve something different, something "authentic," something other than such things as the on-base Chili's Grill & Bar and the off-base McDonald's. Curious, we walked in.

Porky's III bustled with energy. Enthusiastic waiters and waitresses dressed in leather jackets and poodle skirts hopped between circular tables scattered throughout the room. American movie posters, some of films produced in the 1950s and others made in the 1980s about the 1950s, covered the walls. Small mounted televisions playing these movies reinforced the references. The bar had karaoke, too; an older man seated at a table in the corner was soulfully singing Elvis's "Suspicious Minds."

With a big smile and welcoming hand gestures, a young employee near the front door urged us to sit. Orion beers in our hands, we watched in amazement as the staff began to cheer and jump down the aisles between the tables. They headed toward guitars, microphones, and a drum kit assembled at the far end of the room. The rolling beats of the surf-rock instrumental "Wipeout" urged the crowd forward to dance.

Porky's III embraced an interpretation of American culture unfamiliar to us. Aiming to recreate 1950s America, the bar melded together both accurate images of the era and pop-cultural misinterpretation in a way that stood apart even from mainland Japan's embrace of the sock hop. Black-and-white photos of smiling American girls in tea-length skirts shared space on the walls next to posters from the entire Porky's franchise, a series of raunchy 1980s films that portrayed 1950s America as a time of widespread bawdy, inappropriate behavior. Even the sock-hop music at times morphed into something entirely new as it carried distinctly Okinawan melodies and lyrics. Unlike The Alligator, Porky's III did not recreate a familiar representation of American culture to attract a foreign crowd; its theme belonged entirely to the Okinawans, created by them and for their entertainment and enjoyment.

Its quaint existence as a local bar deceptively hid the larger narrative to which it belonged. Since April 1, 1945, when Okinawa became a contested World War II battleground, the population had contended with the persistent pull of two strong, influencing countries—the United States and Japan. During the war and afterward, Okinawans faced the grueling challenge of constructing their own identity in a manner that would afford them relative safety and advantage while caught between two battling foes. In 2006, Porky's III stood as another example of the continuing dialogue about race, ethnicity, and identity on the island. Within the distinct design of the bar, the Okinawans consciously constructed their own place among the competing cultures. Porky's III, neither a Japanese nor an American bar, became a reinvented space where the Okinawans asserted their own unique influence.

The Battle of Okinawa introduced the Okinawans living on the island to the violence and destitution of World War II, but the Americans and Japanese had been engaged in heavy and brutal combat against each other since 1941. The attack on the US naval base of Pearl Harbor on December 7, 1941, formally catapulted America into a world war involving battlefields in a number of countries and across multiple oceans. Despite heightened tension in diplomatic relations between the United States and Japan in the 1930s, the raid on the Hawaiian base on Oahu shocked the American public and dislodged any hopes many had held of remaining isolated from the wars brewing in Europe and Asia.[1]

Japan, which had been allied with Great Britain, France, and the United States during World War I, initially continued its cooperation with the Western powers in the years immediately following the Great War. At the Washington Conference in 1922, the Japanese signed a disarmament treaty that limited shipbuilding and prevented any construction of additional military fortifications and bases on islands throughout the Pacific. Toward other East Asian nations, however, Japan embarked on campaigns of colonization and subjugation. Taiwan and Korea were annexed into the Japanese empire as early as, respectively, 1895 (a result of the Sino-Japanese War) and 1910 (when the protectorate of 1905 became annexed). In 1931, the Japanese-led Kanto Army forcibly took over Manchuria. In 1940, Japan's government launched an initiative, the Greater East Asia Co-Prosperity Sphere, which urged the unity of Asia under Asian self-determination while simultaneously suppressing other nations under claims of Japanese racial superiority. Western powers, concerned with trade and the security of their own Asian colonial possessions and military bases, grew alarmed by Japan's advance throughout the region. For the United States, Japanese expansion placed the American-owned Philippines in an uncertain position, compromised the movement of raw materials from Southeast Asia to America, and directly countered the growth of a united China—a country already serving US interests through trade and that Americans believed held promise as the next great Asian power. As early as the 1924 Asian Exclusion Act, the United States was restricting Japanese immigration, and, by the summer of 1941, its government had imposed an oil embargo. As Western resistance to Japanese expansion intensified, Japan's desire to hold an equal international position among its former World War I allies waned. Instead, the Japanese turned their focus toward Asian dominance and concerned themselves with contesting the Western nations that held interests throughout the Pacific.[2]

At the onset of hostilities, Japan initially stood as a formidable foe, one with tactical skill earned through their previous campaigns in China and intelligent military leaders, such as Admiral Isoroku Yamamoto, General Hideki Tojo, and Admiral Osami Nagano. In quick succession, Japan followed the Pearl Harbor strike with attacks on US, British, and Dutch possessions in Singapore, the Philippines, Borneo, and Java. By 1942, the Japanese fought at sea and on land in the Pacific, aiming for Port Moresby, New Guinea, and the American fleet at Midway. The attacks aligned with Japan's strategy to exert control throughout the region by establishing a defensive perimeter to protect its main islands. Japan extended its influence from the Kurile Islands south to Wake, the Gilbert Islands, and New Britain and west toward New Guinea and onward to Sumatra, Malaya, and Burma. Within this perimeter, Japanese soldiers occupied every island chain, including the Marianas, the Carolines, the Marshalls, and the Solomons. This expansive area of mostly water spanned 2,561 nautical miles from Japan to New Guinea and 3,408 nautical miles from the coast of China to Wake.[3]

In an attempt to slow the swift operational successes of the Japanese drive and unify the many nations that were defending their Pacific possessions, the Allies established American-British-Dutch-Australian Command (ABDACOM) under the British general Archibald Wavell. The nations, however, worked at counter objectives. With air, ground, and naval forces each commanded by a senior leader from a different country, a collective goal failed to materialize. Disputes between the Dutch and British intensified over the defense of the Dutch East Indies, and ABDACOM splintered. Wavell gave up command after the fall of Singapore and Bali, and after that, British and American air units no longer belonged to ABDACOM. The now Dutch command dissolved as their East Indies possessions fell.[4]

The failure of ABDACOM created an opening for the United States to take control of Allied operations in the Pacific. The British would play a role in India and Burma, and Australia was managing its own defense, but the United States, in the interests of efficiency, retained primary responsibility. Moving forward, successes at sea and on land at the battles of Midway, Coral Sea, and Guadalcanal reduced Japan's naval power, broke the myth of Japanese invincibility, and put the island nation on the defensive. By 1943, the US military continued its offensive by embarking on a multiservice island campaign featuring two simultaneous approaches—one north/northwest along the southwest Pacific, led by the US Army under General Douglas MacArthur, and one west in the central Pacific, led by the US Navy under Admiral Chester Nimitz. American forces progressed north, northwest, and west toward Japan by selectively assaulting islands that had the greatest strategic value and bypassing those that lacked Japanese troops or that could simply be cut off from Japanese reinforcement and resupply. Captured islands served as refit outposts and staging bases for further operations. The campaign demonstrated immense American industrial and military power. Throughout the war, the United States produced approximately

297,000 aircraft, 2.3 million military trucks, 86,000 tanks, 87,000 landing craft, and 8,800 naval vessels, including aircraft carriers, battleships, and submarines. Supported by the strength of its production and a mobilization effort that brought 16 million Americans into service across all theaters of war, the United States fought in the air, on land, and at sea with a large and capable military. Operations in the Pacific, a theater made up mostly of sprawling ocean dotted with small islands thick with vegetation, called for the innovative use of aircraft and vessels in amphibious campaigns, naval battles, and jungle land warfare. Naval bombardments coupled with amphibious landings secured far-flung islands such as Tarawa, Eniwetok, and Saipan and allowed US air forces to move within 1,220 nautical miles of the home islands—a distance the B-29 had the capability to complete. Under MacArthur in the southwest Pacific, the US Army, along with Australian forces, executed several operations along the northern coast of New Guinea and onward to the Philippines that secured routes of supply, captured airfields, and led to the establishment of a major refit outpost.[5]

Since April 1943, when the Joint US Strategic Committee produced a comprehensive plan for the defeat of Japan, the United States recognized the necessity of an attack—by air and, possibly, by land—on Japan's home islands. Soldiers, sailors, and Marines fought hard along the two simultaneous drives to narrow the distance between Allied ports and resources and Japan proper. Okinawa, the primary and largest island in the Ryukyu Archipelago, sat only 360 nautical miles from Kyushu, the southernmost home island. In preparation for an invasion of Japan proper, Okinawa would serve as a staging area and supply depot; possession of the island would give the Americans the necessary proximity to their intended target both for invasion and bombing, the latter already made possible by operations in the Marianas. Given the earlier prolonged battles in the Philippines and at Guadalcanal in 1942 and the subsequent grueling island-warfare campaigns that followed through 1944 into 1945, the Americans expected the troops landing on Okinawa to struggle through a bitter, bloody engagement against an enemy that had proven its tenacity to fight and unwillingness to surrender. The Americans feared the intense banzai charge, the deeply dug defenses, and close combat fought at bayonet point. Okinawa's location at the threshold of the Japanese mainland convinced US military leadership that the experience on Okinawa would showcase a Japanese soldier with an even more elevated commitment to engaging in combat. With their home islands threatened, the Japanese would act with even fiercer dedication to Japan's defense.[6]

The Battle of Okinawa, named Operation Iceberg, began with offshore aerial and naval bombardments from the Fifth Fleet's Task Force 58 in March 1945 on the Kerama Islands, located sixteen nautical miles from the island of Okinawa. Along with minesweepers working around Kerama and the southwestern shore of Okinawa, the artillery attempted to disable enemy antiaircraft fire, gun positions, and defensive beach installations. Hagushi Beach, located on the western side of Okinawa between Nago and the Motobu Peninsula to the north and the port city of Naha to the south, would serve as the landing beach for the April 1 assault by the Tenth Army, a joint force of both US Army and Marine divisions commanded by Lieutenant General Simon Bolivar Buckner Jr. The Tenth Army consisted of the III Amphibious Corps, under Major General Roy S. Geiger, with the 1st, 2nd, and 6th Marine divisions, and the XXIV Corps, under Major General John Hodge, with the 7th, 27th, 77th, and 96th infantry divisions.[7]

Buckner was well aware of the possible impact of US interservice rivalry on the effectiveness of the invasion. In 1944, he served as the appointed head of the investigating committee that reviewed the removal from command of Major General Ralph Smith, 27th Infantry Division, by Lieutenant General Holland Smith, V Amphibious Corps, on Saipan. Buckner's investigative duties gave him access to details he would not have otherwise known; his inquiry uncovered an unsettling ugliness to the conflict between the services. Throughout the Pacific War, tension between the US Army, Navy, and Marines had plagued operations. Information and intelligence stalled within one service branch without passing to the others. Army troops bitterly jockeyed for Navy resources within an ocean-based theater, and, despite providing sound military advantages, the strategic twin drives of the Army and Navy became beacons of disagreement and symbolic lines of defiance against the other rival service. Real differences in tactics and logistics between the services caused further frustration as leaders wrestled with divergent approaches, often reluctant to modify their own systems. Rather than cooperate, the Army, Navy, and Marines bypassed one another out of competition, partiality, and aggravation. By the spring of 1945, Buckner had little desire to fuel the interservice conflict, which he deemed toxic and contrary to effective military accomplishment. His intricate knowledge of the command controversy on Saipan and his awareness that the unit it concerned—the 27th Infantry Division—now resided under his care gave Buckner strong convictions about rectifying the issue. As commander of the Tenth Army, a joint force postured to conduct a military operation demonstrative of long-sought-after cooperation, Buckner saw an opportunity to move forward with a cohesive American fighting force. Fortunately, he found a combat-proven leader in his senior-ranking Marine commander;

Geiger had displayed skill in fostering positive Marine-Army relations in 1944 at Guam. At least from the highest ranks of the Tenth Army, Buckner had the right leaders in place to help assuage the damage of interservice rivalry. The lower-ranking soldiers and Marines of the Tenth Army, however, arrived to the unit with predisposed ideas about the ineffectiveness of their sister service, which they had gained from their experiences in previous campaigns or from the widespread derogatory banter forming part of their respective service cultures. The division commanders within the Tenth Army reinforced these cynical views. Buckner would also find little support from his fellow Army general officers, most notably MacArthur.[8]

The Tenth Army landed on a silent Hagushi Beach on April 1; at first, the Japanese did not stage much resistance against the American landing force. The United States had executed many successful operations, which by 1945 saw American forces sitting as far north as the Philippines and the Mariana Islands. But these operations had also offered lessons to the battered Japanese on effective tactics. The Japanese deliberately avoided punishment by US shore bombardments by positioning themselves within the interior of the island, so as to draw the invading forces into areas of concentrated firepower deeper inland. On Okinawa, natural limestone cave formations, untouched by the relentless bombardments, provided protection as well as firepower positions. As the Americans landed with assumed ease, the Japanese laid in wait along heavily constructed defensive lines in the south—the main fortifications ran along the Uraseo-Mura escarpment and the Naha-Shuri-Yonabaru line—as well as in multiple forward-positioned outposts.[9]

Operation Iceberg called for the 1st and 6th Marine divisions to secure central Okinawa, with the 6th Marine Division turning north and assaulting through the Motobu Peninsula and on to Hedo Point. The 7th and 96th infantry divisions had orders to turn south. Beyond the beachhead, the Americans continued, to their surprise, to encounter only negligible enemy confrontation throughout the early days of April. The 1st Marine Division arrived on the eastern side of Okinawa by April 4 and secured the central portion of the island relatively effortlessly. By April 6, the 6th Marine Division secured Nago, and while the Marines did eventually confront an established enemy that bore down on them from high ground on the Motobu Peninsula, the Americans dominated the area by midmonth. Success in the north caused Buckner to accelerate the Marine advance; the Marines, therefore, moved simultaneously with Army operations to the south, despite initial plans that had called for the completed seizure of the south before full actions in the north.[10]

The Army divisions, charging toward the south and thus directly toward the Japanese defensive lines, hit enemy troops, who fought with an expected but still brutal aggression, much sooner than their Marine counterparts. As early as April 3, along Futenma to the west and Kuba to the east, approximately four miles in front of the first defensive line at Urasoe-Mura, the Army faced a few hundred soldiers occupying outposts. The Japanese pounded the American soldiers with machine gun fire, mortars, and hand grenades and then moved in to close fighting. Pushing past the outposts, the Army hit the first major defensive obstacle at Machinato-Kakazu, a sloped area fortified with minefields, barbed wire, and antitank ditches that overlooked American movements. American soldiers found themselves embroiled in a fight against a well-protected and well-placed enemy; movement stalled, and casualties rose steeply. Slipping on ground made up of an unstable and grisly mixture of mud, blood, and freshly dismantled bodies and squinting through blinding streams of fire and driving rain, the soldiers slogged up hills and cliffs, exposed to dug-in Japanese defenders.[11]

The US Army finally broke Japanese resistance on Kakazu Ridge by April 24 but then faced two more defensive lines that further protected General Ushijima Mitsuru's 32nd Army headquarters, situated at Shuri Castle. Recognizing the difficulty encountered in the south, Buckner moved the 1st and 6th Marine divisions and brought in the 27th and 77th infantry divisions into the fight to the south. Building off of their defensive success, the Japanese launched a counterattack on May 4, which the Americans forced back the next day. By May 6, the Japanese had moved all of their forces up along the Naha-Shuri-Yonabaru line. The month of May witnessed gruesome, hard fighting over land defended fiercely by the Japanese and assaulted relentlessly by the Americans. Under severe driving rains that pooled into small lakes and churned dirt into glutinous mud, the Americans used flamethrowers, tanks, and artillery against the intricate defensive cave system of the Japanese, woven within looming hills and ridges, in attacks that at times culminated in bayonet confrontations. By month's end, the Japanese 32nd Army abandoned its positions and retreated south from the Shuri line. On May 29, the Marines climbed over the rubble that remained of Shuri Castle, the historic royal structure that had not only protected the Japanese headquarters a few days before but had also housed the government of the old Ryukyu Kingdom from 1429 to 1879. Throughout June, the Americans pushed further south until the Japanese 32nd Army fell apart; June 21 marked the end of the battle.[12]

Amid the scorching flamethrowers, flights of bullets, and concussions of mortars, half a million Okinawan civilians scurried through the thick mud and unrelenting rain, looking for shelter, food, and a chance at survival.

Okinawa was different from all the other islands that the Americans had landed on in the Pacific theater; it was a prefecture of Japan, and its residents were considered subjects of the emperor. The Okinawan people, however, had suffered from long-term discrimination at the hands of the Japanese. A long and complicated history of unequal relations with Japan set the conditions for treatment that denied the Okinawans full rights as subjects.[13]

In the centuries before the invasive arrival of the Japanese in 1609, during the early Tokugawa shogunate (1603–1868), Okinawa enjoyed independence as its own kingdom. Seated in the magnificent Shuri Castle, the queens and kings of the Ryukyu Islands had established a country that maintained relative peace and traded smoothly with neighboring Korea, China, and Japan. Sho Shin, the ruler from 1477 to 1526, avoided conquest and conflict with other nations and instead focused on the internal improvement of his kingdom. Shin brought art, music, and public parks to his people; maintained positive relations with China as a tributary nation; and established an enduring, stable economic system. While some aspects of Okinawan life reflected foreign influences introduced through trade, Shin's government fostered the development of unique Okinawan ceremonies, a distinctive language used in poems and stories that celebrated Ryukyuan history, and original handcrafted luxury goods made of silk and lacquer. The court also banned the feudal Japanese practice of *junshi*—suicide committed in allegiance to a lord.[14]

During Sho Shin's reign, instability in Japan caused by warring factions and social turmoil (the Sengoku "Warring States" period) threatened not only the Ryukyus but Korea and China as well. As Toyotomi Hideyoshi gained control over Japan in the late sixteenth century, he made plans to expand forcibly into Korea and China. Okinawa, maintaining peace and autonomy as a tributary of China for centuries, refused Japan's overtures for military assistance and shunned Hideyoshi's demands for men and supplies. Following the end of Hideyoshi's campaign into Korea (1598) and the rise of Tokugawa Ieyasu (1603), the Ryukyuan king Sho Nei (1589–1620) continued to refuse diplomatic advances from Japan in favor of maintaining Chinese loyalties. No longer distracted by the campaigns in other Asian nations under Hideyoshi, the Satsuma clan under Ieyasu in the Tokugawa period (1603–1868) greeted this perceived insubordination with an invasion of the island kingdom by three thousand skilled samurai warriors in 1609. Despite a desperate defense staged by the Okinawans, the Japanese easily subdued the Ryukyu Kingdom, took over Shuri Castle, and captured Sho Nei and his court. The king lived in exile in Edo (present-day Tokyo) for two years, and Japanese advisors took control of all trade, funneled any revenue toward Japan, and collected a high annual tribute. Although the Satsuma clan increased its control over Okinawa, Sho Nei, seen as a foreign dignitary with perceived origins from a line of warriors, received privileged treatment from the shogun during his time in Edo.[15]

The Japanese interest in the Ryukyu Islands lay with economic gain, not territorial or political growth. The Satsuma clan thus established practices that diverted all trade to them in an exclusive monopoly and defined an economic structure that gave the shogunate firm control of monetary gains. However, the lack of Japanese interest in fully incorporating the kingdom into the home islands' political life gave Okinawa a reprieve from colonialization and allowed the kingdom to retain many of its traditions and a semblance of autonomous governance. By 1611, with the consolidation of shogunate power in Edo, Sho Nei and his ministers returned to Shuri, where he resumed his position as king. While the influence of the Satsuma clan and the subsequent subordination to Japan did affect Okinawa, the kingdom still enjoyed a satisfactory autonomy under the new arrangement.[16]

The Meiji Restoration of 1868, however, ended the long-standing Tokugawa feudal system and replaced it with centralized political power under the emperor. The resignation of the shogun required the redesign of feudal power structures and government positions throughout Japan. In the early 1870s, powerful clan leaders stepped down, and feudal land designations were dismantled. The end of the Ryukyu Kingdom, therefore, coincided with the political reorganization of Japan as a nation-state. The last Ryukyuan royal, King Sho Tai, quietly relinquished the kingdom and his throne in 1879, and the islands, the last territory of Japan to transition, took on the new name and organization of Okinawa Prefecture. As the king and his family left Shuri Castle in late March, the people of Okinawa grieved the end of royalty. Despite the sadness, however, the kingdom ended peacefully. For hundreds of years, Okinawa had existed with relative tranquility under the direction of Japan. The people had retained their own traditions yet also learned Japanese ways. The peasants lived in humble but not destitute conditions, and the ruling classes lived dignified lives esteemed by the Satsuma clan, despite their subordination to Japan and the suspension of some of the privileges they had previously enjoyed before 1609. The end of the Ryukyu Kingdom and the incorporation of the islands into the fabric of Japanese political and social life thus did not cause a major adjustment for the Okinawans, who had lived under Japanese rule for 270 years.[17]

Through the imposition of Japanese laws under their new status as a prefecture, Okinawans adopted Japanese fashion and modified their names in the Japanese style. Okinawa as a whole, however, remained excluded from Japanese society. Cultural differences and practices stemming from the Okinawans' ethnically Ryukyuan heritage offended the ruling Japanese. Certain aspects of customary Okinawan life, such as the eating of pigs and the wearing of tattoos, appalled the Japanese. Rural regions retained a more humble, traditional lifestyle, which Japan viewed as dirty, ignorant, and representative of individual incompetence. Japan sent its own officials to Okinawa to oversee political life and education; they limited the school curriculum by terminating higher-education classes in subjects such as English and seized political offices. Despite their status as subjects of the emperor, Okinawans suffered discrimination both at home and on Japan's home islands, where they had trouble securing employment or housing. The government of Japan imposed heavier military burdens on the Okinawans by conscripting a disproportionate number of them into military service as compared to subjects of other prefectures.[18]

Okinawa's relationship with Japan over the centuries thus developed along a different trajectory, unlike other Asian countries in the region that Japan would forcibly subjugate in the late nineteenth and early twentieth centuries. Ethnically, Okinawans were Ryukyuan and not of Japanese blood, a difference that led to the relegation of Okinawa to a less desirable and secondary position in politics and social construction. The ease of dismantling the Ryukyuan Kingdom, however, meant that Japan never treated Okinawa as a colony or its people as the conquered; the Okinawan population experienced the transition from an independent kingdom to one under the influence of Japan and then to a Japanese prefecture with relative ease and comparative inclusion. This key distinction meant that by the end of the nineteenth century, Okinawans considered themselves subjects of the emperor and a part of the Japanese nation-state despite the prejudices and disadvantages the Japanese government expressed toward them. At the same time, however, Okinawans remained aware of their second-class status and harbored a certain amount of bitterness toward Japan.[19]

When Brigadier General William E. Crist, the Tenth Army's deputy commander for military government, identified in May the problem of discerning the loyalty of the Okinawan population as "the most vital question" in planning military government and operations on Okinawa, he had witnessed almost forty-five days of armed conflict on the island. Throughout the Pacific theater, wartime occupation received little attention from operational military planners. US occupation policy generally focused on removing civilians from the battlefield by corralling them into encampments. While the use of military government camps still provided the foundation for occupation policies on Okinawa, the size of the Okinawan population posed a new challenge for the American military in the Pacific. Numbering approximately 463,000, the people of Okinawa, whose route of flight caused them to intermingle with Japan's military, significantly affected operations and forced the Americans to deal with the pervasive integration on the battlefield of noncombatant children, families, and the elderly. Crist recognized the complications posed by the population and correctly assessed that a complete analysis of the potential effects of civilian refugees on combat and military government operations stood as a crucial step in the planning of Operation Iceberg—one that if miscalculated could result in the failure of the invasion.[20]

Race and ethnicity lay at the center of this analysis.[21] Crist correctly noted the large size of the population and the close yet strained association between the Okinawans and Japan and assessed how fundamental an educated understanding of the ethnic and racial dynamics would be to conducting military operations of any type on the island of Okinawa. Gauging the reaction of the population to a foreign invasion held paramount importance to the success of the mission. As Japanese subjects, the Okinawans could significantly increase the size of the enemy force by fighting. The people's bitterness toward Japan, however, could inspire them to see the Americans as liberators. The safety and security of the American troops depended on a sophisticated attempt at determining the allegiance and identity of the Okinawans.[22] Only by comprehending the complex ethnic, racial, and historical background of the Okinawans in relation to Japan could American planners make informed decisions about military government practices and the proper employment of troops. Crist's observations reflect the open, analytical role of race and identity in military decision making. Neither practical military considerations nor deliberations on race could accurately inform military policy alone.

Within the greater context of the war with Japan, Crist's comment about the importance of decoding the Okinawans' sense of identity when conducting military planning points to an issue of intellectual discourse among scholars of the Pacific War. Noting the brutality of the combat between Japan and the United States, historians have dissected the relations between the two nations and the possible role of racism in shaping the nature of the fighting. The violent entry of the United States into World War II at Pearl Harbor generated fear toward the Japanese that translated into the internment of Japanese Americans and their exclusion from employment and housing opportunities throughout the United States. American prejudice toward Asians both in America and abroad had already existed in the centuries before the attack at Pearl Harbor, ranging from ill feelings toward Chinese laborers in the nineteenth century to exclusionary immigration policies toward both Japan and China that predated the outbreak of World War II. Throughout the war, Americans believed in the inherent and biological inferiority of Asians, and such an attitude led to displays of unrest between Asian and white Americans in public spaces, from physical and verbal confrontations to passive racist graffiti to the denial of access to community resources. Despite a political position that favored China and government-sponsored propaganda aimed at building a pro-China American public, Americans still held discriminatory attitudes toward all Asians. John Dower's *War without Mercy: Race and Power in the Pacific War* argues that negative racial feelings drove policy makers and individual actors within the military to interact with the Japanese in a darker, more vicious manner that pushed the boundaries of acceptable violence in war. Craig Cameron followed Dower's influential work by examining the details of one unit's actions on Okinawa in *American Samurai: Myth, Imagination, and the Conduct of Battle in the First Marine Division, 1941–1951.* Cameron reinforces Dower's thesis that racism defined action by depicting gruesome deeds the American military committed against its enemy and arguing that negative racial stereotypes served as the primary motivator. John Lynn, however, counters both Cameron and Dower in his work *Battle: A History of Combat and Culture.* Lynn asserts that military organizations shape policy and strategy around practical military considerations such as troop strength, resource allocation, and enemy disposition. According to Lynn, military leaders make balanced tactical and strategic decisions based on mission needs, not fueled by irrational, emotionally charged racism.[23]

The actions of the military planners for the invasion of Okinawa, both in the US Army and the Marine Corps, complicate the arguments of Dower, Cameron, and Lynn. While not disregarding the importance of calculating the strength of supply lines that stretched from the Pacific back to the United States or the dynamics of terrain on the tactics employed, military leaders embraced what Crist promoted—complex, educated, sophisticated, mindful consideration of identity, race, and ethnicity during planning and execution of the mission. Military planners acknowledged culture and ethnicity from a stance of balanced evaluation meant to inform objective military decisions; they did not use impassioned racist sentiments to drive action and provide an excuse for wanton violence.

This study looks at the US Army, Marines, and Navy as each service planned and carried out wartime occupation duties on Okinawa. This work also examines the Okinawan people as involved actors rather than as hapless victims subjected to a great trauma inflicted upon them by the various branches of the armed forces. Okinawans actively contributed to their experience and played a role in the outcome of their plight. Beginning with American planning in Washington, DC, Hawaii, and California as well as with pre-battle positioning by the Japanese on Okinawa and through to the disarmament of American troops in 1946, both the Americans and Okinawans consciously examined identity as they devised ways to survive and later establish an environment that supported long-term stability and, in the case of the Americans, adherence with international priorities.

Under the direction of Crist, the Army spearheaded the preparation for Tenth Army military government operations and developed a document, called the GOPER, which provided a general plan for military governance.[24] The GOPER offered little guidance on how to treat the civilians and instead gave the subordinate commanders the authority to run a military government within the parameters of how they perceived the situation. Planners acknowledged that they could not accurately predict the reaction of the Okinawans to the American invasion and therefore urged the US soldiers to approach the civilians with caution. Through training, the soldiers understood the complexity of Okinawa's relationship with Japan. Full awareness of the uncertainty of Okinawan loyalty to Japan allowed the soldiers to reassess the intentions of the people based on what they encountered on the island. As a result, the Army loosened restrictions within military government camps when the Okinawans demonstrated their obedience and cooperation with US regulations.

The Marines also examined the complex historical and political relationship between Japan and Okinawa through intelligence studies and reached the same conclusion as the Army in regards to the uncertainty of the Okinawans' loyalty. Like the Army, the Marine planners could not determine with confidence whether the population would fight in support of the Japanese emperor or feel liberated by the American forces. Unlike the Army, however, the Marines gave little priority to such studies. Lacking a high-ranking officer to oversee the development of military government plans, the Marines assigned the duty as an ancillary task to a logistics colonel. Marine officers trained at the Civil Affairs schools did not receive permission to attend planning meetings. While the military government plan produced by the Marines, called Annex "Able," copied the GOPER in many ways, Marine leaders added unambiguous statements that identified the Okinawans as Japanese and therefore as the enemy. As the Marines landed, they considered the population unwaveringly hostile and upheld their military government policy, which dictated harsh treatment of enemy civilians.

The Okinawans, uprooted by the impact of the battle, suffered from dislocation and loss. They did not, however, experience the ordeal passively. Instead, the civilians fought hard for their survival and used their identity as a means to secure safety and fair treatment. Japanese indoctrination had sought to align the Okinawans with Japan despite relegating them to a secondary status. The propaganda program had met relative success; before the battle, most Okinawans did associate themselves with Japan. The horrific conditions of war, however, combined with cruel acts inflicted upon the population by the Japanese Army, shocked the people and made them reevaluate their loyalties. Realigning their sense of self with Okinawa rather than Japan served the practical purpose of providing them protection and improved conditions under US military government programs by disassociating themselves with the enemy; it also allowed the people to grapple with the mental anguish caused by the betrayals of the Japanese. The ability of the people to determine their own identity consciously demonstrates the malleability of race and ethnicity and also lends a better understanding to the US military government's observations of the behavior of the population.

Following the surrender of Japan, the US Navy assumed responsibility for military government on Okinawa. It inherited a dislocated population suffering from the impact of war and with urgent needs for medical assistance, food, clothing, shelter, and family reunification. Unprepared partly because of the immediacy of the situation and partly because of the exodus of qualified seamen whose war commitments had expired, the US Navy spent the first months issuing ad hoc orders that reached the field officers at the camps too slowly. Innovative and motivated young officers worked hard to convince their unimaginative superiors that the solution to the ineffectiveness of naval military government lay with granting the Okinawans greater leadership in the development of their community. The transition toward peace erased the imperative wartime necessity of locating the enemy within the chaos of battle and thus eliminated the last remnants of fear felt by the American military toward Okinawans as possible combatants. As a result, the relationship between the sailors and the Okinawans improved, and eventually higher leadership published directives that reinforced the ideas of the young officers. Okinawan leadership not only eased the burden of running military government for the dwindling American forces but also allowed the creation of a government structure that sat on a foundation of culturally familiar practices. The US Navy now saw the Okinawans as a culturally progressing and capable people unique in their own ethnicity.

The US military's efforts to decipher the culture, history, and ethnic background of the Okinawans did not derive from warm feelings of cultural sensitivity and enlightened acceptance of Asians as equals. On the contrary, in alignment with the thoughts of the American population at home, planners and executors of all services held firm racist beliefs toward all Asians. Rarely did those involved with the Okinawan operation, both in combat and military government, harbor radically progressive sentiments of racial equality out of sync with the social reality of the United States in the 1940s. Concerted efforts to study the Okinawans as a people grew from a wartime necessity to fully understand the enemy so as to bring defeat. Policy deriving from information gathered as a part of cultural studies held the sole purpose of contributing to Allied victory; in no way did the US military's handling of Okinawa intend for in-depth cultural studies to lead to profound reforms to promote social equality. Most American planners and executors retained derogatory opinions about the island's population while simultaneously crafting policy that innovatively assessed identity and painstakingly evaluated and defined the capability of the population. Cultural awareness, consideration, comprehension, and understanding did not equate to cultural sensitivity. Work done to distinguish cultural characteristics unique to the Okinawans was done to protect the integrity and success of the military mission and that of the American soldiers, Marines, and sailors; the planners of Okinawan operations valued American lives and strategic objectives above all else. No one stood as a greater example of the dichotomy of holding racist thoughts while also devoting resources to the nuanced study of a group considered inferior than Buckner himself. Buckner viewed the Okinawans as unworthy, lesser humans, yet he endorsed and ordered policy that hinged on the importance of gaining an understanding of the defining aspects of the very people he viewed as unsavory.[25]

Just as widely accepted racism toward Asian populations did not correlate directly to disadvantageous, discriminatory, or brutal policy, destruction of property, artifacts, and lands on Okinawa during the battle did not signify a grotesque hatred toward the population. Military orders directed the preservation of the Okinawan environment to the greatest extent possible; specifically, the Tenth Army's orders for the execution of military government dictated the protection of cultural artifacts and structures.[26] Battle, however, causes unavoidable damage. Certain buildings and monuments, despite their historic and cultural importance to the Okinawans, suffered complete devastation because of military necessity. As the Japanese 32nd Army's headquarters sat firmly entrenched in Shuri Castle, for example, the American forces had little choice but to demolish the ancient seat of the Ryukyu Kingdom. Racism, despite its presence in the hearts of many American military men, did not motivate such destruction; ensuring the success of battlefield operations and winning the war against Japan drove the military decision to fire on the castle.

The Marines stand out as the service that maintained harsh policy and behavior toward the civilians throughout the wartime occupation. While the racism of the Marines toward the Okinawans cannot be dismissed, attributing Marine behavior only to such prejudiced views oversimplifies the interaction between the two groups. In addition to disregarding the Okinawans as culturally backward, the Marines' steadfast conviction of the combatant nature of the local population contributed greatly to their adherence to military government policy that punished more than it protected. Marines' ill feelings toward the Okinawans extended beyond thoughts of racial superiority; they also identified the locals as a group that consorted with the enemy.

Some segment of any large demographic will act contrary to endorsed policy. Overall, though, the planning and execution of early military government policy on Okinawa demonstrates that the American military, despite inherent feelings of superiority over Asian people, operated with a greater level of sophistication, complexity, and erudition than scholarship has previously acknowledged.

My study examines the occupation of Okinawa from the wartime planning stages in late 1944 and early 1945 through to the end of the US Navy's responsibility for occupation duties in July 1946. In engaging in the historical discourse about the role of race in the Pacific War, two analytical choices drive the structure of this work. First, civilians that ethnically bore more resemblance to the enemy than the invading US forces served as the focal point of American racialized interactions. By examining the contact between a besieged civilian population and the US military rather than the contact between two combatant militaries, the study contests the misleading argument that issues of race in the Pacific War stemmed only from dehumanizing an enemy. A large, mostly docile civilian population complicates the term "enemy" and allows for an exploration of American racism in the Pacific expressed outside of the confines of force-on-force conventional warfare. Second, the environment of combat, central to this historical debate, also features predominantly in my work. The confusion, energy, heightened emotions, delirious exhaustion, life-threatening situations, and trauma of combat pushed the actors involved into dramatic decision making. During the battle for Okinawa, US soldiers, sailors, and Marines made quick, weighty decisions that carried grave consequences. Within the intensity of hostilities, the complexity and magnitude of determining the identity of the civilians increased. My study purposefully ends at the termination of the US Navy–led occupation in July 1946, when the Americans stored their weapons and armed the Okinawans as the local police force—the point at which the occupiers finally created enough space between themselves and the end of the war that they no longer had to contemplate the possibility of the local population acting as an enemy.

The 1945 Battle of Okinawa marked the beginning of a long US presence on the island. Okinawa sits in a strategically advantageous geographic position; extended American occupation and the garrisoning of troops on the island following World War II gave the capitalist superpower the ability to forward project force in the Pacific region throughout the Cold War and after. The United States retained control over Okinawa until 1972— twenty years after the reversion of Japan in 1952—and still maintains a decent-sized military there today. Fifteen US military bases on Okinawa today house more than 23,000 US servicemembers.

This study does not attempt to unwrap the complexities of the Okinawan experience for the duration of the US occupation or the period of sustained American troop presence following the reversion of Okinawa to Japan. This is because the Okinawan occupation lacks both linear logic and simplicity. Throughout the decades, treatment of the population by both the Americans and Japanese ranged from congenial to cruel. In reaction, Okinawan allegiances adjusted as the residents continually sought the group—the Americans or the Japanese—that offered them the best treatment. As a result, neither the entirety of the occupation (1945–1972) nor the years following it easily fit into a singular category. A sweeping overview of American and Okinawan relations throughout the years reaches beyond the scope of this work. Instead, this study more specifically examines race and identity as it influenced policy making during the Pacific War and avoids offering a sweeping overview of American and Okinawan relations throughout the years.

In addition to its importance to historical understanding, studying the effects of race and identity on military planning carries significance for future military operations and occupations. As the United States continues long-term commitments in regions containing populations of various races and ethnicities, a closer look at historical examples of wartime occupation provides insights into the potential of American policy makers and those on the ground to handle complex ethnic interactions positively. Much like in Okinawa in 1945, troops working today in volatile areas overseas must differentiate between enemy and civilian in order to fulfill their duties. As the wartime occupation of Okinawa reveals, a deliberate, contemplative, and analytical approach based on the facts of ethnicity, race, and identity opens up the possibility for positive, and therefore productive, interactions between soldiers and local populations that allow for a greater chance of accomplishing military objectives.

On the island of Okinawa in 1945, American soldiers, sailors, and Marines encountered a large population that had lived as subjects of the emperor but still suffered under discriminatory Japanese policies that relegated them to second-class status. Through deliberate, conscious consideration of Okinawan ethnic heritage and the island's complex political relationship with Japan, American military planners made determinations about Okinawan allegiance that shaped occupation policies. By assessing the identity of the populations, troops interacted with the local people from an informed and educated vantage point that, in turn, better allowed for the promotion of the military government's goals. In instances where contact with the population carried negative consequences, this happened because the Marines disregarded the malleability of race and clung to preconceived definitions of identity that did not accurately reflect the circumstances. Alongside the analysis of race and ethnicity, the American military did not discount the importance of practical military considerations such as supply lines, enemy disposition, and the security of troops and information. Military leaders ensured the success of operations on Okinawa by not only evaluating the pragmatic military aspects of the mission but by having the acumen to assess the ethnic dynamics as well.

1 Identifying the Enemy
US Army Wartime Occupation Policy

On May 31, 1945, two American soldiers sat cross-legged on the floor of a small hut in the gutted village of Nodake on the island of Okinawa. Their hostess, a middle-aged Okinawan woman, stooped over them as she poured hot tea into small round clay cups. Many different families shared the hut with the woman, and some of them crowded into the main room to join in the tea ceremony with the Americans.[1] Bombings, begun in October 1944 preparatory to the American invasion, had destroyed numerous homes in the village. Under the direction of the US Army, several families now lived together in the homes that survived.

Military Government Detachment B-5 had operated Camp Nodake for two months. Outside its perimeter, the Battle of Okinawa, which had begun with the invasion of the Kerama Islands in March 1945, still raged. The Japanese were preparing to fall back to their second line of defense, and the Americans had seized Shuri Castle, the headquarters of the Japanese 32nd Army.[2]

In the quiet hut, over a steaming cup of traditional tea, the mood felt welcoming and congenial; the Okinawans and Americans exchanged peaceful gestures and expressed kinship.[3] Months before, during the planning of Operation Iceberg, the Americans had not foreseen such a friendly exchange. Planning efforts had considered the possibility that the Okinawan population could act with hostility toward the invading forces. The commanders and planners who devised the US Army's military government strategy based their work on an overriding commitment to successfully securing the island of Okinawa with the smallest number of American casualties possible. Grappling with the heavy challenge of transporting food and supplies across an ocean and the pivotal importance of the security of both sensitive information and soldiers, consideration of the population entered the planning mindset as a factor related to the protection of American soldiers and the mission. The large size of the population meant that the Okinawans could have a dramatic effect on the outcome of the battle. Analyzing the complicated relationship between Okinawa and Japan, planners recognized that they had to gauge the reaction of the Okinawan population to a foreign force invading their land. Assessing the civilian temperament related directly to the practical military planning considerations of provisions and security yet also required the planners to define the level of allegiance that the Okinawans felt toward Japan. The Americans, therefore, made determinations about the Okinawans' identity that influenced the construction of military government policy.

The American planners who devised military government policy and the commanders and soldiers who executed that policy carefully considered practical military matters in their decision making; however, contemplation of the complex ethnic and political situation of Okinawa as a prefecture of Japan stood as a paramount element of policy construction.

On January 6, 1945, Lieutenant General Simon Bolivar Buckner Jr. sat at a desk in Washington, DC, reviewing the final version of his "Operational Directive #7 from the Commanding General of Tenth Army" (GOPER).[4] For the past three years, the United States had been engaged in world war in numerous theaters of operation. American troops invaded North Africa and Sicily, destroyed German submarines in the Atlantic Ocean, liberated France, combated subversion in Latin America, sent supplies to the Soviets through the North Pacific and the Middle East, provided limited mortars and artillery to the Chinese, and committed over $50 billion to Great Britain for war materials through the Lend-Lease Act. In the Pacific, American forces proved victorious in battles fought from aircraft carriers at sea and amphibious landings on various islands, drawing ever closer to Japan for the inevitable invasion, seizing islands including Guadalcanal, Tarawa, Kwajalein, Saipan, Leyte, and part of New Guinea along the way.

In June 1944, Buckner traveled to Washington to take command of the Tenth Army and participate in the planning for the unit's first mission. Originally identified as the seizure of Taiwan, the objective shifted to the island of Okinawa in October. As American military progress in the Pacific moved closer to Japan's home islands, military planners viewed Operation Iceberg as a crucial preliminary step in the plan to invade mainland Japan. Admiral Chester W. Nimitz, Admiral Raymond A. Spruance, and Vice Admiral Richmond Kelly Turner believed the successful capture of Okinawa would prevent the war from lasting another year.[5] Located 360 nautical miles from Kyushu and equally as close to Formosa and China, Okinawa sat in a militarily advantageous position in relation to Japan, its occupied lands, and its deployed troops. Capture of Okinawa would jeopardize Japan's ability to send supplies to Southeast Asia and allow the Allies to launch missions against multiple Japanese possessions.[6] As a staging ground for the proposed attack on Japan, Okinawa offered airstrips, harbors, and troop-staging areas. The island could also operate as a supply depot and help alleviate the increasingly difficult task of transporting resources from the United States to the western Pacific.

Buckner spent months in Washington planning the details of the up-coming Okinawa mission with top military leaders from both the US Army and Navy, while Brigadier General William E. Crist, his deputy commander for military government, worked from Schofield Barracks in Oahu, Hawaii, with the rest of Buckner's staff.[7] Admiral Nimitz, Admiral Spruance, General of the Army George C. Marshall, Lieutenant General Robert C. Richardson, and Rear Admiral Forrest P. Sherman all participated in the planning of Operation Iceberg. The planners, from the beginning, recognized the mission as a joint operation of the Army, Navy, and Marines that would include amphibious landings, heavy shelling from ground-based artillery, warships and carriers, and an aggressive infantry landing force. Buckner offered his combat plans for Admiral Spruance's review on the morning of November 1, 1944. Buckner had only one voice in the joint planning. On January 8, 1945, he submitted alternative combat plans to Vice Admiral Turner that were then accepted. Separated from his staff in Hawaii, all his plans—combat plans, military government plans, and operational annexes—were written at separate intervals, submitted, revised, and approved at different times.

The GOPER, approved on January 6, was the plan for handling the large civilian population on Okinawa through the use of military government units attached to Marine and Army combat divisions. Based on training manuals used in the US Army's Civil Affairs schools and CINCPAC-CINCPOA Bulletin #161-44, produced from intelligence summaries, the plan provided a general outline of the initial tasks of the military government units.[8] It began with the mission of military government: to "assist military operations by maintaining order, promoting security, preventing interference, reducing active and passive sabotage, relieving combat troops of local administration, and mobilizing local resources in the aid of military objective."[9] The GOPER explained the structure and function of the military government units. It also gave general directions on the proper conduct of the units under the immediate conditions of battle. Primarily, the document established short-term policies aimed at providing the units with just enough information to establish rudimentary camps immediately upon landing.

In the appendices, Buckner and his staff detailed the composition, including personnel and equipment, of the military government units. During the combat phase, he specified that the units would fall under the combat commander and divisions to which they were attached.[10] The headquarters element for all military government activities on the island lay at the Tenth Army level. The separate military government units attached to the combat divisions each consisted of four detachments with different individual missions. "A" detachments were to move forward with the combat units and seek out dislocated civilians for evacuation. The civilians would then move away from the frontlines toward the "B" detachments, which were to follow closely behind the "A" detachments and establish temporary camps that processed civilians. Further back, the "C" detachments were to build more stable camp environments that had the capacity to sustain a large civilian population for an extended period of time. The "D" detachments would process even larger populations—sixty thousand to one hundred thousand people—and potentially would build permanent settlements.[11] The basic concept funneled civilians gradually from the dangerous battlefront to the relatively safe rear areas through a series of detachments and camps that increasingly became more established and larger in size.

Buckner gave little guidance about the personal conduct of his troops toward civilians.[12] He only addressed their relationship in one statement. Under the title of "Degree of Control," he ordered the commanders to "demand and enforce obedience," thus directing that civilians could earn back their freedom only by following the instructions of the occupiers. He delegated to his subordinate commanders the "powers of government as international law and military necessity may require." The GOPER was a flexible document that allowed for interpretation by subordinate commanders as conditions warranted. As the battle changed, commanders on all levels had the freedom to decide based on their own judgment. With language like "to the extent required" and "take necessary action," Buckner made the GOPER as useable a document as subordinate commanders could desire. It clearly stated, however, that "rigid control of civilians will be exercised."[13]

Policies for the immediate occupation outlined in the GOPER addressed supply, medical needs, and civilian labor forces for use both within camps and with tactical units. An initial supply of food for the civilian population would arrive with the assault divisions. The plan calculated rations of foods typical of an Okinawan diet, such as rice, beans, and fish, per individual and per thousand civilians. After the depletion of the initial supplies brought ashore by the Americans, policy called for soldiers to use procured local island resources. Policies for clothing and transportation followed similar guidelines—an initial stock would land with the assault, and resupply became the responsibility of military government by means of reconnaissance and recovery of local items. The policy forbade the issuing of US military rations except in cases of undefined emergency. The GOPER emphasized the ingenuity of the soldiers to procure the necessary supplies while at the same time planning for an adequate initial stock. The policy designated the requirements of food and clothing as those "minim[ally] essential."[14]

Medical policy involved treating casualties, containing contagious disease, and creating a sanitary environment. The guidance directed American military medical personnel to dispense care only "to the extent required to prevent interference with military operations and meet humanitarian needs."[15] Guidance dictated that medical personnel transport the urgently sick or wounded patients to hospitals, quarantine those with contagious ailments, and maintain strict supervision over conditions to ensure proper cleanliness. The order also stated that Okinawan medical doctors and nurses, local facilities, and local equipment should be used only for civilian patients.[16]

Buckner and his staff viewed the Okinawans as a potential source of labor that the combat units could use as long as the population received food, water, and transportation as they worked. Civilians would not receive pay. The policy also directed the combat units to guard civilians as they labored. The responsibility of organizing and coordinating the work force fell to the military government commander of each camp, who handled the labor assignments.[17] Civilians would not have a choice about participating in the labor program.

The GOPER included a section that briefly mentioned locally run government as an eventual goal but an impractical reality for the initial occupation. The majority of the government section dealt with censorship and Okinawan cultural institutions. Civilians residing in camps could not communicate with those outside the camp. The policy denied the use and/or creation of a postal service and empowered military government personnel to "take necessary action to prevent communication with enemy civilians." Policies ordered the protection of cultural arts and monuments and suggested instituting educational programs for civilians.[18]

Buckner thus laid a base for military government operations. Naturally, his policy emphasized the primacy of the tactical military mission over the comfort of the civilians and thus set the standard for the needs of the civilians at the lowest level possible to meet the minimal essential requirements for sustaining life. Despite its varied guidance on numerous aspects of military government, the GOPER neglected any significant discussion of interaction between soldiers and civilians. The GOPER laid out broad expectations of programs but did not address the conduct of American soldiers.

As the commanding general of the Tenth Army, General Buckner wanted first to secure the island in order to sever Japanese supply lines, then organize and launch the final attack on the home islands. In the GOPER, the mission of the military government included a statement about "preventing interference with military operations."[19] He ordered the military government to remove civilians from the battlefield because their presence could jeopardize the tactical mission; he did not order their evacuation out of a concern for their safety. "As for the civilians, the main idea is to keep them out of the way," he told an interviewer on March 21, 1945, "and to minimize difficulties for our own forces."[20] While he and his staff worked on the GOPER, he also worked simultaneously on the invasion plans. The men focused on balance of fire through the combined use of artillery and infantry, decided where to land, and analyzed intelligence reports and maps in an attempt to identify the location of the Japanese forces. Buckner based his decisions related to military government on an assessment of the potential combat situation and how that situation could produce an American victory. The GOPER did not in actuality focus on the conduct of military government. Instead, it focused on how to minimize the impact of civilians on the battle.

Buckner's command emphasis on the battle shaped military government policy completely. He directed the "A" detachments to conduct reconnaissance and locate civilians in forward areas where they might be hiding out of fear. Buckner did not plan for the possibility of stray civilians intermingling with Japanese troops; he assumed the military government detachments would flawlessly execute their responsibility of removing civilians as quickly as possible. Buckner's tactics involved using flamethrowers to kill Japanese troops in caves, regardless of other cave residents, such as Okinawans, who would die as well. His priorities lay with the safety of his soldiers in combat. He aimed to obtain his objective with the greatest conservation of American lives.

Supply also concerned Buckner deeply. The distance between Okinawa, the Philippines, and the United States, coupled with the complication of the continuation of a two-front war, challenged supply operations.[21] Buckner and his staff actively manipulated loading doctrine and managed initial supply and resupply in order to stretch the Tenth Army's assets. His emphasis on supply carried over to his guidance for military government. The detailed supply section in the GOPER, which included extensive appendices about specific food ration amounts and equipment allocation, demonstrated his preoccupation with resources. The document repeatedly ordered soldiers to salvage local property for additional food, clothing, and transportation and assigned a noncommissioned officer to handle the salvage effort.[22] The directive banned the practice of giving US military rations to civilians because Buckner lacked provisions beyond those needed for American troops. Proper control and rationing of all types of supply occupied a central component of mission success. Buckner emphasized supply conservation in the mission statement to military government: The "mobilizing [of] local resources [is] in the aid of military objective."[23]

Buckner's strict yet sparse procedural guidance on medical aid also demonstrated his fear of a supply shortage. He approved the limitation of medical care to the bare necessities and assumed the cooperation of Okinawan medical doctors and nurses.[24] His staff included medical supplies on a list of salvage items, and the GOPER proclaimed that "maximum utilization of local resources and salvaged equipment [was] essential."[25]

In addition to legitimate command concerns about mission success, minimizing casualties, and adequate resources, Buckner, Crist, and their staff faced a unique demographic on Okinawa. While American forces had encountered thirty thousand Japanese, Okinawan, Korean, Chamorro, and Carolinian civilians on Saipan in 1944, Saipan did not have a distinctive political relationship with the mainland in the same manner as Okinawa. Okinawa's status as a prefecture of Japan meant that Allied forces would confront civilians who were subjects of the emperor and might therefore display intense loyalty. American planners categorized the population as "essentially Japanese people, of partly Japanese stock."[26] Yet the years of subjugation as second-class citizens also meant that the Okinawans could harbor disgruntled feelings toward Japan. Numbering 463,000, Okinawa's population dwarfed that of Saipan and had the potential to affect military operations severely. Planners had to seriously consider possible reactions, both positive and negative, of the inhabitants to the invasion. Crist regarded the issue of the mindset of the Okinawans as "the most vital question in connection with military government."[27] In devising policy, Buckner, Crist, and their staff assessed the temperament and loyalty of the Okinawans to the Japanese in an effort to determine the civilian response to the American presence.

All commanders and planners and most soldiers had access to a number of resources that addressed the cultural background of the Okinawans and their historical ties to Japan. Intelligence produced the CINCPAC-CINCPOA Bulletin #161-44, and the Civil Affairs schools distributed the *Ryukyu Handbook*. Popular magazines and books about Japan, its prefectures, and its colonies also were available. The magazine *Fortune*, for example, devoted its entire April 1944 issue to the population, politics, economics, and militarism of Japan.

Each publication had a different intended audience. The wide readership of *Fortune* included everyone from Buckner, Crist, and other staff members to ordinary soldiers waiting for transport ships and their families in the United States.[28] Fairfield Osborn wrote his book *The Pacific World: Its Vast Distances, Its Lands and the Life upon Them, and Its People* specifically for Pacific-theater American military persons and their families.[29] Osborn called Okinawa a "province" of Japan, and *Fortune* emphasized that "Japan coveted not only pieces of the continent but islands, and from China she wrung Formosa and the Ryukyus."[30] *Fortune* also asserted that the people of Japan had different ethnicities: "The Japanese people are not a homogeneous race. They are a mixture of half a dozen distinct Asiatic and South Sea peoples of different physical and cultural characteristics."[31]

The Army's Civil Affairs schools issued the *Ryukyu Handbook* to its officers slated for assignment in the Pacific. In three hundred pages, the handbook covered geography, agriculture, economics, culture, and history. Like the popular publications, the handbook attempted to understand the complicated political situation of Okinawa and the ethnic background of its people. It acknowledged the Japanese invasion and conquest of the island by the Satsuma clan in 1609 and described the current position of Okinawa "as an integral part of the [Japanese] state."[32] It depicted the Okinawans as a racially mixed subordinate group who spoke both Japanese and the local dialect, Luchuan. Japan, according to the handbook, had successfully integrated Okinawa into its own government as a prefecture.[33] Okinawa housed four branch prefectural offices, and its men voted for representatives who served both locally and in the Imperial Diet in Tokyo.[34]

Along with the *Ryukyu Handbook*, Tenth Army staff studied the CINCPAC-CINCPOA Bulletin #161-44, which served as the "enemy situation" supplement to intelligence summaries.[35] Like the handbook, the publication acknowledged the ethnic differences between the Okinawans and the Japanese while simultaneously linking the two groups based on "similar characteristics."[36] It also recognized that Okinawans spoke the Luchuan dialect in rural areas but that schools taught the Japanese language. Politically, the bulletin explained the historical relationship of Okinawa and Japan and addressed Japan's invasion of the island and Okinawa's current status as a legitimate prefecture of the empire. Unlike the handbook, however, the bulletin alluded to a tension between the Okinawans and the Japanese. Despite the current incorporation of Okinawa into the Japanese government, the differences between the two groups in practiced customs and religion as well as their shared history of Okinawa's invasion complicated the political relationship. The bulletin concluded that the Japanese considered the Okinawans more like the Chinese than like themselves and mentioned the Japanese indoctrination program created to integrate Okinawa into the empire culturally.[37] The document also more accurately explained how much influence Okinawa Prefecture truly had in the Imperial Diet. Okinawa's government did fall within the Japanese system and had representatives and voting districts, as the *Ryukyu Handbook* explained. Japanese subjects from the home islands, however, served in the most important government positions in Okinawa and thereby prevented the Okinawans from participating fully in their own governance. Among the Okinawans, the lack of true representation created resentment toward the Japanese and contributed to oppressive feelings of inferiority.[38]

Intelligence summaries of Okinawan culture, geography, politics, and history made the task of predicting the disposition of the civilians complicated. The Okinawans had lost their independent kingdom to an invading force that viewed them as ethnically different and inferior, yet the incorporation of Okinawa as a prefecture and integral part of the empire meant the island was not a colony. An invading foreign country could either inspire the Okinawans to support Japan or ignite long-repressed feelings of resentment toward the Japanese. Crist lamented that the intelligence studies of Okinawa yielded "no satisfactory answer [about] the attitude of the Okinawans."[39]

CINCPAC-CINCPOA Bulletin #161-44 offered a recommendation. "It would be dangerous," it stated, "to conclude that anything less than active resistance to invasion can be expected from the population." With time and an extensive propaganda campaign, the bulletin suggested, the Okinawans would succumb peacefully to American authority.[40] The recommendation made sense to Buckner, Crist, and the subordinate commanders. "At worst," Crist thought, "military government expected to find a fanatical population, typically Japanese in attitude, which would resist to the death and commit mass suicide rather than surrender."[41] Soon to confront a population that politically may have allegiance to Japan but ethnically was alienated, Buckner acted responsibly as a commander and approved a military government policy that best supported the combat mission. Despite his Southern upbringing and racist tendencies, he planned for the worst-case scenario in order to best prepare his troops for unpredictable situations on the battlefield and to minimize American deaths.[42] Throughout the GOPER, he instructed the military government units to proceed carefully with the civilians and safeguard not only themselves but also secret information. His

order for the "rigid control of civilians" served the dual purpose of eliminating the people as battlefield obstacles and preventing them from acting
as enemies once inside the camps. His orders prohibiting a postal system,
ordering censorship, and forbidding the communication of civilians with
any person outside the camps were designed to prevent access to and distribution of information to Japanese troops.[43]

Buckner's combatant commanders, who had access to the same intelligence summaries, also concluded that preparing for the possibility of hostile
civilians was the best course of action. Major General John Hodge, XXIV
Corps Commander, who considered the Okinawans similar to the Japanese
in perceived cunning, "anticipated great trouble with civilians and soldiers
dressed as civilians on target." He wanted the Okinawans kept behind barriers and away from the American soldiers. He warned that fraternization
could put valuable information, and subsequently soldiers' lives, at risk.[44]

US Army policy rested on predictions and possibilities. As Crist had
so ably noted, no definite answer to the question of the actions of the Okinawans existed. While Buckner, his commanders, and his staff opted for
policies that ensured the best chance for mission success, they also acknowledged that the plan to anticipate a hostile population lay on a foundation
of educated, well-researched guesswork. Buckner allotted his commanders
freedom of action, therefore, to readdress the situation with the population based on what the soldiers encountered upon landing. Civilian behavior could dictate an adjustment in military government conditions. In
the meantime, as planning continued without any concrete evidence to
comfortably assume a friendly population, soldiers prepared to encounter
Okinawan hostility.[45]

In line with the recommendations in the bulletin and staff intelligence
estimates, the Tenth Army launched an intensive propaganda campaign.
In hopes of exploiting the ethnic differences between the Okinawans and
the Japanese, propaganda aimed at Okinawans emphasized the inequalities
that the Japanese imposed on them. Leaflet 527 asked the civilians: "What
obligations have you to the Japanese? Is this your war? Or is it really the
war of Japanese leaders who have dominated you for many decades?"[46]
American forces attempted to capitalize on the ethnic tension between the
Okinawans and the Japanese in an effort to turn the Okinawans into friends.

Army planners and commanders, therefore, used cultural information
about the Okinawans to shape military government policies. They actively
assessed the complicated relationship between Japan and Okinawa and thus
attempted to predict the civilian reaction to the American landings. The
policies took seriously Okinawa's status as a prefecture but also sought

to exploit Okinawan feelings of disadvantage and inferiority. Despite following such violent engagements as Peleliu and Iwo Jima, however, occupation policy for Okinawa did not contain overtly harsh procedures based on irrational, emotional race hate. American planners' consideration of race and ethnicity produced logically reasoned policies instituted to ensure the success of the combat mission. The Americans' understanding of the identity of the Okinawans, whether as Japanese subjects or as conquered people with a separate ethnicity, contributed greatly to how they devised military government policy and how they envisioned the conduct of the military government units.

2

US Marine Discipline
Strict Directives in Wartime
Marine Military Government

A large crowd of old men, children, and women walked casually down the road running in front of Marine Private Joe Drago. It was late May 1945, around one in the morning, near Sugar Loaf Hill. Drago, a combat novice from Boston, and his squad had prepared an attack position overlooking the road, with hopes of trapping Japanese soldiers. Despite the dark, Drago could see the approaching group clearly; these were civilians.

Drago and his squad leader, Corporal Ed Yahara, jumped into the middle of the road, faced the oncoming crowd, drew their .45-caliber pistols, and fired continuously until they depleted all their ammunition. In the melee, the rest of the squad, observing from along the side of the road, reactively opened fire. As the crowd fled, Yahara and Drago ran back to their positions, grabbed their machine gun, and sprayed the civilians with bullets, slowly sweeping from left to right and back again.[1]

The Battle of Okinawa had been fiercely ravaging the island for forty-six days. Destruction had forced hundreds of thousands of Okinawans seeking shelter, food, and relative safety into American military government camps that served as refuges to help stabilize the movement of civilians on the battlefield. Within the camps, the Okinawans acted obediently and cooperatively, traits acknowledged by most American soldiers. The Marines, however, saw any Okinawan compliance with American military directives merely as expected behavior for prisoners of war, not as a characteristic of innocent refugees. To Drago, Yahara, and the rest of their squad, the people that lay dying on the road were no different from the Japanese soldiers they had been waiting for; those old men, children, and women were the enemy.

III Amphibious Corps, like XXIV Corps, agonized over the depth of their supply and prioritized the lives of their Marines and the successful execution of the mission above all else. The Marines also conducted intensive intelligence investigations into the cultural background and disposition of the Okinawans.[2] Despite collecting the same data as the Army and falling under the same Tenth Army guidance from Buckner, the Marines reached a different conclusion about the identity of the Okinawans and unequivocally stated in their military government plans that Okinawans, despite a cultural background different from the Japanese, devoted themselves to Japan as loyal citizens. Shocking displays of civilian suicides on Saipan, committed in reverence to the Japanese empire, influenced the Marines, to a certain extent, toward imagining a fiercely loyal Okinawan population. At the same time, the Marines recognized the difference between the size and ethnic composition of the populations on Saipan and on Okinawa and acknowledged the uniquely complicated political relationship between Okinawa and Japan. Ultimately, the Marines chose to erase any ambiguity for their subordinates by authoritatively assigning an identity to the Okinawans that predicted a hostile response. Unlike the Army's preparations, which considered a dangerous civilian population as one possibility among several, Marine leadership did not leave any analytical room for its subordinates to reassess the actions of the civilians upon landing. Orders dictated that Marines and those assigned to Marine units process the local population as enemy civilians without question and thereby eliminate the danger of miscalculating civilian intent on the battlefield. The edict of Okinawan hostility ensured that all Marines viewed the population as the enemy and granted a greater degree of security to the operation by preventing any well-intentioned young Marine from exposing himself to danger by relaxing his guard around the civilians. Marine leadership based their argument for perceived Okinawan hostility on nationalism for Japan; as vehement nationalists, the Okinawans could only greet the American troops with antagonism.[3]

III Amphibious Corps briefed their Marines with definitive clarity: Treat the Okinawans with suspicion. As loyal Japanese, the Okinawans posed a real threat, one that overrode their civilian status.[4] Stating that the population would resolutely defend themselves and their country, the orders rallied the men and encouraged them to approach the civilians aggressively. The instructions for the Marines in regards to the civilians devalued the culture of Okinawa and its people by calling the island "insignificant" and "useless."[5]

The disparity between the Marines' and the Army's expectations of the behavior of the Okinawans displays the contested nature of the American definition of Okinawan identity and the malleable nature of race and ethnicity. Regardless of specific conclusions reached through cultural examination, scrutiny along lines of ethnicity proved pivotal in mission planning. The

American military acknowledged the complexities of each cultural group; assigned a well-researched, purposeful identity; and molded policy around this assignment. The emphasis on cultural analysis did not undermine the centrality of military concerns such as security and supply demands. Considerations based on military factors and battlefield analysis continued to drive the planning of military government operations, although not in isolation. Together, military and cultural factors combined to provide the US forces with a robust picture of the battlefield and allowed them to make decisions that evaluated all aspects of the enemy and environment.

On December 7, 1944, at Admiral Nimitz's headquarters in Hawaii, Major General Roy S. Geiger, commanding general of III Amphibious Corps, listened intently to preliminary briefings about upcoming operations in the Pacific. General Buckner's staff officers briefed developing plans for future operations in Iwo Jima and Okinawa to the senior commanding officers of all the services that would execute the missions. Geiger, a combat veteran who had already commanded at Guadalcanal, Bougainville, Guam, and Peleliu, realized the importance of a mission conducted so close to the home islands of Japan. A man who had spent his combat time far forward with his Marines, Geiger fully immersed himself in every aspect of war fighting. From December 7 to December 20, Geiger and his staff of Marines worked closely with the Army and Navy as they began planning Operation Iceberg.[6]

On December 21, armed with preliminary plans and prepared to translate Marine Corps priorities down to division missions, Geiger and his staff flew from Hawaii to Guadalcanal and Guam to meet with the commanders of the assault divisions. As L-Day drew nearer, refinement and distribution of the plans became paramount. By March 16, 1945, his staff conferred in his office aboard the USS *Panamint* at 0830 every day. Geiger believed in open discussions among his staff members, and each major staff section attended the meetings and presented their work on designated days. In the months prior, Geiger's staff and subordinate commanders had worked tirelessly to intricately plan the mission and prepare their Marines. They trained on amphibious operations and street-fighting techniques using mockups of Japanese-style fortifications. Geiger heard plans from the Marine Corps' surgeon, engineers, signal, artillery, and ordnance elements. His staff considered the complications and benefits of air support, naval gunfire, and debarkation. They carefully thought out the actions of the shore party. Geiger, a persistent, determined, decisive, and fair-minded man, insisted his staff and commanders address every component of the mission.[7]

Marine Colonel F. B. Loomis, assistant chief of staff of the Logistics Section, wrote a small annex to Administrative Plan 1-45 on January 16, 1945. Annex "Able," based off of the Tenth Army's GOPER, covered the procedures and the responsibilities of military government for III Amphibious Corps. Loomis, with the assistance of two additional field-grade officers and a team of enlisted men, handled all aspects of the Marine logistical plan in addition to crafting the military government operation. Loomis wrote a military government section that focused on his expertise: supply, transport, and debarkation for a mission that demanded detailed logistical coordination in order to support fighting forces out on Pacific islands.[8] Geiger, similar to Buckner, wanted to ensure that his Marines had enough food, clothing, and ammunition to sustain a fight at such a great distance from the United States. Although they would use the Philippines as a logistical base, goods still needed to travel across the ocean. Under Geiger's watchful eye, Loomis and his staff focused on the movement of supplies. Military government procedures, normally tasked under a Civil Affairs section, held little interest for Loomis among his many responsibilities. At the morning meetings in Geiger's office, Loomis briefed the major components of the supply plan; he did not brief military government. In fact, when Brigadier General M. H. Silverthorn, Geiger's chief of staff, set the agenda for the meetings, he did not allot a time for issues with military government or invite school-trained military government Marine officers to attend.[9] While Geiger did pay attention to the fact that a large civilian population resided on Okinawa, he considered only how that population would complicate combat operations. He did not overly concern himself with the survival needs of the civilians or the further issues of rehabilitating a war-torn community.

On December 13, 1944, three Marine officers specially trained in military government received orders to III Amphibious Corps to serve as advisors and liaisons. Lieutenant Colonel Donald Winder, Captain Wynne L. Van Schiak, and Captain Hector C. Prud'homme Jr., along with three privates first class, transferred from Fleet Marine Forces, Pacific. Each of them had extensive experience in civil affairs. Winder and Van Schiak had already served in Saipan; Prud'homme had worked with V Amphibious Corps. None of these officers, however, attended any planning meetings for Operation Iceberg with either the Army or the Marines, despite the Army soliciting for advice from Marine military government experts, in accordance with Civil Affairs policy that required Marine officers to attend interservice planning meetings before operations. Brigadier General William E. Crist, deputy commander for military government, invited the Marines' Civil Affairs section to participate in Tenth Army planning in Hawaii before departure to the staging area at Guadalcanal.[10] III Amphibious Corps, however, had no military government officers available to Crist in December 1944 and early January 1945. Prud'homme returned to the United States on emergency leave from October to early December 1944 and only worked three days in November at the Department of the Pacific in San Francisco.[11] Van Schiak and Winder did not arrive to III Amphibious Corps until February 2, 1945. Winder's experience and rank awarded him the position of officer-in-charge. Since no military government section formed in the Marines until well after February 2, however, Winder worked as a special staff officer, as a lawyer in the Disciplinary Section of the headquarters of the Marine Corps, and as the acting director of the Army JAG War Crimes Desk, Navy Division, as he waited for the creation of his military government section.[12]

The Marines created military government liaison positions because joint military government teams consisted of only Army and Navy officers and enlisted men.[13] Despite its close organizational relationship with the Navy, the Marine Corps retained an independent identity. Since 1942, rivalry among the services had complicated the planning and execution of campaigns in the Pacific theater. By 1945, jurisdictional disputes continued to hinder true cooperation. Buckner, in naming Geiger his successor, sparked controversy with key commanders, such as Admiral Nimitz, who "mortally fear[ed] and distrust[ed] the Marines." General Douglas MacArthur, commander in chief of the US Army Forces Pacific (AFPAC), felt irritated that Admiral Nimitz had any opinion over what an Army commander decided yet also expressed dismay at Buckner's choice of Geiger, believing that Buckner had "sold out to one of our sister services." On an inspection visit of the Tenth Army, General Joseph Stilwell found the genial way in which the Army handled interservice relations "nauseating."[14] Brigadier General Oliver P. Smith, Marine deputy chief of staff for the Tenth Army, commented, "if you are going to conduct joint operations successfully you have to tread softly." Smith ensured that planning done by the Marines aligned as cleanly with Army plans as possible in order to avoid undue criticism. Army planners still censored their speech around Smith.[15] Buckner and Geiger, friends since their time together at the US Army Command and General Staff School, tried to minimize conflict. Besides choosing Geiger as his successor, Buckner tried to ensure that news media gave credit to all services involved. He publicly announced that "the Marines form a powerful and essential part of Tenth Army . . . it is most desirable that the Marines . . . be not ignored in any publication relative to the composition of Tenth Army. The cordial relations existing among elements of various services . . . are always menaced by . . . partiality in matters of publicity."[16] Perceptions of unequal treatment plagued interservice team work. Rumors of better living conditions and privileges given to other services added to the friction. The Navy supposedly "lived well ashore. They made themselves far more comfortable than the Army." Marines ridiculed one another, calling one another "crazy" if they expressed any small amount of respect for the combat performance of another service.[17] Buckner penned a memo directly to Geiger insisting that he and his commanders enforce punishments for wayward Marines that aligned with Army justice policies to ensure the "unity of the Task Force."[18] As his subordinate, Geiger respected Buckner as the commander of the Tenth Army and attempted to model a positive interservice working relationship to his subordinates and superiors. When Buckner visited III Amphibious Corps in late January 1945, Geiger found it important that his unit present a clean and orderly appearance. In his report to headquarters, he expressed the worth of pleasing his Army commander and also emphasized the attention and care that Buckner devoted to the Marine units.[19]

Despite Geiger and Buckner's efforts, rivalry continued to undermine the mission. Each service created programs and policies to prevent other services from usurping their control or resources. To counter other services distorting Marine prerogative, the Marines sent a few officers to Army and Navy Civil Affairs schools to train for positions as military government liaisons. Schools in Charlottesville, Virginia, and at Columbia University in New York City trained officers in a country's culture and language and in military tasks such as cargo ship loading. Graduates from the program at Columbia even earned master's degrees. Prud'homme and Winder entered the same class at the Naval School of Military Government and Administration at Columbia University on April 1, 1943, and Van Schiak graduated from the United States Army School of Military Government at Charlottesville, Virginia, on May 6, 1943.[20]

Fewer than twenty Marines served as military government liaisons in the Pacific. The absence of Winder, Prud'homme, and Van Schiak from planning meant there would be minimal input from specialized Marines in an environment where the other services were jockeying for overall control and resources. The slow arrival of Winder, Prud'homme, and Van Schiak, who were then misdirected to other unrelated duties, wasted their field expertise and school training. The Tenth Army, therefore, produced the GOPER with nominal input from the Marines who would execute it. Loomis, lacking a sufficient military government background, produced the Marine Corps–level order as an ancillary task.

Based on the GOPER, the Joint Army-Navy Manual of Military Government and Civil Affairs (Navy Department OpNav 50E-3, War Department

Field Manual 27-5), and intelligence summaries, Annex "Able" outlined the mission and responsibilities of military government units attached to combat Marine units.[21] Despite the inexperience of Loomis or the low priority of military government, as with all III Amphibious Corps orders, Annex "Able" reflected Geiger's intent. Indicative of Buckner's concerns and priorities, Geiger placed the combat mission above the welfare of civilians. Minimizing American casualties and preserving operational secrets outweighed the comfort of the foreign population. Mission success meant defeating the Japanese and gaining unfettered access to Okinawa for launching subsequent operations toward the home islands, not constructing a new society for the Okinawan population after the destruction of battle.

Just as Buckner had done, Geiger molded his military government policies around combat mission priorities. With limited resources, the needs of his Marines took precedence. Marines would receive priority to food, water, shelter, and medical care; civilians would receive life-sustaining items "to the extent necessary to comply with the minimum standards of humanitarian treatment and to the extent that the same can be done without neglect of, or detriment to, our own personnel."[22] While each division would travel with 70,000 units of rations intended for the civilians, Geiger and his staff planned for the Marines to salvage local foods first. In addition to food, the men also received orders to salvage items such as building materials, clothing, fishing equipment, stray animals, vehicles, cookware, and any possible medical provisions found. Geiger expected the military government units to accomplish their tasks with the most minimal of resources. While he did authorize his division commanders to issue military rations to civilians in an emergency, he did not intend to expend vital military resources on a possibly hostile local population.[23]

Through Annex "Able," Geiger also directed his Marines to execute a certain level of control. Using the exact rhetoric of the GOPER, Geiger directed his Marine commanders to "demand and enforce obedience" and to use "such powers of government as international law and military necessity may require." Civilians could earn their freedom back only through compliance with military government orders. Geiger and his staff also quoted the GOPER and authorized "rigid control of civilians" while also allowing for commanders to exercise their own discretion dependent on the conditions they encountered. With priority on the combat mission, Geiger directed his Marines to displace civilians away from the fighting and contain them in separated areas. He intended to prevent civilians from "jeopardize[ing] public order" by restricting their movement and limiting their responsibility for their own lives. He banned religious practices in an effort to prevent the mass organizing of people. In the interest of safeguarding secret operational information, he stopped the mail and thus limited the ability of the population to maintain communication outside their encampment. Consistent to that of the Tenth Army, Geiger's purpose for military government lay with "control [of] the civil population . . . in order to facilitate military [operations and] to relieve combat troops of civilian problems."[24] Geiger did not envision military government as a humanitarian mission. The tasks of civil affairs officers were to directly support the objective of the fighting forces to overtake the island.

Beyond stating the mission, Annex "Able" covered organization, command and control, food allocation, labor, shelter, civilian estimates and handling procedures, and daily reports. The required reports, used to manage limited resources and track the volume of civilian movement, recorded the number of civilians collected, any deaths or births from within the camp, communicable diseases encountered, location of the camp, military rations used, labor requests, and on-hand salvageable materials.[25] Expecting a maximum of 60,000 civilians to appear during the combat phase, Geiger and his staff issued a thorough annex. While not a primary concern, Geiger recognized that the movement of thousands of displaced civilians, if handled poorly, had the potential to disrupt combat seriously. He thus expected Loomis and his staff, despite their specialty in logistics, to write as robust and wide ranging an annex as they could.

In most ways, the Marine orders for military government at the corps and division levels reflected the intent of Buckner and the Tenth Army. The documents the Marines produced used the same format and rhetoric and shared the same mission and tasks as the Tenth Army's GOPER.[26] Unlike the Army, however, the Marines included definitive information about the assumed race and identity of the Okinawans and provided directives for their treatment.

The Army and the Marines both researched the culture and characteristics of the Okinawan population extensively.[27] Military planners needed to predict, as best they could with the available information, how the Okinawans would react to an armed American presence. While Okinawans held status as subjects of the emperor and had a comparatively better relationship with Japan than did colonized countries such as Formosa or Korea, the population felt oppressed and threatened by the Japanese government. As one Okinawan war publication explained, "Under Japanese rule, it's kind of tough to be an Okinawan."[28] The island population could either view the arrival of American troops as an opportunity to separate themselves from Japan, or they could feel threatened by a foreign invader and resist.

Marine planners acknowledged that they lacked sufficient informa-
tion to predict the actions of the Okinawans. Like Crist, who recognized
that the intelligence summaries did not definitively determine a probable
Okinawan reaction, Colonel John McQueen, the chief of staff of the 6th
Marine Division and whose staff wrote the 6th Marine Division Military
Government Plan and Special Order 124-45, applauded the work of the in-
telligence staff but also knew that the information lacked clear conclusions.
McQueen felt that intelligence estimates for earlier operations gave "pretty
accurate accounts . . . more so than [the estimates for Okinawa] did [about]
Okinawa."[29]

For the Army, such uncertainty underwrote a combat policy that urged
caution and prepared for the most threatening possibility. The Army informed soldiers about the potential of civilians to attack American units
and referred to Okinawans as "enemy civilians."[30] Soldiers received the
CINCPAC-CINCPOA Bulletin #161-44, the *Ryukyu Handbook*, and the
Tenth Army Technical Bulletin on Military Government approved by Crist,
documents that detailed cultural information, but the Army did not ensure
the soldiers fully comprehended the material and the intricacies of the
Okinawan-Japanese relationship. For their purposes, the soldiers received
a message that made them wary of the population based on the potential
of the Okinawans to react with violence to foreign invasion. The policy of
caution, however, was defined by the mercurial nature of civilian behavior.
Soldiers needed to gauge how they should approach civilians "depending
on how [the civilians] act."[31] Army planners did not feel that they needed
to definitively align the Okinawans with the Japanese to ensure that their
soldiers would safeguard themselves against possible civilian sabotage.

The Marines, however, under Geiger's direction, clearly and absolutely
stated in their military government plans that Okinawans, "while . . . not
of native Japanese stock, are Japanese nationals of unquestionable loyalty"
and referred to them as "enemy nationals" and "national loyalists." Orders
about religion banned "nationalistic practices." Local goods procured for
community use were to be "captured," a term indicating acts against an
enemy, rather than "salvaged," a term that referred to public or private
property owned within a village. Military government teams would execute a "hostile occupation." "Inmates," "refugees," and "civilian POWs" lived
in military government camps. Propaganda campaigns "for use against Japs"
referred to the Okinawans as "Japanese civilians," constructed messages
enunciating the ties of the civilians to Japan, and discredited the Japanese
military.[32] Marine planners assigned a fixed Japanese identity to Okinawans,
which implied a solidly predictable reaction from the Okinawans toward

the American military. The Marines' categorization of the population as fervently loyal predetermined their interpretation of the motives and actions of the Okinawans as unchangeably hostile.

Aligning Okinawan allegiance with Japan stemmed in part from small methodological and analytical differences between Marine and Army intelligence summaries. While both services agreed that they could not accurately ascertain the response of the Okinawans to an invasion of their island, the Marines compared Okinawa to previous engagements in the Mariana and Marshall Islands and Palau, where American forces had also encountered civilian populations.[33]

As early as 1942 on the Solomon Islands and again in 1943 on New Guinea, US forces faced small groups of civilians. The people displayed congenial attitudes and did relatively little to obstruct military operations. On Guam, the harsh occupation by the Japanese since 1941 led the Chamorros to welcome the Americans in 1944. Likewise, Filipinos on Leyte and Luzon generally responded well to the US presence.[34]

On Saipan, however, the Marines encountered more than 30,000 civilians, including Japanese, Okinawans, Koreans, Chamorros, and Carolinians. The people protected themselves from aerial bombing with fire-fighting capabilities and ran warning systems and home-watch organizations. They worked as laborers, constructed food-storage facilities and airfields, and served in local civil defense units. As the possibility of an American ground attack became real, most civilians retreated into shelters and caves in the hills to avoid the danger the best they could. When the progression of the battle pressed the civilians, they evacuated their caves. Wearing discarded military uniforms because of rationing and a shortage of textiles, their appearance confused the attacking Marines. Any overtures of combat the civilians made against the Americans remained limited to defensive posturing with makeshift weapons, but people did commit suicide as a desperate act of defeat, using grenades distributed by the Japanese military, by drowning, or by jumping off cliffs. The Marines interpreted the stands of defense and the suicides as evidence of the local populations' deep commitment and loyalty to Japan. In many cases, the Marines referred to all people they encountered on Saipan as Japanese, despite the number of different ethnicities.[35]

Marine intelligence used these combat examples as predictors of an Okinawan response to the American landings. Conclusions based on previous experiences in other combat areas, however, did not consider the specific circumstances of Okinawa. For one, the population on Saipan consisted of a large number of native Japanese as well as Okinawans. As the Marines assessed the behavior of the local people, they included the Japanese in their assessment. This inclusion caused the Marines to further amalgamate the actions of the Okinawans with the actions they observed of the native and loyal Japanese. Second, Okinawans who lived on Saipan were geographically removed from the immediate discomfort of inferiority that the Okinawans living in Okinawa Prefecture experienced from the Japanese. Marines who participated in the invasion and occupation of Saipan observed the actions of these Okinawans, who had a different connection to the Japanese government. Saipan, as an outer island rather than a prefecture, did not threaten to disrupt the ethnic balance within Japan in the way Okinawa Prefecture did. Okinawans living on Saipan, therefore, had a less contentious relationship with Japan and intermingled with the Japanese people on their island in a more neighborly way. The Marines, however, applied their conclusions about the Okinawans on Saipan universally. Examining the behavior of local military formations on Peleliu and Saipan who lacked weapons and had never fought, Marine intelligence concluded, while still believing in the population's potential for lethality, that "civilian resistance [on Okinawa] will probably not be organized [in actual military units] to any great extent." Assessing the loyalty displayed by the civilians on outer islands, Marine intelligence summaries produced for the Okinawa mission stated that "the Okinawans . . . in general regarded themselves as completely Japanese." In explaining the history of the Ryukyus, Marines drew upon information from previous operations and assumed incorrectly that "the natives [of Okinawa] were Japanese in race, language, and tradition. They differed . . . only in being more primitive and less affected by western civilization."[36] Assigning a Japanese identity to the Okinawans resulted in postulations about possible action. The "toughness and independence" of Okinawan fishermen, combined with their ability to swim, prompted the Marines to assume that the fishermen were training as suicide swimmers. By wrongly categorizing Okinawa as part of the Japanese homeland and improperly identifying the island as "Japanese soil," analysts predicted "that fanatical as his resistance has been . . . his efforts will be redoubled in defense of his home islands."[37] Marine intelligence described an enthusiastic, nationalistic populace that differed greatly from the actual character of the inhabitants of Okinawa. Okinawans who fought did so because of conscription laws under the Nationalization Act in 1944, not because of a supposedly martial spirit and nationally driven motivation. Any allegiance the Okinawans would display to Japan lacked depth and had the potential to waver under the duress of wartime conditions. Marine estimates misunderstood conscription policies and disregarded the percentage of Okinawans who spoke English, had lived in Hawaii, or had relatives serving in American units.[38]

Intelligence summaries formed the foundation for operational orders; planners used the summaries to determine how the enemy would fight so that their own forces could integrate effective counterstrategies. For military government, intelligence determined the needs and temperament of a civilian population that required handling and herding. An accurate understanding of the cultural leanings of a populace assisted military government in administration and helped avert forms of resistance and acts of sabotage.[39] Intelligence estimates, therefore, were relied upon for their accuracy. The estimates the Marines produced, however, established an explicit yet erroneous kinship between the Okinawans and the Japanese. Despite acknowledging that they lacked enough information to make a confident, clear assessment of potential Okinawan behavior, Marine leaders largely accepted the conclusions that Marine intelligence reached. Published military government plans duplicated the cultural content of the estimates. Both the orders and the estimates, with their unambiguous declarations of loyal Okinawans, left no room for reassessment by the ground forces.

Marine military government plans gave specific guidance to the ground forces about how to treat the Okinawans. Directly connected to the assertion of Okinawan loyalty to Japan, orders directed military government units to collect civilians by "searching out every ravine and village," search them for weapons and important enemy documents, and process them as prisoners of war, following the procedural guidelines put forth in the Enemy Situation Annex. In addition to living in camps, the civilians were prohibited free movement within the enclosure unless "under close surveillance of properly armed personnel." Orders did not allow military government personnel to evacuate wounded civilians to facilities outside camp boundaries. Military proclamations set curfew times and established punishments for disobedience.[40]

Geiger's directives for the treatment of civilians generally aligned with mission priorities of safeguarding American lives and secrets. Military government rightfully needed to conduct initial screenings of the population and restrict movement so as to prevent the infiltration of Japanese troops and the interference of civilians on the battlefield. In comparison to Army orders for military government, however, Geiger's restrictions for civilians were excessive. Marine orders regulated camp life so tightly that every civilian remained an adversary regardless of conduct or situation. Geiger and his staff prevented civilians not only from leaving the camps but from unsupervised movement within them. Based on the assumption of Okinawans' loyalty to Japan, the Marines viewed Okinawans as permanently hostile combatants, not as victims of war.

Geiger and his staff laid the groundwork for possible catastrophic interaction between Marine military government units and civilians. The orders described a warlike populace and guided the men to handle the people sternly. Geiger envisioned Marine military government camps that herded the Okinawans like prisoners, but he did not want harsh treatment to cause deaths. The Tenth Army's mission for military government provided for only the minimum humanitarian needs, but it also urged basic humane treatment of the Okinawans. Orders dictated that troops move civilians away from the battlefield to reduce interference and, despite their potential for sabotage, not harm them unnecessarily. Since Marine orders described the Okinawans as loyal Japanese willing to disrupt American operations, Geiger had to set boundaries for his Marines. He "indoctrinated [his Marines] against wanton destruction . . . looting." He made it "expressly forbidden to kill, injure, or mistreat any persons acting in good faith. . . . Rape [would] be severely and quickly punished. The clothing of captured civilians [would] not be removed." Marines that damaged enemy supplies or equipment or participated in the "willful killing or mistreating of civilians" would be tried by courts martial. He ordered his Marines to give "particular care . . . not to fire on innocent civilians while mopping up villages." Civilian labor parties working in support of combat units "must not be fired upon."[41] Geiger devoted significant time to setting guidelines for the treatment of civilians, a topic never addressed in Army military government orders. He felt strongly that the parameters of Marine behavior needed clarification. While he viewed the Okinawans as an enemy and purposefully communicated this to his subordinates, he feared that the hostility felt by his Marines might lead them toward destructive, dishonorable behavior. Buckner echoed the same concern. He produced a memorandum for the Marines on discipline that authorized the death penalty for acts of violence against civilians.[42]

Geiger recognized the power of the assumption of Okinawan identity on the conduct of his Marines. Although the Marines' analysis of the cultural and historical relationship between Japan and Okinawa led them to an inaccurate conclusion, it still influenced operational orders. Once again, American planners processed cultural information when they devised their military government plans. While practical considerations of geography, resources, and the availability of military personnel contributed heavily, cultural considerations and identity assignment, whether accurate or not, shaped military government policy just as dramatically.

3

"Japanese" Warriors?
Okinawan Preparation for Battle

After Okinawa's integration into the Japanese nation as a prefecture in 1879, Japan embarked on a program of propaganda and indoctrination to instill loyalty in its new Okinawan subjects. Unlike the indoctrination practices used by the Japanese toward the colonies, practices that dissolved existing traditions, manipulated work conditions, and enslaved the population, propaganda for the Okinawans sought to assimilate the people into a shared Japanese culture and nationhood. In practice, indoctrination caused the Okinawans to compromise their ethnic distinctiveness as the Japanese directed them toward the national cultural consensus. Japan expected the Okinawans, as subjects of the emperor, to conform to national policies and customs and support the principles of the nation. But Japan also excluded the Okinawans from full participation in government and politics because of their Ryukyuan heritage. Okinawa held a position as a demoted minority within the Japanese family. While regulated by the same rules as the home islands' population, the Okinawans lacked full privileges in contrast to domestic Japanese.[1]

War waged by Japan against the Allies throughout the Pacific did little to hamper the daily lives of the Okinawans in the early 1940s. Families tended their small plots, young children spent their days outside at play and at work, and older children attended school.[2] No military infrastructure existed on the island, with the exception of a small submarine base at the port of Unten in northern Okinawa. Small islands within the Ryukyu archipelago, such as Yaeyama, accommodated air wings and naval units. On Miyako, the Japanese built five airstrips and housed three complete Japanese divisions. The primarily rural central island, Okinawa itself, provided few economic or technological advantages. Okinawans contributed to the war effort through conscription; sons served in the Japanese military in Japan or fought in China or on one of the Pacific islands.[3]

The trajectory of the war, however, aimed northward toward the island of Okinawa as the southernmost prefecture of Japan. Successful combat operations on Okinawa would provide the Americans with bases and air-strips from which to stage an invasion of the main Japanese islands. Recognition of the looming danger of American invasion from the south led to the arrival of the 32nd Army on Okinawa in March 1944 and the enactment of the National Mobilization Act of 1944, which enlisted all able-bodied Okinawans in the war effort. Japan's mobilization plan had a broad scope that encompassed the skills of all fit people and capitalized on the strengths of Okinawa's environment. In addition to building infrastructure and standing up military organizations composed of Okinawans of all ages, the Act mobilized farming assets. Ordered by the government, local families provided food from their small farms to arriving Japanese units. An Okinawan man who raised his four children alone provided sweet potatoes to a Signal Corps unit training near his home. His responsibility to feed the Signal Corps soldiers exempted him from Civilian Defense Force duty. Women and children also worked for the war cause. Children enlisted in youth corps as soldiers and nurses, and Japan encouraged Okinawan women to reproduce for the war effort. Japan published an eleven-point edict to encourage population growth. It banned birth control, modified taxes, encouraged marriage, and established employment policies that kept women of childbearing years out of work. Japanese war slogans circulated around Okinawa proclaiming "Umeyo fuyaseyo!" (Reproduce and multiply!). The prime minister distributed personal congratulatory letters to Okinawan women who had over ten children. Despite a perceived racial difference, Okinawan women still possessed an acceptable, albeit second-class, biology to the Japanese; their offspring could contribute to the advancement of the Japanese empire as rightful subjects.[4]

Japan mandated that all civilians resist and fight if the battle came to their village. Colonel Hiromachi Yahara, senior operations officer of the 32nd Army, stated that "any person who can be of help must march under the battle flag in time of war . . . for Japan, survival as a nation is hanging in the balance."[5] Resistance required civilians to engage in martial activities outside the scope of traditional military actions. Civilians received orders to "infiltrate deep into enemy territory" as spies, "assassinate enemy leaders, [and] destroy army barracks."[6] Japan demanded the same steadfast endurance from the population that it did of its trained soldiers; assaults against the enemy could only end in victory or death by either the enemies' actions or by self-infliction.[7]

Japan invoked images of civic duty and obligation to the nation in its appeals to its civilians to use guerilla tactics. Japanese soldiers, ordered that "indoctrination [toward the population] must be thoroughly carried out," tied the civilians to the empire through an onus of civic honor by rhetorically including Okinawans in the central ethnic structure. Mobilization slogans referred to the Okinawans as Japanese to create one like group against a common threat, mutual nationhood, and a collective commitment to defense. The soldiers gave "thorough instructions [to the civilians] . . . to the effect that the embodiment of the characteristics of the Japanese [people] is to fight the enemy without regard to the danger of your own life" and called for "civilians [to] demonstrate this spirit and . . . fight for glory as Japanese."[8]

The National Mobilization Act transformed Okinawa into a military campus; every resource supported the war effort, and every person prepared for war. Under total mobilization, little tolerance existed for those who could not contribute because of physical limitations. The Japanese government even published a civilian evacuation order to remove from the island Okinawans who required care or who had impairments. Many stayed in Okinawa out of a real fear of Allied torpedoes aimed at transport ships. In fact, Japan limited evacuations because of a legitimate concern about submarine attack. Under the order, however, 80,000 infants, elderly, sick, handicapped, and their caregivers traveled to Formosa and the home islands. Successful evacuations served as propaganda; Japan used identity rhetoric to disguise the true purpose of discarding the useless. As a way to further inspire Okinawan devotion to the nation, Japan touted the passages as examples of the government's commitment to the well-being of the people. Japanese government officials serving in Okinawa also used the ships to transport their families to temporary safety, an option likely too expensive for most Okinawan families. Instead, healthy, strong, able-bodied Okinawan children as young as fourteen received orders to serve in military corps on the island.[9]

The residents of Okinawa generally accepted the roles they were expected and exhorted to play in the upcoming fight. While most Okinawans recognized the entitlements they lacked under the Japanese, they also felt that the Americans had no claim on their island. Mobilization policy, supported by years of propagandistic rhetoric, did not strike a false note with the population. Okinawan schools had followed curriculum regulations from the Japanese government for decades. Called Tennoist education, instruction centered on obedience and veneration for the emperor. Teachers recited sayings in the classroom such as "out with the enemy!" Children learned "to respect and honor the country and the Emperor" at an early age.[10] Parents expressed pride in their sons' service in the Japanese military. Although Okinawans felt bitter about filling a disproportionate percentage of the conscripted army, families respected the bravery of their sons and fathers and framed their feelings in expressions of national pride for Japan. One sister articulated her reverence by saying that her brother "fought for his country."[11] Before the battle touched the shores of Okinawa, most Okinawans saw themselves as Japanese subjects working hard to protect the empire.

Young Okinawans rallied to Japan's cause with an innocent fervor unmatched by their elders. Since children learned propaganda as curriculum in school, it penetrated deeply in their minds.[12] Pro-Japan ideology looked exciting to young Okinawans, whose age lent them naivety, a lack of experience, and little understanding of the weight of responsibility and hardship. Playing into a child's need to belong and to form peer bonds, patriotic youth organizations served as delivery mechanisms of the pride-in-nation message. Okinawan boys and girls readily joined the groups as thrilling outlets and opportunities to build friendships. Young female students aged fourteen and older joined student nursing corps; young boys joined military fighting units.[13] Organized by schools like the Okinawa Normal School and the Prefectural First Middle School, the Blood and Iron Corps (Tekketsu Kinnotai), under the supervision of the Japanese armed forces, would employ young boys as a "suicidal attack corps."[14] Fumiko Nakamura, a young Okinawan girl, led the Girls' Youth Organization. The group supported Okinawan military men serving overseas. Girls stood on the docks of Naha Port and waved farewell to soldiers sailing off to war; the girls attended funerals and sent packages and letters. The organization supported Japan's military conquests and practiced Japanese customs. The girls proclaimed mantras of Japanese solidarity like "Kyokoku icchi" (National unity) and "Jinchu hokoku" (Do your best for your country!). They stitched *senninbari* belts for soldiers to wear in battle under their uniforms. The belts, sewn with a thousand brightly colored stitches, each stitch completed by a different woman, provided luck and protection on the battlefield.[15]

Juvenile Okinawans shocked their parents with their eagerness to die for the emperor. As children filled the membership of the newly formed military organizations, they quickly vowed to die with honor. Miyagi Kikuko, a nurse in the Himeyuri Student Corps (also called the Lily Student Corps), sought approval from her parents for her forthcoming glorious end when she told them she "would win the Imperial Order of the Rising Sun, eighth class, and be enshrined at Yasukuni." Kikuko so strongly believed in the virtue of death for Japan that her father's disgust with her desire to die repulsed her. She "thought he was a traitor to say such a thing."[16]

Japanese soldiers, prevalent on the island by early spring, emerged as heroic figures for imaginative Okinawan children. During mobilization, Japanese soldiers readily offered their companionship to the young, eager Okinawans that brought supplies or lingered curiously close to the encampments. Children saw the newly arrived soldiers as their friends, protectors, and countrymen. One young Okinawan girl became close with the troops while delivering sweet potato crops to their unit. The soldiers "thank[ed her] heartily, and [gave her] sweets." In return, she built a special relationship with them and called them "good friend[s]"; she enjoyed piggyback rides and shared stories.[17] The kindness the soldiers showed the children built trust and comfort; the compassion affirmed feelings of sameness between the young Okinawans and the Japanese and confirmed for the children their own Japanese identity as taught to them in school. The soldiers looked strong, mysterious, and safe: emblems of national pride. Playful interactions with the soldiers convinced the children that the Japanese Army had arrived on Okinawa as their protector. Children loved the soldiers as their nation's military and aspired to join them.[18]

The older population did not share the intensity of the young's interest in nation, nor did they innocently accept all arriving Japanese troops as saviors and equals. While all Okinawans identified as Japanese subjects before the battle, maturity and a closer connection to the former Ryukyu Kingdom separated older Okinawans from the enthusiasm of the young. Japan's cultural impact on the Ryukyu Islands started in 1609, with the invasion of the Satsuma clan, but Okinawa's definitive transition into a Japanese prefecture had occurred within living memory; the independent Ryukyu Kingdom under King Sho Tai had ended only sixty-five years earlier. Older Okinawans still practiced distinctly Ryukyuan traditions in their homes. They played Okinawan instruments such as the *sanshin* and sang early Ryukyuan songs. They spoke fluent Luchuan, an Okinawan dialect not mutually intelligible with the Japanese language. The structure of village life honored the Okinawan practice of collective community support. At harvest, villagers pooled efforts to help one another with the crops. The leaders of the villages established *moai*, a customary way of collecting communal money for loans among the villagers.[19]

Practicing Ryukyuan customs in the home, however, did not derail older Okinawans' commitment to serving the Japanese empire as its subjects. Okinawans identified as Japanese with a Ryukyuan heritage, and, despite discontent with unequal treatment, claimed the nation of Japan as their own. Okinawa's status as a prefecture rather than a colony contributed to a greater sense of belonging because the people felt like a marginalized second class but not like powerless captives.[20] Adult Okinawans accepted

Japanese propaganda messages of shared nationhood even if they lacked the youthful spirit of younger generations.

As parents, however, older Okinawans at times retained a relatively cautious view toward the most extreme Japanese propaganda messages, especially those targeting their children. Parents expressed distress at their children's passionate and earnest proclamations of loyalty to the emperor until death. One parent exclaimed in horror, "I didn't bring you up to the age of sixteen to die!" To the young, the wholesale acceptance of all propaganda by their classmates proved its veracity. Adults had the mature ability to process the details of the messaging and to contextualize it within their roles as subjects of the emperor. Parents introduced Ryukyuan customs but also imparted values of Japanese loyalty to their children and instructed them about the importance of fitting their vernacular into the Japanese message. "It doesn't matter what you hear or who tells you," one father told his children, "you mustn't ever say that Japan is losing, even if you're wrong."[21]

Adult Okinawans prepared their families for the hardships that may result from a battle waged on their land. As early as 1944, mothers and fathers talked to their children frankly about the rough conditions to come. One father explained: "Okinawa may soon become a battlefield, and when that happens there may be terrible confusion and families may become separated."[22] The warnings parents issued to their children grew more serious and urgent by early 1945 as Okinawans overheard military information from Japanese troops stationed throughout the island. Parents tried to teach their young children survival but offered mostly general advice such as "keep your head" or "decide for yourself what to do." Children struggled to comprehend as they listened to warnings from their parents that clashed with the glamorous depictions of war used by the schools. One young girl recalled, "I looked at [my siblings'] faces and at my father's face in turn, for I had no way of knowing how to react on my own."[23]

Parents directed their children toward Japanese values as a guiding source of protection and stood by their identity as Japanese subjects. Having lived long lives under the Japanese flag in relative peace, indoctrination played no less of a role in defining their senses of self than it did for the young. On the brink of a battle, Okinawans saw Japan as their country and felt compelled to protect it along with their families. Adult Okinawans took very seriously the civil defense roles dictated to them by the Japanese government.[24]

4

The US Fights Overseas
Americans Charge toward the Battlefield

While Buckner attended meetings and developed plans in Washington, his forces were spread across the globe in various states of preparation. Crist and his staff, working closely with Geiger and his III Amphibious Corps, continued to plan and produce orders from Hawaii. Army combat divisions waited on Leyte after successfully securing the island under the leadership of General MacArthur, and the Marine divisions were refitting for combat on Pavuvu, Guadalcanal, and Saipan.

The Tenth Army's military government units, both those assigned to the Marines and the Army, struggled with the challenges inherent in constant mobilization. Soldiers, sailors, and Marines slated to serve in the units found themselves scattered around the world, between military schools and deployment ports in the United States and in bases throughout the Pacific. Each service had to consolidate their personnel, provide adequate training within the constraints of a mission timeline, and move their units toward the battlefield. The hard deadline of L-Day forced the Marines and Army to administer poorly resourced training programs aboard the transport ships.

Military government officers assigned to Army units arrived at Fort Ord, California, from the Civil Affairs training schools at Princeton University and Columbia University on December 28, 1944, and, once there, received their assignments to specific military government units with an undisclosed overseas mission. Enlisted soldiers also arrived at Fort Ord between late December and early January from various other units or as draftees. They had not received training at the military schools in New Jersey and New York; those institutions existed for officer education only. Their arrival in California marked the first time that the enlisted men learned that they would work in civil affairs, so at Fort Ord they began their first classes on what their jobs would entail.[1]

Within four days of arriving at Fort Ord, the soldiers boarded their transport ships and headed across the Pacific. Over the two-month voyage, the units received their mission, instructed the soldiers in the basics of their duties, and conducted preparations ranging from equipment issue and task training to tracking soldier pay. The absence of any previous civil affairs training for the enlisted soldiers challenged the unprepared officers.

Officers drafted the onboard training plan at Fort Ord. In addition to generic Army topics such as rifle familiarization and disease prevention, they taught the basics of civil affairs using the *Ryukyu Handbook,* CINCPAC-CINCPOA bulletin #161-44, the Tenth Army pamphlet "Information on Military Government," and the Tenth Army Technical Bulletin on Military Government approved by Crist.[2] Officers with experience in Japanese language and culture, like Captain E. H. Horn of Detachment B-5, Company A, who had spent nineteen years in Japan, instructed all soldiers in Japanese language and "characteristics."[3]

The enlisted soldiers, therefore, received the same information about Okinawa as the officers who planned the operation. The Tenth Army pamphlet, written specifically for the troops and approved on February 13, 1945, further enforced the idea that the Okinawans could act in dangerous ways toward American forces. The pamphlet emphasized the threat of civilians, calling them "weapons of war" and "enemy civilians." It warned that Japanese soldiers might insert themselves into the population as spies.[4] The document also advised against soldiers interacting with civilians for fear of catching diseases that infected people "regardless of color or race."[5] In its conclusion, it instructed soldiers to report suspicious civilians to their superiors.[6]

Soldiers, therefore, received training that instructed them to approach the civilians with caution and to view them as potential enemies, and, in an effort to communicate this directive clearly, the pamphlet purposefully avoided calling the civilians Okinawans. Despite receiving the CINCPAC-CINCPOA bulletin and the *Ryukyu Handbook,* the training consistently referred to the Okinawans as "Japanese civilians" or "enemy civilians."[7] As a result, soldiers did not always feel as if they received training that clearly differentiated between the two groups, and each soldier interpreted the ethnicity of the Okinawans in his own way. One explained that while he realized that the civilians came from Ryukyuan descent, he viewed Okinawa as Japanese land peopled by Japanese. "You have so many walking on two different cultures that, gosh, it's hard to explain," he remembered, "And that's what we were all taught, you know, in the military that, hey, they're all Japanese so there's no need to separate them."[8] Another soldier stated that "no one had heard of Okinawa . . . [only] that the island was infected with poisonous snakes . . . [and that] the natives were not Japanese but a more primitive people called Hairy Anus [*sic*]."[9] The complicated situation of Okinawa's relationship with Japan perplexed the soldiers as much as it did the planners. The training did, however, communicate one thing clearly about mission security and operational safety: Regardless of whether the soldiers fully understood Okinawan culture and ethnicity, they should not trust the civilians and should remain fully aware of their potential for sabotage.[10]

Soldiers also received instruction that granted them the authority to assess an interaction they might have with civilians on its own merit. Training on board the ships described the population as "proper prisoners of war [or] war criminals, or they can be civilians, depending on how they act ... [but they] cannot pose as civilians and still try to help the enemy, either acting as spies, blowing up stuff, or anything like that."[11] By acknowledging that civilian action may not follow the prescribed predictions, the training taught soldiers to reassess the situations they would encounter with the population once they landed. While training clearly emphasized the potential of the civilians to act as an enemy, it also empowered the soldiers to reevaluate if the predicted disposition of the civilians proved false.

On January 13, 1945, the troop ships stopped at Pearl Harbor, Hawaii, to allow the detachment commanders to confer with the military government staff of the Tenth Army. Only commanders attended the four-day meeting; all other soldiers—officers and enlisted men—remained on board. Crist distributed the finalized GOPER during the meeting. Additionally, he defined the mission of the "A" and "B" detachments as "confined almost entirely to providing suitable concentration and assembly areas."[12] Crist's verbal guidance contradicted the GOPER. The document specified that "A" detachments collect civilians and that "B" detachments construct temporary camps as assembly points for evacuating civilians. Crist's input narrowly defined the duties of the "A" and "B" detachments to reconnoitering space for and establishing more permanent camps, respectively. The contradiction caused major confusion for the military government commanders, particularly because Crist delivered both conflicting missions at the same meeting. The distribution of the GOPER should have clarified duties for the commanders and their men and provided much-desired insight into their overseas mission and new civil affairs duties. Crist's brief instead raised more questions. The soldiers—commanders, officers, and enlisted—mostly arrived at their new units with no previous experience in conducting the actual duties of military government. Now they faced their mission with limited time to train and only a vague notion as to how the different detachments should function and connect with the combat units.

Four days later, on January 17, the troop transport ships left Honolulu for the Philippines with liaison officers from the Tenth Army military government staff aboard. These men led and supervised instruction on the mission and military government duties using the GOPER. In accordance with the GOPER and Buckner's intent, "anticipation of more complex and elaborate civil administration was discouraged."[13] While the addition of these officers aboard the ships made the document accessible to the soldiers, the officers also further modified the duties of the "A" and "B" detachments. The officers decided to consolidate "the effort of the 'A' and 'B' teams toward taking care of displaced persons and paving the way for camp teams."[14] The various descriptions of the detachments' duties, even though the differences were slight, made the conduct of the operation unclear to the soldiers and commanders.

The arrival of the liaison officers also marked a shift in the command structure for the training program; instruction was now consolidated under a single commander on each ship. Previously, each detachment team had conducted its own training, which meant that the soldiers received their instruction in small groups from their own superiors. The new plan combined all the enlisted soldiers on the ship into one large training group. The focus of the training also shifted; rudimentary subjects such as Army organization and map reading now replaced Japanese culture and language. The officers who had previously taught the material moved into assignments specified in the GOPER. Captain Horn, for example, no longer conducted language training because he now served on the censorship board. As L-Day neared, all soldiers found themselves busy with important preparatory tasks, and the training program dwindled.[15]

On February 19, when the transport ships reached Leyte and the military government units joined up with their combat divisions, training in the Japanese language resumed. Only five enlisted men per detachment, however, participated in the training. While in the Philippines, the debate about the mission and purpose of the detachments continued, and new questions arose about how the combat divisions would function with the military government units. Officers discussed issues of supply support and the scope of the units' responsibilities on the actual battlefield. Out of these discussions developed a new directive addressing the interaction of the soldiers with the civilian populace, a subject the GOPER did not address. The detachment commanders ordered the separation of civilians and soldiers into fenced enclosures constructed by Army engineer units to prevent fraternization and to restrict civilian access to military information.[16] These regulations were based on the governing view of Okinawans as a potential enemy.

By the time Buckner joined his troops in the Philippines, the training program for the treatment of civilians had been going for a month. Supported by testimony that Japanese paratroopers in civilian clothing had played a part in the fighting on Leyte, the training program enforced the notion that the handling of Okinawans should involve the utmost scrutiny and caution. The instruction informed soldiers that civilians on Okinawa, while not from the Japanese islands, "will be regarded as enemies and as likely to do us harm whenever opportunity offers, and [should be] treat[ed] accordingly."[17] The soldiers continued to acknowledge the cultural differences of the Okinawans but aligned them more with the Japanese.

By February 28, the mission of the "A" and "B" detachments had diverged so far from the original instructions in the GOPER that the detachment commanders began to speak of their task in loose, assumptive terms. E. R. Mosman, the commander of B-5, attached to 96th Division, wrote that "it *appeared* that the function of the 'B' teams in this operation would be concerned almost entirely with internal administration of civilian collection stockades and providing labor. No other duties outside the collection areas were contemplated."[18] In reality, the "B" detachments had received formal and informal instruction describing a range of duties as wide and varied as locating camps, establishing both temporary and permanent camps, and searching for misplaced civilians in an effort to prepare them for any task that may ultimately be assigned.

On March 31, the eve of the landings on Okinawa, Mosman expressed exasperation about the uncertainty of his unit's mission and recorded yet another version of their possible duties in his command notes: "Experiencing considerable difficulty in appraising position in the coming operation as related to Division plans regarding civilians but it appears this unit will serve as an 'Advanced Team.'"[19] With those words, Mosman went to bed, only to wake the next day and send his men into combat with no clarity on the particulars of their duties.

Ten days earlier, on March 21, 1945, an estimated 1,400 ships left Ulithi and steamed across the Pacific Ocean toward Okinawa. The convoy, carrying the military government units attached to the Marines, stretched for miles, and, to the men who chose to find a vantage point to appreciate the enormous trail of steel, it made the impending mission quite real. Raymond Johnson, an electrician who traveled on the heavy cruiser USS *San Francisco*, called it a "spectacle." Most men, however, slept all day and all evening. They debated the ability of the body to store sleep for increased energy and stamina to use on L-Day.[20] Such arguments helped the men in their struggle against the demons of boredom and fear.

Despite the sleep patterns of the men aboard, life on the ships en route to the landing zone buzzed with activity. Each day, they trained on the detailed tasks related to their specific job. Like the Army, most enlisted men sent to serve in Marine military government units had never heard of "civil affairs" before boarding; the training on the ships served as an introduction. Those few who had received prior training found that it only provided cursory information. Interpreters, for example, received language instruction specifically tailored to interaction with civilians but no additional military training in civil administration. Military police assigned to military government received hasty lectures on board about public safety, the law of belligerent occupation, and the treatment of property. Others traveled on the wrong transports and missed all instruction. As a result, with the exception of Prud'homme, Winder, Van Schiak, and three privates first class, the majority of the teams had no prior military government experience and began their training en route to the battlefield.[21]

Besides technical expertise, Marine military government personnel also lacked basic military skills. Most had no weapons training, had never driven a military vehicle, and had never endured the hardships of field duty. Officers that had attended the military government schools at Charlottesville and Columbia took a pistol-familiarization course that made the officers no better than amateurs at weapons handling. Those who shot well, like Prud'homme, had acquired those skills independently, not from military training.[22] Under the cramped conditions on the ships, the men did not receive training on these tasks sufficient enough to resolve their individual deficiencies.

In addition to training, Marine planners and commanders held daily meetings and continually refined their plans. This, in turn, meant that leaders would pass new information to their men daily.[23] The Marines circulated the division-level military government plans, based on Annex "Able," to the men on board. Mere days before debarkation, the Tenth Army distributed additional military government materials to the Marines; these were incomplete and of questionable value. The Tenth Army Technical Bulletin offered no additional information beyond division plans and simply presented the orders in the format of an Army manual. The Marines units never received the Tenth Army pamphlet written specifically for soldiers and Marines and containing information about the Okinawans. Military government officers attached to Marine units felt they worked in "an atmosphere of uncertainty." They had no information about the rate at which their rations were to arrive, the protocol for posting proclamations, or where to acquire equipment.[24]

Lacking detailed guidance for the conduct of military government from the Army and having only the instructions from Annex "Able," the

Marines wrote their own guidelines, knowing that the Tenth Army could change their plans. With a dearth of input from the Tenth Army, Geiger's assumption of Okinawan identity and correlating orders for action filled the void. In addition to the operational orders and Annex "Able," the Marines wrote and distributed Corps General Order Number 33, Executive Officer's Memorandum No. 94-45, and a memorandum from Geiger entitled "Additional Instructions relating to Military Government."[25] Corps General Order Number 33 gave specific instructions to the Marines concerning the civilian population and included Geiger's warnings to Marines about excessively confrontational behavior. The order declared local buildings inaccessible, limited the destruction of religious sites to those impeding military operations, and urged the use of receipts when acquiring local property.[26] Geiger's memorandum forbade his Marines from making any statements about the future of the emperor and ordered the protection of previous prisoners of the Japanese associated with the United Nations.[27] Ultimately, these documents promoted the policy of suspicion toward the civilians and strengthened the idea that the Okinawans posed a threat. In efforts to rally the men, the documents stated that "no holds are barred. . . . Let's give it to them." They also taught the Marines that Okinawa bore no value and discredited it as a "worthless place."[28] Created without a model from the Tenth Army to use as a guide, these documents further demarcated the points of deviance between Army orders and conduct and that of the Marines.

As the ships traveled closer to the target area, Japanese planes attacked the convoy. Beginning on March 26, kamikazes, along with suicide boats and swimmers, dove toward the massive ships. For those on board, the battle of Okinawa had effectively already begun. The Marines and those assigned to their units began to harden their concepts of the identity of the enemy. Raymond Johnson took relief in watching the Marines blow up suicide swimmers and their rafts. In a display of survival instinct, Johnson "was sure glad to see [a kamikaze pilot] hit the water and not us."[29] Geiger's orders to regard civilians as an unwavering, committed enemy fed into the natural human reaction of the Marines to value themselves over their foes. Further compounding this tendency was the apparent lack of any civilians along the shore. The men of III Amphibious Corps observed that they could not "see any other life." Bombarded by a plethora of rumors about what they might encounter upon landing, the men searched for the tangible.[30] The early assaults on the convoy, combined with the visual absence of meek civilians, added validity to Geiger's assessment of the Okinawans as a force that would fight; the men of III Amphibious Corps felt that they were already under attack and did not see anything or anyone to disabuse them of that idea. Under these circumstances, Geiger's assumption that the Okinawans intended harm as a deliberate Japanese enemy force seemed valid, unquestionable, and definite.

Marine planners carefully considered the meanings of Okinawan allegiance and its effect on combat operations, yet the issued orders and estimates finalized Okinawan identity and left no room for debate or reconsideration. Receiving the orders immediately before disembarking on hostile land, the Marines and those assigned to the Marines had little time to analyze the reasoning behind the orders, even if they wanted to. As the bombardment continued and the Marines saw no civilians on shore, they accepted the conception of Okinawans as the enemy and charged forward without asking questions or considering the cultural nuances of the Okinawans on their own.

As the ships neared Okinawa, the roars of preinvasion bombardment echoed for six days.[31] Hours before the men landed, the bombardment increased in magnitude. The war correspondent Ernie Pyle, watching from one of the ships, described it as "ghastly. Great sheets of flame flashed out . . . gray-brownish smoke puffed up . . . then the crash of sound and concussion carried across the water and hit you. . . . Smoke and dust rose up . . . the land was completely veiled." The combined noise from carrier planes, naval guns, and machine guns deafened the incoming troops.[32]

The night before L-Day, a message from each ship's captain attempted to inspire and motivate the Marines and others on board. They applauded American strength and instilled faith by pronouncing that the operation was already running smoothly. The captains also made one last mention of the civilian population to their attentive Marine passengers and restated the predicted reaction of the populace. The people, some half-million strong, would display "determined resistance."[33]

Troops heading for Okinawa beaches on L-Day. *Source*: US Army Photo Interpretation Group 2, Commanding Officer, Lt. Reinhart T. Kowallis.

Shuri Castle shortly after L-Day. First battle damage is evident. *Source*: US Army Photo
Interpretation Group 2, Commanding Officer, Lt. Reinhart T. Kowallis.

Okinawan woman and her two children found hiding in a cave, May 1945. *Source*: US Army Photo Interpretation Group 2, Commanding Officer, Lt. Reinhart T. Kowallis.

Okinawans submitting to US troops with leaflets dropped by American planes. *Source:* US Army Photo Interpretation Group 2, Commanding Officer, Lt. Reinhart T. Kowallis.

Okinawans en route to military government camps with their belongings. *Source*: US Army Photo Interpretation Group 2, Commanding Officer, Lt. Reinhart T. Kowallis.

Army military government camp on Okinawa. *Source*: Courtesy of the Institute on World War II and the Human Experience.

Gathering of old Okinawan men and women in a military government camp, May 1945. *Source*: US Army Photo Interpretation Group 2, Commanding Officer, Lt. Reinhart T. Kowallis.

Young children and baby. *Source*: US Army Photo Interpretation Group 2,
Commanding Officer, Lt. Reinhart T. Kowallis.

Army MPs (military police) lighting cigarettes for Okinawans. *Source*: US Army Photo Interpretation Group 2, Commanding Officer, Lt. Reinhart T. Kowallis.

Army captain talking to Okinawan children, July 1945. *Source*: US Army Photo Interpretation Group 2, Commanding Officer, Lt. Reinhart T. Kowallis.

Movies provided entertainment. *Source*: US Army Photo Interpretation Group 2, Commanding Officer, Lt. Reinhart T. Kowallis.

Typhoon damage to camp area, October 1945. *Source*: US Army Photo Interpretation
Group 2, Commanding Officer, Lt. Reinhart T. Kowallis.

5

In early summer, outside the village of Maehira, a small Okinawan family huddled inside a limestone cave for protection against a recent barrage of bombs. The family—two young children, a teenage girl, a middle-aged woman, and an elderly woman—had survived battle conditions for over two months. They had cowered in caves, abandoned houses, and under rock overhangs. They had scavenged through old crops and slurped from drying creeks for nourishment. Now, with the silence signaling a pause in the on-slaught, the teenage girl ran from the cave in search of water. The quiet was both a relief and a new source of tension, as the Japanese military also used the stillness as an opportunity to move. One Japanese soldier, looming in the entrance of the cave, cast a dark shadow over the faces of the Okinawan family inside. Blocking the sunlight, he peered into the blackness in front of him. Abruptly, he asked the family if any other people lived in the cave. The old woman, fluent only in Luchuan, the Okinawan dialect, attempted to answer, but her Japanese came out incoherently. The soldier, in a flash of anger and frustration, severed the head of the old woman with his sword; the head plopped into the lap of the other woman. After a moment's pause in horror, the two children scrambled past the soldier and rushed toward the cave's entrance. They did not travel far; the soldier pursued the young ones and, upon catching them, disemboweled them.[1]

For the rest of the cave's residents, the nightmare continued. Retreating from the American troops that surrounded them, the Japanese soldiers of the 24th Division systematically executed almost twenty civilians in order to occupy the cave themselves.[2] The killings in Maehira and other similar incidents around the island jarred the Okinawans, who had identified as Japanese subjects. The violence ignited feelings of betrayal, confusion, and insecurity. Most of all, the brutal episodes conflicted with the lessons the Okinawans had learned through indoctrination programs preaching ideals of shared nationhood and aimed at aligning their loyalty with Japan.

Inculcated on their responsibilities as Japanese subjects since the acquisition of Okinawa as a prefecture in 1879, the Okinawan population had adopted a belief system that hinged on devotion to the emperor and allegiance to the nation; every Okinawan dutifully fulfilled prescribed roles as dictated by Japan. The population served the emperor through military service, supported government offices, and displayed a level of commitment to Japan similar to that of a soldier. Enthusiastic mobilization programs enforced service to the nation for the entire Okinawan population.

The chaos of battle created insufferable conditions for the people. Hundreds of thousands of Okinawans fled their homes and struggled without adequate food, water, or shelter. In their desperate wanderings, the Okinawans had numerous encounters with the Japanese military, sometimes seeking out the troops for protection. Many encounters, however, ended in violence and brutality. Shaken by the dissonance between the rhetoric of indoctrination and the soldiers' acts of cruelty, the Okinawans processed the duplicity of the Japanese by reevaluating their own identity. The severity of the Okinawans' experiences with the Japanese military during the war derailed years of teachings and propaganda. Okinawans felt discord both physically from clear threats to their safety and psychologically, suffering from feelings of betrayal and the dissolution of their sense of self and community. The Okinawans began to question their commitment to Japan and their identity as Japanese subjects.

In response to the wartime conditions on their islands, the Okinawans actively reconstructed an identity in efforts to improve their situation, whether that meant protecting themselves from physical harm, gaining better access to food, or alleviating the psychological anguish of contradiction and duplicity. They formed this identity consciously, through interaction with both the Japanese and the Americans, and came to a collective understanding of themselves that they then branded and distributed. This process of identity reconstruction, however, was difficult. Each individual Okinawan wrestled personally with the harsh conditions of the battle and the treachery of the Japanese. Molded by the particular confrontations they experienced and their own perceptions previous to the conflict, each Okinawan followed his or her own path at his or her own pace toward identity reevaluation. Young Okinawans, who idolized the Japanese soldiers and aspired to battlefield glory, suffered from the abrupt destruction of their idealized fantasy and the sting of disillusionment, often experienced through pain and violence. Adult Okinawans, more aware of their second-class status within Japan, capitalized on the benevolence of the American troops as a catalyst to reject Japanese association and responsibility. Okinawans who fought alongside the Japanese in official military units as soldiers recoiled at battle's end as their combat brethren deserted them and left them to question their own decency after their willful participation in the cruel acts sponsored by their units.

All paths, however, eventually led to a new collective identity as Okinawan. Not chosen as a default because of historical or ethnic familiarity, an Okinawan identity provided the people with distinct advantages—whether that meant food, shelter, protection, or relief from the psychological discord that resulted from Japanese deceit—that increased the likelihood of survival. A strong identity as Okinawan, forged out of deliberate choice, built a collective community of sameness, fostered good relations with and treatment by the American victors through disassociation with the enemy, and quieted the cacophony of the mental trauma of betrayal. Through deliberate choice, the people of the islands elected an Okinawan identity in a conscious effort to improve their situation. The active participation of the population in forming this new identity demonstrates the malleability of race and ethnicity.

The thunderous cacophony of American aerial and naval bombardments hitting the shores of the Kerama Islands just south of Okinawa in March 1945 alerted Okinawans and Japanese alike that the battle had finally arrived; the bombing signaled a call to prepare for the imminent land battle. Final civil defense measures and the full activation of the student military corps started before the Americans landed on the beaches of Okinawa proper.[3] The concussions of the artillery also popped the rising pressure of anticipation of the past year. Okinawans were relieved, happy, thrilled; the feelings of glee came from a release of "indecisive gloom" and "the constraints of deadlock."[4] The battle had opened, and, with it, all anxious, tense waiting disappeared as focus turned toward both the execution of emergency plans and the defense of the land and villages. The First Okinawa Prefectural Girls' High School became the Himeyuri Student Corps; the "loud thunder of the guns" prompted the students to "mobilize straight from the school dormitory to Haebaru Army Hospital," which consisted of bunks in numerous caves. The children had not yet graduated; the ceremony occurred in a barracks building lit only by candlelight, while the noise of guns echoed outside. The children sang "Give your life for the sake of the emperor, wherever you may go," and one young girl "went to the battlefield feeling proud of [her]self."[5]

The deafening impacts of almost three million shells gutted fields and crops. Artillery destroyed homes and displaced hundreds of families. Dead bodies, floating in wells and streams, contaminated the water supply. The people experienced such severe dehydration that they went days without urinating. Unable to wash, lice and fleas covered their bodies. Makeshift shelters built of soft earth caved in at the slightest tremor. Numerous shells did not detonate; their weight pushed them deep into the sucking mud created by the rains of the monsoons, where they waited for a misstep by a civilian. The loss of their homes emotionally crushed the Okinawans. "As I walk among what are literally the ruins of our hometown, I am overcome with emotion," one Okinawan man cried, "but if there was even a single wall left of that house we all loved, I saw no sign of it."[6]

Many Okinawan men headed toward the battle as part of organized military units such as the Boei Tai (Okinawan Home Guard).[7] Military service often pulled the men from their occupations. Teruya Eihan left his job as a math teacher at the Shuri Girls' School in March 1945 to fight with the Boei Tai. His duties included food and message delivery to the Japanese troops. As senior operations officer of the 32nd Army, Hiromachi Yahara explained, "All people young and old, men and women, along with military forces, devoted themselves to protecting the imperial motherland. This was the guiding principle that our military leaders had been emphasizing."[8] Eihan told his school principal that he intended to "do [his] bit for the country."[9]

Work as farmers, fishermen, and schoolmasters also forced men away from their families. One farmer traveled to Makabe to collect meat, milk, fruits, and vegetables for the Japanese soldiers. The trips, which took days, separated him from his family as the shifting battle lines made any passage impossible to complete. He left behind four children, the eldest a girl seventeen years old.[10] With most men gone, young children and women, along with elderly family members who had refused passage on ships to Formosa or Japan's home islands, searched for safety by themselves. One woman traveled with her five-year-old son, five-month-old baby, and her asthmatic mother-in-law. The old woman needed to rest often; the younger woman carried both the elderly woman and her baby on her back.[11]

The Japanese initially allowed the Americans to land on the shores of Okinawa with little confrontation. Deep inland, the 117,000 men of the 32nd Army waited for the US invaders from strong, well-fortified positions.[12] Along with the mainland Japanese, Okinawan men built defenses, shouldered weapons, and secured terrain.[13] Committed to combat against the Americans, the conscripted Okinawans lived, trained, and waged battle as Japanese soldiers. Maintaining cohesion within their units, they set up defensive perimeters, kept guard, ate collective meals, and occupied key ground. Fighting under the flag of Japan, they shared the hardships of war with the Japanese. The two ethnic groups worked together, protected each other, and formed a bond against the common American enemy.[14] Even those who fought in ethnically pure formations, like the 16,000 Okinawan men of the Boei Tai, united with the Japanese against a mutual foe. Under the traumatic stress of combat, the Okinawan soldiers strengthened their sense of Japanese identity through shared mortality. One badly wounded Okinawan explained, with pride, in his final hours that he had "fought hard for the emperor and the country." Okinawan soldiers also noted similarities between themselves and the Japanese. One observed, "Yamatunchu [mainland] soldiers were no different." Dying in the caves alongside Okinawans, Japanese soldiers cried for their wives and mothers rather than shouting "Banzai" or "Long live the emperor." Okinawans took surprising comfort in these shared raw human experiences. "We thought we were just the same as the Japanese," one local soldier said, "that we fought together as one."[15]

As a part of martial units, Okinawan soldiers absorbed the cultural military beliefs of the Japanese. Soldiers from Okinawa viewed seppuku, or death by disembowelment, as an accepted practice, and some did complete the act on their own initiative. Those who carried out the ritual suicide tended to do so in dire situations where death loomed certain. Severely wounded soldiers in intense pain willingly chose self-elimination over slowly succumbing to wounds. The drastic nature of the practice, though, caused shocked outcries from fellow soldiers who witnessed the act.[16] Seppuku remained a controversial practice for Okinawan soldiers, entered into with hesitation and rarely executed under a cry of glorified sacrifice to country. Although the conscripts would dutifully execute seppuku if ordered to do so, retreat remained the favored option for able-bodied Okinawans facing a military defeat. Okinawan soldiers' view of ritualized suicide did not deviate greatly from the feelings of Japanese soldiers toward self-extinction. Even the Japanese responded to seppuku with natural human trepidation despite their professed belief in the honor of the act.[17]

The benefits of serving in a military unit extended beyond emotional support. Despite expectations placed upon the civilians to resist the invading foreigners, the people had little means to defend themselves or their homes. They lacked adequate weapons, training, and organization beyond the village leadership. Japanese troops briefly organized some of the population from villages into groups and armed each with two grenades—one to throw at the Americans and one to use against themselves—but the military offered only limited instruction on what to do against the advancing forces.[18] The civilians did not have surpluses of food, clothing, or medical supplies in the quantities needed to offset the damage caused by shells, bombs, and bullets. Okinawan soldiers received basic rations, uniforms, weapons, and military training. The military units took over homes, villages, and caves as leadership positioned their troops and planned attacks and counterattacks.[19] Civilians faced displacement from deadly artillery, unexploded shells, advancing foreign troops, and the needs of their own side's military.

The shock of war immediately affected the population and especially stunned the once energetic and innocent youth. Within the opening days of the battle, young, enthusiastic nurses saw Japanese soldiers missing entire faces, arms, and legs. Child nurses fainted at pools of blood in hospital caves. Children watched their school friends attempt to stuff their intestines back into their gaping abdomens. Some young boys, misled into thinking that service in the girls' nurse corps provided safety, modeled their hair in feminine styles to avoid fighting and death in the boys' Blood and Iron Corps. Of the two thousand students mobilized as nurses or soldiers, 1,050 died.[20]

Working in hospital caves or traveling through fields in search of safety, children's observations of war rattled their concepts of the rewards and glories of battle. Shaken by the grisly violence of war injuries, many insufficiently trained student nurses responded clumsily to emergency trauma. The Japanese reacted to the young girls' hesitation by screaming at them and calling them names. "You idiot!" they would chastise, "You think you can act like that on the battlefield? . . . Fools! Idiots! Dummies!"[21] Frustrated with the inadequacies of the nurses under urgent, life-threatening conditions, the soldiers' demeaning treatment was understandable. It did, however, awaken the girls to their own "naïve and unrealistic" fantasies about the glory of war. "Victorious battle! Our army is always superior! That was all we knew," one young girl proclaimed, "We were so gullible, so innocent."[22]

As the fighting spread across the island, children witnessed behavior by the Japanese military toward the population that contradicted their education and indoctrination. Propaganda had convinced the Okinawan people that they stood as contributing subjects of the emperor and shared a stake in the battle and the future of the nation; Okinawans augmented troops and fulfilled distinct and defined roles, from childrearing to farming, in preparation for war. Once the battle began, however, the tactical usefulness of the large population waned. Soldiers found the mass of civilians cumbersome and a hindrance to battlefield activities. The Japanese troops were able to loosely consolidate civilians that still lived in villages, but the destruction of war forced many civilians to abandon their damaged homes. Roaming the island haphazardly in disjointed, small groups, the people inadvertently interrupted combat operations with no intention of engaging in the fighting. A group of soldiers pushed along a small band of people found sleeping in makeshift divots in the ground by screaming, "Move off, move off! There's going to be fighting here soon. Go somewhere else!"[23] Where the family went did not matter. The Okinawans soon discovered that the military they supported and called their own was exposing them to danger, not safeguarding them; children watched in confusion as the Japanese denied them protection. Battle damage destroyed food sources on the island, and the Japanese soldiers forcibly took food from the civilians at gun- or knifepoint or by brute force.[24] With bombardments raining down and close fire pressing in, soldiers claimed some caves for exclusive military use and refused civilians entrance. Outside the caves, the people faced an uncertain fate, with no shelter from the monsoon rains and little hope of finding food. Most concerning, the Okinawans feared possible deadly confrontation with the Americans.[25] A young mother, whose infant's constant shrieks led to her exile from a cave, was soon slaughtered in a torrid round of machine gun fire. The people in her cave, including young children, watched Japanese soldiers forcefully pull the woman out of the shelter and were witnesses to her death moments later. They then listened to the baby's continued cries as he lay strapped to his dead mother's back.[26]

In their efforts to conceal their positions, the Japanese military also directly and deliberately killed civilians and children.[27] One abandoned girl searched numerous caves for her lost sisters. She made excessive noise calling out their names, and a soldier charged out of his cave brandishing his sword, intent on killing her. Terrified for her life, the girl also "was flabbergasted" that her assailant was a Japanese soldier. "My father and the soldiers at the Signal Corp unit had always told me that soldiers were there to protect us, and here was one raising a sword to kill me!" Another teenage girl watched in stunned silence as a group of soldiers strangled a crying four- or five-year-old boy with a medical bandage. According to one eyewitness, some soldiers threw babies up in the air and speared them with their bayonets. The Japanese also ordered Okinawans to kill themselves. Instructions distributed with grenades to the population stated that "in defending the Imperial soil not only soldiers are obliged to give their lives but all."[28] While the population did not hold any official military status, civilians felt obligated to obey military orders as if they served as soldiers themselves, and most followed soldiers' instructions, ranging from relocation edicts to participating in acts of violence. Many Okinawans committed suicide out of feelings of obligation to Japan and duty to the emperor. Several student nurses killed themselves at Arasaki. One boy explained with exasperation, "you have to grasp here the relationship between the military and the residents as a whole or you'll never understand. . . . We . . . await[ed] orders from the military."[29] Trust, built on the foundation of propaganda that rallied all Okinawans together with the Japanese under a fabricated shared sense of nationhood, compelled the young to follow the orders of the Japanese military.

Japanese soldiers also killed members of their own ranks who threatened the security of their unit. Accompanied by sobs and apologies, soldiers stabbed their injured friends to death to silence their painful cries or as a part of their duty to safeguard military information. Soldiers offered milk laced with cyanide to the badly wounded and nobly instructed their victims to "achieve your glorious end like a Japanese soldier." The prospect of surrender, an unacceptable compromise to the Japanese, also prompted soldiers to shoot each other.[30]

Children watched killings occur directly outside the caves, and young nurses were ordered to poison their patients. The experiences of war weighed heavily on the hearts of the youth who earlier had spoken of willingly sacrificing their lives in defense of the nation. The heroes they strived to emulate now threatened their families and neighbors; soldiers that had once given them piggyback rides now tried to kill them.[31]

The nationalistic pride of the young, however, was firmly rooted in peer pressure, respect for authority figures, and desire for self-discovery and independence. Moreover, its core was fueled by systematic indoctrination so strong that it held captive the minds of the adult population as well. Shock at watching grotesque displays of brutality did not automatically transform young Okinawans once fiercely committed to Japan into vehement denouncers of the empire. Many children excused much of the cruelty they experienced at the soldiers' hands. They rationalized their suffering as vital to the success of the military mission and the men in battle. The youth considered it "unthinkable . . . that one of [their] own soldiers could kill a defenseless mother, a small child like [them], or a baby, just to save his own skin." And when witnessing such devastating acts, they justified them as essential for military victory.[32] Within the turmoil of battle, the children sought security in the stability and consistency of previously indoctrinated values. Okinawan youth often contrived reasons to cling to a Japanese identity and to validate the teachings of honor in the Japanese military. Solidifying this identity, the young used the pronouns "we" and "our" in reference to Japan, its soldiers, and the battle; they practiced Japanese courtesies and called themselves subjects of the emperor, "we Okinawans, Great Japanese all."[33] As the Japanese soldiers delivered commands to the population, the Okinawan youth followed the orders under the duty-bound teachings of commitment to the emperor.[34] Memories of pleasant interactions with the Japanese in 1944 sustained the children's convictions even in the new face of violence. One young girl still referred to a soldier friend of hers as "young, and gentle, and kind" and comforted dying soldiers with assurances of national victory.[35] The Japanese, despite their behavior toward the population, represented the familiar and therefore retained the trust of the eager youth, who had so willingly accepted the ideals of nationhood and military might.

Fear was another factor in young Okinawans' continued loyalty to the Japanese. The Japanese told explicit and grotesquely detailed stories of what the Americans would do to the Okinawans if captured. The stories exaggerated Japanese stereotypes of Americans to mythical proportions and exploited the darkest fears of the Okinawans. Mighty US tanks, products of industrial production and material extravagance, would crush the Okinawans under their treads. The unclean, demonic Americans would sexually violate young girls to satisfy their brutish desires and hedonistic ways. "We knew that if we were captured we'd be chopped to pieces," one teenager explained. "They'd cut off our noses, our ears, chop off our fingers, and then run over our bodies with their tanks. Women would be raped." One story threatened children: "[The Americans] were killing children by ripping them apart from the crotch."[36] Terror at the possibility of death or torture ignited hatred. One five-year-boy wanted to survive the battle so that, once grown, he could avenge the havoc brought to his home by killing Americans himself.[37] During the early weeks of battle, propaganda taught the young Okinawans to seek refuge with the Japanese and avoid the Americans.[38]

The conflict, however, lasted far longer than weeks. As the battle stretched into months, more people died, and children, left alone, scavenged for scarcer amounts of food. As the situation for the civilians grew more desperate, it became harder to ignore or justify the actual brutality and death the Japanese were inflicting on the population. Repeatedly, children fell victim to cruel acts by the Japanese. Soldiers killed family members and stole their food. While the young Okinawans feared the possibility of American aggression, the Japanese were actually harming the civilians during most of their interactions with them. The more frequent and severe the encounters with the Japanese, the more difficult it became to excuse the cruelty; the children started to lose confidence in the might of Japan and the loyal role of Okinawans. Japanese cruelty devastated the young's understanding of themselves and their world; it betrayed an alleged kinship that propaganda had ensured existed.[39] Continued exposure to recurrent acts of betrayal eroded the strong patriotic feelings of the young over time. Many reluctantly recognized the duplicity of the Japanese, sometimes holding tight to the illusion of protection despite many months of intense fighting, death, hardship, and atrocities until the aggregate of their experiences made denial impossible.[40] For others, a single act of cruelty of an intensely devastating or personal nature propelled them toward disillusionment. One sixteen-year-old boy watched his brother and niece, both under three years old, die when Japanese troops injected the children with a lethal substance. The soldiers believed the children's noises would alert the Americans to their location in the shared cave. The Japanese refused the boy's offer to leave the cave with the small children and, the next morning, attempted to kill the boy as well. Previously, the boy had justified minor acts of cruelty; when soldiers stole his family's food, he reasoned that "it was the soldiers who had to do the fighting." The death of his brother and niece, however, caused the boy to feel "so shocked [he] didn't know what to say." The event stripped away the illusions he had clung to and broke down his gallant convictions of patriotism. He now saw the theft of his food as a selfish act merely ensuring the soldiers' own survival.[41]

Weak devotion by some soldiers to national Japanese standards of honor dismantled the trust between the young Okinawans and the Japanese as much as acts of violence. Young Okinawans committed themselves as warriors for Japan; they fought in child military units, served as nurses, or protected their families as devoted subjects. Living the Japanese ethos of valuing nation over life, some youth even harmed weaker civilians under the auspices of honor or in support of alleged battlefield necessity.[42] While Japanese soldiers did support the same principles, Okinawans reacted to any Japanese deviation from complete commitment with disdain and distress. The realization that some Japanese troops had committed atrocities simply to preserve their own survival shocked and enraged young Okinawans who had dedicated themselves to the principle of self-sacrifice for the advancement of the nation. Two teenage boys, watching the horror of mass suicide and murder among Okinawans at the demand of the Japanese, delayed their own suicide in the hopes of killing one enemy before they died. As they left the cave to join the fight, surrendering Japanese troops ran past them, clearly alive and avoiding death. The experience enraged the boys: "We felt . . . anger and distrust, boiling up in us. Could it be possible that we, alone, had gone through this horror? Our sense of unity with the military—that we would be forever tied together in death, which had reached its peak in those deaths—dissolved completely."[43] A young nurse who may have euthanized the wounded with cyanide as a part of her dictated duties watched a Japanese soldier climb down a cliff toward the Americans in capitulation. She was stunned. "A Japanese soldier raising his hands in surrender? Impossible! Traitor!"[44]

Betrayal, whether by harming the population or by failing to meet the national commitment to sacrifice that the Okinawans upheld, undermined the trust in the Japanese soldiers to which the young had clung so desperately at the onset of the battle. The actions of the Japanese contradicted the propaganda campaign of unity and created an environment of instability and unpredictability for the children. When the mounting death toll made it harder and harder to rationalize away the dissonance between Japanese actions and the rhetoric, the young Okinawans became fearful of the Japanese troops. They could no longer deny that the Japanese were taking their lives, shelter, and food, and, in efforts to avoid the treachery of the Japanese, some jumped off cliffs to their death. "Now," said one teenage boy, "the Japanese more than the Americans became the object of our fears."[45] Abandoned children, roaming the island by themselves, found dead soldiers useful because their carcasses tended to carry uneaten food in their satchels. Inanimate dead soldiers posed no harm to the children but instead offered a chance at survival. Living soldiers, on the other hand, chased the children and threatened to kill them. "I always felt that dead soldiers were my friends, providing me with things to eat, and was no longer afraid of them, but I was really afraid of the live soldiers," explained one girl.[46]

The erosion of patriotism in the young realigned their sense of identity. As the battle progressed, the young pulled away from a shared Japanese identity and started to see themselves as separate from Japan, as innocent victims of propaganda lies. Burning under the slap of betrayal and seeing clearly where the responsibility for the atrocities lay, the young chose to disassociate with the Japanese and define the Japanese military as an organization with loyalty outside of and at odds with Okinawa. The young quipped that what motivated the Japanese troops was a desire to "get back to the mainland" and spoke about the home islands as an alien place to which the Okinawans did not belong.[47] By stating the troops' desire to return home, they implied that the Japanese in Okinawa stood on foreign land. As the battle grew progressively worse for the Japanese, young Okinawans witnessed soldiers shouting statements of devotion to the emperor during final stands. Amid the constant violence, destruction, and carnage, which was wearing down their own resolve, the Okinawan children could no longer understand how some Japanese troops still proclaimed faith in the Japanese nation and its future, nor did the Okinawan children share those ideas of nation any longer. The confusion the children felt signified a growing chasm between the Japanese and the young Okinawans; any statement of nation by the Japanese now seemed unconnected to the young's experiences and lives. The youth referred to themselves as "we islanders," which referenced the geographic relation of Okinawa as an island separate from Japan's mainland; they consciously moved toward an Okinawan identity that provided them a defining source of strength from which to combat the mental and physical anguish of Japan's betrayal.[48]

Children comprised only one part of the refugee population that crowded into caves and walked on thin shoes along waterlogged roads. Although many of the young traveled only with other children, such as their siblings, the Okinawan refugee population consisted of many women and elderly as well. Older Okinawans, who bore responsibility as providers and caregivers, instinctively protected their wards above all else. With bombardments raining down and cratering rooftops, they scrambled to pack food, spare clothes, and a few cooking utensils, hopefully enough supplies to sustain the lives of their entire traveling party for as long as possible. They fled their homes in attempts to outrun the battle and find makeshift shelter. Some hoarded ammunition and weapons they found along their route. Others, desperately thirsty but finding only contaminated streams, drank their own urine. Traveling families started out as large groups; one woman had ten people under her care, even with all the men gone to fighting units or civil defense duties.[49]

Before the battle began, the adult Okinawans unquestionably considered themselves Japanese, yet concern for family often overrode political or patriotic gallantry. Under the stress of combat and the struggle for survival, adult Okinawans found it difficult to abide by the Japanese state's ideology that linked the integrity, stability, and growth of the family to national strength. As artillery leveled their homes and gutted their fields and errant bullets threatened their lives, they found it impossible to maintain the housekeeping and childrearing duties expected of them by Japanese propaganda. No longer receiving congratulatory letters from the prime minister for pregnancies, women now gave birth on the side of the street without medical help.[50] Absconding among cratered, empty homes and unattended fields, they felt an eerie sense of abandonment despite walking amid gunshots on an active battlefield.

Unlike the youth, older Okinawans held no lofty ambitions crafted in school classrooms and refined during mobilization for glory, nor did they idealize the Japanese soldier as hero. Their maturity and wisdom produced a realistic viewpoint that drove their priorities toward the survival of loved ones rather than toward the promotion of patriotic nationhood, as the children did. The opening of the battle shook the comfort they once felt in their homes, but, without preconceived convictions of patriotic grandeur, the harsh conditions did not dismantle any pre-battle concepts they held about their relationship with Japan. As they rushed to protect their charges in the immediate opening shots, they acknowledged only that they were Japanese subjects and that their homes suffered under fire.

Defenseless infants and slow-moving grandparents relied upon the able-bodied women for their survival. The women, as caregivers, remained wary of all who carried weapons. To the best of their ability, they challenged any acts by the Japanese military that placed their families in further jeopardy; if they noticed the potential for harm, they pushed back against the soldiers in any way possible. One woman had only a tea kettle filled with boiled sweet potato vine for her family's food. When Japanese soldiers took it from her, she grabbed it back. "My children would have starved to death without it," she retorted. In contrast to the young, who attempted to justify such thefts, the adult Okinawans immediately reviled such crimes and pushed against them. Adults did not make excuses or extend understanding for the cruelty. When they watched Japanese troops in shared caves strangle noisy children to death, they called the murders "unbelievable . . . so horrible [they] couldn't watch to the end." Yet despite their strength to retaliate against the Japanese at times, the troops' capacity for such horrific violence triggered fear in the adults as well. Some did not even need to witness the brutality to feel dread and anxiety toward the Japanese military; simple talk of soldiers killing children caused fear to build. Threats proved just as powerful. "They would demand food from us," one woman lamented, "rattling their bayonets and saying they'd been ordered to kill any civilians who'd become a nuisance to military operations."[51]

Survival drove the actions of the adult Okinawans. Preserving a kettle of sweet potato water meant a few more days of life. Fleeing from destroyed communities offered a chance of finding water, food, or refuge.[52] Aware of the vicious deeds committed against them by the Japanese, older Okinawans knew that avoiding the Japanese military was the best way to protect their families from harm. The trajectory of the battle, however, made circumventing the military a nearly impossible task. Civilians and soldiers both flowed into caves. Soldiers passed through areas with large congregated civilian populations with the intent of commandeering re-sources and organizing the communities into fighting forces. Facing the demands of the armed military, some adult Okinawans believed that com-pliance gave them the best chance of preserving their family and dutifully accepted grenades for suicide. Coerced by the threat of punishment, women silenced their smaller children, sometimes by abandonment, in hopes of protecting their older children.[53]

While horrified by the behavior of the Japanese troops, the atrocities did not immediately alter the adult Okinawans' sense of identity. Amid growing fright, full awareness of the brutalities, and the mettle to stand up to the troops in small ways, the adult Okinawans still classified the Japa-nese troops as friendly forces. "I was most afraid of friendly troops," one woman said as she described her feelings toward the Japanese.[54] As before the battle, the older Okinawans saw themselves as subjects of Japan with a unique Ryukyuan heritage that set them apart from the home islands and, at times, politically disadvantaged them. The acknowledgment of their ethnic background did not divorce the adult Okinawans from their belief in their place in the Japanese empire and their role as subjects; they thought of Japan as their nation. Although the battle brought unheard-of brutalities, the older Okinawans had come to accept the inequalities and disadvantages they had experienced at the hands of the Japanese over the years.[55] For over sixty years, Japan had limited the rights of the Okinawans. Unlike the young, who had bolstered the image of the troops to romanticized epic myth, the adults maintained a more grounded view of Japan and their re-lationship with the home islands. A more levelheaded and realistic per-spective better prepared the older Okinawans to absorb the horrific events without immediately dismantling their sense of self. They saw Japanese brutality during the battle as another instance, albeit extreme in nature, of the unfairness with which Japan treated its Okinawan subjects.[56] Older Okinawans immediately abhorred the Japanese for the cruelty that served as the latest offense against them, but, as already acclimated to the tense relationship between Ryukyuans and Yamato Japanese over the years, the violence of the battle did not yet rattle their identity as Japanese.[57]

As the opening volleys of the battle pounded the shores, a prepared Okinawan population and Japanese military force stood ready to defend the island. The shock of the brutality of war, the devastation and danger that fighting brought to their homes and families, however, jolted the island's population. The Japanese military delivered grotesque—and unforeseen— violence upon a population that had previously believed in their inclusion in the nation. Reeling from betrayal and frightened by the instability that betrayal had caused, enthusiastic youth forged a new sanctuary out of a constructed Okinawan identity, while the adult population, as caregivers and protectors, put contemplation about their relationship with Japan on hold. For all Okinawans, though, the onset of war on their island created more than just physical upheaval; war disrupted their society, their political relationships, and their very definition of how their Ryukyuan heritage informed their sense of self.

6

Policy into Action
The US Army Hits the Shore

Army Corporal Robert L. Hostetler landed on the beaches with the initial assault on April 1, 1945. At twenty-four, he was not the youngest enlisted soldier in his battalion, but he still looked fresh faced and youthful, with combed-back sandy blond hair and a wiry, thin physique. A veteran of the Pacific theater since December 1942, Hostetler had seen Bougainville and New Caledonia and had prepared for the Okinawan operation from Oahu and Eniwetok. As he worked his way inland, Hostetler had confronted civilians that bristled at the US presence as they protected their homes and land. He described their behavior as "obnoxious"; they showed frustration with the foreign invaders through their off-putting body language, such as firm stances and darting eyes. Despite the tension and terseness, however, Hostetler categorized the conduct of the civilians as "fine for the most part." His primary worry lay with protecting himself and his unit from enemy fire. In his observation of the civilians, Hostetler thought the people, regardless of their expressed distaste for the upheaval of war, appeared to pose no threat. "We came into a situation," he explained, "you got a little boy and a family . . . naturally you're gonna treat 'em right." Two months later, in June, Hostetler received a reissue of supplies and food. He walked away from the distribution point, and when he was alone, he separated his gains into two relatively equal piles. Half of the pile he packed away. With the other half, he walked still farther from his fellow soldiers and toward an encampment area holding civilians. He handed the Army clothing, food, and shoes to a meek group of women. Then he turned away silently and walked back up the small hill to return to the distribution point for a second issue.[1]

Initial landings and first encounters with civilians required careful vigilance and judicious evaluations of the potential of the population to fight. Exercising caution in order to minimize unnecessary risks to operational secrets and American lives, military government units worked under guidance that resulted in intense security measures aimed to firmly control civilian movement. As the battle expanded inland by early summer and the possibility of the people acting violently toward the soldiers seemed less likely, however, Hostetler's generosity did not stand out as a rare occurrence. Acting under orders that allowed the soldiers to "decide [them]selves" about the temperament of the civilians upon landing, other soldiers also offered charity and extended goodwill to the dislocated population. As the soldiers continually dealt with the civilians, they encountered a cooperative, obedient population that they began to perceive as more akin to the Americans than to the Japanese. Gradually, the military government units relaxed their strict parameters. Firsthand experience with the civilians led the soldiers to reevaluate the Okinawans' loyalty to Japan and the population's identity as a group. The conclusions reached by the military government units assigned to Army combat units about the Okinawan identity caused the modification of Army military government policy, and strict regulations in the camps gave way to congenial living arrangements.

Military government units attached to the US Army landed with the main assault on April 1. The "A" detachments came ashore alongside the combat units, followed by the "B" and "C" detachments. The teams began setting up processing centers and registering retreating civilians in areas like Sunabe, Chatan, and Nugun.[2] Army engineers attached to the military government units quickly constructed barbed-wire fences, and military police acted as guards in order to separate the civilians from the prisoners of war and the American soldiers.[3]

The relentless bombardment destroyed 75 percent of the island's houses and forced the civilian population to retreat to limestone caves. In shock, starving, lice ridden, disease stricken, and suffering injuries from bullets and shelling, civilians needed the temporary camps hastily set up by the American forces for preliminary medical care and food. In letters to family members that had evacuated the island under Japanese direction in 1944, the civilians cried out that "everything is so totally different from how it was before the war. We think about nothing other than finding enough food to stay alive."[4]

The battle's destruction created conditions that made the mission of military government exceedingly difficult. Both combat soldiers and military government personnel reeled at the scale of the devastation. The battle flattened most of Okinawa's structures and cities. Private E. B. Sledge described the landscape as "shell blasted . . . treeless and increasingly low and flat." The extent of the damage also complicated combat operations. Buckner described large cities such as Naha as "deserted ruins . . . most of it burned out . . . of no value except as a port." As the fighting continued and rain fell steadily, the destruction grew. Okinawa, once considered "picturesquely beautiful," now sat bogged down in mud so thick that vehicles couldn't move through it. The mud and knee-deep water hindered soldiers' efforts to distribute ammunition and evacuate the wounded. Eventually, even Naha's use as a port diminished as sunken ships blocked the harbor.[5]

An estimated 200,000 people—Okinawan, Japanese, and American—had died, with most of their corpses rotting in the humid air. A young Okinawan girl, near starvation, observed, "Here and there were rotten parts of bodies, and the mud-covered corpses were so grotesque you couldn't tell the men from the women. Somehow they reminded me of sweet potato tempura covered with kneaded flour." As part of the cleanup effort following the hostilities, Americans dug mass graves in the once productive fields and thus prevented the planting of new crops.[6]

In the few areas that did not suffer much bomb damage, sturdy homes and healthy crops lay abandoned. With limited American supplies, such wasted resources contributed to the tight rationing of food and required a communal living environment within the military government camps. The close accommodations, combined with the Okinawan custom of saving human feces for use as pig feed, increased the likelihood of disease and the presence of rodents, flies, and mosquitoes. The abundance of casualties overwhelmed the early temporary camps and produced a "relative absence of public health and sanitation measures." Staff Sergeant A. G. Karpen wrote a poem entitled "Japanese Garden" describing the desecration of Okinawa. In it, he juxtaposed imagery of Okinawa as a beautiful and exotic Asian island next to the brutality and carnage of the war. "Come walk with me in gardens of the dead," he wrote, "What lily-beds, the skulls, and yellow gentians the old unburied bones, what sacred odor of disintegrated flesh, what ample altars for glad offering to kind divinity are tanks shattered midst the garden's carnage. Naha's rubble, all so delicate; and Itoman, sequestered, proudest bed of roses, red with blood and piles of roof slate." Seizen Nakasone, a professor at the University of the Ryuykus, lamented, "I thought that this land, soaked with the blood of countless people, would never be fit for human habitation again."[7]

Within the desolation and near-total destruction, the military government units had to create living conditions that would preserve and protect life. Camp conditions varied depending upon what each location had available for salvage and how much time the Americans had spent on each site's improvement. The camp at Sunabe, for example, lasted for only five days. Described as "rigorous," the camp held 2,039 civilians but only had two tarpaulins for shelter and no blankets for the cooler night temperatures.

Given the size of the population, the tarpaulins covered only the elderly. In contrast, the camp at Nodake, set up within a village, had the advantage of 167 houses available for use (only twenty-two houses had burned down). With Nodake's population at 6,000, civilians lived crowded together in the remaining structures. The "C" detachment camp at Shimabuku created ten districts fifteen days into the battle while at the same time struggling to secure an adequate water supply.[8]

Despite the variation in the conditions, all camps operated under the basic principles outlined in the GOPER as further modified by detachment commanders. Every camp kept a meticulous headcount and filled out daily reports signed by the detachment commander, who submitted the documents through the division and XXIV Corps to the Tenth Army military government staff. The staff then combined the data into a memo addressed to Crist, the deputy commander for military government. By requesting specific data, the reports laid out the Tenth Army's priorities for the detachment—maintain an accurate headcount, control disease, provide basic needs through local salvage, and organize the civilians into an Army-wide beneficial labor force. The reports required a demographic tally of the civilians by gender, location, and medical status and also a brief citation on sanitation and an extended paragraph on communicable diseases. Instances of typhus, meningitis, and skin conditions appeared most frequently, but even these were only as isolated cases. Two reported cases of leprosy at the field hospital in Koza, however, prompted discussions of evacuation and command involvement from the Tenth Army.[9]

The reports also dealt with supply and the status of salvage. Buckner's concerns about supply were warranted; the military government units saved their initial stock of food and construction material for use as emergency rations and focused on local salvage immediately. As the war continued and local resources were slowly consumed, the failure of the promised resupply to arrive worried Americans and Okinawans alike. The Tenth Army recognized the effect that the availability of local materials had on the living conditions of the camps and tracked salvage efforts closely.[10]

The reports provided information on the labor projects of the civilians as well. The GOPER directed the availability of civilian labor to any unit, including combat units, and the military government designed its program around the intent of the GOPER. Most combat units, however, did not request the additional labor; civilians worked almost exclusively within the camps, doing cooking, laundry, nursing, construction, and, if possible, farming.[11]

American soldiers interacted with both the Japanese and the Okinawan civilians immediately upon landing. Information received during training, combined with hasty observations once on the island, meant that most soldiers were able to differentiate between the Okinawans and the Japanese through simple, though sometimes inaccurate, methods.[12] The ability of the soldiers to distinguish between the two ethnic groups did not reflect an acute awareness of the intricacies of culture and race. Instead, the soldiers separated the groups based on rudimentary visual differences. The Okinawans, rendered homeless by the intense shelling and fighting, walked in the muddy roads looking for shelter and carrying all their possessions. They were filthy, scared, and unarmed. Japanese soldiers wore military uniforms, carried weapons, and organized attacks against the Americans. As American soldiers encountered tired, weary, weak, scared, grimy local people not wearing Japanese uniforms or carrying weapons, they assumed they were Okinawan, whom they categorized as "pathetic . . . pitiful . . . totally bewildered by the shock of [the] invasion . . . and scared to death of [the Americans]." Soldiers noted the "debilitated condition physically and mentally" of the local civilians. Wrote one soldier from Camp Sunabe: "The attitude of the natives toward the American forces at this early stage can be described as one of passivity resulting from great shock and fright . . . completely docile."[13]

The American soldiers thus identified the Okinawans based on superficial, general, imprecise, and not always accurate assumptions.[14] Okinawans did wear soiled, threadbare clothing and felt fearful, sick, and injured, but this was the fault of the destructive battle, not fundamental attributes of the people. To the soldiers, however, the destitute state of the Okinawans invoked a paternalistic, racially driven feeling of superiority. The soldiers viewed the population as uncivilized, primitive, and unintelligent rather than as war victims.[15] Soldiers denigrated the condition of the locals by describing their belongings as "pitifully few and pathetically poor."[16] The training they received about Okinawa supported their paternalistic views. The *Ryukyu Handbook*, for example, described the Okinawans as "mild-mannered, courteous, and subservient" people who "do not value orderliness and cleanliness."[17] Despite the devastation of war being the obvious cause of the grimy look of the civilians, such training instilled a belief in the Americans that filth was intrinsic to Okinawan culture. "They violate sanitary regulations," explained Crist, "because they have no real knowledge of sanitation."[18] Local practices such as using human excrement as fertilizer contributed to the Americans' false assumptions about Okinawans as unclean. Military government soldiers said the civilians "carefully hoarded" the excrement; soldiers worried that the sanitation situation, "including the

odor, would probably deteriorate."[19] Adherence to their own Western no-
tions made the military government units emphasize a few unfamiliar farming practices as representative of the nature of the Okinawans as a group.

While the American observation of the distressed Okinawans as docile,
weak, and primitive translated into xenophobic feelings, the majority of
the Okinawans did, in fact, behave in a friendly manner. To the surprise of
the Americans, few civilians under the custody of the US military in the
camps carried out subversive acts or committed suicide. Frightened at such
close interaction with the American enemy, Okinawans complied with the
directions of the military government officers. Obediently moving between
locations by truck or by foot, the civilians calculated their chance of survival
in the camps by observing the number of people the Americans processed.
"I thought that we were probably going to be killed because there were too
many POWs for them to handle," a middle-school boy at Sunabe thought.
When the Americans handed him shorts, a shirt, and eating utensils, he
relaxed.[20] A XXIV Corps report stated that "the processing of civs posed no
problems during the first months of the operation."[21] Captain R. W. Appleman, the XXIV Corps historian, recorded that "the civilians presented no difficult problem and took care of themselves by and large, no serious difficulty
developed."[22] Military government units observed no aggressive actions
against Americans by civilians during the first eight days.[23]

Even while noting the harmless nature of the Okinawans, however, the
soldiers did not disregard the potential of the civilians to incite violent chaos
or spy.[24] One soldier observed many years later that "every culture has their
good people and their bad people."[25] Heeding the horror stories told on the
transport ships about Japanese soldiers disguised as civilians, the Americans
still viewed the Okinawans with suspicion, despite their helpless appearance.[26] New rumors and stories about the covert actions of civilians against
American forces circulated once the soldiers landed, and, while these reports went unproven, they did fuel distrust.[27] Consistent with the soldiers'
training and orders, a generally wary attitude toward the locals worked in
harmony with the soldiers' vigilant efforts at self-preservation in a wartime
environment. Soldiers worried that "intelligence was getting to the enemy
forces via itinerant civilians" who had run away from the military government camps. When Americans saw civilians wearing US military uniforms
given to them out of charity, the image heightened fear of espionage because
it blurred the informally established visual identification lines.[28] In both
official and unofficial written correspondence, the term "enemy civilian"
continued to appear in reference to the Okinawans.[29] Displaying the unease
with which military government units approached civilians, XXIV Corps

identified the "doubtful attitude" of "240,000 Ok[inawans]" to be "one of the major problems" that military government personnel sections had to contend with.[30] American soldiers tried to identify possible hostile Okinawans by using the same simplistic, flawed method they used to differentiate the Okinawans from the Japanese—how they looked. As one soldier explained, "you could tell by their eyes."[31] Ultimately, the Americans recognized that there existed no way to sort out the enemies from the innocents accurately. In the first month of battle, sheer survival suggested that caution be the ruling principle.[32]

While the majority of the Okinawans living in the military government camps complied with American authority and posed no threat, not all Okinawans on the island acted as noncombatants. In addition to the few civilians who spied from within the camps, a sizeable portion of the Okinawan population had served in military units on the Japanese side.[33] Okinawans fought in organizations ranging from the Boei Tai (the Okinawan Home Guard), which employed adult men as soldiers in formal military units, to children's groups such as the Blood and Iron Corps and the student nurse corps. American forces keenly noticed that "the middle-aged group of men were missing" from the evacuation camps.[34] Out of a population of several thousand at Camp Tobaru, military government officials reported only fifty men aged seventeen to forty-five years.[35]

Okinawan mobilization contributed significantly to Japanese fighting strength. Between December 1944 and March 1945, Japanese troop strength increased by 16,000 after the incorporation of the Boei Tai.[36] Although the US forces did consider that some Okinawans could act as spies, they underestimated civilian participation in actual combat units. Only when realizing the inconsistency between their after-action estimates of the number of enemy casualties compared to the estimated number of enemy troops engaged did the Americans notice the active combatant role of the Okinawans. Cultural training received by the American forces before the invasion emphasized the rural background and ethnic differences between the Okinawans and the mainland Japanese and contributed to this miscalculation. Stated one officer, "[The] advanced propaganda [campaign] about an enchained race seeking liberation has perhaps clouded appreciation of the full extent of Ok contribution to the defense of their native land." Of 1,113 prisoners of war tallied over a three-week period, 424 were Boei Tai and 121 were military civilian employees.[37]

Differentiating the Okinawans from the Japanese lacked the precision and tendency toward accuracy of a scientific process. American soldiers tried their best to separate innocuous civilians from those civilians who intended to harm them and from the uniformed enemy troops. Forming assumptions based on training material and observation, the Americans recognized not only passivity and compliance but the potential for infiltration and deceit among the Okinawans. For soldiers fighting in combat units, the intricate process of separating the Okinawans from the Japanese bore less import; as combatants themselves, their concern lay with those who actively fought against them, regardless of ethnicity.[38] Combat soldiers ignored crowds of dislocated civilians along the roads or swiftly transferred them to the military government units attached to the divisions. For the military government soldiers administrating the camps, however, identifying Okinawans and Japanese as separate groups required extensive care and carried real consequences if done incorrectly. Military government personnel slept in the same camps, mere yards away from the local residents. To them, separating Japanese soldiers and Okinawans loyal to Japan from the majority of Okinawan refugees seeking relief was of paramount importance. Their personal security depended upon it.

The detachment commanders' orders, issued on the transport ships, for rigid security measures existed "for their protection and ours." Each civilian arriving to the camp underwent a screening process in order to discover any dangerous intentions and to find and remove any threatening weapon-like object. Civilian men aged seventeen to forty-five stayed in stockades overnight. Perimeter fences enclosed the camps, and internal fencing separated American and Okinawan living areas. No civilians could leave the camp without an American soldier escort. Labor parties worked under guard. Military police, when available, augmented some camps, conducted patrols, and enforced antifraternization rules. Dog patrols consisting of twelve men and thirteen dogs guarded the camps while the military police rested in the evenings.[39]

XXIV Corps ordered strict security measures, and each camp implemented the regulations with as much rigor as their resources allowed. Nodake, for example, did not have a perimeter fence because the area lacked adequate amounts of both the military and local materials necessary for construction.[40] Personnel shortages posed the greatest difficulties. B-5, for example, consisted of only twenty-three soldiers yet processed thousands of civilians; the camp reached a resident population of 6,999 by mid-April.[41] Units short on people sent requests for military police augmentees to XXIV Corps regularly.[42]

To ensure that the civilians followed the directives of the Americans, military government units devised a set of punishments for rule breakers. In the first few days of the battle, the soldiers only issued warnings to those civilians who disregarded the camp regulations.[43] Before a week had passed, however, they realized that the penalties had to increase. Punishments included placing offenders in the stockades or denying the daily rice ration.[44]

Civilians committed infractions out of their own need for survival, not a desire for deviance. Still anxious and uneasy from the destruction and their displacement, the civilians felt more comfortable fending for themselves, scavenging for food scraps such as empty fish tins discarded by the Japanese army. Civilians left the camps searching for family members or salvageable food in abandoned fields. American forces understood why civilians escaped and organized salvage parties to procure food and supplies for all camp residents. Military government lacked the manpower, however, to escort every forlorn, anxious, restless Okinawan and denied most requests. The civilians' urgent desires to leave the camps, combined with shortages of material and personnel, resulted in "numerous problems [with] civilian control."[45]

XXIV Corps issued an order in response to this lack of control. By April 11, eleven days after the initial landings, XXIV Corps authorized military government soldiers to shoot any resident found leaving the camps or stealing food.[46] The order unambiguously directed perimeter guards to "stop all civilians leaving the village for crops or any reason, and upon failure to stop when ordered back, to fire at such civilians."[47] Each individual camp displayed standardized warning signs issued from XXIV Corps to alert the residents about the punishment of death.[48] Written in Japanese, the public notices were illegible to older Okinawans who only spoke and read Luchuan.[49] American forces not only knew that the Okinawans spoke a different language than Japanese but also acknowledged that "sentences may be translated [between the two languages] word for word without comprehension" and that the two languages were "mutually unintelligible."[50] Lack of training in Luchuan and its five dialects limited the language options for the bulletins, but the Americans also knew that "standard [Tokyo] Japanese [was] understood by many in the cities and towns."[51] The posted bulletins, though unintelligible to some of the camp population, signified an honest effort by military government officials to communicate with the population and, while not always able to accommodate it, an awareness of the distinction between Okinawans and Japanese.

Unfortunately, the threats in the postings, coupled with the limits of language, meant that some camp residents learned of the penalty only by witnessing at first hand the consequences. In Nodake, seven civilians died from bullet wounds under the April 11 edict. One civilian each met a similar demise at Chatan, Maebaru, and Tobaru. Military government soldiers shot two escaping civilians at Shimabuku.[52] When guards fired at fleeing civilians, they rarely, if ever, delivered less than a death blow, thus proving that the intent of the order was to kill, not merely to stop. Though the number of civilians killed remained low in comparison with the thousands residing in the camps, military government units followed the XXIV Corps order universally.[53]

The civilians shot had not threatened American soldiers or disclosed American secrets to the Japanese. They had attempted to leave camp unaccompanied, stolen food, or lingered around the ration dump.[54] While the Americans had a real fear that Okinawans could return to Japanese lines after they had lived in close proximity to American military information, such fears only partially explained the extreme punishment of death. Notably, the American forces knew that most fleeing Okinawans were doing so to locate lost family members or food. While death stood as a drastic consequence against crimes unrelated to enemy acts, civilian freedom of movement threatened security within the camps by diminishing the control of the undermanned military government units. Severely outnumbered, the soldiers needed to enforce discipline to reduce the possibility of organized civilian treachery. XXIV Corps issued the order in response to the military government units' loosening grip on the control of their camps. The American knowledge of the Okinawans' motivations for escaping meant that they did not shoot civilians because they considered them enemy combatants, yet neither did they consider them harmless.

The last shooting of a fleeing civilian occurred on April 26, at the Shimabaru camp, when a civilian attempted to leave after sunset.[55] For the remainder of the wartime occupation, ending with the surrender of the Ryukyus on September 7, US Army military government units did not shoot any more civilians.[56] Throughout the last four months of intense fighting, the military government units no longer saw a need for strict, deadly control over their camp populations. As soldiers recognized the Okinawans' quick obedience to the regulations and as close living increased familiarity between foreigner and local, individual military government units began to loosen the rigid restrictions.

Punishment programs—whether stockades, food denial, or death— alerted the Okinawan camp populations to the seriousness with which the Americans dealt with violations. While the Okinawans discovered to their relief and surprise that the Americans did not intend to harm them through consistent mistreatment, Japanese horror stories about American torture made the Okinawans mindful of the structure imposed on them.[57] As soon as they witnessed the consequences of disobedience, they complied.

Military government soldiers quickly noticed the effectiveness of their punishment policies in restoring order and maintaining control over the thousands in the camps. With death as a punishment, they observed the "virtually complete solution of the problem" of civilians leaving the camps on their own. A stockade constructed at Nodake for escapees who turned back before the military police could fire "was seldom required after the first few days." Within a month, "the penalty of cancelling the rice ration was threatened but not found necessary to be used."[58]

Not only did the Okinawans choose cooperation over rebellion, but they readily participated in the daily operations of the camps and assisted the Americans in camp administration. One Okinawan man made additional leaflets about the consequence of death and posted them on paths that led away from Nodake. Even given that the man's motivation was likely primarily to protect his fellow Okinawans and not to lighten the Americans' workload, the soldiers viewed such actions as signs not only of compliance but of teamwork toward a common goal.[59]

During the month of April, American soldiers began to link Okinawan obedience and cooperation in camp life to Okinawan culture and identity. Soldiers compared Okinawans to other cultural groups, such as Filipinos and Japanese, and used these comparisons in their favorable assessments of Okinawan behavior. They viewed the Okinawans as "a lot more amenable to discipline than Filipinos and [with a] better standard of living."[60] They observed that "the rigid and arbitrary Japanese authoritarian disposition appeared strangely absent" in the work demeanor of the Okinawans.[61] In observing the civilians' compliant attitude during his visits to the camps, Buckner called Okinawan women meek and claimed that, in contrast, Japanese women attempted to destroy American equipment with explosives during night attacks. Buckner's successor, General Joseph Stilwell, similarly described the Japanese as ferocious, brutal, and animal-like and the Okinawans as beautiful people.[62] The Americans even compared the Okinawans to Americans and found that the way they took initiative in camp life resembled an American leadership style characterized by compromise and rationality.[63]

The military government units made special note of those few Okinawans who had spent time in the United States, and, rather than inspiring sentiments of fear, the close ties to America emphasized commonalities between the soldiers and civilians.[64] In contrast to the apprehension felt toward Japanese American citizens back home, connections that the Okinawans had with America encouraged understanding between the interned civilians and the American camp administrators. Okinawans' personal associations with America also further estranged the Okinawans from the Japanese in the minds of the Americans. More than just visitors to places like Hawaii and Los Angeles, some Okinawans had children stationed in Hawaii serving in the US Army. The soldiers gravitated toward those Okinawans with such shared experiences and gave the commonality great weight in the formation of their opinions. Soldiers began to view the Okinawans as being on the American side and described civilians that aided camp activities as "responsible."[65]

With such familial ties to America, the soldiers interpreted Okinawan efforts toward cooperation as larger gestures in support of the American viewpoint of the war. "Indeed," wrote one soldier, "the fact that some of them had lived in the United States undoubted ameliorated there [sic] attitudes."[66] By April 30, soldiers recognized a trend in the attitude of the civilians; most expressed a preference for the influence of the US government on Okinawa over the Japanese government.[67] In Nodake, questioning exposed that "civilians generally refrained from expressing views hostile to Japan, but did state they would prefer the rule of the United States."[68] Though the military government soldiers who queried the civilians at Nodake considered the pro-American response to be linked to Okinawan concerns about economic distress, the sentiment nonetheless contributed to an increasing comfort felt by the Americans toward the Okinawans. The local people, initially viewed with suspicion and dismissed with culturally biased, insulting assumptions about their childlike nature, gradually represented a cooperative populace that might share principles with their foreigner invaders.

By the end of April, obedience, cooperation, and a feeling of kinship resulted in an adjustment in policy at the individual camps.[69] The loosened restrictions did not originate from XXIV Corps or the Tenth Army. Instead, they grew gradually as each camp commander assessed the situation through careful consideration of the improvement in overall control, the positive contributions of the civilians, and the perceived growing rift between the Okinawans and the Japanese.[70] Many of the situations each commander encountered by late April and early May bore resemblance to incidents dealt with in early April at the outbreak of the battle. The camp commanders, however, chose to handle the incidents quite differently. When confronted with possible espionage more than a month into the battle, camp commanders displayed more trust toward the Okinawans and favored their innocence.

American suspicion and demeaning, prejudiced paternalism toward the Okinawans did not disappear, however. Improved interaction among the Okinawans and the Americans in the camps did not eliminate the widely

held characterization of the Okinawans as a backward, primitive, and uncivilized people. The battle still raged fiercely, and the possibility of treachery
also still loomed. The military government units, for example, continued
to record the names of civilians who had relatives in the Japanese Army.[71]
The Americans, however, trusted the Okinawans to collect this information
themselves, and the list did not lead to additional vigilance by the military government. Despite remaining cognizant of their vulnerability living
closely with the Okinawans, the Americans trusted the camp residents on
a level unseen earlier in the battle. Compared to decisions made soon after
the landing, when suspicion quickly turned into accusation, the leniency
signified a change in the Americans' view of the Okinawans and their identity as a people.

In Nodake, for example, the precise shelling of a nearby American gun
position alerted the military government soldiers of B-5 of a possible breach
of security. After the 96th Division Counter Intelligence Corps (CIC) detachment finished interviews with the civilian camp population and submitted
them for review, the camp commander decided that no evidence existed
against any Okinawans and ruled against any disciplinary action of any
type. He cited as reasons for his decision the cooperation and usefulness of
the Okinawans in camp productivity and their identity as Okinawans, not
as Japanese. "It may be noted," he wrote, "that while a number of Japanese
flags were taken from arriving civilians, the inhabitants on questions as
to being 'Japanese' asserted themselves to be 'Okinawan,' not Japanese."[72]
A similar situation during the first month of battle would probably have
caused the suspected offenders to spend at least one night in the stockade.
By April 30, the military government soldiers disassociated the Okinawans
from the Japanese; military government no longer viewed the Okinawans
as enemy civilians.

The realignment of identity of the Okinawans altered military government policy within the individual camps.[73] In addition to ending the
use of death as a consequence after April 26, military-aged men no longer
spent their evenings in guarded barbed-wire enclosures in the center of the
camps.[74] At Shimabaru, the value of the Okinawans as workers outweighed
any fears of organized rebellion. Military government soldiers found it important to send the civilians to work some of the few surviving crops and
increase the food supply. While a few soldiers still guarded work parties that
tended gardens outside of the camp, civilians conducted their work within
the camp under little to no supervision. From the beginning of the battle,
civilians had received tasks from the military government; by late in the

month, civilians completed those daily tasks with a greatly increased level of independence.[75]

Okinawans held camp leadership positions by April 30. The Americans divided up the living sectors and assigned locals to oversee them. They interviewed each candidate about their previous experience with government, their social and economic status within their village, and their attitude toward the United States.[76] Chosen leaders had some English-language skills, ties to America, and credibility within their community. One man chosen as the civilian public safety headman in Nodake had served as the mayor of Ginowan for fifteen years. Another, named Kamajo, had lived in California for twenty-seven years.[77]

The selected local leaders underwent a three-week trial period and, upon assuming their positions, possessed only limited authority. Local leaders oversaw food-ration distribution and assisted in rule enforcement by communicating the regulations to the population.[78] They also served on firefighting teams and recommended other civilians who they believed deserved positions of responsibility. The soldiers retained the right to demote locals who they believed had failed in their management roles; however, the use of civilians as organizers increased the stability and control of camp life.[79] The decision by Americans to identify civilian leaders demonstrated confidence, reliance, and some degree of trust in the Okinawans. The rapid emergence of local leadership in the midst of battle, although rudimentary, signified progress on the part of the Americans toward reevaluating the Okinawans and their identity.[80]

Military government units now diverted the low supply of salvaged construction materials to projects unrelated to security.[81] Camps became more permanent communities; Americans constructed playgrounds, schools, orphanages, and nursing homes with materials that had once built stockades.[82] Soldiers also began to share their military rations and old uniforms more readily with cold and hungry civilians despite previous regulations forbidding such actions.[83] By May 31, military government supply officers sought out discarded American uniforms from salvage dumps and issued them to civilians. To dispel any apprehension when viewed by tactical units, the military government supply sections painted the word "civilian" in white on each shirt.[84] The relaxed restrictions fostered an environment of friendship and encouraged the soldiers to interact with the civilians in casual, social settings; as a result, the people had access to more intimate views of the soldiers. A young Okinawan boy observed soldiers shaving and drinking coffee. "I couldn't believe it," he exclaimed, "It was a completely

different world from what I was used to. They even had toilet paper." Two
soldiers enjoyed tea with a family, and several local nurses had to be moved
away from Nodake to the camp in Koza after beginning romantic relationships with American soldiers.[85]

The mission of military government to remove the civilians from the battlefield and support the main combat operations to secure the island never
changed throughout the battle. Likewise, the priorities of safeguarding
American lives and maximizing resources also continued to drive policy.
American perceptions of Okinawan identity, however, changed as the battle
progressed. Continual interaction with the Okinawans revealed an obedient
and cooperative population. The ability of the military government soldiers
to interpret some traits of the Okinawans as relatable promoted a degree
of trust. Contrasting sharply with pre-battle assumptions of the Okinawan
disposition, Okinawan behavior caused American military government personnel to reassess their perception of Okinawan identity and allegiance,
which in turn modified policy. American camp commanders and military
government soldiers continually evaluated the culture and ethnicity of
Okinawa as well as its political connections to Japan when making decisions
about the conduct of the occupation.

Inside the military government camps, the soldiers encountered the
complexities of race when faced with two ethnic groups—Okinawans and
Japanese—that appeared racially alike at first glance. As military government soldiers, their job required them not only to safeguard their fellow
American soldiers but to sustain the lives of thousands of civilians who appeared more similar to the enemy than themselves. Broad generalizations of
the racial and ethnic character of the enemy promoted by combat planners
to protect American soldiers' lives conflicted with the war experience of the
military government soldier. Within the camps, the military government
soldiers had to make a sophisticated distinction between two ethnic groups
from the same country.

Military government personnel held racist opinions about Asians, yet
the conduct of military government on Okinawa demonstrates that racist
ideas did not always dissolve into ill-informed generalizations and assumptions that bore negative consequences. Nor did such ideas translate into
unorthodox and unnecessarily cruel policies or behavior. By embracing the
Okinawans, US military government soldiers challenged the widely publi-
cized negative images of Americans that the Japanese had promulgated; the
Americans responded to people of a different ethnicity through conscious
evaluation based on experiences of actual interaction. While the Americans

and the Japanese fighting on the battlefields of the Pacific carried out the tasks of war in an extremely brutal manner, the ability of the US Army military government on Okinawa to contemplate the various ethnicities rationally dispels the idea that racial hostility dominated American behavior. Military government commanders and soldiers' contemplation of race in the early occupation of Okinawa resulted in the modification of policy through the constant evaluation of ethnically different people.

7

Benevolent Captors?
Okinawans Encounter the Americans

Yasutaka Aza found himself trapped with his back to the ocean and Americans, tending to their war dead, holding ground on the other three sides of Mabuni Hill. Aza, along with thousands of other dislocated Okinawans, crouched on the beach at night and hid in a nearby cave during the day. At first, Aza did not want to surrender and spent some time foraging for food and drink in blood-tainted waters. His existence grew intolerable. Believing that the Americans would crush him under their tanks, Aza walked to the other side of Mabuni Hill prepared for death. To his surprise, an American soldier calmly searched him and simply took him into custody.[1]

By the end of April, the Japanese forces had fallen back from their defensive positions along a ridgeline south of Machinato and Kakazu and toward Shuri Castle, the symbolic seat of the erstwhile Ryukyu Kingdom. The Japanese defenses along the Shuri Line held for only a few weeks before American forces took both Conical Hill and Sugar Loaf Hill. Situated on the eastern and western ends of the line, the capture of the high terrain enabled the Americans to outflank the Japanese. By May 29, the Americans captured the nearly abandoned Shuri Castle as the Japanese retreated toward Kiyan Peninsula. On the northern part of the island, the Americans had quickly sealed off the Motobu Peninsula as early as April 7; by April 13, they reached Hedo Point, the northernmost area of Okinawa.[2] As the battle advanced up and down the island, with the American forces aggressively uprooting both northern and southern Japanese strongholds, the Okinawan population came face to face with the feared foreign invaders.

Confrontation with Americans both frightened and confused the Okinawans. Believing the Japanese propaganda that described the foreigners as demonic, sadistic monsters, the civilians tried to avoid capture. Failing at evasion, the corralled population gasped in surprise at the conditions they found in the military government camps; compared to foraging on the battlefield, the meager camp resources looked abundant. Okinawans found a relatively safe refuge and access to medical care, fresh clothes, and food. Surprised, civilians discovered that most Americans did not torture or overtly cause harm—and that even those that did participate in inappropriate behavior did not rise to the horrific level described in Japanese tales; Americans did not crush Okinawans under tanks, grind up bodies, or gouge out genitals. More importantly, the Americans did not inflict the level of pain upon the civilians that the Japanese had readily imposed on the population in caves and on the battlefield.

US military government camps and the behavior of American troops offered an opportunity for the Okinawans to redefine their identity in order to capitalize on favorable conditions. Transformation toward an appreciation of the foreigners did not necessarily come easily for the Okinawans. Shaped by years of indoctrination and hiding behind a new layer of distrust as a result of their recent interactions with the Japanese, the population wrestled with the contradictions between what they witnessed of the Americans and what they had heard from propaganda. The Okinawans, however, recognized the advantages of relating to the Americans and proving their worth through productivity and cooperation within the camps. By deliberately aligning their identity either more closely with the Americans or more strictly as Okinawans—and thereby fracturing their association with the Japanese—the civilians found that they could dismantle American fears and confusion as well. Each demographic, whether adults or children, soldiers or refugees, eventually reached a well-defined collective identity as Okinawans, an identity developed through their own unique experiences and used to gain advantage and ensure survival.

Okinawan men and boys who fought with the Japanese units interacted with the Americans primarily through exchanges of fire. Side by side with the Japanese soldiers, the Okinawans that fought saw a hardened, hated, and faceless enemy on the other side of the battlefield. Loyalty to their unit, the country of Japan, their fellow soldiers, their homes, and their families compelled them to fight the enemy. An Okinawan soldier who found himself separated from his unit knew he "had to get back to [his] company, and that determination kept [him] going." Encountering the Americans in battle spurred even more commitment to the ideals encouraged by Japanese propaganda than his military training had inspired during mobilization. In the heat and intensity of combat, the Okinawans who fought as official soldiers reviled the foreign invaders. Americans, engaged in direct combat with them, stood as a well-defined enemy. Hard fighting also drew the Okinawans closer to the Japanese with whom they fought; they shared a survival mentality and equally disregarded the civilian population. One Okinawan soldier dismissed the needs of fellow Okinawans he encountered out of concern for his own necessities. Although he realized he had no means to offer medical help to the badly wounded, he also refused water to people who begged for a simple drink.[3]

The collapse of the Japanese defensive lines brought the Americans cascading into every area of the island. Civilians in both the northern and southern portions of the island found themselves pushed to the edges of the land, trapped on peninsulas, and cornered in caves. In all these areas, the civilian population sat deeply intermingled with the Japanese military, a situation that placed them in serious danger of getting caught in the crossfire. The Americans rooted out pockets of Japanese resistance and thus inflicted casualties among Okinawans. Into the openings of even the smallest caves, Americans threw incendiary charges, ignited gasoline, and aimed flamethrowers. As they closed in on the caves, they attacked from positions above the opening to prevent the escape of anyone inside. The method, called "blowtorch and corkscrew," or "straddling a cave" (*umanori* by the Japanese), killed thousands of civilians and military men. One student nurse recalled the devastating effects of a gas bomb sent into a hospital cave. The bomb was "thrown into the cave with the—fifteen-year-olds! The way they died! Their bodies swelled up and turned purple. . . . It was like they suffocated to death. . . . Forty-six of fifty-one perished there." While the Americans did not target the civilian population specifically, they also did not take special precautions for the Okinawans at the risk of allowing the Japanese to escape. In caves that housed an inordinate number of military compared to a few civilians, the risk for the Okinawans increased. A teenage girl found temporary refuge in a cave in Makabe called Sennin-Go, or Thousand People Cave. The cavern held mostly Japanese military and only a few civilians. The Americans mortared the entrance, sealing it and trapping everyone inside. Deaths of civilians also occurred outside of caves. Rifle fire decimated groups of Okinawans hiding in foliage or moving on roads if the people intermixed too densely with Japanese troops. In one episode, an American rifleman opened fire on a Japanese soldier and, in the same burst, also killed three Okinawan students. Firing on the students stopped once the teacher, carrying the dead body of one of the students, stood upright in front of the rifleman. An observing student commented, "Random firing stopped. The American, who had been firing wildly, must have noticed he was shooting girls."[4] In most instances, though, US troops did not explicitly attempt to kill civilians directly. If a cave appeared to house civilians, for example, they would bring an interpreter to coax the people out.

Children encountered Americans in sizeable numbers after the momentum of the battle favored the foreign invaders. Battle interactions between the population and the Japanese military, however, had occurred at the very opening of the conflict. The young, therefore, had already lost their trust in the Japanese military before facing the Americans. Experiences with the Japanese taught the youth to remain wary toward any soldier. For the young, safety only existed among themselves. Knowing nothing about the Americans outside of the propaganda describing them as vicious animals, the young Okinawans felt threatened, convinced that the foreign troops intended harm. Most children lacked the clarity to understand why their family had perished in crossfire and instead believed that the Americans had deliberately aimed their rifles and flamethrowers at them. Smoked out of the depths of a cave by a charge singeing the entrance, young Okinawans crawled out to face armed Americans who herded them with the barrels of their rifles. "If we stand up, they'll shoot us," the children thought. As they saw ships offshore, they believed the Americans would use naval guns against them as well. "We were in full view of the ships at sea. If they wanted to . . . they could kill us with a single salvo," one youth imagined. "I shuddered. I was completely exposed." As mortars rained down near a village, a teenage boy remarked, "I guess the killing had already started," as he assumed that the Americans were dropping the mortars intentionally on the population for the purpose of mass slaughter.[5]

The young held tightly to the image of the Americans as created by the Japanese. Tragically, fear of torture prevented the children from accepting earnest offers of safety from the US troops. Using translators to persuade civilians away from cliffs, beaches, and out of caves, Americans corralled the people into military government camps that provided food, shelter, clothing, and medical help to the limits of what US resources could support.[6] The Okinawans, however, had no way to trust the sincerity of the offers. Hundreds of civilians died from American rifle fire and incendiaries thrown into caves. The Japanese warned of rape, mutilation, and torture at the hands of the foreigners. The young, who still reeled from the betrayal of the Japanese, presented the stiffest resistance to the coaxing words of the Americans. The children recoiled and called the rescue pleas from the US translators the "voice of the enemy . . . the voices of demons."[7] The interpreters declared, "We'll save you . . . We have food! We will rescue you," but the young Okinawans stubbornly ignored the offers and ran away. As one girl explained, "We'd only been educated to hate them . . . we didn't answer that voice but continued our flight . . . we were simply too terrified . . . we never dreamt the enemy would rescue us."[8] Resistance and hesitation placed the young in danger. Without hearing any responses from fearful youth huddled silently in caverns, the interpreters considered the caves empty of civilians and, therefore, clear for engagements with the enemy. US troops would then fill the cave with gasoline and light it with a tracer round.[9] With the American military dominating the island, few routes devoid of soldiers existed. Young Okinawans that fled from the Americans found themselves in dire situations such as being cornered on the edges of cliffs or facing desperate and deadly Japanese troops. Losing whatever hope they once had, some youths resorted to suicide. Bands of students cried in despair, "We can't take it anymore. Teacher, please kill us. Kill us with a grenade!"[10]

Regardless of their attempts at evasion, the children did interact with the Americans. Ever observant, the young deeply considered what they experienced. In the same way that they recognized insincerity and discord between the promises and behavior of the Japanese military, they noticed dissonance between the actions of the Americans and the stories they had been told about them. Despite the apprehension with which the young approached all militaries, the Americans provided tangible evidence of their sincerity. The stunned youth watched the US troops fulfill promises of safety and nourishment. The Americans administered medicine and bandaged the wounds of their classmates. "Until that moment, I could think of the Americans only as devils and demons," one girl thought. "I was simply frozen. I couldn't believe what I saw."[11] An injured girl, after watching Japanese soldiers kill their wounded with cyanide, crawled away as best she could. US forces picked her up near Haebaru and took her to a medical dispensary. She survived, later saying that she "hated and feared these Americans, but they treated me with great care and kindness, while my classmates, my teachers left me behind."[12] A child, choking on smoke as she exited a burning cave, regained her breath thanks to a US soldier sticking a piece of sugarcane into her mouth. Her two sisters, unconscious from blood loss, also survived after receiving aid from the Americans. Just as the continually aggressive actions of the Japanese toward the population drove the youth toward distrust, the persistent acts of humanity by the Americans left an indelible impression on the young that eventually overrode their fear of the foreigners.[13] While shocked by the positive interactions in contrast to the threatening, mythical stories of torture fabricated by the Japanese, the consistency of charitable acts by the foreigners caused the youth of Okinawa to rethink their definition of enemy. American encounters also made the perceptive children appreciate the additional advantages of an Okinawan identity, advantages beyond the relief of the mental and physical anguish brought on by Japanese duplicity. Identified as Okinawans, the young received treatment as innocent refugees and found themselves herded into military government camps that offered relative protection, food, and shelter.[14] The children's ability to analyze their circumstances, purposely adjust their conduct, and redefine their identity produced conditions that increased their chances of living.

Adults, influenced by the same storytelling about the evil Americans as the young, reacted with similar initial hesitancy toward the foreigners. A twenty-one-year-old woman "never thought of surrendering [to the Americans]." Instead, she and her grandmother chose to follow a Japanese military unit, which exposed them to sparring between the two forces. Hiding among the Japanese soldiers under a cliff's overhang, she watched American grenades kill one man and injure her grandmother. From this experience, she believed that the United States targeted civilians and represented a great threat to her family.[15] Hopelessly trapped between the reality of Japanese cruelty and the assumption of American torture, several adult Okinawans opted to end their own lives. One woman tried to strangle herself with her obi. Another woman gave detailed instructions to the civilians with her on when and under what circumstances they should kill themselves. "If the Americans kill men only," she advised, "then we women should kill ourselves." She also instructed her group against fleeing from the Americans because "they would shoot anybody who would try to escape." Death by the foreigners seemed guaranteed; far better to end their own lives as they saw fit.[16]

Adults reacted with pleased bewilderment when the Americans unexpectedly offered assistance or carried weaker civilians to safety. Older Okinawans felt surprised relief when they experienced the benevolence of the US troops.[17] After the dismay at the poor behavior of the Japanese, American kindness created an opportunity for the adult Okinawans to seek benefits that did not exist before the US military advancement. With survival and caring for their families still priorities, the adults actively sought advantages that might bring comfort or safety; the Americans offered such possibilities. The older Okinawans deliberately appealed to and allied themselves with the Americans to gain favor. A group of fifty Okinawans from the village of Aragaki approached the Americans, waving a white flag and seeking refuge. Adults highlighted any associations they had to America. Locals with medical skills worked as doctors and nurses in US military hospitals, their efforts described by the Navy as a "willingness . . . to cooperate with American authorities."[18] Whereas the young stumbled upon the benefits of military government camps, the adults purposely positioned themselves with the Americans as counterparts; they built kinship and actively sought treatment as equals.

Ingratiating themselves to the Americans, however, required a departure from the Japanese. Unlike the young, who wrestled emotionally with betrayal and broken trust, many of the adults weathered the discord between the expectations and the reality of the behavior of the Japanese and the Americans with more resilience. Older Okinawans were more cognizant of Japanese inconsistencies and the inherent disadvantages of membership in the Okinawan prefecture. Their mature awareness allowed them to transition away from a Japanese identity when the opportunity for improved conditions required such a shift. Making a deliberate choice about their identity protected themselves and their families. Informal, collective communities, under the extreme duress of war, used comparisons of sameness and distinctiveness to select the Okinawan identity consciously.[19] In dialogue with the Americans, the people purposely redefined themselves as exclusively ethnic Okinawans and spoke out against the Japanese as a disparate group.[20] The conscious realignment of their identity earned them relaxed security in the US military government camps and had such a high level of effectiveness that US troops began to believe that the population supported the American way of life and governance.[21] Recognizing the benefits of American benevolence, adult civilians fully committed to their new identity as full Okinawans and dismissed their civil obligations as subjects of the emperor. Not only did they draw similarities between themselves and the Americans, but they actively fought against the Japanese. They helped locate and capture over two hundred resisting Japanese soldiers and, at times, beat up any Japanese that attempted to hide among them.[22] The strained historical relationship between the two ethnic groups allowed the Okinawans' close interaction with the Americans to spawn a drastic divergence from their previous sense of Japanese identity. While the abuses at the hands of the Japanese had not turned away adult loyalty as sharply as it did with the young, the older Okinawans nonetheless recognized the disadvantages they faced in the empire. The Americans offered a chance to improve their lives not only in the immediate situation but potentially in political, larger, and more fundamental ways. While motivated by present concerns of safety and survival, Okinawan abandonment of any dedication to Japan was neither temporary nor meant only to ease the present hardship; adults fully internalized a shift in their identity that redefined their views and actions. The Okinawans now stood by the Americans as opposed to the Japanese; they blamed civilian deaths caused by errant US fire on the Japanese troops intermixed with the population.[23]

As the days pushed into late June, the weather on the island of Okinawa turned to heat and sunshine. The hot sun dried up the wet of the rainy season. Throughout the fighting, mud had sucked shoes right off of feet, and standing water had made waist-deep ponds out of fields and roadways. As full summer arrived on the island, however, the ground cracked from dryness.[24] Official military and political dialogue announced the conclusion of hostilities in favor of the Americans on June 21, 1945.[25] To the Okinawan people, the shift in weather marked a distinction in their environment more clearly than that high-level declaration did. In the months following the end of the battle, much stayed the same for the civilian population. Americans and Japanese still engaged in firefights that placed civilians in danger. The population still scurried around for food and shelter in a setting where little or none existed. In what officials called mopping-up operations, the Americans often encountered sizable resistance in their efforts to bring the Japanese in compliance with the surrender.[26]

Despite their sometimes considerable size, the post-battle engagements took on a different quality. Under the punishment of the American military's momentum, the Japanese forces began to disintegrate. Days before the Americans claimed victory, Japan dissolved several units heavily manned by Okinawans. The Blood and Iron Corps, for example, disbanded on June 19, 1945.[27] As their last defensive lines fell and defeat loomed, many senior officers committed suicide, including General Mitsuru Ushijima, commander of the 32nd Army, and his second-in-command, General Isamu Cho.[28] The lack of leadership on multiple levels led to sporadic resistance fighting. Weakly organized and lacking structure, the post-battle clashes changed much of the camaraderie that fueled the Okinawan fighters' sense of Japanese loyalty. The Okinawans that fought in the battle, therefore, experienced first the impact of the cessation of formal fighting. Much of the security that they experienced via their inclusion in the Japanese military fell apart as the units resorted to individual survival.

In the disorder of a crumbling army, the fighting Okinawans splintered off in the same way as the Japanese did; they dodged the enemy and fought with the same devotion to principles that had inspired their earlier, organized fighting. Each soldier strived to return to the normalcy that had provided them comfort over the past few months by continuing their wartime duties or by seeking reunion with their unit.[29] As the Americans sought to eradicate pockets of opposition that still waged battle, Okinawan soldiers

felt hunted in an unrelenting predator-prey game. "The hunting for us stragglers was severe," one Okinawan soldier said. "Every day Americans came to
the heights of Mabuni with automatic rifles, stripped to their bare chests. . . .
When we went looking for food along the beaches, they would shoot at us
from the heights, as if it were sport." While some Okinawan soldiers did
surrender in the chaos of defeat, many of the military Okinawans continued
to define the Americans as a dangerous enemy worth fighting. Actions by
the American forces aimed at the opposing military, such as puncturing
food cans to cause rot, so the stragglers could not eat the food, and writing
profanities on Japanese graves, ignited anger within the hearts of the Japanese and Okinawans who faced them in armed conflict. [30]

As their units fractured, however, Okinawan fighters saw the first displays of Japanese indifference and bias against them. While the rest of the
population had months earlier processed the shock of Japanese cruelty, the
Okinawan fighters encountered such duplicity directly only with the onset
of military defeat.[31] Okinawans who worked actively as spies, for example,
tasted bitter betrayal as the Japanese became wary of the close relationships
that espionage necessitated between the infiltrators and their subjects. Despite units like the Okinawan-populated Chihaya Unit, a spy organization
under the intelligence section of the 32nd Army Headquarters, the Japanese
published secret orders that called for the "investigation of the [Okinawan]
men who are in the enemy-occupied area."[32] Japanese suspicions of cooperation between the Okinawans and the Americans ran high and bore a deadly
penalty. Conscripted Okinawan spies, along with civilians both innocent
and guilty, were executed after accusations of such collaboration.[33]

Okinawan fighters captured by the Americans found themselves in
prisoner of war camps. US troops separated the Okinawans from the Japanese in the camps and thus allowed the civilian fighters to talk with one
another and share their experiences.[34] Under tolerant prison conditions,
the Okinawans questioned the teachings of the Japanese and reevaluated
what they had witnessed and participated in as soldiers of the 32nd Army;
they found themselves reflecting on the violence that their units had visited
on the population. Caught in the hypocrisy, the Okinawan soldiers placed
blame on the coercive Japanese. Okinawan fighters who carried out violent
acts under military orders against the population disclaimed responsibility
by attributing their actions to a temporary, uncharacteristically confused
state. "I was in a sort of daze myself," reasoned one Okinawan soldier. "I
could hardly care for other people."[35] They also disassociated their actions
from the outcome, often claiming that they did not know what happened

after they fired their weapons, thrust their swords, stole food, or pulled people from caves. Some Okinawan soldiers only admitted to bearing witness to such events and denied any participation at all.[36] The prisoners commiserated and tried to understand why such events had occurred at all. In their efforts to deny any active role they may have played, they accused the Japanese of acting like "bullies" both to the civilian population and to the Okinawan soldiers.[37]

Okinawans in the prisoner of war camps arrived there with the help of fellow soldiers that had surrendered. While not an accepted practice, some soldiers did choose to submit to the military victors. Okinawans did so in groups along with the Japanese or when unit disintegration left them with a low chance of survival on their own. Some surrenders also began as unsuccessful suicide attempts. One Okinawan, crouched in hiding with fellow soldiers for months, offered the remainder of his food ration to his comrades before he rushed toward the enemy.[38] Okinawans that had capitulated then worked for the Americans; they were formed into "placation squads" to coax soldiers and civilians out of hiding. The small groups were dispatched to known refuges to shout messages that broadcast the Japanese defeat. "We've lost. We were defeated," they called. "Your friends and teachers are all in a camp."[39]

Placation squad missions demonstrated to the Okinawans the different ways the two countries treated the population; where the Americans expressed empathy, the Japanese conveyed contempt. Despite noting the different behaviors, Okinawan fighters, both those in prisoner of war camps and in the placation squads, did not attempt to ingratiate themselves with the Americans. The experience of engaging with the foreigners in deadly, armed conflict for months kept the Okinawan soldiers from viewing the US troops as anything but an enemy; they continued to see the Americans as a force that had fired at them with malice and desecrated the graves of their dead. Rejecting the notion of appeals to the Americans and reeling under the splintered military units' exposure to the falsehood of Japanese brotherhood, the civilian soldiers awakened to a newfound sense of being Okinawan. Bolstered by a collective share of the combat trauma, the imprisoned Okinawan fighters questioned the order of the empire both verbally and physically.[40] Nightly, they rose in anger and violence against those who they believed had subjugated them or those Okinawans who turned too slowly toward the new group consensus. As they watched or participated in the beatings, they thought, "What's the difference between Okinawans and people from outside the prefecture?"[41] The revelations profoundly resonated with the Okinawan soldiers and brought them to a definitive conclusion. "For the first time I began to be awakened to differences in our cultures," one soldier said. "I began to see that I was an Okinawan."[42]

The population continued to have complicated feelings toward the Japanese, however. One boy found a pair of Japanese officer's leather leggings in the bushes while gathering sannin ginger leaves and recoiled in fear; one young girl attributed her resilience during the fighting to the Japanese teachings she received in school before the war.[43] The Japanese military still waged a propaganda campaign for Okinawan inclusion. Rear Admiral Minoru Ota, commanding officer of the Japanese Navy Underground Headquarters, described Okinawan actions during the battle as those of allegiance with the empire. "In their heart," he telegrammed, "they wish only to serve as loyal Japanese."[44] The experience of the battle, however, had altered the population's perceptions of the Japanese to such a great extent that rhetoric alone, particularly contradictory rhetoric, could no longer significantly influence the people. The Okinawans witnessed actions by both the American and Japanese militaries that derailed years of propaganda designed to inspire loyalty under claims of national inclusion. As munitions cratered land, scorched crops, flattened homes, and pulverized people, the Okinawans faced violence at the hands of the Japanese, not safety. Stunned by the dissonance between promises of nationhood and the soldiers' violent behavior, the population distrusted and rejected the Japanese by battle's end.

In their denial of a Japanese heritage, however, the Okinawans did not adopt the American culture. Okinawans that did appeal to Japan's foe did so seeking refuge, not assimilation. The dismissal of their Japanese association resulted in a full embrace and elevation of their already recognized Okinawan roots. Each Okinawan—young, old, fighter, or refugee—processed the severe experience of war at his or her own pace and in a unique way, yet all demographic groups ultimately reestablished a definitive connection to an Okinawan identity. The trauma of the war forged shared experiences of hardship that promoted solidarity built around experience. Mutual destitution drawn along lines of similar ethnicity led to a renewed embrace of their likeness as they sought reason and reassurance within the chaos of war. Gravitating toward others that shared the traits that made them outsiders, collectively the people found strength in understanding themselves in terms that not only led to communal comfort but also shunned the oppressor; they were Okinawan above all else.[45] As more of the population pooled together in military government enclosures and prisoner of war camps, relatively safe environments with food, water, and shelter, their conversations led to *consciousness*—a sociological process of realizing that a group exists and understanding its position in relation to other groups—which further united the people in a collective Okinawan identity.[46]

The Okinawans reached their determinations about identity through active and deliberate consideration of the conditions of their environment. Okinawans fully participated in the formation of and commitment to an identity that brought safety, reassurance and comfort and gained them an advantage, no matter how small, in a grave situation. A strong Okinawan identity worked to secure relative physical safety and assuaged the mental discord brought on by Japanese duplicity and war. Okinawans participated as full actors in their identity formation and thus helped shape their own fate during the volatile conditions of war.

8

No Initiative
Unbending Policy, Rigid US Marine Action

Nightfall on the island of Okinawa made all shadows look like monsters and all movement sound nefarious. Rustling grasses, moved by the wind, made the Marines prickle and twitch in tense expectation of an approaching Japanese soldier. The quiet beaches encountered upon landing were not only a source of relief but also of concern. The enemy, by not engaging in an aggressive defense on the beaches, had acted unexpectedly and therefore increased the danger of the battlefield. The Okinawan civilians also surprised the Marines by not acting as predicted; unorganized groups of civilians greeted the foreign invaders on the beaches in misguided attempts to flee the hazards of war. At night, in the early days of the battle, the uneasiness of an enemy acting with chicanery and a civilian population moving freely between the two opposing forces caused some US Marine units to hesitate in the dark. Crafty Japanese soldiers took advantage of the confusion and disguised themselves as women to slip past the Marines and lob grenades into their positions. Confusion gave way to anger and determination as the Marines quickly resorted to their typical tactic of indiscriminately killing anyone that moved in the darkness.[1]

In the confusion and tension of combat, the Marines' landing on the beaches of Okinawa concentrated primarily on the mission objectives: the cohesion of their teams, the effectiveness of their weapons, and the strength of their resupply. Consistent with their lack of emphasis during pre-battle preparations on comprehensive planning for the large civilian population, the Marines stepping onto the battlefield relegated concerns for the welfare of the Okinawan people to the lowest priority. The assaulting Marines haphazardly grouped the unarmed Okinawans that cluttered the beaches into clusters and then pushed inland. In the first days after landing, Marine military government retained the unstructured clusters so as to speed the attack. Undermanned and short on resources, the military government units ignored the nourishment needs of the growing number of relatively free-roaming civilians. Marines found the sight of the war-ravaged civilians offensive; they saw the Okinawans as vile and inhuman. By marginalizing the people, these impressions allowed the military government to rationalize their insufficient handling of the population.[2] At quick glance, the composition of the groups of Okinawans encountered on the beaches (children, old men, and women) appeared to pose no threat. Never wavering in their belief that the Okinawans stood as a definitive enemy, disgusted by the population that they encountered, and naively disregarding the strength of the too young and too old, the Marines postponed the establishment of functioning refugee camps, reluctant to devote the massive effort for such a vile people. Negative attitudes, combined with a lack of adequate personnel and supplies, and therefore ability, contributed to a lack of formal military government procedures. Civilians, therefore, traveled unfettered throughout the battlefield, obstructing both the operational and military government missions.[3]

Unstructured, disorganized military government hampered aid distribution and increased the number of accidental civilian casualties. The ability of the Okinawans to wander anywhere within American lines also increased the likelihood of exposed military secrets and compromised security. An inadequate, weak military government structure that allowed civilians unrestricted movement gave the Japanese opportunities to attack cagey Marine combat units. By mid-April, attacks against Americans were occurring from within the local populations residing in the Marine-occupied military government areas. The Marines, however, did not take the time to determine the ethnicity of the attackers. Reports about the incidents dismissively stated that the offenders could have either Japanese or Okinawan origins.[4] The shock of the attacks caused the Marines to reassess the level of control they exercised over the population; creating established camps with restrictive regulations, as originally planned, would minimize the threat of hostile acts against Americans. While the absence of a military government structure at the onset of the invasion resulted from the apathy and inability of an overstressed, undermanned workforce, the transition toward firmer controls stemmed from concerns about troop safety and extreme misgivings about the Okinawans that reinforced the original assessment of the population as "nationals of unquestionable loyalty."[5] The Marines, despite neglecting to ascertain the ethnicity of the attackers, believed that the incidents proved the combative nature of the Okinawans as unquestionably allied with the Japanese. With the attacks considered as evidence of hostility and resolute cooperation with the Japanese, the Marines' adverse feelings toward the

Okinawans increased. Identifying the Okinawans as Japanese, combined with agitation caused by the attacks, translated into occasional aggressive action from the Marines toward the civilian population.[6]

By mid-April, operations in Marine military government camps resembled the Army camps far more than they had earlier during the landing. The Marines had learned from their own experiences that loose policies and absent systems made their mission of controlling the population and providing for basic humanitarian needs much more difficult. Despite maintaining their distrust of the Okinawans, the Marines had exposed themselves unnecessarily to danger by executing their duties with minimal effort. Now hardened in their conviction of the malicious nature of the Okinawans—despite never verifying the veracity of the claim—the military government units attached to the Marines began establishing a camp system that promoted security. The barbed wire, guards, accountability, rations, and movement restrictions looked similar to those used by the Army detachments. By basing those measures on an unwavering belief in the aggressive intentions of the Okinawans, however, from the very beginning the Marines carried out their military government duties with an element of harshness absent from the Army camps.[7]

The differences between the running of Marine and Army military government camps demonstrates the great extent to which the assignment of identity shaped the actions of the American combatants. Marines landed on the beaches of Okinawa with a predetermined, definitive definition of Okinawan identity as enemy. Unambiguous assignment of identity meant that Marines—military government personnel and combatants alike—did not receive guidance, permission, or any expectation that they should reevaluate the identity of the Okinawans based on the behavior of the population they encountered. The predisposed notion of a combatant Okinawan deeply influenced the actions of the Marine units despite any witnessed civilian behavior to the contrary. As military government units assigned to the Marines transitioned from having no structure to imposing strict regulations in their camp design, the idea of the enemy Okinawan remained steadfast. Marine military government camps distinguished themselves by overtly harsh treatment inspired by a mistrust of a supposedly adversarial population.

As they landed, the Marines should not have seen any civilians on shore, because an Okinawan district order on February 25, 1945, followed by an order from the Japanese military on March 23, had evacuated thousands of civilians out of the central area around Naha and toward the rough northern wilderness.[8] By the time the American forces landed on April 1, war had darkened the beauty of the warm island of Okinawa. As the pressure of military vehicles and marching men on ground wet from the rainy season churned out a muddy paste, one hospital corpsman described the mud in a letter to his parents as "so deep it's like getting a perpetual enema. And I mean a high colonic."[9]

Just back off the beach, Marines encountered scattered civilians who neither followed the Japanese and district orders nor paid attention to preliminary instructions dropped from American B-29s during the bombardment and in the first days after the landing. Meant to minimize initial confusion by instructing the civilians on how to react to the battle, the airdropped pamphlets "discouraged [civilians] from coming through [American] lines." The Marines also distributed proclamations of authority upon landing.[10] Geiger hoped that such information would encourage Okinawans to follow American direction and thus alleviate disorder as a means to establish control sooner.

Military government detachments A-1 and B-1, attached to the 1st Marine Division, found seventy-five Okinawans in their sector. The group, consisting primarily of old men, women, and children in poor health, had lived on the beach since the loss of their homes during the preinvasion bombardment. Farther off the beach, elderly Okinawans, having abandoned their homes during the initial bombardment, crouched in crumbling, soft earth, hand-dug caves. Military government personnel searched for structures further inland in Sobe but found only skeletons of buildings still standing. For the first night, they simply held the people on the beach without any shelter or within any enclosure.[11]

The next day, five hundred Okinawans turned up homeless. To deal with this increase, military government personnel attempted to use the shells of the buildings for containment. Military police units attached to the divisions guarded the civilians, but Civil Affairs still did not erect any type of enclosures to hold the growing population. With food difficult to find, Marines offered their own rations to the Okinawans on L-Day; military government could only provide each person one meal a day.[12]

Quickly, the number of civilians grew larger than estimated by the Tenth Army planners. Some nine thousand Okinawans had wandered into the rapidly advancing American-occupied territory by April 5, 1945.[13] Most lacked shelter or food, and those that came from villages that had withstood the bombardment often needed medical care or assistance with basic sanitation. Soon the loose plans created on board the ships fell apart. Teruto Tsubota, an interpreter assigned to the 6th Marine Division, described the situation as a "madhouse, no control, no nothing."[14] Contrary to the orders stating that the Okinawans should be treated as prisoners of war and restricted, the rapid influx of civilians forced the military government soldiers attached to the Marines to allow, though reluctantly, a permissive environment. Short on personnel and resources, units that encountered villages chose to leave them alone. Without enough men to assist, military government personnel did not search civilians for weapons or documents. Except for the limited control of appointing a local Okinawan as overseer, they allowed the civilians to stay in their homes, salvage what remained of flattened crops, and roam freely throughout the area.[15]

Supply shortfalls, particularly in transportation and equipment, contributed to an inadequate military government system by severely restricting what the civil affairs programs could accomplish. To transport and house thousands of dislocated civilians, many of whom suffered wounds, military government units required transportation and ample tarpaulin and tents.[16] The allocated two vehicles per detachment fell well short of being able to handle the number of civilians the military government needed to move. As for shelter, the predicted size of the civilian group determined the allotment of tentage for each detachment. Large "C" detachments, which had been allocated 110 sleeping cots, had received sufficient tents. Forward-operating "A" and "B" detachments, however, designed as smaller and more temporary units and meant to process fewer civilians, had only one small command tent and two tarpaulins. On the beaches of Okinawa, the inadequate tentage left many civilians exposed to the Okinawan spring rainstorms and defeated any efforts to contain the crowds. The arrangement risked security because of the difficulty of addressing defensive concerns. Despite its necessity in mitigating fraternization and preventing any exposure of American military secrets, the idea of separating the civilians from the Americans proved impossible to enforce in the first week of April. Shortages in equipment also prevented the detachments from providing basic humanitarian needs and precluded the development of established systems for long-term or advanced care. Lieutenant Colonel Donald Winder argued that the detachments needed "heavy trucks [2½ ton]. . . . Three-quarter ton weapon carriers and jeep trailers are not sufficient . . . [the 'A' and 'B' teams need] hundreds of 20 × 40 foot tarpaulins for emergency shelter . . . an absolute necessity for assault shipping." The two tarpaulins allotted to the teams did not even arrive on time. "Practically no equipment had been landed . . . for two or three days" for teams A-3 and B-3.[17]

Overwhelmed and inexperienced military government personnel saw the villages as an opportunity to ease their workload and used the preexisting village structure to provide for the population.[18] From shelter to local government, the quasi-stability of the village community made the overworked military government units assign much of the responsibility for the civilians' well-being to the civilians themselves. Use of such villages was only a temporary solution; their size could not sufficiently support the large groups of wandering, homeless Okinawans. Military government personnel's acceptance of the temporary nature of the situation, however, inspired them to ignore their responsibility to enact any policies of their own. Identifying local leaders among the village residents did not signify a heightened trust between the Americans and the Okinawans; military government personnel simply needed more people to work for them.

Beyond using the village structure, the military government units improvised in other ways. Military Government Detachment B-10, attached to the 1st Marine Division, salvaged building materials, clothing, and food from the local population. They used discarded American rations and acquired household goods such as cooking pots and sleeping mats from abandoned homes. They obtained four Japanese trucks and used them to move civilians from forward collecting points to rear areas for medical assistance. Most military government detachments forced all but the non-ambulatory to march toward collection areas miles away. Others asked for assistance either by loading Okinawans on empty American military trucks driving by or by augmenting their organic trucks and acquired Japanese trucks with vehicles and Marine personnel from combat units.[19] Such cooperation caused tension between the operational units and the military government units. The mission of civil affairs was to alleviate the intrusion of civilians into frontline operations; borrowing combat resources for military government was simply another form of such intrusion. In essence, civil affairs became a burden upon the frontline fighters. Empty military vehicles commandeered for civilian transport and combat Marines that ferried Okinawans back to rear areas were diverted from the combat missions. Winder quickly realized that his efforts at civilian control, rather than providing support, had become a "burden" and "retard[ed] the combat effort."[20] As civil affairs tasks strained combat assets, the divisions, which tended to retain interpreters and military police for use by the intelligence staff for interrogations, showed increased reluctance toward offering support to the military government agenda.

While the Marine military government plans, conceived late and without input from the Tenth Army, crumbled upon landing, the belief that the Marines held about the Okinawans as fervent nationalists loyal to Japan stood strong. The majority of the Okinawans that streamed into American-occupied areas within the first week of the battle were docile, posed no threat, and only desired assistance in the form of food or medical attention. Despite meeting thousands of disheveled, meek, and helpless Okinawans on the beaches and throughout the island, the Marines still categorized the local people as "Japanese civilian enemy." The Marines considered Japan and Okinawa one nation; they assigned the Japanese heritage to any cultural artifact or behavior encountered. In letters sent home, they inaccurately described Ryukyuan handicrafts, clothing, and cookware found in abandoned Okinawan homes as traditional Japanese items.[21] Despite behavioral evidence to the contrary, the Marines' association of the Okinawans with the Japanese remained immutable. Hatred toward the fighting Japanese enemy translated into repugnance for the weak Okinawans suffering from war's fallout. The Marines categorized the Okinawans as subhuman; Corporal James Johnston, while bemoaning the size of the population, referred to them collectively as an overgrown pest infestation.[22] The Marines lamented that "the worst crosses to bear [as part of overseas duty in the Pacific] were the mosquitoes, the fleas, and the sight of the pathetic people."[23] By not differentiating between the effects of war and the characteristics of culture, Marines viewed the dismal living conditions they encountered as indicative of the population's way of life and not as the result of heavy bombardment and island-wide ground battle. They saw the Okinawans as "not very clean personally . . . their homes were utterly filthy." One Marine remarked, "This would be a nice country if the people weren't so dirty." Private First Class John David Jackson called them "nasty . . . nasty people."[24] Such categorization inspired no ingenuity from the men to devise creative programs and systems to improve the Okinawans' circumstances.

The Marines, seeing the Okinawans as adversaries and bestial, dirty vermin, exhibited reluctance to contribute the herculean effort needed to establish functional—let alone comfortable—camps for the refugees. To justify the desire for inaction further, the Marines identified the particular Okinawans they encountered as physically incapable of causing harm; they described them as "so old and decrepit or young and harmless-looking that the best thing was to leave them alone and let them stay in their homes, tilling their fields, provided they did not get in the way of troops, keeping only the homeless ones in camps."[25] The Marines' disgust at the appearance of the Okinawans also translated to assumptions about their intelligence, demeanor, and worth. They thought of the Okinawans as naive and simple, people to pity and mock rather than help. In the opinion of the Marines, the Okinawans seemed scared, shocked, and unable to comprehend the battle around them.[26] Joking among themselves, the Marines ridiculed the civilians as being like children. One Marine called the Okinawans "poor devils" whose primitive comprehension caused them to interpret the war as the fulfillment of apocalyptic prophecy.[27]

The Marines' unwavering conception of the Okinawans as dirty and as enemy, along with the limitations caused by inadequate civil affairs resources, stunted the implementation of Marine policy to force the population into restrictive, guarded camps. In the opening days of the battle, an undertrained, overstretched military government chose the easiest option to deal with the growing number of homeless Okinawans—they ignored them. The demographics of the population they encountered, predominantly groups perceived as weaker (old men, children, and women), eased their fears of attack. Even though the Marines assessed the Okinawans found on the beach as non-threats, the men still believed the population "belonged" to the enemy. As a result, the Marines detested offering assistance to the civilians.

Civilians, therefore, roamed haphazardly throughout American-occupied territory and created problems for both the operational and military government missions. The detachments had no control over the massive number of Okinawans, and this impeded their ability to provide rations, clothing, or medical care. Without a system of distribution, military government personnel parceled out goods to any eager civilians that requested them. Okinawans that avoided the Americans received none; those who asked received as much as the Americans could offer. The free-roaming Okinawan civilian population intermixed with the Japanese soldiers and made it difficult for the American combat troops to differentiate fighter from farmer. The Marines killed civilians in their efforts to engage enemy soldiers and also fired at any unidentified human form that crossed into their area. Units with previous battle experience in the Pacific theater, such as the 1st Marine Division, found that the indiscriminate shooting, while also having occurred in other island campaigns, was producing an inordinate number of dead civilians on Okinawa.[28]

The number of Okinawans that found their way behind American lines continued to increase, exacerbating the problem. Detachments A-1 and B-1 encountered 12,000 civilians in Chibana alone by April 6.[29] Placing further strain on the disorganized detachments, the "C" camps, designed to handle larger numbers of dislocated civilians, did not receive them because the lack of control that the "A" and "B" detachments had over the population prevented the detachments from uniformly processing and moving groups of people.[30] Buckner observed with consternation 40,000 civilians wandering around the 1st Marine Division area of Chimu and Nakagusuku Wan. The military government units lacked control to such a degree that civilians "[were] left practically to their own devices."[31]

In addition to hindering aid distribution and increasing accidental civilian casualties, loose military government practices also increased the likelihood of exposing military secrets and compromising security. On April 5, in the area of Chibana, an attack by two armed men resulted in casualties on both sides. Similar incidents of attacks from within the local populations occurred at Taira, Zahana, and Itoman.[32] The attackers could have been Okinawan, possibly conscripted soldiers serving in the Okinawan Home Guard (Boei Tai) or the Blood and Iron Corps.[33] Just as likely, however, the attackers could also have been from a Japanese unit, that is, Japanese soldiers disguised as civilians. Military government detachments loosely estimated "hundreds of military personnel disguised as civilians" and had difficulty with prisoners of war infiltrating the civilian population.[34]

The Marines, however, did not generally care to determine the ethnic background of the instigators of the incidents. Most often, their reports indicated that the offenders could have possessed either an Okinawan or Japanese background and did not suggest that any time was spent determining the difference.[35] Trying to separate an aggressive Okinawan from a Japanese soldier disguised as a civilian proved difficult. The Marine interpreter Teruto Tsubota acknowledged the presence of Japanese soldiers among the population but felt it pointless to determine the attackers' origins. "Yeah. Some of them [are Japanese soldiers], but we don't know who they are. Because they all look alike to us; they dress alike. They try to look as much like the Okinawans as possible."[36] One Marine found it humorous that the "Japs and Okinawans and kids and old people and ducks and dogs and cats . . . everything was being smashed together. And it's hard to sort them out."[37] The Marines also projected their own American brand of patriotism onto the Okinawans and assumed that the sole motivation an Okinawan could have for attacking American combatants stemmed from proud allegiance to country. In the minds of the Marines, the violent acts served as tangible evidence to solidify the already absolute notion that the Okinawans displayed loyalty to Japan at such an intense level as to spur violence.[38]

The incidents inspired a stark realization: Military government units needed to implement tight restrictions, as originally planned, to protect American lives from any hostile actions staged in areas under American control. By mid-April, the military government detachments began formally establishing controls and imposing restrictions upon the population. The new policies expanded on the original preinvasion plans and limited the access of Okinawans to American personnel and military secrets, thus increasing the security of both, and monitored the movement of the Okinawans to maintain better awareness of the residents of the camps. In compliance with orders from the Marine division commanders to detain all civilians, the military government detachments erected barbed-wire enclosures to cordon off areas and thus created definitive boundaries and camps. In some areas, for example Berger Beach, the detachments added fences around groups of people who had already formed themselves into informal communities. With larger, less organized populations, military government personnel consolidated the civilians and transported them to predetermined locations away from the frontlines. Detachments working in the 1st Marine Division area cordoned off the entire Katchin Peninsula and moved 30,000 civilians to within its boundaries. Separate inner enclosures contained men ranging in age from sixteen to forty-five, a demographic that mimicked the composition of American forces.[39] Marines screened the male population in an attempt to identify any potential adversaries and did not allow them to re-integrate with the women, children, and old men regardless of the results of the screenings. Men considered of military age lived under guard and were questioned as if they were captured Japanese soldiers. The intense interrogations infuriated the men, since the tactics used by the Marines made the Okinawans appear untrustworthy to their fellow villagers, as if they served as spies. Military police and military government soldiers guarded both the all-male inner enclosures and the outside perimeter camp enclosures. No Okinawan could travel outside the designated camp area unless escorted by an American guard; groups could be no larger than five people.[40]

As an unintended secondary consequence, measures put in place to safeguard American lives also greatly improved the efficiency of the camps and therefore, ironically, allowed the detachments to organize the provision of more aid. Newly implemented programs that dealt with supply distribution and accountability stemmed from the need to maintain control and restrict the population. Each Okinawan received a rations tag that allowed the detachments to track both the amount of food consumed and the number of people present. Detachment soldiers guarded towers of military ration cans in efforts to deter thieves.[41] Every Okinawan had to register upon arrival so as to ensure the proper documentation of every resident. To minimize movement within the camps, families lived together within shelter compounds as much as feasible.[42] With such programs in place, the detachments could accomplish more tasks without additional men.

To encourage compliance with the new regulations, the detachment soldiers wore armbands designating them as military police. The soldiers did not fulfill any police functions, but the armbands gave them a certain authority that allowed them to corral the Okinawans.[43] The detachment soldiers also identified Okinawans that held prestige within their communities and had them assume informal leadership roles. These local leaders either had already held prominent positions within their villages in politics or education or could speak English. For the Marines, the use of local leaders helped dissolve language barriers and eased the perceived caginess of the population. Military government did not consider the local Okinawan leaders as equals in terms of authority but as workhorses to aid the outnumbered Marines, who remained suspicious of them and kept them under close observation.[44]

The Marines had learned from their own experiences that loose policies and absent systems made their mission of controlling the population much more difficult and exposed them unnecessarily to danger. While the idea for minimal restrictions had stemmed from the apathy that grew out of a workforce inundated with more tasks than they had men to complete them, the move toward stricter controls grounded itself in the concept of self-survival and deep distrust toward the Okinawans. Despite neglecting to identify the ethnicity of the attackers, the Marines believed that the Okinawans had proven themselves combative and had aligned themselves squarely with the Japanese. Military government personnel assigned to Marine units viewed homeless Okinawan women as combatants and captured them as prisoners of war. New regulations barred military government troops from sharing transport vehicles with the civilian population. Dubbed "enemy aliens," the Marines feared that their men would get killed if they traveled too close to the Okinawans.[45]

With the attacks seen as proof of hostile intent and concerted coordination with the Japanese, the Marines' adverse feelings toward the Okinawans increased and aligned even more squarely with negative racial assumptions. Following the attacks, Private Charles Miller, 6th Marine Division, directed his hostility toward the Okinawans because "they had slant eyes. We [are] very anti-slant eyes. Guys [say], 'There goes a slant-eyed chink, pow-pow.'"[46] Intense racist feelings, combined with agitation over the attacks, translated into occasional aggressive action toward the civilian population. The 6th Marine Division knowingly opened fire on large groups of civilians traversing the roads and, when observing the carnage, felt no empathy and refused to care for the bodies respectfully. One group of Marines kidnapped and took turns raping Okinawan women in their tents for days. After they lost interest, they covered up their debauchery by presenting the women to their commanding officer as captured Japanese nurses. Those Marines who did not participate in the sexual assaults chose not to because they categorized the Okinawan women as subhuman and inferior, not because they found the acts morally reprehensible. Okinawan women "represented filth," they stated. "God, who would want to go into the tent with that thing?"[47]

The sudden imposition of structure and the threat of harm did not mean that the Okinawans immediately became willing participants in camp life. The abrupt move toward managing the population came with distinct limitations and consequences. In the confusion of war, the Okinawans distrusted the Americans as much as the Americans distrusted them. Japanese propaganda told lurid stories about how the Americans treated prisoners and portrayed the Americans as racially biased and viciously cruel.[48] The Okinawans, while desperate for help, remained wary of the Americans, particularly when the actions of the Marines in and out of the camps tended to lean toward violence. Some Okinawans resisted the Marines by avoiding the camps and, once in the camps, purposefully moved slowly through processing. Some even spat on the Marines. One Okinawan wrote furiously in a letter about how his "blood boiled over with uncontrolled hatred for the American bastards."[49] Military government units assigned to the Marines processed the civilians as captured enemy combatants, and this classification resulted in an environment that lent itself to prison-like standards.

The level of treachery that the Japanese attributed to the Americans, however, still remained inaccurate, even in the camps run under Marine guidelines and regulations. Barbed-wire enclosures, guards, regulations, and screenings did not compare to the Japanese accusation that the Americans "would chop [the Okinawans'] legs off, would ship them to Frisco to be used as dog meat," or "slice [them] up like a piece of vegetable."[50] Measures such as enclosures and guards allowed the detachments to maintain accountability of the residents of the camps, and, while the civilians could expect an austere environment with minimal room for independent action and occasional outbursts of violence in the form of rape or abuse, they also found that the horror stories of grotesque mutilation were not grounded in the truth and that the camps at least provided a steady source of food and refuge from the rampages of the battlefield. Some Marines did exhibit exemplary behavior, as well. Two scared seventy-five-year-old women and a paralyzed child offered a group of Marines that darkened their cave entrance money in exchange for their lives. To their surprise, the Marines refused the money and instead offered food and medical care as they escorted the trio back to a camp. An Okinawan man expressed gratitude toward the Marine who revived him after a failed suicide attempt. Okinawans found that they could tolerate the violent abuses experienced in the Marine camps as sacrifices outweighed by the security of food and shelter. Death and abandonment suffered at the hands of the Japanese for simply getting in the way remained an unacceptable alternative.[51]

The barbed wire, guards, accountability, rations, and movement restrictions of the Marine security system may have appeared similar to those used by the Army detachments. Military government camps assigned to the Marines, however, were held to notably harsher and more stringent standards than the Army's camps. By basing the design for security measures on an unwavering belief in the aggressive intentions of the Okinawans, the Marines carried out their military government duties with an element of severity absent from the Army camps. Upon reception in a Marine camp, Okinawans received a crude identifying badge, which was to hang around their necks at all times. Military government soldiers "bartered" with the civilians as they entered camp by withholding certain amenities until the civilians agreed to the policies governing the camp. Newly arriving Okinawans did not receive any bed or shelter until the military government soldiers running the camps felt confident in their obedience. Men separated for screening were "thoroughly grilled" through a series of questions indistinguishable from fierce interrogations.[52] Okinawan men deemed strong enough to work were sent to prisoner of war camps so they could be used as a labor force. Called "civilian prisoners," the men served as forced labor, suffered stringent discipline, and remained under close guard. While working in forward areas on tasks such as filling sandbags, some men died from misdirected fire. Okinawan men who stayed in the male-only enclosures in the military government camps lived in quarters so cramped and overpopulated that the men stood shoulder to shoulder with no room to sit down. Marines argued that the overcrowded population occupying Katchin Peninsula "lived in freedom" and did not deserve their own homes. They proclaimed that "Japanese Army camp followers and prostitutes [were] uniformly superior in intelligence, cleanliness and discipline to the run of refugees."[53] They unsympathetically viewed the Okinawans as useless because they disassociated them from humanity. Even Okinawans who spoke English or had ties to America and who served as interpreters and informal liaisons to the populations fell into the forced labor category with no authority over other civilians.[54]

The attacks on the camps put all the detachment soldiers on edge. Following the incidents, any movement of unknown people along the outskirts of the gathered populations caused the men to fire their weapons indiscriminately, which resulted in the deaths of innocent civilians. Begun by individuals independent of orders, shooting civilians that were moving about unauthorized gradually became a common and accepted practice. The

Marines placed the responsibility for the shootings on what they considered the careless actions of the civilians. They reasoned that civilians who wandered in and out of territory held by armed Americans, sometimes at night, placed themselves in danger. "Of course they were fired upon," the Marines rationalized.[55]

The first shooting of a civilian by Marine military government on Okinawa occurred at dusk on April 6, in Chibana, the day after the attack against the 1st Marine Division by a person within the population. Civilians moving about in the dim hours caused anxious men from Detachment B-1 to open fire.[56] The shooting occurred five days before the first shooting of a disobedient civilian by Army military government and, unlike the Army, whose soldiers acted in accordance with an issued XXIV Corps order, the Marines as a whole informally adopted the practice on their own by accepting the behavior of their men. Despite not having an explicit order authorizing civilian shootings, however, aggression toward the population aligned with the Marines' association of the Okinawans with the Japanese enemy.

In Marine military government camps, the shooting of civilians who wandered without authorization in and out of the perimeter devolved into a cruel ritual that extended beyond boundary infractions. Marines knowingly shot civilians, at times without a clear purpose, and justified their actions by arguments of "survival of the fittest" and the complacent attitude that the civilians would have died anyway. Said one Marine, "There's always somebody who would shoot them."[57] Shooting civilians became so commonplace and so obligatory that Marines felt they "had to shoot [the Okinawans]." The sight of wounded children and women failed to produce visceral, human reactions of remorse.[58]

Hostility continued through interactions with civilians outside of the camps as well. Military government soldiers both passively received Okinawans that made their own way into the camps and actively traveled forward into combat areas to collect those still hiding in fear. The limestone caves dotting the landscape of Okinawa housed both Japanese fighting troops and refugee civilians fleeing the advancing Americans. Marine military government units used dynamite to clear the caves or seal them shut without first allowing the civilians to exit. Those few soldiers that disagreed with the practice and actively sought to secure civilians before the explosives ignited often faced discipline from their commanding officers. One officer placed a pistol to the temple of an American interpreter whose efforts to persuade the residents of a cave to evacuate delayed a dynamite charge.[59]

On April 11, Major General Pedro del Valle, the commander of the 1st Marine Division, repeated to his men in an official order that all "civilians and prisoners of war will be treated with humanity and their persons and honor respected" and restated that Marines who disobeyed the directive would receive "severe and quick punishment."[60] Del Valle opposed any treatment of civilians that would constitute a war crime and felt it necessary, in observing the conduct of his Marines toward civilians and prisoners of war alike, to reiterate in a threatening manner the limitations of their roles as prison guards and keepers of the people. His words, however, betrayed the distinct difference between the development of the Army military government camps and those of the Marines. Grouping civilians and prisoners of war together in both speech and identity, del Valle insisted on keeping both groups detained involuntarily.

The Marines disagreed with the Army on the precise parameters of humane treatment, and the disagreement played itself out at all levels of command. A product of rivalry and the poor working relationship between the services, Marine commands under Buckner broke some of the orders he issued. One directive routinely broken by the Marines prohibited all soldiers under the Tenth Army from consuming local livestock and its dairy products. Issued with detailed guidance that specified the prioritized use of dairy and meat products for the Okinawan population, Buckner believed the preservation of local assets for local people would safeguard military rations exclusively for American forces. By protecting the resources of the island, the Tenth Army could preserve Okinawan access to a basic food supply and thus minimize the amount of American rations consumed by the locals. Consumption of local farm goods by Americans also increased the likelihood of contracting foodborne diseases and conflicted with the standing order against looting and pilfering the population unnecessarily.[61] Marines, however, milked goats and butchered pigs. While some livestock had roamed from their original pens unaccounted for, Marines also stole pigs and goats from struggling families in villages and from abandoned farms that starving Okinawans would scavenge as they wandered the battlefield. While the Marines enjoyed the milk and roast pork as welcome delicacies after months of military rations, the local people were desperate to recover their livestock.[62]

In addition to lower-ranking enlisted Marines wrangling the local livestock, division commanders brazenly disobeyed the order as well. In an ostentatious show of defiance, del Valle served Buckner fresh pork chops when the Tenth Army commander visited the operating area of the 1st Marine Division. After awkwardly eating the meal, Buckner announced, "Now, General, this is a disobedience to my orders. You have evidently killed one of the local animals." Del Valle beckoned to the mess sergeant, who then explained that an attack last night had claimed the life of a local pig. Del Valle cockily proclaimed after Buckner left, "I don't think the General swallowed it, but he couldn't say 'no' because he [doesn't] know the local situation [has] been perfectly calm for days and we [haven't] had any shooting around here."[63] Buckner's order prohibiting farm theft originated from his concern for the health and sustenance of his American forces, but it also had the secondary effect of conserving the scarce resources of the local population. Del Valle's smug disregard for the authority of Buckner, an Army commander, also had the consequence of endorsing more poor treatment of the local population. Del Valle's attitude toward both the Army and the Okinawans spread infectiously among the Marines.[64]

In efforts to assert their authority and as a display of the adversarial relationship between the services, the Marines took further control over the military government units assigned to them by reorganizing the composition and command structure of the detachments. Composed of both Army and Navy personnel, the detachments suffered from mismanagement and proved inefficient. Conflict arose largely from duplications of effort and strains on resources. Confusion over responsibilities between the services caused four different officers to attempt to draw the same supplies for one detachment. It also complicated food distribution and salvage operations and contributed to overseas pay problems for Navy enlisted men. Tensions among the team members increased as minor annoyances developed into mission-impeding issues. Navy officers brought heavy "A" boxes filled with extraneous comfort items, such as mattresses and rain boots, which bogged down transportation and infuriated the Army officers, who had no such items. Army military police prohibited the commander of A-1, a Navy lieutenant commander, from transporting civilians on his truck without Army guards, despite the presence of a Navy shore patrol. The Army military government commander of A-5 "belittled navy personnel" and used "extremely offensive language and epithets." Interservice conflicts delayed essential mission tasks and tied up higher officers in dispute resolution.[65]

To fix these issues, the Marines wanted to assert greater influence. Organically, Marines did not compose any part of the detachment teams and only served as liaisons with limited authority and scope.[66] The Marine commanders, as well as the liaisons, believed that continuity and efficiency could improve by appointing a Marine officer overall in charge of the detachment. They favored an all-Marine detachment or at least a "nucleus of Marine personnel" to merge the other two services into a workable team. Furthermore, they recommended that any non-Marine personnel should belong to the Navy, not the Army.[67]

Marine division commanders reorganized the detachments to resolve immediate conflicts. Major General Lemuel Shepherd Jr., 6th Marine Division commander, combined detachments A-3 and B-3 and merged them into one team. He placed Army Lieutenant Colonel M. A. May, the B-3 commander and most senior officer, in overall charge. Del Valle and the 1st Marine Division placed all military police under the direct supervision of the "B" teams. Army officers typically commanded the "B" teams and, since Army military police outnumbered the Navy shore patrol within the teams, the consolidation aligned with the objective of separating the services.[68] Despite placing Army officers into positions of higher authority within the modified military government structure because of seniority, the moves both Shepherd and del Valle made shifted control of military government more firmly over to the Marines. Shepherd and del Valle kept a Marine in the position of division military government officer, a key billet that served as a link between the detachment commander and the division commander, and empowered the position holder to impose directives upon the detachments. More importantly, both division commanders exercised initiative to change the organization to their liking without requesting or securing approval from Tenth Army command. In this way, the modification of military government structure flaunted their disregard for Army rules and authority and served as a gateway to further deviations—from simple daily procedures to the demonstration of new standards of conduct.

The violent attacks internal to the camps confirmed to the Marines their concept of Okinawan identity formulated during preinvasion training; in the minds of the Marines, Okinawans shared a likeness with the Americans' sadistic foes, the Japanese. Growing from this belief, the necessary security environment of the Marine military government camps turned severe in comparison to the Army camps. Compounding the tendency toward ruthless conditions, interservice rivalry prompted the Marines to resist some Army directives and act counter to Army policy, which thereby further solidified trends of callous treatment toward the Okinawans.

With the internment of civilians in camps now governed by stricter regulations, aggressive actions against the camp residents from within the captive population decreased. Whether such a result signified actual confirmation of the resistance of the civilians or lessened opportunities for Japanese soldiers to infiltrate the populations remained unconfirmed by the Marines. It did, however, demonstrate that, regardless of the exact source of the hostilities, greater American control over the area created a safer environment for the Americans. In most areas, acts of belligerence "ceased almost entirely," and detachment soldiers faced massive populations that

generally displayed good will and acted meekly to avoid negative interactions with the Marines. Civilians who sought informal leadership positions or attempted to maintain their role as the head of a household initiated
the most contentious confrontations. Even these Okinawans, though, generally displayed eagerness, not belligerence.[69] The Marines acknowledged
the behavior of the Okinawans and reported that "civilians of the occupied zones submitted to new rule with equanimity." They characterized the
Okinawan manner as "co-operative, docile," and noted that there were "no
suspected cases involving sabotage, espionage, or subversive activities."[70]
The Okinawans came to recognize both the futility of acting independently
and the benefit of remaining in the camps. While they had risked getting
shot while attempting to secure their own individual food at nearby farms,
Okinawans soon learned that labor parties, traveling under guard, procured
the same food and distributed it to all camp residents. It became apparent
that patience and cooperation would sustain them and their families struggling under the rough conditions of war.

The Marines acknowledged the cooperative nature of the Okinawans
but did not modify their own behavior in response.[71] Instead, counter to
the reality of the situation, military government leaders saw the accommo-
dating Okinawans as the exception to the general attitude of the masses.
In selecting local leaders, they chose from a batch of what they considered
"the most intelligent and cooperative internees": men viewed as rare so still
categorized as prisoners.[72] Feelings of distrust persisted, and restrictions
remained in place well into July and August. As late as July 2, detachment
B-10, despite acknowledging that "there was no problem of discipline either
within the stockade or on work parties in the field," still assigned guards
to supervise the involuntary work parties closely. Local men still received
intense screenings and separate enclosures, the Katchin Peninsula still stood
as a holding area for "enemy nationals," and able-bodied civilians continued
to form out the ranks of a forced labor pool.[73]

As the Okinawans not only resigned themselves to Marine regulations but also relied upon them for sustenance and survival, the Marines
exploited the weakened state of the population both in and outside the
camps by destroying or personally using what little shelter or food they
had. Throughout the summer, the Marines continued to kill livestock for
sport and food and forcibly took up residence in any Okinawan structures
that still stood, a practice rendering any remaining occupants homeless.[74]
As the American battle successes mounted, the way the Marines conceived
and implemented camp restrictions and their treatment of the population
appeared increasingly out of place and unnecessary to the mission. The

6th Marine Division herded and tagged civilians like cattle.[75] Camp shootings in Marine military government camps continued excessively into late June, well past the initial confusion of the battle and the notable shift in Okinawan behavior, and thus beyond any reasonable concerns over uncertainties about perimeter security or Okinawan motivation.[76] Despite an end to hostilities in late June, Marine violence toward Okinawan property and people continued. Throughout the months of July and August, a group of Marines routinely traveled into an Okinawan containment that retained its village structure and kidnapped women for afternoons of forced group sex and sodomy. As late as June 22, 1st Marine Division soldiers burned down village homes that still housed civilians.[77]

Infuriated Army leaders described such actions as "wanton destruction" and measured the personal cruelty and property devastation as outpacing the actions of other services on Okinawa and in previous operations. After spending the day with military government units attached to the 6th Marine Division, Buckner reprimanded both Shepherd and Geiger for excessive damage to both the environment and the populace.[78] In a visit to the 1st Marine Division moments before his death on June 18, Buckner further chastised the division leadership about the predicament of the Okinawans and the division's lack of involvement in improving the situation. Such acute observations by the Tenth Army commander were truly extraordinary. Buckner's focus stayed primarily on battle tactics and logistical challenges; consistent with his opinions toward Asian people, he did not hold any overly charitable sentiments about the Okinawans. His continual distress about the Okinawan condition, therefore, demonstrated an acknowledgment of notably inappropriate behavior on the part of the Marines.[79] Military government leadership attempted to underplay the severity of the mistreatment of people and property. Winder argued that "military necessity has been confused with military convenience"; he meant to minimize the motivations behind the damage to an explanation about simple soldiers seeking the comforts of home.[80] Geiger's response, however, harshly exposed the deeper driving forces behind the actions of his Marines and the units operating under him. In a letter to Admiral R. H. Jackson dated May 20, Geiger described the Okinawans as "a very backward type of humanity" who lacked "anything of value."[81]

Geiger, like his soldiers, separated the positive behavioral changes from his assessment of Okinawan loyalty. For the Marines, the new demeanor of the Okinawans did not signify a shift in their allegiance and certainly did not lead the Marines toward drawing comparisons between themselves and the population. They continued to identify the Okinawans as Japanese, and the wholehearted acceptance of this identity molded Marine behavior toward the civilians and prevented them from reassessing the dynamics of the relationship between the Okinawans and the Japanese. This unwavering assessment differed greatly from the changing conclusions reached by Army personnel and command. By late April, an overwhelming majority of the Okinawan population displayed docile behavior and complied with American directives in both Marine and Army areas of responsibility. The Army found that the obedience forged a kinship between the Okinawans and themselves; the Marines downplayed any similarities. The Marines saw the Okinawans as "tiny oriental creatures . . . who could speak a little English" and ate in areas referred to as "gook-galleys." The Marines took advantage of Okinawan submission and opted to further subordinate and disrespect the native population under the rubric of paternalism. The better the Okinawans communicated, the more the Marines used them as "office boys," calling them Western names like "Clarence" and dubbing themselves their "masters."[82] In contrast, Army paternalism toward the Okinawans served as a backdrop to a budding relatable bond between the two cultures; by late April, the Army identified the Okinawans as more akin to Americans than to Japanese and used their limited resources to build extraneous recreational structures such as playgrounds. Engineer units attached to Marine military government units restricted their work to jobs associated with security and the basic necessities of life, even if they had extra salvage materials. Official Marine documents published in May and June still referred to Okinawans as "Japanese civilians" and "enemy nationals."[83] The Marines, in continually viewing the Okinawans as a less sophisticated subset of the enemy, attributed the new, openly positive attitude of the population to a sudden disillusionment with the cause and a sense of defeat. "Apparently aware of the hopelessness of the enemy's cause," the Marines reasoned, "[the civilians] began surrendering in overwhelming numbers."[84]

Both the Marines and the Army conducted the wartime occupation of Okinawa with primary attention given to such practical wartime concerns as security and mission accomplishment; both branches also researched and made determinations about Okinawan identity and allegiance. The Marines, however, never adapted their initial assessment of Okinawan identity despite the changing combat environment and true combat posture of the population. The Marines continued to perceive the Okinawans as fiercely loyal Japanese subjects. In late June, a published Marine report described the actions of Operation Iceberg as the "first conquest of Japanese soil" and further identified the local inhabitants as "Japanese in race."[85] The continual misunderstanding of the Okinawan disposition caused the Marines to implement harsher and more restrictive policies than those practiced by the Army, and these policies endured for months after battle's end. The inability of the Marines to revise their original assessments of the Okinawans stunted the growth and development of their military government program and limited its ability to establish procedures for sustained support. The disparity between the Marines and the Army in expectations and conduct of military government displays the contested nature of the American definition of Okinawan identity and the malleability of race and ethnicity.

Like their Army counterparts, before the battle started the Marines researched and analyzed the complex cultural foundations of Okinawa and its political connection with Japan's home islands. They considered the differences between the Okinawans and the Japanese and also attempted to categorize the relationship between mainland Japan and its farthest outlying prefecture. Despite obtaining and processing the same information, the Marines' conclusions did not match those of the Army. Whereas the Army determined that the disposition of the Okinawan people was inconclusive, the Marines declared definitively and without question that the Okinawans felt strong nationalistic ties to Japan. As a result, the Army units were afforded more freedom to allow situational encounters to provide any missing information and analysis; a combination of intelligence data in history, culture, language, and government structure, supplemented by interaction with the local people, would yield the most accurate representation of the Okinawan disposition. As the Okinawans acquiesced to American military demands, the Army recognized this cooperation and modified their cautious stance toward an unknown population into congenial, welcome relations. The Marines, on the other hand, by stating as a definitive, unarguable fact that the Okinawans stood as loyal Japanese, closed all discussion and further analysis of the situation on all levels. Marines and military government soldiers attached to the Marines received instructions about exercising caution toward the volatile locals not because of the instability of the unknown but because of the hostility of positively identified enemy combatants. Such a label bred a level of distrust that stood firm even within the context of battle. The capitulation of the population was seen merely as the white flag of an enemy's surrender, not as proof of a large body of innocent victims caught in the battle's crossfire.

Interservice rivalry worked to push the Marines further toward their already unbreakable conviction of Okinawan loyalty to Japan. Antagonism between the services, compounded by the subordinated position of the Marines under the Tenth Army, led to rebuffing and sometimes blatantly defiant actions on the part of the Marines. The Army's shift toward empathy in its actions toward the civilians moved the Marines in the opposite direction. Okinawans became pawns in the authority struggle between the American services in the Pacific theater; Shepherd and del Valle applauded actions from their Marines that countered Buckner's policies as long as such actions retained the integrity of the operation. Policies that indirectly affected the civilian population presented the perfect opportunity to display noncooperation without endangering the overall mission. Lower-ranking enlisted soldiers from both services judged the others' opportunities, privileges, conditions, and exploits. In their jealous quest to validate the superiority of their own affiliation, they often embraced actions that contradicted the goals of the other services. As the soldiers of the Army acknowledged the amenable attitude of the Okinawans, the Marines fixed tighter to their notion that the civilians completely embodied the Japanese ideology; they took action against the civilians to prove the veracity of their claim and the erroneous ways of the Army.[86]

Regardless of what specific conclusions were reached through the various services' cultural study, scrutiny along lines of ethnicity proved pivotal in mission planning and execution. The US military acknowledged the complexities of each cultural group; assigned a well-researched, purposeful identity; and molded policy around this assignment. The emphasis on cultural analysis did not undermine the centrality of military concerns such as security and supply demands. Considerations based on military factors and battlefield analysis continued to drive the planning and execution of military government operations. Together, however, military and cultural factors combined to provide the American military with a robust picture of the battlefield and allowed the military to make decisions that evaluated all aspects of the enemy and environment.

9

Lieutenant Commander John Tyler Caldwell sat in his Quonset hut in Okinawa on a slow, lazy Saturday morning in late 1945. Composing a letter to his family, Caldwell felt despondent, dissatisfied, and frustrated. As a labor officer for naval military government following the end of the war, he had spent months involved in tasks aimed at securing the peace and restoring some order to the island community. It seemed almost impossible to build up any momentum, however; instead, every day consisted of quick reactions to emergencies. Caldwell questioned whether it made any sense for him to remain in Okinawa. As the morning crept on, he received a visitor. The executive officer, Commander Firman, came with a message from the commander, Colonel Murray. Murray wanted Caldwell to stay on; he valued the young lieutenant commander's work above everyone else's. Caldwell, however, begrudgingly disturbed from his morning funk, found no good in the news. While he appreciated the compliment of the offer, he curtly replied, "The way we're running this outfit now, I'm not needed, and whoever stays around here much longer is going to be in deep trouble." Caldwell did eventually change his mind and remain on, but his exasperation at a mediocre and inefficient operation matched the sentiments of many who served with him in the early stages of the US Navy's administration of military government on Okinawa.[1]

War between Japan and the United States of America ended in September 1945. As the countries transitioned to peace, the responsibility for military government on Okinawa transferred to the US Navy. American combat troops on Okinawa adjusted their priority from enemy engagement to demobilization, and military government changed its mission from collecting and controlling the population to full occupation of a prefecture of a defeated country. The Navy took control of a program in progress; unlike the Army and Marines, who had planned their military government operations before encountering the people, the Navy assumed responsibility for a large, dislocated population that had urgent needs for basic sustenance and medical treatment. Overwhelmed, the Navy issued ad hoc directives while simultaneously handling existing concerns; little effort was put into building strategically toward a defined, long-term goal. The loss of dedicated planning time stunted the Navy's ability to analyze the changes brought on by the termination of the war and the effect that the end of hostilities had on the Okinawan people. As a result, many of the Navy's policies reiterated practices adopted from the Army and grounded in battle-field realities. Early Navy military government failed to adapt to the new peacetime environment; it did not attempt to rebuild, and its assumptions regarding Okinawan identity stagnated in a wartime state. Furthermore, the attrition of men whose service contracts had expired stripped military government of leaders and sailors with expert knowledge of military gov-ernment operations.

Navy leadership expressed concern for the malaise of military govern-ment and solicited input from their officers to reform the program. With a military manpower shortage, a new idea was to place administrative con-trol of local government in the hands of the Okinawans. Inefficiency and uninspired leadership, however, caused such innovative proposed plans to stagnate. Enthusiastic young officers waited as their ideas received praise but lagged in implementation. Overwhelmed by the situation it faced, Navy military government struggled so profoundly in completing daily tasks that developments toward improvements in the program failed to reach fruition in 1945.

On June 21, 1945, Major General Geiger declared the end of the Battle of Okinawa.[2] To the soldiers and Marines fighting on the island, Geiger's statement seemed premature. Despite the suicides of the defeated senior Japanese military leaders, Japanese soldiers continued to resist. Throughout August, Americans continued to lose their lives in Okinawa, with casualty rates reaching well into the hundreds. American bombs still harassed small groups of enemy troops moving in the early morning hours, and Japanese planes continued to fly menacingly overhead. The tenacity of the Japanese fighter made mopping-up operations dangerous and unpredictable; hun-dreds of Japanese were holed up in caves, and thousands mounted offen-sives.[3] General Joseph Stilwell, appointed by General Douglas MacArthur to replace Geiger as commander of the Tenth Army, arrived on Okinawa on June 23. Two days after Geiger's announcement, Stilwell wrote "Operations about over" but also gave credence to the idea that American troops would still encounter sporadic armed conflict on Okinawa. Stilwell viewed the persistent enemy action as a "bad set back"; only five to ten Japanese troops were surrendering per day.[4]

As commander of the Tenth Army, Stilwell immediately focused on preparations for the next stage of the war. With the end of the battle, Okinawa began to transform into a garrison for approximately 90,000 troops and a staging area for an attack on Japan's home islands. Observing the devastation left by the long battle, Stilwell prioritized engineering projects. He ordered the creation of three engineer battalions, including one for construction. The battle had destroyed many key pieces of infrastructure necessary to support the launching of an attack. Submerged ships obstructed ports, and uneven terrain hindered airstrip construction. The grim task of burying the approximately 12,000 American dead also affected the use of the ground. In his reports, Stilwell repeatedly described areas around the island—Naha Harbor, Naha city, Shuri—as a "mess" and equated the condition of the land to the bombed-out craters of World War I's no-man's-land. "We have *got* to get tough," he lamented. The Tenth Army started rebuilding ports, constructing airstrips, and erecting barracks buildings on makeshift bases. In addition to rooting out Japanese troops that continued to resist, combat units trained and refined military plans for future battles.[5]

On June 21, the American forces transitioned to a new phase of military operations on Okinawa, the central tasks of which focused on rooting out Japanese resistance and corralling all civilians into military government camps. From the military standpoint, June 21 designated a definite shift in priorities and operations. For the civilian population, some of whom had already found their way to US military government camps during the battle, the transition appeared gradual, if not invisible, throughout June and early July.[6]

The end of the battle did not put an end to the camp policies already in place. By the end of April 1945, restrictive policies and strict punishments in the Army camps were relaxed as the Okinawans demonstrated cooperative and obedient behavior that contributed to the effective control and management of large camp populations and built kinship between the civilians and the Americans. Even in the Marine-run military government camps, where a mutual respect between the people and the military did not exist, the civilians adapted to the austere camp environment, and an acceptance of the conditions set in; both groups lived communally with minimal conflict. The end of the battle only helped to reinforce the preexisting camp environments and policies.[7]

Within the harsh environment of decimated farmland, cratered ground, and unexploded minefields, nearly 320,000 Okinawans lived as refugees. The battle left an estimated 75 percent of the island's population dislocated; nearly 90 percent of structures and associated household items had been destroyed. By late June, most Okinawans resided in temporary American military government camps, which provided limited amounts of resources and relative stability in a postbattlefield environment. The few Okinawans who still lived outside the camps scavenged for food and fled from combat troops. Despite the contributions of the camps to the survival of the people, the population still required more than the camps could adequately provide. The Okinawans suffered from war wounds caused by stray munitions or direct exchanges of fire. They wore threadbare, dirty, lice-infested clothes, which hung off their emaciated bodies. The people needed medical care, food, and water. Separated from their families as they fled, they anxiously wanted to return to their now uninhabitable home areas or reunite with lost loved ones.[8]

The pressing needs of the Okinawans did not derail the Tenth Army from their operational missions aimed at the defeat of Japan. Stilwell did not commit additional leadership, manpower, or material resources into solving the problem of the large, dislocated local population. Similar to Buckner's concerns during the battle, Stilwell only required that the population not interfere with military operations. Island Command (IsCom), an organization originally conceived in early 1945 to manage the military government detachments—a task it never fully assumed—acquired responsibility for military government in late June 1945.[9] Its authority for the program, though, only accounted for a small portion of the command's obligations. IsCom handled logistics, administration, base development, and base defense in addition to military government. It tracked enemy aggression, pacification, surrender, resources, and morale; it accounted for prisoners of war; recorded the progress of airfield, runway, and work structure construction; calculated requests for troop replacements; and managed supply. IsCom also handled the entirety of garrison operations.[10] The day-to-day tasks of military government, a small piece within a vast remit, received negligible consideration.

IsCom did produce a nine-page cultural study about Okinawa intended to analyze the potential of Okinawa to house semipermanent military facilities in support of IsCom's mission of base development. Along with topics such as geography, climate, and resources, the study explored the people of Okinawa and the historical question of sovereignty.[11] Major General Fred C.

Wallace, IsCom's commander, directed the study as a tool to further plans for base development, not as a robust plan for military government. IsCom's analysis of the temperament of the Okinawan people and the state of their society provided useful data for determining the feasibility of a longer-term American military presence on the island. Although not the purpose of the study, it also presented information important for military government program building and post-battle planning; no matter the project type or length, no plans for the island of Okinawa could exclude even the most cursory acknowledgment of the 320,000 Okinawans struggling to reconstruct their lives.

Consideration of the Okinawan population slightly improved when military responsibility for the Ryukyu Islands shifted to the Army on July 31, to align with the Army's status as the primary service component for the attack on Japan. Meant as a temporary transfer, its sole purpose was "to facilitate preparation and execution of [Operation] Olympic."[12] Stilwell, as the Tenth Army commander, became the military governor of the Ryukyus, and IsCom was renamed Army Service Command I (ASCOM I).[13]

ASCOM received a new mission that expanded its role in military government. While simultaneously converting Okinawa into a base for a final attack against Japan's home islands, ASCOM sought to relocate the "population into the Okinawan hinterland and to adjust the people to new and greatly restricted ways of life."[14] The command's mission of resettlement signified a change in military government thought; whereas early military government efforts during the battle had focused on temporary answers to an immediate concern, post-battle resettlement plans sought to lay foundations for more solid communities. ASCOM defined resettlement as the return of Okinawans to their home areas, a necessary objective to set the stage for longer-lasting and better-functioning villages. Resettlement planning began by first asking the military government detachments to submit recommendations.[15] The submissions included proposed timelines, transportation concepts, and suggested methods of identifying village areas. Plans included information on providing basic needs such as a decent water supply, adequate food, and inhabitable structures.[16]

Within the camps, the Okinawans demonstrated docile behavior and acted as a people who "passively accept ... change." Consistent with the Okinawan village tradition of community cooperation, they contributed to camp life by laundering, harvesting food, and caring for patients. Informally, they designated leaders, distributed tasks among themselves, and contributed to policing. Such group involvement demonstrated their desire and ability to live in functioning communities. Not only did the cooperation improve camp life, but it also inspired military government to add the establishment of social structures to the resettlement agenda.[17]

Japan surrendered on September 2 to General Douglas MacArthur aboard the USS *Missouri*. Five days later, on September 7, Stilwell accepted the Japanese surrender of the Ryukyu Islands on Kadena Airfield. The Japanese delegation waited, rigidly standing at attention for ten minutes, until Stilwell walked out toward the surrender table to the tune of "The General's March," played by an Army band. The Japanese signed first, followed by Stilwell, who then ordered the delegation to leave. "We threw the hooks into them," Stilwell said. "Just cold, hard, business."[18]

Following the surrender, the War Department prioritized the demobilization of combat units and the return of war-weary troops to the United States. Swiftly returning the fighting men to civilian life appeased Congress and the public and aligned with military commanders' concerns for the well-being of their troops. In a memorandum to Geiger, Major General Pedro del Valle, commander of the 1st Marine Division, explained with empathy that his division had fought "on the front line continuously for the past fifty five days . . . sustained 1200 dead and 6200 wounded . . . [and had] not seen civilization or lived in a prepared camp for over twenty two months."[19] Movement of troops began within a few days of the surrender; Navy ships transitioned from combat roles to transports for military personnel returning to the United States.[20] A system where each man earned points based on time overseas, months in service, medals earned, number of campaigns participated in, and number of children determined which men qualified for release from the service. For the Army and Marines, eighty points earned a discharge; sixty points disqualified them from overseas duty. For the Navy, forty-four points allowed men to return to civilian life. Men short on points watched others return home while they remained overseas.[21]

Yet the War Department also considered the "job of [occupation to] take priority over everything. . . . Therefore, [the] No. 1 task [was] to get enough men on the spot as soon as possible and in the right places to ensure a real peace." The mission of combat forces adjusted to "consolidat[e] . . . victory [through] occupation, disarmament, and enforcement of surrender policies," tasks that required an estimated 2.5 million men.[22] Since occupation duties naturally occurred alongside demobilization, the War Department's personnel policy for postwar Okinawa contradicted itself. Occupation required manpower, but demobilization required the return home of American troops. The point system did not make special consideration for military occupational specialties and failed to effectively retain troops skilled for occupation duties.[23] Many trained military government personnel, including those educated at the university Civil Affairs schools in New York City and Charlottesville, were released from service once they reached the appropriate points thresholds.[24]

September 21 marked the transfer of military government to the Navy despite the Army retaining operational control of Okinawa. Rear Admiral John D. Price, the commandant of Naval Operating Base, Okinawa (NOB), became chief military government officer, and Colonel Charles I. Murray, US Marine Corps, continued as the deputy commander of military government. Murray held most of the responsibility for the planning and execution of Okinawan military government. With the exception of approximately one hundred enlisted Army translators, the transfer of Army civil affairs officers to Korea and mainland Japan caused the composition of military government on Okinawa to become almost entirely Navy.[25]

A modest group of devoted, college-educated lieutenant commanders and ensigns with military government experience opted to stay in the service and overseas.[26] After spending years away from their families, the officers and ensigns that chose to continue their military service in the Pacific did so with great gravity. Navy Lieutenant John Tyler Caldwell, a labor officer, originally had no intention of staying past his obligation. He wrote to his parents, "I'm resolved not to volunteer to hang around here when my points mature. . . . I feel no compunction to stay on the job. . . . So, boy, I'm pulling out when the day permits." Caldwell did choose to stay, but not because of the offer of promotion; he stayed because he believed in the mission of military government, sought to improve it, and was granted a position with authority to create change. "The extra half stripe in rank to Lieutenant Commander was not important," he wrote. Most who extended their overseas service shared an enthusiasm and devotion to military governance.[27]

Officers like Caldwell were the exceptions; few troops chose to stay. To compensate for the exodus of experience, replacement troops came in slowly from deactivated units on Okinawa. A lack of formal military government training limited the usefulness of the replacements, and their accumulation of points meant that their contributions would be temporary. Although grateful for the extensions of officers such as Caldwell, Murray still complained that the "trouble with [the] outfit [was] we've got too many damn college professors."[28] The Navy sought to adjust its personnel requirements, both along lines of skill level and rank, in coordination with the Navy's assumption of full responsibility for military government. Redesigning the requirements, however, did not result in their fulfillment.

Even combined, the volunteers that extended their overseas service and the replacements could not offset, either numerically or by skill set, the personnel shortfalls created by demobilization. The military government mission was expanding just as trained personnel departed. Occupation duties encompassed programs for rebuilding and rehabilitating the island. In addition to the immediate humanitarian concerns of food, clean clothing, and sanitary conditions for the dislocated population, the Navy military government's mission called for programs to restore farmland and reconstitute community structure. With only 2,700 men, the Navy faced a gap in manpower that leaders sought solutions for with increasing urgency.[29]

The Navy's military government program, called "United States Naval Military Government, Okinawa," separated from ASCOM. Three organizations now handled operations on postwar Okinawa: ASCOM; US Naval Military Government, Okinawa; and NOB. The responsibilities of each differed greatly. ASCOM focused on tasks necessary to enforce the surrender, such as disarmament and demobilization, because the Navy now handled civilians through military government programs. NOB completed missions congruent to Navy base operations, such as providing sea and air transportation. All three organizations' duties overlapped in some ways. ASCOM, for example, handled opening ports, which required coordination with NOB. To combat any confusion over priorities or resource allocation, both NOB and US Naval Military Government assigned a liaison officer to each other's headquarters.[30]

The Navy grew its military government program into a large, centrally run organization by dissolving all field detachment teams and reorganizing the island into sixteen districts. US Naval Military Government had a headquarters and various departments, operational units, and institutions, including a port and a bank.[31] The Navy combined multiple departments created under ASCOM into one Civilian Affairs Department, which served as the planning cell for resettlement, economic development, and education.[32]

The Navy did not have the luxury of a protected planning period to devise and refine policy before implementation. As US Naval Military Government officers and seamen assumed duties at the camps, they soon discovered that they could not wait for higher guidance before distributing food or erecting medical facilities. Mopping-up operations and the declaration of surrender caused camp sizes to swell, as captured Okinawan men who had fought in Japanese units and in the Boei Tai were released from prisoner of war camps and reunited with their families.[33] Even though the bombings and carnage had stopped three months earlier, the destruction remained. The Okinawans, having lost their homes, belongings, and farmland in early

April, lacked the capacity to rebuild or recover on their own. US Naval Military Government headquarters thus relied on operating parameters established by ASCOM to provide continuity and initial direction. Research into resettlement and land viability continued. Labor tasks assigned to the population kept the people occupied and content. Adherence to the standard of providing "minimum humanitarian needs . . . [that] include basic food, clothing, housing, and medical care" also derived from ASCOM.[34]

Building on ASCOM's resettlement initiatives, the Navy expanded the mission of military government to include "actively and materially . . . encourage[ing] the rehabilitation of the island socially, economically, and politically" but "within the limits of military demand." By aiming to develop the foundations of an Okinawan society, the Navy hoped to strengthen the Okinawan community and improve its agility and responsiveness for whatever unknown purpose Okinawa may serve to the US government and military in the future. Resettlement became identified as the necessary first step that, once accomplished, would better facilitate the growth of societal institutions.[35]

The Navy also sought to "admini[strate] the civilian population."[36] Such language signified further commitment to an American attitude in favor of the Okinawan people. During early combat, US military personnel had referred to the Okinawans as "enemy civilians." A few months after the end of organized combat, and several weeks following the surrender, the term "civilians" without the qualifier of "enemy" became the norm. Since American forces still encountered stiff resistance from Japanese combatants during mopping-up efforts, this shift in language bore significance; it indicated a more widespread acceptance of a fundamentally different interpretation of the relationship of the Okinawans to the Japanese and the Okinawan disposition toward the Americans.

Despite a noteworthy expansion of the mission, the US Naval Military Government headquarters did little in its early directives to define any achievable goals or provide any framework to build toward long-term accomplishments. In published orders, the Navy carefully used words that allowed seamen to exercise their own initiative. They directed sailors to "supervise" the reestablishment of societal constructs without explaining how to reconstruct economic or political institutions. The orders assigned military government personnel to supervisory roles yet did not define whom they would supervise. Vague, general definitions of duties allowed the Navy to react and adapt to ever-changing conditions. Conversely, the lack of any goals, procedures, or standards left sailors and troops working with civilians in camps and makeshift villages with little day-to-day direction and no tangible targets to strive for.[37] Planning efforts by headquarters moved slower than the urgency the situation demanded, and, since planning and execution happened concurrently, directives often arrived at the camps far after field actions had occurred. Military government officers felt uninformed and critical of higher headquarters. Caldwell "felt the Military Government was *not* moving, was sort of in the doldrums, and did not have its sights set either high enough for full realization of its possibilities and responsibilities . . . most action we take is based upon decisions dictated by circumstances, not imagination or planning ability."[38] Field officers contributed to the disconnection by failing to report their projects or results to headquarters.[39]

Disagreement about occupation policy also occurred at the strategic levels of the Navy. Naval Affairs Committee hearings addressed the precise locations of future US Navy bases in the Pacific and debated the details of a strategic military government plan for the region. The "Plan for Post-War Civil Government," written by the Office of Island Governments, was a generic policy meant to apply to all Pacific islands under Navy jurisdiction. Immediately, it created friction. As the plan moved slowly through different levels of approving authorities, the comments it received varied widely. Captain L. S. Sabin, an author of the plan, diligently incorporated the input only to discover that, as the document continued to circulate, concepts deleted to appease one authority would reappear when another high official offered their contribution.[40]

Two issues created the widest fissures: authority to oversee military government activities and removal of the resident populations from the islands. Admiral Richard S. Edwards, deputy chief of naval operations, issued a directive in early September in response to the plan. He instructed the Office of Island Governments to keep the civil administration independent from the military administration. Military government, when dealing with camp and village residents, did not require a military command chain. Edwards's concern lay with public perception of undue military control and influence outside the bounds of declared war. "It must be made clear to the public," Edwards wrote, "that we propose to set up a system of civil administration separate and distinct from the chain of military command."[41] Military authority would control military compounds only, a viewpoint consistent with the Navy as a whole. Admiral Nimitz, the commander in chief, US Pacific Fleet, disagreed with Edwards. While Nimitz agreed that "civilian commissioners from other Federal agencies" should head the administration of the islands, he strongly felt that a military command chain, with himself as governor general, would improve the efficiency of the operation.[42]

Clashes over policies regarding the removal of certain groups from Navy-administered Pacific islands revealed unresolved misconceptions about local ethnicities. Without question, both Edwards and Nimitz agreed that the return of the Japanese to mainland Japan aligned consistently with strategic efforts to dismantle the Japanese empire and its holdings. For Edwards, such a removal sufficiently met the objective. "We will kick out the Japs," he stated. "Others, including Okinawans, should be left." Removal of other groups, he reasoned, would make America appear as a victorious conqueror. He clearly identified Okinawans as a distinct ethnic group from the Japanese and as bystanders to the violence of war.[43] Nimitz, however, desired the removal of all groups, even including those residing on the islands whose ethnic roots tied them to Spain or Germany.[44] Edwards's view of the Okinawans and others who had served the empire as distinctly different from the Japanese again aligned consistently with the Navy as a whole. Nimitz's preference for complete removal grew from his desire for clear command in the region, not from deep adversarial sentiments. His call for the disposal of Spanish priests and nuns and the appointment of American clergy, for example, would streamline American authority and funnel an approved message to the local populations.[45]

Sabin appealed to both viewpoints and highlighted the benefits of each side when presenting the conflict to higher admirals. He suggested the submission of a previous version of the plan, which contained the military oversight Nimitz required.[46] Sabin's willingness to adjust the document so readily to an earlier draft demonstrated the fluidity of the directive and the lack of urgency on the part of Navy leadership to act directly and decisively in the execution of military government. The plan languished in revisions and approvals for months, while Navy men solved military government problems in the camps and villages daily and in an ad hoc manner. Sabin made his offer of resurrecting an older version of the document, an act that undoubtedly would require additional processing time, in October. Such variability at the strategic level made it difficult for US Naval Military Government headquarters in Okinawa to set definitive guidance for their military government officers to follow.

Naval military government continued to operate with few trained military government officers and ensigns. The US military presence on the island decreased by approximately two thousand troops per month. As the weather cooled, some units fell to as low as six officers and twenty enlisted men. Murray saw his roster reduced by more than 71 percent.[47] The exodus of qualified military personnel placed an increasing strain on military government operations. As the scope of projects expanded from providing basic humanitarian needs to full resettlement, repatriation, and society (re)construction, the Naval military government was pushed to the edges of its capability. Military government policy makers sought more viable solutions to the manpower shortage than the temporary assignment of soldiers borrowed from demobilizing combat units.

One contested option called for the increased involvement of Okinawans in administrating the camps and districts. In various forms, Okinawans had participated in American-controlled military government since the first soldiers landed on the island in early April. During the battle, however, the Army and the Marines had used Okinawans in administrative positions only as a temporary and limited measure, with no plans to build an Okinawan-owned community. The Army entrusted only select individuals with ties to the United States to serve in limited capacities as informal leaders in the camps. The Marines' lack of interest and commitment to civil affairs caused them to divert aspects of military government to the Okinawans in order to avoid conducting such tasks themselves.[48]

In July, ASCOM devised a group of Okinawan advisors that, by August, had evolved into the Okinawan Advisory Council. Fifteen Okinawan men, recommended by one hundred of their peers, served as advisors to the deputy commander for military government. ASCOM described the assembly as a "permanent advisory group of Okinawans as a communication device to assist the [military government] authorities in planning and decision-making."[49] The creation of the Okinawan Advisory Council marked a significant development in the American military's assessment of the capability of the Okinawans. The establishment of the council demonstrated a lean toward an increased contemplation of the potential of the Okinawan people to handle their own affairs. While American leaders did not develop the council out of progressive sentiments about the ability of the Okinawans to lead and think, the formation of the Okinawan Advisory Council still signified a departure from the American view of the Okinawans as helpless. ASCOM selected each member of the council based on exhibited informal leadership, credentials of higher education, and superior business sense.[50] Selected council members had experience as journalists, police commissioners, and businessmen, positions consistent with American definitions of prominence. The formation of the council gave the Okinawans an opportunity to shape their own society, contribute to the trajectory of their lives, and demonstrate to the Americans that they could govern themselves.[51] The organization elevated Okinawan influence above the rigors of daily village life and broke them out of the constraints of minor leadership roles, such as laundry supervision or food rationing, within the camps.

The full launch of the council moved slowly. By mid-September, the men had only received orientations but not yet offered advice on any issue. By design, the council did not transfer any responsibility or power to the Okinawans. As mere advisors, the men provided input to Murray, who retained sole decision-making authority.[52] Military government still remained an endeavor strongly controlled by the Americans. Military government officials consistently placed themselves in positions to dictate action and direction.[53] Okinawan council members could not devise or lead a project. Practically, the disorganization of the Navy's military government apparatus precluded the option of releasing any control from American authorities.

While still limited, Okinawans exercised slightly more influence within the sixteen newly formed districts and at the camp level than at the higher levels of military government administration. In efforts to build the economy, local industries such as handicrafts, laundry, carpentry, and tea and tobacco production were put under the auspices of the Okinawan population. US Naval Military Government directed that "the leadership and management of various industries should be placed in the hands of skilled native leaders." District commanders supervised the work, albeit with directorial responsibilities. In addition to economic benefits, the Navy encouraged Okinawan efforts in sewing, cutting hair, and peanut farming because it "aid[ed] in the health and comfort" of the population. While Okinawans gained more ownership over daily community routines, their contributions to the commerce of their district remained restricted to manufacturing. Few, if any, Okinawans oversaw mass production of a local industry, and services rarely grew beyond the individual district; the products almost exclusively benefitted the district residents. Military government cultivated local industry projects to assist in the establishment of the community but also to keep its residents occupied. By retaining a supervisory role, district commanders contained Okinawan local leadership initiatives and regulated the direction of economic growth.[54]

The involvement of Okinawans in both goods production at the district level and in the Okinawan Advisory Council helped alleviate some of the strain on military government operations caused by a lack of military manpower. Okinawan participation in military government programs, however, served a greater purpose than simply offsetting personnel shortages. The Navy sought to establish economic, political, and social structures that reflected Okinawan customs and traditions, a task they could not complete without the contribution of the Okinawan people. Practically, a shortage of sailors made reconstructing the Okinawan community in an American image impossible. Okinawa bore no resemblance to America; creating institutions based on American principles would require work beginning at the most fundamental levels and expertise in complex areas such as law and democratic government. An Okinawan society built on a foundation of its own traditions and customs presented many advantages: With a limited work force, the Navy could build off of the basics that already existed, and the Okinawans would readily accept the improvements because of the cultural familiarity. Participation of the population became a key component; the Navy lacked the in-depth cultural knowledge to restore a viable Okinawan community. For the civilians, military government programs now presented more opportunities for involvement and leadership. Okinawans played a role in resettlement; elected local mayors, called *shicho*, organized the people by their former villages, or *muras*, and compiled manifests for movement.[55] Committees of Okinawans mediated conflicts among the civilians. "Okinawans themselves managed the details of the resettlement," military government reports acknowledged. They "determined the location and layout of the new settlement . . . the allocation of land for farming purposes, the establishment of community projects such as schools."[56] An Okinawan police force augmented the military police, assisting with escorting the resettlement movements and handling local disputes as well.[57]

While the Navy's decision to base economic and political institution building on Okinawan practices stemmed from practical considerations, such as a lack of personnel and resources, the emphasis on Okinawan traditions forced the Navy to consider the differences between Okinawan and Japanese customs and to commit to the conclusion that the Okinawans were ethnically distinct. Enthusiastic young officers like Caldwell began laying the foundations for programs that greatly increased the role of the Okinawans beyond participation and toward ownership. Their work rested on the belief that the Okinawans had the intellectual capacity to handle the intricacies of government and the leadership abilities to form strong, united communities. "The Okinawans have demonstrated convincingly that they possess sufficient indigenous leadership to manage their own affairs in much larger degree than is allowed them at present," they wrote.[58]

The proposed plans championed a new view of the Okinawans as a culturally progressing group rather than as a docile, obedient people. Ideas such as the creation of a *chiji*, or Okinawan governor, went beyond an advisory body of local men; the *chiji* would be responsible for the design of the government. The military government officers did recognize the ethnic differences between the Okinawans and the Japanese, but, in keeping with the simplicity of using structures already in place, the plan proposed the continuation of the Japanese prefectural system.[59] The *chiji*, however, could shape the substance of the government in the model of his own traditions and customs; he would "develop and appoint a central administration and would propose local units of government."[60] The Okinawan Advisory Council, also referred to as the Civilian Advisory Council, would remain as an advisory body to the deputy commander. Consistent with the Navy's requirement to ensure that military government development stayed within the boundaries of the budget and the political interests of the United States, the military would still retain some oversight; the deputy commander would appoint the *chiji*, and the Civilian Affairs Department "supervised [the] activities" of the Civilian Advisory Council.[61] The plan included a "competent [military government] inspection system" as a mechanism to monitor the work of the Okinawans and safeguard the evolving government from drifting outside of what the United States could support.[62] Despite Navy oversight, the proposed plan greatly increased the influence of the Okinawans; it even assigned authority for establishing civilian conduct regulations to a civilian administration.[63]

The plan circulated through higher levels of military government leadership throughout the fall to generally positive responses, and, by late October, the commandant of Naval Operating Base granted Murray authority to enact any changes he desired. Thorough planning did not translate into immediate implementation, however. Despite his enthusiasm for the plan, Murray remained bogged down in immediate emergencies and daily decisions. Even though he complained of a small staff, he failed to manage them efficiently. The plan stayed with Murray for months; he did not distribute responsibility for projects among his staff.[64] From November to mid-December, the Navy military government continued to operate in an ad hoc, disorganized manner. Innovations stalled, and military government officers at the district level continued to handle immediate problems within their areas on a day-to-day or month-to-month basis. While the Navy did begin to rely on civilian participation to round out its military government programs, disenchanted officers that worked in the districts described the use of the local population as "clumsy and inadequate."[65]

Despite its deficiencies, the level of civilian involvement in Navy military government in 1945 had increased in a purposeful and significant way. Military government officers used the Okinawans on lower levels within the districts to account for the limited availability of American personnel and in initial efforts to stabilize the war-torn communities. The steady rise of a reliance on the population to promote military government initiatives differed from the limited way that the Army and Marines had sought assistance from the Okinawans; while the Navy shared the racially biased viewpoints expressed by the other services, the Navy meant for the use of civilians in military government programs to develop toward permanency rather than fill gaps temporarily. Such involvement of the Okinawans laid the foundation for the success of official policy that would provide the push needed for apathetic military government leaders to catapult ideas into action by late 1945 and early 1946.

10 New Visions, New Interpretations of Identity
The Expansion of US Navy Military Government

On April 24, 1946, Mr. Koshin Shikiya stood in front of a small crowd crammed into the office of Colonel Charles I. Murray, the deputy commander for military government. Dressed simply in American casual clothes—slacks and a shirt—he had a kind face and a reassuring smile. Well-known in the Okinawan community, Shikiya had extensive experience as an educator; he had served as a middle school principal and founded a secondary school in Naha. Selected by a group of Okinawan peers, Shikiya accepted the office of *chiji*, or Okinawan governor, in front of officers of the US Naval Military Government and members of the Okinawan Advisory Council. Lieutenant Commander John Tyler Caldwell, director of civilian affairs, stood in the audience. Caldwell, who had pushed for Okinawan ownership in military government and whose plans had created the position of *chiji*, felt an immense sense of accomplishment and pride. He described Shikiya's inauguration as "the most satisfying moment of my adult career of service to my fellow man."[1]

Despite the continuation of rough living conditions, by mid-December 1945 circumstances finally allowed the Navy to execute its plans to further incorporate the Okinawans into the administration of military government. Changes at the higher levels of military leadership, in particular Admiral Raymond A. Spruance as the new commander in chief, US Pacific Fleet and Pacific Ocean Areas (CINCPAC-CINCPOA), shifted priorities and placed more emphasis on a civil administration that featured the inclusion of the local population. Officers that had championed such adjustments found themselves promoted into positions that allowed them to implement the plans they had designed and advocated. Once only a labor officer, Caldwell now began work as the director of civilian affairs. In his new role, he built a team that shared his enthusiasm for the people.

Through intricate analysis of the history and traditions of the Okinawan people, the Navy constructed a feasible and sustainable local government structure dependent on Okinawan custom and participation. Okinawans serving in positions of administrative influence demonstrated their ability to govern, the power of their leadership, and the capacity for independent thought. Seamen, no longer under the stress and fear of combat conditions, formed both formal and personal relationships with the Okinawans within the context of their duties. Through close interactions, Navy men reassessed Okinawan identity as not only separate from Japan but also free from congenial comparisons with America. Naval military government identified Okinawans as capable and culturally progressing, a group that formed a distinct, separate, unique ethnic community neither American nor Japanese. The Navy acknowledged the cognitive ability and aptitude of the local people and, along with practically considering its own shortfalls in personnel and resources, devised military government policy that led to Okinawan influence in government, medical structure, education, and crime management.

As the autumn of 1945 transitioned into winter, the island began to settle into a peacetime pace. Engineer units built clubs, messes, and living quarters, while more officers traveled freely in military jeeps for personal use.[2] The absence of a threat relaxed the men and gave them opportunities for individual activities. Sailors could visit movie houses and enjoy beer. Planning for family housing began. John Dorfman, a Navy military government officer who managed the distribution of civilian labor, taught high school mathematics to fellow seamen and learned how to type.[3] Okinawa Base Command (OBASCOM) started a University Study Center for the soldiers, sailors, and Marines. By late November, the United States raised a flag over the newly established Okinawan Base and slightly lifted the restrictions on late-night movement for both civilians and the military. In response to the calm, troops turned in their weapons.[4]

Occupation duties still required seamen to work every day from early morning to late at night. The island lay in ruins; its land, riddled with half-buried, unexploded munitions, was unable to support sufficient farming. Movements of tactical military units still dominated routes.[5] Typhoons ripped through the island and destroyed construction projects, living areas, and ports. Stilwell complained that typhoons made it "a struggle to get to the mess hall." He tersely described damage caused by the storms with one simple word: "Bad."[6] Despite the terseness of Stilwell's assessment, the typhoons leveled manmade structures and foliage and affected the safety, health, and lives of both the seamen and the Okinawans. Flying debris and flooding brought deadly peril and contaminated water sources. The high winds and rains destroyed 15 percent of the few crops planted and forced the civilians to continue to rely on military government support for food. Some civilians resorted to foraging outside of the districts.[7]

Devastating typhoons and the prioritization of the occupation of Japan caused delays in supply shipments. The Navy military government's tendency to operate with temporary programs and its failure to have foresight or patience caused many initiatives to fall short of completion as well. Mismanagement by the Navy placed strain on the Okinawan people; poorly planned relocation movements forced civilians to walk long distances to destinations that ended only at another district, rather than at an established *mura*, and uneven food distribution caused a cut in rations by half. Despite some military government officers setting aside excess food without adding it to the quota, Okinawans still rummaged through dumps and refrigerated vans for spoiled food.[8] Above all, the Okinawans longed to return home and reunite with family members. Relocation moved slowly; months passed, and the population continued to reside in districts and camps. Even Okinawan participation in organizing resettlement did little to increase the efficiency.[9]

Dissatisfied with the unsuccessful efforts of the Navy, some Okinawans abandoned the camps to search for homes and food by themselves. Most of their efforts only caused additional hardship. Those that left the camps and districts were abandoning what support the military government did provide. The civilian population depended on military government for 75 percent of their food supply. "If [the Okinawans] had anything, it was from the military," explained one military government officer.[10] Okinawans that trekked out on their own encountered unspent munitions and barren land that prevented farming. Rarely did they locate family members.[11]

Okinawans that wandered outside designated military government areas encountered idle American combat troops, but those that stayed within the districts did as well. With most significant mopping-up missions culminating by early winter, approximately 30,000 tactical troops found themselves less engaged in military work. Looking to unwind from the tension of combat, the men roamed into areas heavily inhabited by civilians. As a result, two sizeable groups—wandering civilians and inactive warriors—interfered with military government operations by circulating "unauthorized [and] uncontrolled" around the island. Free movement and commingling among the military and civilians outside the parameters of official duties ignited fears of fraternization and disrupted resettlement. Without proper accountability of the Okinawans, the Navy could not accurately send the people to the right villages and homes. NOB, OBASCOM, and Naval Military Government worked together to enforce measures to separate the military from the civilians. Regulations prevented combat troops from entering civilian districts and camps; the Okinawans reserved exclusive access to the area north of Route 6, and military traffic outside of military government required a pass issued from either Naval Military Government headquarters or the provost marshal.[12] As a control measure, the Navy continued the wartime practice of requiring all civilians to move under guard; no civilian could attempt relocation by themselves. Military police delegated some of the guard duty, however, to Okinawan police. Police returned civilians moving freely "at large" back to camps for punishment under a military government court system, a more hospitable development from the wartime death sentence.[13] Unlike control measures implemented by the Army and the Marines during the war, the Navy's military government had no concerns with safety; it did not control Okinawan movement to protect American military secrets or troops from armed civilians. Concern over civilian freedom of movement came from the Navy's distress at watching independent civilian actions disrupt the military's attempts to reestablish a rudimentary, functional Okinawan community. The military no longer viewed Okinawans as a possible enemy; combatant Okinawans had returned to their families from prisoner of war camps, and US soldiers had turned in and locked up their weapons.[14]

Despite restrictive regulations, military and civilians began to live closer together than they had during the fighting. Close living with the Okinawans encouraged increased familiarity between Navy military government personnel and civilians. Military government sailors expressed sympathy toward the tragic circumstances of the civilians and acknowledged "their difficult time." With such philanthropic sentiments came a desire to help and a belief in the nobility of their work. Lauding their accomplishments, they saw the camps as places of great benefit; the population "could get whatever they needed. It really helped their lives." Within the districts, military government personnel related to Okinawans on a human level; they knew them, learned about their families, connected with their personalities, and cared about them. They formed relationships. "[Okinawans were] very friendly, you know—just good," a labor officer stated. "Good people."[15]

Altruistic feelings, however, did not entirely escape from the Americans' early sentiments of belittling paternalism. In many ways, the charitable urge to help the disadvantaged Okinawans grew out of previous viewpoints that minimized the worth of the Okinawans. The Navy, like the Marines and Army before them, still thought of themselves as superior to such a rural population. American racism toward Asians did not disappear with the cessation of bullets in flight. Lower-ranking seamen who worked more along the periphery of military government operations and did not participate in planning initiatives had a tendency to adhere more firmly to negative ideas about the population. A seaman who worked as a driver for a research medical team maintained his distaste for the Okinawans. "It was the filth and how they lived," he said, failing to consider the trials of war as an explanation for Okinawan conditions. "You wanted to get out of there." The young man, twenty years old at the time, did not believe he spoke for the doctors he delivered into the camps and districts, though; he believed the doctors felt genuine concern for the sick and wounded population. Disassociating the doctors from himself, he attributed a greater nobility to the doctors' work. "They went in for a reason," he said. "I just went to take them."[16] The doctors, however, despite the excellence of their work, did not transcend the social norms of the time and view their patients as equals. While the Navy distinctly adopted policies in Okinawa that entrusted the people with more responsibility than before, the congenial sentiments and steps toward affection among the population and the Navy still carried a strain of racial superiority at its heart.

As military government built rapport with the population, the idea of Okinawans as capable contributors became less controversial. Americans began to attribute more characteristics of cognitive aptitude and cultural tolerability to the population. While sailors writing home to loved ones still used "natives" to describe the Okinawans, a term that implied savagery and basic living, references to Okinawans in official documents transitioned to using the words "the people," a term that implied humanity and civic responsibility. As fears of an Okinawan enemy disappeared, military government policy created regulations for Okinawans that differed from regulations devised for the Japanese. American troops continued to patrol for Japanese prisoners of war and still detained them in prisoner of war camps. Okinawans that fought alongside the Japanese left prisoner of war camps for military government camps and then reunited with their families as quickly as practicable. Recategorized as Okinawan civilians, each former prisoner of war had only one minor accountability task: to "report to [the] Chief of Police of [the] district once each week."[17]

On November 24, Admiral Raymond A. Spruance replaced Admiral Nimitz as the commander in chief, US Pacific Fleet and Pacific Ocean Areas (CINCPAC-CINCPOA). A United States Naval Academy graduate, Spruance had performed brilliantly in the Battle of Midway and earned a reputation through his years of service for high intelligence, modesty, composure, and decisiveness and for a willingness to listen to the contributions of others.[18] Spruance's methodical approach to military challenges made him well suited to face the malaise of the Navy's military government. He published two orders related to military government operations. One announced an incentive program designed to retain skilled military government officers, and the other detailed Spruance's policy for military government procedures throughout the Pacific, to include the Mariana and Marshall Islands as well as Okinawa. He issued comprehensive guidance that included a clearly defined mission with five subpoints and identified mission completion criteria. He greatly expanded upon the idea of setting up Okinawa economically and socially and centralized the development of education programs. Spruance's directive contributed far more than simple clarity and defined direction. The directive changed the core program of military government and moved it toward a new intention. Spruance ordered Naval Military Government to assist in establishing "self-governing communities" that, once firmly formed, would serve as the basis of a permanent structure with appropriate authority to regulate itself. The directive took the current program of building communities based on Okinawan traditions and expanded it by minimizing and gradually eliminating the role of the American forces in the construction and sustainment of Okinawan society. Spruance saw the Okinawans as full leaders, administrators, and officials.[19]

Self-sufficient Okinawan communities would allow for the termination of American occupational responsibility. Strategically, Washington recognized the geographic and political advantage of Okinawa; the island extended the influence of the United States into the Pacific Ocean without offending the amiable development of Japan's occupation under MacArthur. Okinawan air bases could serve as strategic deterrence platforms against the questionable intentions of former allies. Okinawa needed a self-reliant population, functional institutions, and adequate sustenance in order for the island to support multiple American airstrips, bases, and military platforms. A lengthy commitment to humanitarian assistance would bog down military manpower and delay Okinawa from transitioning to its long-term role. Spruance understood the strategic interests of the Joint Chiefs of Staff and modified his military government program to support their intent months before they published an order directing him to do so.[20]

The success of Spruance's directive rested on the ability of the Okinawans to administer their own government. While driven by strategic military plans, the investment in Okinawan capability signified the Navy military government's greatest departure from previous underestimations of the possible contribution of the Okinawans as a people. The directive called for structures built on Okinawan organizational and cultural principles and run exclusively by Okinawan leadership. "Local governments,"

Spruance wrote, "should be patterned on the politico-social institutions which the inhabitants evolved for themselves . . . ultimate ownership and management can be transferred." Education programs "fostered and encouraged instruction in the native language and history and . . . arts and crafts," and, although instruction in English remained "a prime necessity," Spruance specifically noted that this reversion to American references should "not . . . be construed as discouraging instruction in native language."[21]

The fundamental driving principle behind the directive was to swiftly eradicate the need for Navy personnel in occupation duties. Rooting the society in Okinawan practices eased implementation and thus supported a quicker withdrawal. Spruance fully recognized the practical military reasons for increasing Okinawan authority, but he also had confidence in the Okinawans' ability to govern themselves to the extent necessary for American release from the military government mission. He authorized the use of training centers on Guam for educating Okinawans "who demonstrate a capability and adaptability for advanced work and who should be considered as a potential source of teachers and government officials," and he approved the Medical Training Center on Guam to train Okinawan doctors and nurses. He condemned cheap labor practices so that the Okinawans could "enjoy the full benefits of their own labor and enterprise." To ensure Okinawan autonomy, Spruance moved officers and ensigns to an ancillary role and ordered the placement of Okinawans at the forefront of military government operations. [22]

Under an incentive program that encouraged motivated and skilled officers to choose to stay overseas, Murray appointed Caldwell as director of the Civilian Affairs Department, endorsed his plan for increased Okinawan responsibility, and allowed him to select his own team of officers.[23] Caldwell took over his new position with full support for his ideas from not only Murray but the CINCPAC as well. In Caldwell, US Naval Military Government had a leader who strongly believed in an Okinawan capacity for management and in the Navy's support role of assisting them. "Our job," he stated, "[is] to take care of these people, to get our feet muddy."[24] With a crew of like-minded officers and an approved plan that now corresponded with the intent of his higher headquarters, Caldwell had full power to create dramatic change. Spruance's vision laid out a comprehensive new approach to military government, and his personnel policies allowed the right officers and ensigns to implement it. As a result, December marked a spectacular shift in military government policy that embraced the already growing acknowledgment of the Okinawans as a group that possessed managerial and organizational skills at a level above what the Americans expected from a rural society.

The Navy began an overhaul of existing programs. Starting with resettlement, military government dissolved and merged districts in order to reconstitute the *mura* in its correct form, complete with settlement subdivisions called *azas*. The construction of the *muras* gave the civilians a more stable place to relocate to, and the camps closed in the late spring and early summer of 1946 as their usefulness as holding areas expired. To aid in the development of the villages, the American military returned unused land. Within five months, over half of the dislocated population had returned to close approximations of their home villages.[25]

Within the *azas* and *muras*, Okinawans served as headman (*soncho*), assistant headman (*joyaku*) and chief (*shunin*). By April 1946, the Okinawan Advisory Council, along with *mura* leaders, selected Koshin Shikiya as the *chiji*, governor of Okinawa. The *chiji's* responsibilities included following directives outlined by the Navy, submitting mandatory monthly reports, working directly with the newly formed Central Okinawan Administration, and expanding the accountabilities of the Okinawan committees and organizations. Shikiya also managed councils at all levels and supplied men to fill vacancies in the interim between elections.[26]

A pleasant man who had enjoyed a long career as a principal and educator, Shikiya approached his duties as *chiji* with the utmost seriousness. He fully exercised the power granted to him by representing the concerns of the population, pushing for changes, and working on comparable footing with the military government officers. His well-presented speeches and eloquently written letters served as vehicles to inspire confidence in the civilians, establish credibility for his administration, and mollify the Americans. His message to his people emphasized that the government belonged to them and urged them to shape their own communities actively. He issued proclamations written by the Navy to the population; his image and title allowed him to influence the Okinawans through positional and charismatic leadership and thus inspire Okinawan agreement. Shikiya's ownership of the only Okinawan newspaper, *Uruma Shimpo*, offered him an outlet for further impact. Through the command of information distribution, he affected the population and garnered their support for military government programs as he saw fit. Most Okinawans recognized the fundamental shift in military government and readily embraced their newfound role in government and society. Shikiya promoted Okinawan rule; his policies and programs further increased the involvement of Okinawans in administration from small, informal actions like voting to larger leadership roles in councils and villages.[27]

To ensure a successful transition from American oversight to Okinawan governance, Navy military government instituted a process of sequential steps that sought to relinquish control gradually. Each administrative department had an assigned military government officer tasked to develop his department on the Okinawan model, staffed by Okinawans. Once the department appeared ready for independent operations, the military government officer would assume an advisory role only.[28] Ultimately, the process would result in a complete transfer of military government over to the Okinawans by means of a structured timetable that ensured the Okinawans assumed control only when ready. Establishing sturdy, permanent Okinawan institutions required time as the people recovered from the damages of the war. Steady, slow implementation safeguarded against failure. American oversight continued as a stabilizing force that aided Okinawan recuperation while paving the way for their inheritance.[29]

Military government worked meticulously to reconstitute an amenable Okinawan society based on accurate Okinawan traditions and practices. The importance placed on the correctness of the structures and institutions did not indicate that the Navy valued Okinawan culture but rather that the Navy was working under the principle that the more legitimate the rebuilt society, the longer it would last; only authentic structures had any chance of gaining permanence. Additionally, the Navy did not have the resources to construct a society based on American-modeled institutions. The men that Caldwell chose as his top advisors had backgrounds in political science and extensive knowledge of Okinawan culture. In building the framework for the Okinawan-run programs, they carefully analyzed Okinawan customs and history and separated Japanese practices from Ryukyuan tradition. Caldwell's men had an elevated understanding of the ethnic differences and political strain between Japan and Okinawa. They acknowledged not only Okinawan potential for management but also the civilians' identity as a group disparate from the Japanese; military government efforts did not rehabilitate an enemy but rather revitalized a victimized island people. Lieutenant Commander James Watkins believed that laws firmly grounded within the cultural beliefs of a society built a strong foundation for civil order. The economist Henry Lawrence "advance[ed] any way possible the human welfare of the people" and championed initiatives that worked within the framework of the present Okinawan economy. Willard "Red" Hanna, described as "absolutely determined," worked to restart schools and invigorate the handicraft industry; he empowered Okinawans by assigning them the responsibility of beginning and managing community projects. School subjects included Okinawan history and geography, taught by Okinawan teachers. The reorganized Okinawan Public Works designed homes with traditional Okinawan-style porticos. "The attitudes and characteristics of the Okinawans," stated Murray, "in great measure conditioned all Military Government."[30]

As they fulfilled their military government duties in accordance with Spruance's directive, soldiers and seamen began to feel as if they had gained a basic understanding of Okinawan ethnicity and how it was different from that of the Japanese. By January 1946, the men could visually differentiate between Okinawan and Japanese people with an eye that discerned more than just filthy clothing and states of duress. Sailors could identify distinct physical characteristics, which they were able to attribute to ethnic lineages. They classified the Okinawans as "really, really tiny people" with mixed roots from New Guinea, China, and Japan. Seamen explained that "you could tell [who the Japanese were] because they were generally taller. And their heads were a different shape; their heads were slightly pointed."[31] The ability to differentiate between the Japanese and the Okinawans during peacetime military government under the Navy did not hold the deadly consequences that it did during wartime for soldiers and Marines. Under battle conditions, the men needed to accurately separate friendly from enemy to ensure their own survival. In contrast, military government sailors needed clarity between the two ethnicities to properly distribute benefits and correctly execute repatriation and community building. Dorfman, as labor paymaster, needed to be able to identify and weed out the Japanese who waited hopefully in line for pay or work. Like all its benefits and programs, military government reserved the opportunity for work for the Okinawans. The Japanese scared Dorfman, but he related to the Okinawans, whom he called "the nicest people."[32]

Navy military government officers like Dorfman viewed Okinawans as a people ravaged by war and exploited by Japan.[33] Hatred toward the Japanese held a corollary of pity for the Okinawans. Navy men expanded their ability from distinguishing between the Okinawans to actively seeking to sever the institutional ties between the two ethnic groups. Sailors, noting the pride with which the Okinawans recounted the history of the Ryukyuan Kingdom, referred to the population as "independent operators," despite accepting their status as imperial subjects. Repatriation initiatives transferred 105,000 Okinawans away from Japan and back to Okinawa. Several military government officials sought the restoration of an independent mail service and international trade. By 1946, Okinawan theatrical performers entertained Americans in military base theaters; museums in the United States exhibited Okinawan oil paintings and watercolors. The Navy even went so far as to call Okinawa a "former" prefecture.[34]

Regard for the Okinawans did not mean the Americans accepted the people as cultural equals. Sailors still maintained racially distorted opinions of the Okinawans that aligned with the widely accepted beliefs about Asian inferiority expressed by most Americans. In personal journals and letters home to receptive family members, seamen made derogatory statements about the local population, denoting a barrier between the Americans and the Okinawans that existed despite the gradual peacetime development away from fear of an enemy threat and toward benevolence toward a re-covering population. The Americans believed in an ethnic hierarchy. The Japanese, assessed as inferior and animal-like and blamed for extinguishing the comfortable yet primitive rural life Okinawa had enjoyed before the war, held the bottom rung of development. America naturally placed itself, with its deemed-superior Western way, on the civilized top. The Okinawans, still notably categorized as "oriental" and "native," remained relegated to a middle space, the benchmark for societal success set at a much lower standard than that for Western nations.[35] Nevertheless, among the men of the Navy, the ethnic hierarchy elevated Okinawa ever so slightly above Japan in terms of its capability to form a functioning society, despite the rural backwardness the Navy attributed to the Ryukyuan heritage. Marred by American opinions of Japanese wartime militarism, fervent nationalism, and malicious behavior in war and international politics, Japan could not overcome, in the early months following the surrender, the American idea of Japanese society as a defunct and shameless producer of war. Marking a development beyond the initial impression of the Okinawans as a sub-servient, ingenuous group, Americans now viewed Okinawans as a rational people with an identity independent from Japan.

Increased opportunities for interaction between Okinawans and Ameri-cans led to increased incidents of fraternization. As military government sailors began to recognize a capacity for thought in the Okinawans, their curiosity and desire for interaction grew. Not all contact involved sex and love; some sailors found themselves fascinated with the lifestyle of the islanders. Fraternization, however, signified a massive nightmare in order, discipline, and control. Overly friendly encounters disrupted operations be-cause they threatened the sailors' ability to remain unbiased and distracted them from their duties. Pregnancies and births also strained the medical and supply systems. Despite regulations restricting intermingling, military police arrested 904 soldiers and sailors for trespassing into off-limits areas.[36]

Okinawans expressed conflicting feelings about the Americans' interest in building personal relationships. They recognized the advantages of closer associations with Americans; even though the island remained a prefecture of Japan, the political and economic future of Okinawa did best on a global stage if closely bonded in positive diplomacy with America. Some Okinawans even genuinely fell in love with and married Americans. A substantial number of military government personnel expressed goodwill toward the Okinawans and commingled peacefully with the population in business and romance. Unfortunately, some American troops committed crimes against the population that included rapes and assaults. The military police themselves contributed to the violence. On multiple occasions, large bands of approximately sixty military police would search numerous houses in Okinawan villages without a clear explanation or understandable reason. Some raids would only disrupt the family while they slept; the Americans would steal property or yen. Other times the raids would reach high pitches of violence, with rapes or beatings. In these incursions, the military police failed to remove their shoes upon entry into the house—a culturally disrespectful act that scorned the Okinawans more than the crimes.[37]

The incidents of poor conduct happened at such a frequency that military government officials felt they needed to cover up the misconduct; Lieutenant Commander Paul Skuse, the chief of police, tore up most reports of American criminal wrongdoing, and Murray wrote in his closeout report on July 1, 1946 that the Naval military government had had no courts martial and that its members had exercised high discipline. The deliberate destruction of the reports called into question law enforcement's ability to protect civilians from troops; it also clearly signified a failing by senior military government officers in their "responsibility for discipline of [their] officers and men."[38] The Okinawans did not accept the inappropriate behavior and, empowered by their increased ownership in their communities, took a stance against fraternization. As their leader, Shikiya spearheaded a campaign to remove offenders by methodically cataloging the crimes committed against his people. Some Okinawans acted within their communities; residents of one *mura* allegedly killed three Americans for repeatedly raping the women. The civilians demanded that antifraternization laws be kept in place well past most other postwar occupied territories.[39]

By the spring of 1946, the Okinawans began to move into roles of greater responsibility within the government. Work in textiles, pottery, lacquerware, and woodworking blossomed into full industries that benefited beyond the immediate village. Common elections for local government positions happened as early as July. Okinawan doctors and nurses took over primary responsibility for treatment and care of patients. With the exception of US supplies and cadaver disposal, which the Navy regulated within American health and sanitation regulations, Okinawans ran their own hospitals and clinics, with minimal interference from the Navy. Okinawan doctors numbered in the sixties and handled patients in over 120 dispensaries. An additional workforce of 1,100 people handled administration, supplies, nursing, and cleanliness. The local police established a police department with a commissioner who reorganized and expanded his forces to over one thousand men. At the forefront of local dispute resolution, local police served as first responders for civilian matters; military police provided backup only as needed. Previously relegated to augmenting the military police and handling only the civilians, by spring the Okinawan police had expanded their authority even to arrests of American military men. Okinawans presided over legal actions as well. Effective April 15, low-jurisdiction civilian courts run by Okinawan court officials backed up police action.[40]

Okinawan life in the *muras* improved throughout 1946. With Okinawans at the helm of government, the people felt industrious, useful, and galvanized. They lived in rebuilt houses in areas relatively close to their original homes. As much as feasible, they reunited with family members that had survived. They physically healed from war wounds and ate more regularly. They attended council meetings, farmed collectively on recovering land, and created wares that aided the economy. As the Okinawans returned to a life of routine and productivity, recreational and relaxing tasks also found their place. One man, for example, spent his time sculpting. Within a budding political, economic, and social structure, the Okinawan people found a way to reconstruct their lives. Returning to prewar conditions took time, though. *Mura* construction moved slowly; repeated storms, combined with the low priority of Okinawa's rehabilitation from Washington, DC, caused the restoration of Okinawa to lag behind that of Japan. Comparatively, though, the state of the *muras* represented a great improvement from tent living in the districts. Spruance's policy, invigorated by passionate men like Caldwell and executed by dedicated Okinawans, had pulled the civilians out of a state of urgent distress. Okinawans still lived on meager resources, but, with the bones of society in place and the facilities to foster growth established, the Okinawan people moved beyond the critical poverty brought on by the war.[41]

The Navy officially retained responsibility for military government for only a short duration. The Army, who still held the battlespace, started sending military government personnel back to Okinawa as early as May. On July 1,

1946, military government officially transitioned from the Navy back to the Army.[42]

In a short ten months, the Navy made tremendous progress toward rehabilitating a war-torn community. Recognizing the impossibility of constructing a community based on American laws and regulations, the Navy restored Okinawan society by laying a foundation based on Okinawan tradition. Okinawan participation in government allowed for the Navy's release from the military government mission by not only providing manpower to take the places of seamen returning home but by entrenching the society in practices familiar to the people. Firmly cementing the military government design in common Okinawan practices and customs led by the Okinawans themselves ensured the permanence of the emerging society and increased the rate of demobilization.

As Okinawans served in the forefront of military government operations, they demonstrated their capability for independent action to the Americans. The proven managerial ability of the Okinawans, combined with the increased daily interactions between the population and Navy military government personnel in a nonthreatening, postwar environment, yielded a new interpretation of Okinawan identity that further severed the cultural correlation between Japan and Okinawa. Navy military government viewed Okinawans as capable and culturally progressing. The Americans assessed the Okinawans as more sensible and calmly rational than the Japanese and categorized the rural islanders as an advanced Asian people with the ability to manage political, economic, and social structures capably and with an even temperament. Okinawans themselves fundamentally shaped the execution of Navy military government; the practical US military requirement to offset the loss of demobilized troops yet continue to establish Okinawa as a strategic base placed the Okinawans at the head of constructing their society. Once the Okinawans sat in positions of influence, the gradual acknowledgment by the Americans of the population's aptitude for managing their own communities led to a US reassessment of Okinawan identity as independent from Japan.

Conclusion

War begets destruction. War involves blood, weapons, disease, and fire. War kills people, levels buildings, and burns crops; it dismantles economies, destroys political bodies, and places social constructs in peril. Successful war, as an instrument of politics, despite its purpose to impose, via force, an alternative political will, does not seamlessly transform the losing country or belligerent group into a less volatile yet still functioning entity. War brings ruin; it does not create.[1]

War, therefore, is only one of the steps toward achieving a nation's geopolitical objectives. Following the resounding defeat of an enemy, a victorious country or governing body must face the perplexing question of what to do with the carcass of their foe. Leaving the enemy in a distressed state is an option, but long-term political stability often requires the victor to rebuild their devastated opponent to at least some minimal level of self-sufficiency. Occupation and reconstruction gives the conqueror a say in the future development of the defeated nation and allows the victor to mold the vanquished into a body that poses minimal threat. Militarily, an occupation ensures the security of the winning state and stands as a necessary step to establishing peace. In practice, however, an occupation disrupts a foreign culture because the occupying military is rarely organized and equipped for gubernatorial duties. The necessary eradication of elements of the offending society believed to have caused the war can produce deep cultural conflict, often to the detriment of the occupied people. Reconstruction in the American South following the Civil War serves as such an example. The imposition of blacks' rights caused such a disruption in the racial hierarchy that it provoked Southern white violence.[2] US Marine occupation in Haiti from 1915 to 1934 devolved into a "police state" punctuated by massacres of the civilian population.[3] Occupation duty compels military officers to adopt unfamiliar government roles, which can create further tension between the population and the military enforcing the policies. Dissatisfied with the selection of the Haitian president and the earlier establishment of a US high commissioner, violent protests erupted in Haiti in 1929.[4] During American

Reconstruction, General Philip Sheridan asserted his military authority by removing civilian government officials. President Andrew Johnson fired him.[5] Occupations carry weighty consequences for the longevity of the country that prevailed in war, yet they remain complicated undertakings that stretch the capabilities of their military executors and unavoidably disturb the cultural fabric of the conquered society. Miscalculations of the situation or a dismissal of the gravity of the responsibilities to government can place a hard-earned victory in jeopardy or ensnare a country in an undesirably prolonged commitment in an area.

Wartime occupation begins at the same time as the combat begins, since battle commences among the population. Therefore, the roots of reconstruction start within the violent conflict itself. Initial contact between a foreign army and the local population builds the groundwork for the military government operations that follow the conclusion of hostilities. An army that fails to consider the interruption to military operations caused by local infrastructure puts its campaigns at risk. Local communities pose logistical challenges: They stand in the way of linear battlefields, redefine routes, disrupt supply distribution, obscure targets, and hide the enemy. Practically, military commanders must consider how to preserve the integrity of their mission while minimizing the amount of interference caused by—and casualties to—the population.

Focusing only on military tactics on the battlefield and how to manage challenges to military maneuvers, however, ignores the inherent cultural nature of occupation and reduces the understanding of the local people to two dimensions. Occupations born out of strictly military considerations struggle to find commonality with the population and thus impose regulations that consequently fail because they are unable to adapt to the environment. Ultimately, militaries conducting occupations in this manner impede the population from regaining control over their community following the conflict and thus extend the commitment of the foreign government in administering the occupied land.

The wartime occupation of Okinawa demonstrates the crucial role that considerations of race and ethnicity have on the conduct of military government. American military government planners recognized both the possible threat a population of 463,000 civilians might pose and the complexities of the relationship between Okinawa and Japan. Without losing sight of the impact that the civilians would have on military operations, planners from all services, including the Marines, analyzed the ethnicity of the Okinawans and how their cultural distinctiveness might inform their behavior. While the Marines' policy prohibited further assessment of the population upon landing on the island, preliminary analyses provided the military leadership of all services with a more robust understanding of the battlefield that they faced and thus better prepared them to preserve military lives, safeguard American secrets, and win the battle.

Planning for the Battle of Okinawa began in the fall of 1944 as American military leadership recognized the strategic importance of Okinawa in relation to mainland Japan. Buckner, as the commanding general of the Tenth Army, primarily concerned himself with the tactical and operational plans of the invasion yet empowered his subordinate staff to analyze carefully what effects the sizeable population of the island might have on the mission. As Crist identified, the determination of Okinawan allegiance to Japan held crucial importance in the conduct of the battle. Balancing, on the one hand, operational concerns about supply, mission accomplishment, and minimizing casualties with, on the other, the potential of the civilians to form a fighting force, Army planners opted for a strategy that prepared the soldiers for a worst-case scenario: that the Okinawans would honor their prefectural status with Japan and engage in combat, both by augmenting Japanese troop levels and as irregulars. In execution, the plan called for the removal of civilians from the battlefield so they did not interfere with the mission. Soldiers learned to approach civilians with caution and to consider them as potential spies and enemies. Consistent with Buckner's priority on mission success, the policy meant to preserve the safety of tactical military secrets and minimize the loss of American soldiers' lives. Training for the soldiers, however, also acknowledged, to varying degrees, that the true disposition of the Okinawans remained unknown. Once ashore, the recognition of the conjecture involved with assigning an Okinawan identity allowed the soldiers to interpret on their own what they encountered in the field and modify their judgments accordingly. Through increased interaction with the Okinawans, the military government units attached to the Army gradually began to view the civilians more positively and as less of a threat. The soldiers began to give the civilians more independence within the military government camps and provide them with extra facilities beyond their basic needs. They identified the civilians as Okinawans, separate from the Japanese and independent in their motivations and loyalties.

The analytical studies conducted during planning did not lack complications, however, and the different conclusions drawn by the various US services produced somewhat uneven results on the battlefield. The Marines reached the same answer about Okinawan loyalty as the Army and also devised a policy that rested on the supposition that the Okinawans would rally to the Japanese side. Unlike the Army, however, the Marines' strict

adherence to the assignment of a Japanese identity to the Okinawans prohibited their men on the ground from continually reassessing the behavior
of the people they encountered. As a result, the Marines held on to the idea
of the Okinawan enemy longer than practical, which resulted in harsher,
sometimes brutal treatment. Joint operations in the Pacific carried many
complications despite the conscious efforts of Buckner to seamlessly amalgamate XXIV Corps and III Amphibious Corps under his Tenth Army and
monitor interservice discontent and rivalry. Unfortunately, the Okinawans
at times became pawns in the contest of wills between the services.

Following combat operations, the mission of military government on
Okinawa changed from wartime occupation to the occupation of a defeated
country. As Army forces were diverted to perform occupation duties in
Japan and Korea, the Navy assumed responsibility for military government
on Okinawa. In the chaotic aftermath of the battle, the Navy handled the
displacement of civilians by dictating military government activities on an
ad hoc basis through directives issued simultaneously throughout operations. The Navy failed to analyze the changed environment as the island
transitioned to peace and continued battlefield practices, such as guarding
civilians during movement, which were inappropriate under the new situation. The Navy military government settled into a malaise that managed
little more than temporary fixes to the most conspicuous problems.

By the winter of 1945, inspired new Navy leadership began to rectify the
troubles afflicting military government on the island. Admiral Raymond A.
Spruance and a collection of talented junior officers recognized the importance of Okinawan participation in the emerging government structure and
wrote a directive that gradually placed increasing administrative control of
local government with the Okinawans. Meant to address the practical problem of troop attrition from expired military service commitments, the plan
also offered the people a chance to shape their own community. Spruance
and the ingenuity of key officers working directly in military government
recognized that only through a meticulous analysis of the history and customs of the Okinawans could the Navy construct a viable and durable government organization. Just as the Army experienced during the war, Navy
military government found their views of the Okinawans evolving through
increased interaction with the population; they now viewed Okinawans as
capable and culturally progressing, a group that formed a distinct, separate,
unique ethnic community neither American nor Japanese.

In postwar operations, correctly comprehending the intent and loyalty of the Okinawan population allowed the occupying forces to grant
the civilians increased liberties and involvement in the reestablishment

of their government. Under the superior direction of Spruance and young, imaginative leaders such as Lieutenant Commander John Tyler Caldwell, occupation during the transition to peace focused on the utility of the population in achieving US military goals. Even with the ongoing strategic role of Okinawa following the war as an American base and a geographic presence in the Pacific, Okinawan participation in the shaping of their society ensured the long-term viability of their community programs and allowed the US military to reduce its manpower overseas to minimal levels.

Acknowledgment of race and ethnicity does not always ignite emotionally charged racism that then produces racially driven policy devoid of practical reasoning. Conversely, conducting in-depth cultural studies does not singularly erase deeply held racial biases, especially when such discriminatory views align with the norms of one's own society. Racism, in its complexity, defies any simple formula that claims to reduce its manifestation into a clear line from thought to action. As demonstrated by the multifaceted Lieutenant General Simon Bolivar Buckner, who denigrated the worth of the Okinawans as a people yet endorsed policy that provided space for free assessments of Okinawan abilities and opportunities for their influence, inherent racial beliefs do not necessarily align with discriminatory policy. The Okinawan occupation tells the story of the centrality of recognizing racial, ethnic, and cultural dynamics as a useful practice in devising complete and careful military plans. Detailed study about the Ryukyus conducted in preparation for the assault on Hagushi Beach produced a generally deeper comprehension about the Okinawans in 1944–1946 and a better understanding of their unique place within the Japanese empire. Soldiers, sailors, and Marines alike retained paternalistic prejudices against a population they viewed as rural, backward, and crude, but such biases did not overwhelm their commitment to mission success. The knowledge gained through cultural study allowed military planners to grapple with the complex question about the disposition of the population, a vital analysis pertinent to ensuring the well-being of the military operation and the men who fought in it.

Well aware of the importance of positive control of Okinawa in the overall strategic campaign for the invasion of Japan, planners took the challenge of the civilian population seriously. The conclusion they reached—to prepare for Okinawan loyalty to the Japanese emperor and, therefore, a legitimate fight—lay on a foundation of solid and reliable information despite it only carrying the weight of a best guess. Military planners recognized the dichotomy between the governing nation and the people it had relegated to second-class status and appreciated that no simple or guaranteed answer about an Okinawan temperament existed. Cultural studies of an area of occupation expand the image of the occupied population into three dimensions and prompt policy makers to ask questions about the effects of their decisions. Military governments that provide even a small amount of cultural continuity in their policies increase the likelihood of acceptance by the occupied population.

Through cultural analysis, a planner gains insight into the potential of a population to think and contribute to the outcome of their own situation. Thoughtful analysis of the complexities of race and ethnicity reveals its malleability and exposes the aptitude of the occupied people to adapt and modify their identity to gain advantage. As evidenced by the US Army and Navy in Okinawa, military and government officials need to understand the historic foundation of ethnic traditions and loyalties yet also appreciate the contested nature of ethnicity and identity. Successful military government must be flexible in its cultural analysis if it is to account properly for the adaptive nature of the occupied people as they struggle under the stress of the newly and forcibly imposed government.

Today, the small island of Okinawa holds vigils for their war dead at numerous memorial sites, monuments, and annual events and in the memories of the island's centenarians. The American occupation of Okinawa continued officially until 1972, throughout which the islanders expressed their discontent with both governments—the United States and Japan—presiding over them. Most recently, Okinawa's residents protested the continued presence of American troops and rallied against the relocation of Marine Corps Air Station Futenma from Ginowan City to Henoko, demanding its complete closure. While the tension between the Marines and the Okinawans certainly aligns with recent episodes of Marine poor conduct in more current decades, the initial behavior of Marines during the Battle of Okinawa, as opposed to that of Army soldiers, may have stained the reputation of the Marine Corps in ways that the other services avoided. Long-term association of the Marines with heavy-handed, sometimes brutal policy may still influence the perceptions of the population today. Certainly, the Marines compose a vast majority of the American forces on the island today, but, if war memory, memorialization, and the sensitivity of the Okinawans to their tumultuous past serve as indications, the present-day friction between the Marines and the islanders may have deep historical roots. If so, the present-day animosity can potentially serve as a lesson about the long-term consequences of a harsher, unyielding interpretation of cultural dynamics and obstinate interaction.

Nations and belligerents will continue to fight wars and face occupation responsibilities in communities whose cultures, traditions, and beliefs deviate from or conflict with theirs. Race and ethnicity cannot be ignored in occupations because the very nature of an occupation is the imposition of one set of cultural beliefs upon another in order to accomplish a military objective of stability. In 2013, as the United States transitioned from brigade combat team operations to advisor roles in Afghanistan, the need for positive and effective interaction with the local population became paramount. In combating a terrorist enemy that embeds itself among the people, soldiers in Afghanistan, much like the American forces on Okinawa, needed to be able to differentiate between the enemy and the citizens. Thorough, evaluative examination of race and ethnicity executed as an active and evolving analysis provides the military with the ability to fully engage in their environment and renders their policy flexible enough to suit changing circumstances. Acknowledgment of ethnic differences, done in a manner that seeks educative understanding, should hopefully foster cognizant policy that still supports military goals. An examination of the wartime occupation of Okinawa provides an example for effective military government programs now and in the future.

Acknowledgments

I came upon the idea for this project in 2006, when the Army stationed my husband, David, an active duty officer, at Kadena Air Base, on Okinawa. Although I was attending the University of North Carolina–Chapel Hill as a graduate student and Army officer at the time, I visited him on the island as often as I could. As happens when anyone explores a new country, we quickly immersed ourselves in exciting and new experiences. We enjoyed the unique music, tasty food, temperate weather, and stunning natural beauty. We also delighted in the incredible convenience of pulling our car over at any point along a road or path so we could jump in the clear, bright blue water to snorkel. As American soldiers, however, we also became aware of our distinct relationship with the island, its people, and its history. For centuries, the Ryukyuan Kingdom—later, Okinawa prefecture—experienced the imposition of many nations upon their trade, traditions, government, and economics. During World War II, the United States entered into this contested space. My husband and I found ourselves on Okinawa in 2006 precisely because of this history; when the US military arrived in 1945, they never left. Following the war, the Okinawans deftly navigated the demands of two nations—the United States and Japan—on their geographic space, their autonomy, their politics, their economics, and their sense of self. My husband and I soon realized that these international conditions, rooted in a deep and complex history, influenced our interactions with the population. As I saw the long-term effects of past actions and decisions play out in the present, I became more and more interested in researching the US military's behavior in complex situations of race, ethnicity, and identity.

As with all academic endeavors, the scholarly journey is a long one that is not walked alone. First and foremost, it is the people that live with you and love you that contribute and sacrifice the most in support of your success. My husband, David, stands as my greatest supporter, my steadfast partner, and my teammate in life. Through years of constant military moves and demanding jobs, he always ensured I had time for my academic pursuits, challenged me intellectually, and committed our whole family to the accomplishment of this project. He has stood by me every step of the way and genuinely believed in me. He is the foundation upon which I have built my whole life. My little girl, Olivia, has also been crucial to the development of this work. Since she was three years old, she has sat right next to me and colored, drew pictures, and banged away on a children's computer as she worked on her own "book" about mermaids and weddings. As she grew older, she even let me know which sentences did not "sound good." She and I spent many weekends together—her at the playground or playing next to me on the living room floor, while I wrote at a nearby table or studied documents spread across the couch. Her sweet behavior and keen insights allowed me to think and create. To my family, I owe everything.

Dr. Richard Kohn and Dr. Joseph Glatthaar taught me the art of historical thinking and reasoning and how to write intellectually. I am honored to have had the privilege to work with such renowned and brilliant scholars. I will forever be in their debt for teaching and challenging me. Dr. Kohn introduced me to the historical profession and guided me from the initial conception of this project through the successful completion of my master's degree. He molded me from being simply an Army officer into a scholar as well. I would also like to particularly express my sincere gratitude to Dr. Glatthaar, who, through his continuous mentorship, inspired me to finish this work. Through the years, he motivated me and pushed me to the most rigorous academic standards. I would also like to thank the members of my PhD committee—Dr. Gerhard Weinberg, Dr. W. Miles Fletcher, and Dr. Wayne Lee—for their time and extremely valuable insights and critique. The University of North Carolina–Chapel Hill provided an invigorating educational experience that expanded my worldview and developed me as a person.

I am indebted to the fine institutions and exemplary professionals that house and care for the archival materials that provide the foundation for this work. The National Archives and Record Administration, the Gray Research Center at the United States Marine Corps Archives and Special Collections, the United States Marine Corps Historical Division, and the United States Army Heritage and Education Center continue to preserve our history beautifully. I would like to particularly thank the outstanding Veterans History Project at the Library of Congress for providing such excellent resources in such an accessible format, Dr. Gregory L. Mattson at the Kadena Air Base Archives for allowing me into back rooms and old file cabinets, the Hoover Institute at Stanford University, the Western Manuscript Collection at the University of Missouri, and the Okinawa Prefectural Peace Memorial Museum. Thank you also to Mike Kasper, Liesa Abel, and the Institute on World War II and the Human Experience at Florida State University for their tremendous help with locating some truly fantastic images. On a personal note, I am grateful for Robert Hostetler's time, valuable insights, and shared personal experiences and the kindness of Colonel (retired) Gary Montgomery, USMC, who allowed me to look at materials he had collected from limited-access Marine Corps personnel files. I also deeply appreciate the generosity of Dr. Bart Kowallis, who entrusted me with the photos taken by his father, Lieutenant Reinhart Kowallis.

Finally, I would like to express my gratitude to Dr. G. Kurt Piehler, director of the Institute on World War II and the Human Experience, for reviewing earlier revisions and for bringing my work to the attention of Fordham University Press, and to Mr. Fredric Nachbaur and Mr. William Cerbone at Fordham University Press, for their patience and professionalism in bringing this work to print.

Notes

Introduction

1. Ronald H. Spector, *Eagle against the Sun: The American War with Japan* (New York: Free Press, 1985), 9.

2. Spector, *Eagle against the Sun*, 20–21, 35–36; Mark E. Caprio, *Japanese Assimilation Policies in Colonial Korea, 1910–1945* (Seattle: University of Washington Press, 2009), 12–14; Peter Paret, *Makers of Modern Strategy from Machiavelli to the Nuclear Age* (Princeton, NJ: Princeton University Press, 1986), 703–12; John W. Dower, *War without Mercy: Race and Power in the Pacific War* (New York: Pantheon, 1986), 6–8.

3. Christopher J. Anderson, *The Marines in World War II: From Pearl Harbor to Tokyo Bay* (London: Stackpole, 2006); Michael J. Lyons, *World War II: A Short History* (Cambridge: Pearson, 2009), 142–50; Max Hastings, *Inferno: The World at War, 1939–1945* (New York: Vintage, 2012), 198–263; Williamson Murray and Allan R. Millett, *A War to Be Won: Fighting the Second World War* (Cambridge, MA: Harvard University Press, 2000); E. B. Sledge, *With the Old Breed at Peleliu and Okinawa* (Annapolis, MD: Naval Institute Press, 1996).

4. Lyons, *World War II*, 143–44; Spector, *Eagle against the Sun*, 130–33.

5. Hastings, *Inferno*, 198–263, 419–26; Murray and Millett, *A War to Be Won*, 340–48; Spector, *Eagle against the Sun*, 142–46, 217–18, 291, 294, 301; Lyons, *World War II*, 142–50; Sledge, *With the Old Breed*; Richard Overy, *Why the Allies Won* (London: Pimlico, 1995), 235.

6. Richard Frank, *Downfall: The End of the Imperial Japanese Empire* (New York: Penguin, 1999), 70; Spector, *Eagle against the Sun*, 253.

7. Benis M. Frank, *Okinawa: Touchstone to Victory* (New York: Ballantine, 1970), 44–46, 72.

8. Murray and Millett, *A War to Be Won*, 361; Nicolas Evan Sarantakes, ed., *Seven Stars: The Okinawa Battle Diaries of Simon Bolivar Buckner Jr. and Joseph Stilwell* (College Station: Texas A&M University Press, 2004), 7–8, 17.

9. Bill Sloan, *The Ultimate Battle: Okinawa 1945—The Last Epic Struggle of World War II* (New York: Simon and Schuster, 2007), 30; Spector, *Eagle against the Sun*, 533; Murray and Millett, *A War to Be Won*, 511.

10. Frank, *Okinawa*, 62, 66; Sloan, *The Ultimate Battle*, 64–65; Thomas E.

Griess, ed., *West Point Atlas for the Second World War: Asia and the Pacific* (New York: Square One, 2002), map 48b.

11. Frank, *Okinawa*, 67, 70; Griess, ed., *West Point Atlas for the Second World War*, map 47b; Spector, *Eagle against the Sun*, 534; Murray and Millett, *A War to Be Won*, 514; Frank, *Downfall*, 70–71.

12. Griess, ed., *West Point Atlas for the Second World War*, map 49a, 49b; Murray and Millett, *A War to Be Won*, 514–15; Spector, *Eagle against the Sun*, 535; Sloan, *The Ultimate Battle*, 174–79, 255–72; Frank, *Okinawa*, 106, 136.

13. CINCPAC-CINCPOA Bulletin #161-44, November 15, 1944, RG 407, Box 2502, NARA, 5; Frank, *Downfall*, 70; Frank, *Okinawa*, 16; George H. Kerr, *Okinawa: The History of an Island People* (Tokyo: Tuttle, 2000), 381.

14. Kerr, *Okinawa*, 104–16.

15. Kerr, *Okinawa*, 153–55, 158–59, 563; Kenneth M. Swope, *A Dragon's Head and a Serpent's Tail: Ming China and the First Great East Asian War, 1592–1598* (Norman: University of Oklahoma Press, 2009), 6, 62, 292.

16. Kerr, *Okinawa*, 163–65, 566.

17. Kerr, *Okinawa*, 352–53, 381–82, 566.

18. Kerr, *Okinawa*, 442, 448–49, 460–64; *An Oral History of the Battle of Okinawa, Survivor's Testimonies* (Okinawa: Relief Section, Welfare Department, Okinawa Prefectural Government, 1985), 4. From the beginning of Okinawan conscription in 1898, Okinawans failed to meet the height and weight requirements, as directed by the Japanese government, for military service. As a result, the majority of Okinawans that were conscripted served on the mainland in labor units as opposed to in combat units. However, as the threat of American forces bore down on the island, Japan mobilized the population through the National Mobilization Act of 1944 and incorporated more Okinawan men into combat military units stationed on Okinawa. Included in this increase of Okinawan combatants was the 16,000-strong Okinawan Home Guard, or Boei Tai. Young boys and girls were also enlisted to serve as soldiers in the Blood and Iron Corps and the student nurse corps.

19. Kerr, *Okinawa*, 156–66, 381–83.

20. History of Military Government Operations on Okinawa, 1 April–30 April 1945 [L Day to L+29], by BG William E. Crist, May 10, 1945, RG 407, Box 2487, File 110-5.0, NARA; Robert B. Sheeks, Lieutenant, USMCR, "Civilians on Saipan," *Far Eastern Survey*, May 9, 1945, 109; Military Government, General Order No. 2-44, Tinian, September 2, 1944, RG 389, Box 844, NARA; Training Syllabus, Charlottesville, VA, October 21, 1944, RG 496, Box 351, NARA, 1; Military Government, General Order No. 1-44, Tinian, August 26, 1944, RG 389, Box 844, NARA; Plan for the Naval Military Government of the Marianas, RG 398, Box 844, NARA; Political Directive for the Military Government of the Caroline Islands in the Central Pacific, Appendix D, March 1944, RG 389, Box 844, NARA; Plan for the Naval Military Government of the East Caroline Islands, RG 389, Box 844, NARA.

21. Race and ethnicity, as seen within the context of Japan and its relationship with its Okinawan population, are best understood as malleable categories based on cultural factors, such as language and ancestry, and a shared group history. In language, traditions, ancestry, and group history, the Ryukyuan people differed from the Yamato Japanese on the mainland. Japan resisted any diversity within its population and prided itself on an assumed homogeneity. Michael Weiner, ed., *Japan's Minorities: The Illusion of Homogeneity* (London: Routledge, 2008).

22. History of Military Government Operations on Okinawa, May 10, 1945, BG William E. Crist, 17; LTC John Stevens and MSG James M. Burns, Okinawa Diary, March 21, 1945, RG 407, Box 2441, NARA. Note: This is an unpublished diary/log written by soldiers involved in the occupation of Okinawa. It is a small, multipage document located in a box (2441) in record group 407 at NARA. RG 407, which is very large and contains many of documents I worked with, is listed in the bibliography, but I do not list all of the separate documents.

23. Dower, *War without Mercy*; Craig M. Cameron, *American Samurai: Myth, Imagination, and the Conduct of Battle in First Marine Division, 1941–1951* (New York: Cambridge University Press, 1994); John A. Lynn, *Battle: A History of Combat and Culture* (Boulder, CO: Westview, 2003); Adam Schrager, *The Principled Politician: Governor Ralph Carr and the Fight against Japanese American Internment* (Golden, CO: Fulcrum, 2008); Ellen D. Wu, *The Color of Success: Asians Americans and the Origins of the Model Minority* (Princeton, NJ: Princeton University Press, 2014).

24. The short title "GOPER" is not an acronym, and its origin is not known. Arnold Fisch, *Military Government in the Ryukyu Islands, 1945–1950* (Washington, DC: Center of Military History, United States Army, 1988).

25. Sarantakes, ed., *Seven Stars*, 28, 45; *Anchorage Times*, June 19, 1945; Interview with LTG Simon Bolivar Buckner Jr., Okinawa Diary, March 21, 1945, LTC John Stevens and MSG James M. Burns; Nicolas Evan Sarantakes, *Keystone: The American Occupation of Okinawa and U.S. Japanese Relations* (College Station: Texas A&M University Press, 2000), 28–29.

26. Operational Directive #7 from the Commanding General of Tenth Army, January 6, 1945, RG 290, Box 2196, NARA, 9.

1. Identifying the Enemy: US Army Wartime Occupation Policy

1. United States Military Government, Detachment B-5, Diary, April 30, 1945, Western Manuscript Collection, CO445, Folders 1–4, University of Missouri, Columbia, MO, 33.

2. Benis M. Frank, *Okinawa: Touchstone to Victory* (New York: Ballantine, 1970); Masahide Ota, *The Battle of Okinawa: The Typhoon of Steel and Bombs* (Tokyo: Kume, 1984); E. B. Sledge, *With the Old Breed at Peleliu and Okinawa* (Annapolis, MD: Naval Institute Press, 1996); Bill Sloan, *The Ultimate Battle: Okinawa 1945—The Last Epic Struggle of World War II* (New York: Simon and Schuster, 2007).

3. Diary, April 3, 1945, Detachment B-5, 25.

4. The GOPER was the primary document for military government operations on Okinawa; it was the document briefed to all military government units. Its contents were repeated in Annex 15 to Operations Plan 1-45. Two other military government appendices were completed two months after the GOPER and covered command responsibility issues following the battle. Appendix E, Annex 1 to Operation Plan No. 1., called "Tentative Military Government Plan for Phase II," mentioned without details how military government would fall under Island Command (IsCom) after the completion of the battle. Appendix A, Annex X, "Civil Censorship Plan," was completed by IsCom. Annex 15, Tentative Operations Plan No. 1-45, January 6, 1945, RG 407, Box 2487, File 110-5.5, NARA; Appendix E, Annex 1 to Operation Plan No. 1, "Tentative Military Government Plan for Phase II," RG 389, Box 704, NARA; Appendix A, Annex X, "Civil Censorship Plan," March 11, 1945, RG 389, Box 704, NARA; History of Military Government Operations on Okinawa, 1 April–30 April 1945 [L Day to L+29], by BG William E. Crist, May 10, 1945, RG 407, Box 2487, File 110-5.0, NARA.

5. Nicolas Evan Sarantakes, ed., *Seven Stars: The Okinawa Battle Diaries of Simon Bolivar Buckner Jr. and Joseph Stilwell* (College Station: Texas A&M University Press, 2004), 17. Buckner received official orders assigning him as the commanding general of the Tenth Army on September 4, 1944.

6. CINCPAC-CINCPOA Bulletin #161-44, November 15, 1944, RG 407, Box 2502, NARA, 5.

7. Sarantakes, ed., *Seven Stars*, 17–21; Arnold Fisch, *Military Government in the Ryukyu Islands, 1945–1950* (Washington, DC: Center of Military History, United States Army, 1988), 18.

8. The GOPER was not directly based on previous military government policies created for other theaters of battles, nor did it arise from a template. The GOPER followed the US Army standard operations order format and covered typical topics taught in the Civil Affairs schools—local government, medical care, supply, finance, etc.—but because the planners considered the Okinawans possibly similar to the Japanese in culture and allegiance, the contents of the GOPER deviated from previous military government policies created for areas like the Philippines, Guadalcanal, Saipan, and the Marianas. Military Government, General Order No. 2-44, Tinian, September 2, 1944, RG 389, Box 844, NARA; Training Syllabus, Charlottesville, VA, October 21, 1944, RG 496, Box 351, NARA, 1; Military Government, General Order No. 1-44, Tinian, August 26, 1944, RG 389, Box 844, NARA; Plan for the Naval Military Government of the Marianas, RG 398, Box 844, NARA; Political Directive for the Military Government of the Caroline Islands in the Central Pacific, Appendix D, March 1944, RG 389, Box 844, NARA; Plan for the Naval Military Government of the East Caroline Islands, RG 389, Box 844, NARA.

9. Operational Directive #7 from the Commanding General of Tenth Army, January 6, 1945, RG 290, Box 2196, NARA, 1.

10. Upon completion of the assault, the military government teams were to be reassigned to Island Command (IsCom) under Major General Fred C. Wallace, USMC. This transition was originally planned to begin once camps were set up in the rear areas. By the end of the battle (the garrison phase), all military government units were to be under IsCom. In actuality, however, the transition to IsCom took much longer and was not completed until July 2, 1945. The military government units remained under the control of the combat divisions, XXIV Corps, and Tenth Army military government staffs. IsCom existed primarily as a staff section for the majority of the battle. Fisch, *Military Government in the Ryukyu Islands*, 18, 27; Captain Roy E. Appleman, notes, RG 407, File 224-12, NARA, 2; CINCPAC-CINCPOA Bulletin #161-44, November 15, 1944; XXIV Corps Military Government Daily Operations Log, RG 407, File 224-12, NARA; Military Government Operations in the Ryukyu Area, Appendix V, Part I-IV, August 2, 1945, RG 407, Box 2487, File 110-5, NARA; LTC John Stevens and MSG James M. Burns, Okinawa Diary, April 30, 1945, RG 407, Box 2441, NARA.

11. Operational Directive #7, January 6, 1945, Commanding General, Tenth Army, 2–4.

12. Details about the specific treatment of and interaction between civilians and American forces were not included in most literature about military government, civil affairs, and occupation. Only training materials used at the Civil Affairs training schools for officers briefly instructed that all cultural and religious customs be maintained and that civilians be treated with respect. All other information distributed to the soldiers eliminated the topic, stating only that it would addressed as required. Training Syllabus, Charlottesville, VA, October 21, 1944, RG 496, Box 351, NARA, 1; Tenth Army Pamphlet—Information on Military Government, February 13, 1945, RG 389, Box 704, NARA, 7.

13. Operational Directive #7, January 6, 1945, Commanding General, Tenth Army, 1, 2, 9; Interview with LTG Simon Bolivar Buckner Jr., Okinawa Diary, March 21, 1945, LTC John Stevens and MSG James M. Burns.

14. Operational Directive #7, January 6, 1945, Commanding General, Tenth Army, 5.

15. Operational Directive #7, January 6, 1945, Commanding General, Tenth Army, 9.

16. Operational Directive #7, January 6, 1945, Commanding General, Tenth Army, 10.

17. Operational Directive #7, January 6, 1945, Commanding General, Tenth Army, 11.

18. Operational Directive #7, January 6, 1945, Commanding General, Tenth Army, 9.

19. Operational Directive #7, January 6, 1945, Commanding General, Tenth Army, 1.

20. Interview with LTG Simon Bolivar Buckner Jr., Okinawa Diary, March 21, 1945, LTC John Stevens and MSG James M. Burns.

21. Sarantakes, ed., *Seven Stars*, 5. The Americans landed 548,000 troops and docked 1,300 ships. Frank, *Okinawa*, 50; Ota, *The Battle of Okinawa*, x; Sledge, *With the Old Breed*, 192; Sloan, *The Ultimate Battle*, 96.

22. Operational Directive #7, January 6, 1945, Commanding General, Tenth Army, 7.

23. Operational Directive #7, January 6, 1945, Commanding General, Tenth Army, 1.

24. Operational Directive #7, January 6, 1945, Commanding General, Tenth Army, 10.

25. Operational Directive #7, January 6, 1945, Commanding General, Tenth Army, 7.

26. Captain Roy E. Appleman, notes, RG 407, File 224-12, NARA, 1. In reality, the Okinawans were of a different ethnicity completely—Ryukyuan—from the mainland Yamato Japanese.

27. History of Military Government Operations on Okinawa, May 10, 1945, BG William E. Crist.

28. Sarantakes, ed., *Seven Stars*, 22.

29. Osborn's book was not sponsored by the US War Department, and its readership can only be assumed.

30. "The Geography of Conquest," *Fortune*, April 1944, 161; Fairfield Osborn, *The Pacific World: Its Vast Distances, Its Lands and the Life upon Them, and Its People* (New York: Norton, 1944), 184. These publications portrayed Okinawa as a colony, which it was not.

31. "The Citizens," *Fortune*, April 1944, 149.

32. *The Ryukyus Handbook*, Department of the Army, Civil Affairs Handbook, 1944, RG 290, Box 3199, NARA, VII.

33. This assessment was slightly incorrect and misleading. While Okinawa was legally a prefecture of Japan, Japan maintained a higher level of control over Okinawa than its other prefectures. For example, all high prefectural positions in Okinawa were held by the Japanese, rather than by locals. The government structure in Okinawa was the same as other prefectures, but it was dominated by the Japanese. Yenob-PW-188, POW interrogation, May 16, 1945, RG 389, Box 844, NARA; Masamichi S. Inoue, *Okinawa and the U.S. Military: Identity Making in the Age of Globalization* (New York: Columbia University Press, 2007), 55–62.

34. *The Ryukyus Handbook*, 1944, Department of the Army, VIII.

35. History of Military Government Operations on Okinawa, May 10, 1945, BG William E. Crist, 17.

36. CINCPAC-CINCPOA Bulletin #161-44, November 15, 1944, 5, 10.

37. CINCPAC-CINCPOA Bulletin #161-44, November 15, 1944, 10, 11.

38. CINCPAC-CINCPOA Bulletin #161-44, November 15, 1944, 12; POW interrogation, May 16, 1945, Yenob-PW-188; Inoue, *Okinawa and the U.S. Military*, 55–62.

39. History of Military Government Operations on Okinawa, May 10, 1945, BG William E. Crist, 17; Okinawa Diary, March 21, 1945, LTC John Stevens and MSG James M. Burns.

40. CINCPAC-CINCPOA Bulletin #161-44, November 15, 1944, 13; Report of Psychological Warfare Activities Okinawa Operation, September 15, 1945, RG 407, Box 2502, File 110-39, NARA, 20; Interview with 2LT Alfred S. Youkoff, Psychological Warfare—Combat Propaganda Team, Okinawa Diary, March 21, 1945, LTC John Stevens and MSG James M. Burns.

41. History of Military Government Operations on Okinawa, May 10, 1945, BG William E. Crist, 17.

42. Buckner was the son of a Confederate general and shared similar beliefs with his father on race and the South. He lamented the South's loss of the Civil War and considered the Southerners' cause noble. He studied Douglass Southall Freeman's *Lee's Lieutenants* as a guidebook to leadership and command and felt that the incorporation of different races into the fabric of American citizenry would further complicate America's race problem. Should the US forces be successful in taking the island of Okinawa, he felt strongly that the Okinawans should never have rights to American citizenship because their Asian heritage would taint American demography. Sarantakes, ed., *Seven Stars*, 28, 45; *Anchorage Times*, June 19, 1945; Interview with LTG Simon Bolivar Buckner Jr., Okinawa Diary, March 21, 1945, LTC John Stevens and MSG James M. Burns; Nicolas Evan Sarantakes, *Keystone: The American Occupation of Okinawa and U.S. Japanese Relations* (College Station: Texas A&M University Press, 2000), 28–29. Despite his personal feelings toward other ethnicities and races, however, Buckner's decision to view the Okinawan civilian population as an enemy was widely accepted and shared by his fellow commanders and staff planners. In the interest of successfully securing Okinawa and safeguarding the lives of the troops, all American commanders approached the unpredictable Okinawans with caution.

43. Operational Directive #7, January 6, 1945, Commanding General, Tenth Army, 2, 9; Interview with LTG Simon Bolivar Buckner Jr., Okinawa Diary, March 21, 1945, LTC John Stevens and MSG James M. Burns.

44. Interview with MG John Hodge, Okinawa Diary, March 12, 1945, LTC John Stevens and MSG James M. Burns.

45. Interview with MG John Hodge, Okinawa Diary, March 12, 1945, LTC John Stevens and MSG James M. Burns; History of Military Government Operations on Okinawa, May 10, 1945, BG William E. Crist, 17; Operational Directive #7, January 6, 1945, Commanding General, Tenth Army, 1, 2, 9; 7th Division, speech transcript, Inclosure 2, Civil Affairs, RG 407, File 224-12, NARA; XXIV Corps Military Government Daily Operations Log, RG 407, File 224-12, NARA.

46. Leaflet 527, X-1, X-10, 521, X-12, 530, RG 407, Box 2502, NARA; Report of Psychological Warfare Activities Okinawa Operation, September 15, 1945, RG 407, Box 2502, File 110-39, NARA.

2. US Marine Discipline: Strict Directives in Wartime
Marine Military Government

1. Laura Homan Lacey, *Stay off the Skyline: The Sixth Marine Division on Okinawa, an Oral History* (Washington, DC: Potomac, 2005), 73–75, told by Private Joe Drago.

2. D-2 Study of Theater of Operations Okinawa Jima, Part I, 6th Marine Division, February 8, 1945, WWII, Okinawa, 6th Marine Division Collection, Box 7, Folder 2/7, United States Marine Corps Archives and Special Collections, Alfred M. Gray Research Center, Quantico, VA, 2–3, 5; LTC John Stevens and MSG James M. Burns, Okinawa Diary, April 30, 1945, RG 407, Box 2441, NARA; CINCPAC-CINCPOA Bulletin #161-44, November 15, 1944, RG 407, Box 2502, NARA, 13; Report of Psychological Warfare Activities Okinawa Operation, September 15, 1945, RG 407, Box 2502, File 110-39, NARA, 20.

3. Annex Fox to Administrative Plan 1-45, 1st Marine Division, February 10, 1945, RG 389, Box 704, NARA 5, 14; Procedure for Handling Enemy Nationals, 1st Marine Division, Detachment B-10, May 2, 1945, RG 389, Box 704, NARA; Annex "Able" to Administrative Plan No. 1-45, January 16, 1945, RG 389, Box 704, NARA, 5–6, 8–9; Appendix No. 3 to Annex "Able" to Administrative Plan No. 1-45, January 16, 1945, RG 389, Box 704, NARA; Military Government Plan, 6th Marine Division, February 8, 1945, RG 389, Box 704, NARA, 3, 6; Propaganda for Use against the Japanese, 2nd Marine Division, December 29, 1944, WWII, Marine Corps Various, 1941–1945, Box, 1, Folder 24/1, United States Marine Corps Archives and Special Collections, Alfred M. Gray Research Center, Quantico, VA, 1, 3.

4. Annex "Able," January 16, 1945, 5; Military Government Plan, February 8, 1945, 6th Marine Division, 2–3; Proclamations, 1st Marine Division, February 13, 1945, RG 389, Box 704, NARA; Commander's Estimate of the Situation, Okinawa Island (Operation Iceberg), WWII, Okinawa, 6th Marine Division Collection, Box 7, Folder 1/7, United States Marine Corps Archives and Special Collections, Alfred M. Gray Research Center, Quantico, VA, 15.

5. Captain's Message to All Hands, USS *Panamint*, March 31, 1945, Major General Roy S. Geiger Papers, Box 6, Folder 106, Alfred M. Gray Research Center, Quantico, VA; Executive Officer's Memorandum No. 94-45, March 21, 1945, Major General Roy S. Geiger Papers, Box 6, Folder 106, Alfred M. Gray Research Center, Quantico, VA; Ernie Pyle, *The Last Chapter* (New York: Holt, 1946), 107. In addition to the operational orders, the Marines wrote and distributed Corps General Order Number 33, Executive Officer's Memorandum No. 94-45, and a memorandum from Geiger entitled "Additional Instructions Relating to Military Government." Meant for distribution twice, Corps General Order Number 33 gave specific instructions to the Marines concerning the civilian population. Ultimately, these documents promoted the policy of suspicion toward the civilians and encouraged the idea that the Okinawans posed a threat. The

Marines never received the Tenth Army Pamphlet, which was written specifically for soldiers and contained information about the Okinawans. Lacking detailed guidance for the conduct of military government from the Army, they wrote their own guidelines, knowing that the Tenth Army could change their plans. Created without a model from the Tenth Army to use as a guide, these documents further demarcated a point of deviance between Army orders and conduct and that of the Marines. Receiving the orders immediately before disembarking on hostile territory, the Marines had little time to analyze the reasoning behind the orders, if they had wanted to at all. Comments on Military Government Operation, OKINAWA, 1st Marine Division, 1 April to 26 June, 1945, July 6, 1945, RG 389, Box 704, NARA, 1; Corps General Order Number 33: Instructions to Troops concerning Military Government, III Amphibious Corps, February 27, 1945, RG 389, Box 704, NARA.

6. Roger Willock, *Unaccustomed to Fear: A Biography of the Late General Roy S. Geiger* (Quantico, VA: Marine Corps Association, 1983), 284.

7. Willock, *Unaccustomed to Fear*, 289; Memorandum by BG M. H. Silverthorn, March 10, 1945, Major General Roy S. Geiger Papers, Box 6, Folder 106, Alfred M. Gray Marine Corps Research Center, Quantico, VA. The term "L-Day" means the same as "D-Day": the designated start day for a combat attack. Following the pivotal Normandy landings on June 6, 1944, planners chose to preserve the term "D-Day" in honor of that assault. Another example: The beginning of the Battle of Leyte—October 20, 1944—was called "A-Day."

8. Annex "Able," January 16, 1945; Memorandum, March 10, 1945, BG Silverthorn.

9. Memorandum, March 10, 1945, BG Silverthorn.

10. Comments on Military Government Operation, July 6, 1945, 1st Marine Division, 2; Operational Report on Military Government, OKINAWA, Phase I and II, May 1, 1945; US Marine Corps Civil Affairs Officers, Memorandum, April 13, 1944, RG 127, Box 13, NARA, 3; Major Garnelle G. Wheeler, Activities of the Marine Corps in Civil Affairs in World War II, critical study of, March 1946, Montgomery Papers.

11. Major Hector Charles Prud'homme Jr., Record (Personnel Files), January 1946, 000019042, NPRC, 3.

12. Temporary duty, case of Lieutenant Colonel Donald T. Winder, July 13, 1945, Floor 3, Module 5, Row 44, NPRC; Legal Qualifications, First Endorsement on LtCol. Donald T. Winder, December 11, 1950, Floor 3, Module 5, Row 44; Performance of Temporary Duty, report on, case of Captain Wynne L. Van Schiak, July 2, 1945, 000014812; Operational Report on Military Government, OKINAWA, Phase I and II, May 1, 1945.

13. US Marine Corps Civil Affairs Officers, Memorandum, April 13, 1944; Annex "Able," January 16, 1945, 4; 6th Marine Division Special Action Report, Section 11-Military Government, 50.

14. Nicolas Evan Sarantakes, ed., *Seven Stars: The Okinawa Battle Diaries of Simon Bolivar Buckner Jr. and Joseph Stilwell* (College Station: Texas A&M University Press, 2004), 17, 19, 57, 75.

15. BG Oliver P. Smith, "The Tenth Army and Okinawa," Brigadier General Oliver P. Smith Papers, Box 22, Folder 8, United States Marine Corps Historical Division, Quantico, VA, 46.

16. LTG Simon B. Buckner Jr. to CG, United States Army Forces, Pacific Ocean Areas, "Newsmap of Okinawa," April 24, 1945, Major General Roy S. Geiger Papers, Box 5, Alfred M. Gray Marine Corps Research Center, Quantico, VA.

17. Sarantakes, ed., *Seven Stars*, 20; Pyle, *The Last Chapter*, 138–39.

18. LTG Simon B. Buckner Jr. to MG Roy S. Geiger, "Discipline," February 12, 1945, Major General Roy S. Geiger Papers, Box 6, Folder 105, Alfred M. Gray Marine Corps Research Center, Quantico, VA.

19. MG Roy S. Geiger to LTG A. A. Vandergrift, letter, February 2, 1945, Major General Roy S. Geiger Papers, Box 6, Folder 105, Alfred M. Gray Marine Corps Research Center, Quantico, VA; MG Roy S. Geiger to Admiral R. H. Jackson, letter, May 20, 1945, Major General Roy S. Geiger Papers, Box 6, Folder 108, Alfred M. Gray Marine Corps Research Center, Quantico, VA.

20. Captain Wynne L. Van Schiak, School of Military Government Graduation certificate, May 6, 1943, Major Wynne L. Van Schiak, Record (Personnel Files), 000014812, NPRC; "Military Government School: Its Alumni Face a Big Test in the Marshalls," *Bureau of Naval Personnel Training Bulletin* 14916 (March 1944): 2, 7–8; Naval School of Military Government and Administration, *The Luluai* (New York: Naval School of Military Government and Administration); Spot Promotion, November 11, 1944, Captain Wynne L. Van Schiak; Operation Report on Military Government, OKINAWA, Southern Phase, July 1, 1945, 3; Prud'homme Jr., Record (Personnel Files), January 1946, 1, 3.

21. Annex "Able," January 16, 1945, 10–11; Joint Army-Navy Manual of Military Government and Civil Affairs, War Department Field Manual 27-5, November 4, 1943, RG 389, Box 879, NARA.

22. Annex "Able," January 16, 1945, 6; Annex Fox, February 10, 1945, 1st Marine Division, 3; Appendix No. 1 to Annex Fox to Administrative Plan 1-45, 1st Marine Division, February 10, 1945, RG 389, Box 704, NARA.

23. Annex "Able," January 16, 1945, 1, 5–9; Military Government Plan, February 8, 1945, 6th Marine Division, 2, 4, 6; War Department Field Manual 27-5, November 4, 1943, 4, 9–10. III Amphibious Corps was expected to conduct military government operations to the same extent as XXIV Corps despite having less equipment and fewer people. Sarantakes, ed., *Seven Stars*, 8; Comments on Military Government Operation, July 6, 1945, 6th Marine Division; Operation Report on Military Government, OKINAWA, Southern Phase, July 1, 1945, 2.

24. Annex Fox, February 10, 1945, 1st Marine Division, 1; Annex "Able," January 16, 1945, 1, 5–8, 9; Military Government Plan, February 8, 1945, 6th

Marine Division, 1–2, 4, 6; War Department Field Manual 27-5, November 4, 1943, 4, 7, 10.

25. Annex "Able," January 16, 1945, 11–12; Military Government Plan, February 8, 1945, 6th Marine Division, 6–7; Annex "C" to accompany Division Administrative Order #50, 2nd Marine Division, February 15, 1945, Box 6, Folder 5/6, United States Marine Corps Archives and Special Collections, Alfred M. Gray Research Center, Quantico, VA; Annex Fox, February 10, 1945, 1st Marine Division; Appendix No. 1 to Annex Fox, February 10, 1945, 1st Marine Division, 1–2; Annex 15 to Tentative Operations Plan No. 1-45, Headquarters, Tenth Army, January 6, 1945, RG 407, Box 2487, NARA 5.

26. US Marine Corps Civil Affairs Officers, Memorandum, April 13, 1944, 3.

27. D-2 Study of Theater of Operations Okinawa Jima, Part I, February 8, 1945, 6th Marine Division, 2–3, 5; Okinawa Diary, April 30, 1945, LTC John Stevens and MSG James M. Burns; CINCPAC-CINCPOA Bulletin #161-44, November 15, 1944, 13; Report of Psychological Warfare Activities Okinawa Operation, September 15, 1945, 20.

28. Nansei Shoto, Japanese Naval Underground Museum, Document Exhibit Room, Okinawa, Japan; Yenob-PW-188, POW interrogation, May 16, 1945, RG 389, Box 844, NARA; Masamichi S. Inoue, *Okinawa and the U.S. Military: Identity Making in the Age of Globalization* (New York: Columbia University Press, 2007), 55–62; *The Ryukyu Handbook*, Department of the Army, Civil Affairs Handbook, 1944, RG 290, Box 3199, NARA, VIII; D-2 Study of Theater of Operations Okinawa Jima, Part I, February 8, 1945, 6th Marine Division, 3; CINCPAC-CINCPOA Bulletin #161-44, November 15, 1944, 12.

29. LTG John C. McQueen, USMC, Oral History Transcript, 1973, Headquarters, United States Marine Corps Historical Division, Quantico, VA, 94; COL John C. McQueen, Special Order 124-45, 6th Marine Division, May 19, 1945, Box 704, RG 389, NARA; History of Military Government Operations on Okinawa, 1 April–30 April 1945 [L Day to L+29] by BG William E. Crist, May 10, 1945, RG 407, Box 2487, file 110-5.0, NARA, 17; Okinawa Diary, March 21, 1945, LTC John Stevens and MSG James M. Burns.

30. Tenth Army Pamphlet—Information on Military Government, February 13, 1945, RG 389, Box 704, NARA, 7.

31. 7th Division, speech transcript, Inclosure 2, Civil Affairs, RG 407, File 224-12, NARA; XXIV Corps Military Government Daily Operations Log, RG 407, File 224-12, NARA.

32. Propaganda for Use against the Japanese, December 29, 1944, 2nd Marine Division, December 29, 1944, 1, 3; Military Government Plan, February 8, 1945, 6th Marine Division, 3, 6; Comments on Military Government, July 6, 1945, 1st Marine Division, 5, 14; Procedure for Handling Enemy Nationals, May 2, 1945, 1st Marine Division, Detachment B-10; Annex "Able," January 16, 1945, 5–6, 8–9; Appendix No. 3 to Annex "Able," January 16, 1945, 1.

33. Marine report, "Okinawa," Subject File: O, United States Marine Corps Historical Division, Quantico, VA, 1; D-2 Study of Theater of Operations Okinawa Jima, Part I, February 8, 1945, 6th Marine Division, 6–7; Robert B. Sheeks, Lieutenant, USMCR, "Civilians on Saipan," *Far Eastern Survey*, May 9, 1945, 109.

34. Ronald H. Spector, *Eagle against the Sun: The American War with Japan* (New York: Free Press, 1985), 101, 106; Williamson Murray and Allan R. Millett, *A War to Be Won: Fighting the Second World War* (Cambridge, MA: Harvard University Press, 2000), 484–503.

35. Sheeks, "Civilians on Saipan," 109–11; Bruce M. Petty, *Saipan: Oral Histories of the Pacific War* (Jefferson, NC: McFarland, 2002), 140.

36. Marine report, "Okinawa," Subject File: O, United States Marine Corps Historical Division, Quantico, VA, 1; D-2 Study of Theater of Operations Okinawa Jima, Part I, February 8, 1945, 6th Marine Division, 6–7; Sheeks, "Civilians on Saipan," 109.

37. Major General Lemuel Shepherd Jr., 6th Marine Division, Commander's Estimate of the Situation, Subject File: O, Box 7, Folder 1/7, United States Marine Corps Historical Division, Quantico, VA, 15; Marine report, "Okinawa," 1; D-2 Study of Theater of Operations Okinawa Jima, Part I, February 8, 1945, 6th Marine Division, 7; D-2 Estimate of Enemy Situation—Okinawa Jima, Annex Able—Intelligence to Operation Plan No. 1-45, 6th Marine Division, February 7, 1945, Subject File: O, Box 7, Folder 1/7, United States Marine Corps Historical Division, Quantico, VA, 7.

38. D-2 Study of Theater of Operations Okinawa Jima, Part I, February 8, 1945, 6th Marine Division, 5,7; United States Military Government, Detachment B-5, Diary, April 30, 1945, Western Manuscript Collection, CO445, Folders 1–4, University of Missouri, Columbia, MO, 41.

39. War Department Field Manual 27-5, November 4, 1943, 12.

40. Annex "Able," January 16, 1945, 5; Military Government Plan, February 8, 1945, 6th Marine Division, 2–3; Proclamations, February 13, 1945, 1st Marine Division; Commander's Estimate of the Situation, Major General Lemuel Shepherd Jr., 6th Marine Division, 15.

41. Annex "Able," January 16, 1945, 5–6, 10; Annex Fox, February 10, 1945, 1st Marine Division, 3; Military Government Plan, February 8, 1945, 6th Marine Division, 7; Corps General Order Number 33, February 27, 1945, III Amphibious Corps; Annex "C," February 15, 1945, 2nd Marine Division.

42. Buckner to Geiger, "Discipline," February 12, 1945, Geiger Papers.

3. "Japanese" Warriors? Okinawan Preparation for Battle

1. "Asia for the Japanese," *Fortune*, April 1944; Peter Duus, *The Abacus and the Sword: Japanese Penetration of Korea, 1895–1910* (Berkeley: University of California Press, 1995), 313; CINCPAC-CINCPOA Bulletin #161-44, November 15, 1944, RG 407, Box 2502, NARA, 5, 10–12; Masamichi S. Inoue, *Okinawa and the U.S. Military: Identity Making in the Age of Globalization* (New York: Columbia

University Press, 2007), 55–62; Yenob-PW-188, POW interrogation, May 16, 1945, RG 389, Box 844, NARA; Marine report, "Government," Subject File: O, United States Marine Corps Historical Division, Quantico, VA, 1–3; George H. Kerr, *Okinawa: The History of an Island People* (Tokyo: Tuttle, 2000), 467.

2. Tomiko Higa, a young child during the Battle of Okinawa, recalls a peaceful life on Okinawa before the battle. "I led a happy outdoor life at our farm and was as brown as a berry," she recalled. Tomiko Higa, *The Girl with the White Flag: A Spellbinding Account of Love and Courage in Wartime Okinawa* (Tokyo: Kodansha International, 1989), 16.

3. Higa, *The Girl with the White Flag*, 16–17; *An Oral History of the Battle of Okinawa, Survivor's Testimonies* (Okinawa: Relief Section, Welfare Department, Okinawa Prefectural Government, 1985), 4; Kerr, *Okinawa*, 463.

4. Higa, *The Girl with the White Flag*, 36–38, 42; *An Oral History of the Battle of Okinawa*, 4–5; Kerr, *Okinawa*, 466; "Fumiko Nakamura," in Ruth Ann Keyso, *Women of Okinawa: Nine Voices from a Garrison Island* (Ithaca, NY: Cornell University Press, 2000), 37; Masahide Ota, *The Battle of Okinawa: The Typhoon of Steel and Bombs* (Tokyo: Kume, 1984), 196–97; Roy E. Appleman, James M. Burns, Russell A. Gugeler, and John Stevens, *Okinawa: The Last Battle* (Washington, DC: Historical Division, Department of the Army, 1948); Inoue, *Okinawa and the U.S. Military*, 59; Colonel Hiromachi Yahara, *The Battle of Okinawa: A Japanese Officer's Account of the Last Great Campaign* (New York: John Wiley and Sons, 1995), 8; Benis M. Frank, *Okinawa: Touchstone to Victory* (New York: Ballantine, 1970), 19; Miyagi Kikuko, "Student Nurses of the 'Lily Corps,'" in Haruko Taya Cook and Theodore F. Cook, *Japan at War: An Oral History* (New York: The New Press, 1992), 354–63; POW Interrogation Report Number 52, Nishiyama Sakae, June 25, 1945, Box 7, Folder 11, United States Marine Corps Historical Division, Quantico, VA, 1; Rodo, ed., *Nihon fujin mondai shiryo shusei* (Domesu Shuppan, 1977), 3:478–80. The number of large families diminished after the war as a result of the high civilian casualties during the battle. Japanese Imperial Army Statistics, Japanese Naval Underground Museum, Document Exhibit Room.

5. Ota, *The Battle of Okinawa*, 196; Yahara, *The Battle of Okinawa*, 8, 59–60.

6. Japanese military instructions, translated, June 21, 1945, Fred C. Wallace papers, Box 1, Folder 8, US Army Heritage and Education Center, Carlisle, PA; Higa, *The Girl with the White Flag*, 16–17.

7. Japanese military instructions, translated, June 21, 1945, 1–4; Kerr, *Okinawa*, 466–67.

8. Japanese military instructions, translated, June 21, 1945, 1.

9. *An Oral History of the Battle of Okinawa*, 4; Kerr, *Okinawa*, 466; Kikuko, "Student Nurses of the 'Lily Corps,'" 354; United States Military Government, Detachment B-5, Diary, April 30, 1945, Western Manuscript Collection, CO445, Folders 1–4, University of Missouri, Columbia, MO, 30.

10. Nakamura, "Fumiko Nakamura," 39; Kikuko, "Student Nurses of the 'Lily

Corps,'" 355, 371; Masahide Ota, "Straggler," in Cook and Cook, *Japan at War*, 371; Higa, *The Girl with the White Flag*, 36–40, 42.

11. Higa, *The Girl with the White Flag*, 17, 96; Chiyomi Sumida and David Allen, "Prayer for the Past: Thousands Recall Battle of Okinawa," *Stars and Stripes*, June 25, 2007.

12. "Fumiko Nakamura," 37.

13. *An Oral History of the Battle of Okinawa*, 5.

14. Ota, *The Battle of Okinawa*, 197.

15. Ota, *The Battle of Okinawa*, 197; William B. Hauser, "Women and War: The Japanese Film Image," in *Recreating Japanese Women, 1600–1945*, ed. Gail Lee Berstein (Berkeley: University of California Press, 1991), 302–3.

16. Okinawan children did not aspire to die by suicide. The pre-battle propaganda inspired a glorified death by the hands of the enemy as the expression of ultimate devotion to the emperor. Kikuko, "Student Nurses of the 'Lily Corps,'" 355; *An Oral History of the Battle of Okinawa*, 4; Ota, *The Battle of Okinawa*, 197; Japanese military instructions, translated, June 21, 1945, 1–4.

17. Higa, *The Girl with the White Flag*, 37–38, 40.

18. Higa, *The Girl with the White Flag*, 37–38, 40; Kikuko, "Student Nurses of the 'Lily Corps,'" 354–63.

19. The *sanshin* is a three stringed instrument that originated in Okinawa. The practice of Ryukyuan rituals became sources of comfort following the war. Higa, *The Girl with the White Flag*, 19, 23, 26; Christopher Nelson, *Dancing with the Dead: Memory, Performance, and Everyday Life in Postwar Okinawa* (Durham, NC: Duke University Press, 2008), 39–40; Norma Field, *In the Realm of a Dying Emperor: Japan at Century's End* (New York: Vintage, 1992), 65; Haru Maeda, in *An Oral History of the Battle of Okinawa, Survivor's Testimonies* (Okinawa: Relief Section, Welfare Department, Okinawa Prefectural Government, 1985), 29.

20. Marine report, "Government," 3.

21. Higa, *The Girl with the White Flag*, 56.

22. Higa, *The Girl with the White Flag*, 18.

23. Higa, *The Girl with the White Flag*, 18, 36–37, 42.

24. Field, *In the Realm of a Dying Emperor*, 101; Kikuko, "Student Nurses of the 'Lily Corps,'" 355; Kinjo Shigeaki, "Now They Call It 'Group Suicide,'" in Cook and Cook, *Japan at War*, 364.

4. The US Fights Overseas: Americans Charge toward the Battlefield

1. Diary, December 29, 1944–January 3, 1945, Detachment B-5, 3, Western Manuscript Collection, CO445, Folders 1–4, University of Missouri, Columbia, MO.

2. Approved on February 25, 1945, the Technical Bulletin duplicated the contents of the GOPER with slight elaboration and presented the information in the format of an Army manual.

3. Diary, December 29, 1944–January 12, 1945, Detachment B-5, 2, 4, 5.

4. Tenth Army Pamphlet—Information on Military Government, February 13, 1945, 4–5, 8.

5. Tenth Army Pamphlet—Information on Military Government, February 13, 1945, 5.

6. Tenth Army Pamphlet—Information on Military Government, February 13, 1945, 9.

7. One such example: The label under a diagram of a proposed camp restroom facility in the Technical Bulletin said "Jap squatter." Technical Bulletin, Military Government, February 25, 1945, RG 407, File 224-12, NARA.

8. Robert L. Hostetler, interview by author, Okinawa, Japan, December 27, 2007. Hostetler was a corporal in 1945 assigned to the Statistical Section Task Force.

9. See also George Feifer, *The Battle of Okinawa: The Blood and the Bomb* (Guilford, CT: Lyons, 1992, 2001), 126. In the CINCPAC-CINCPOA Bulletin #161-44, the ethnicity of the Okinawans is described as "a branch of the hairy Ainu and Kumaso peoples who inhabited Kyushu and other islands of Japan." This is most likely where the soldier derived the term "Hairy Anus." CINCPAC-CINCPOA Bulletin #161-44, November 15, 1944, 10.

10. Hostetler, interview; Feifer, *The Battle of Okinawa*, 127.

11. 7th Division, speech transcript, Inclosure 2, Civil Affairs, RG 407, File 224-12, NARA; XXIV Corps Military Government Daily Operations Log, RG 407, File 224-12, NARA.

12. Diary, January 13, 1945, Detachment B-5, 6.

13. Diary, January 13, 1945, Detachment B-5, 8.

14. Diary, January 13, 1945, Detachment B-5, 8.

15. Diary, January 13, 1945, Detachment B-5, 7–8.

16. Diary, January 13, 1945, Detachment B-5, 13, 17. The detachment commanders' expansion of the GOPER was consistent with the flexible nature of the plan and Buckner's desire that his subordinate commanders exercise their own initiative.

17. Diary, January 13, 1945, Detachment B-5, 17.

18. Diary, January 13, 1945, Detachment B-5, 15, emphasis added.

19. Diary, January 13, 1945, Detachment B-5, 18.

20. Ken Hatfield, *Heartland Heroes: Remembering World War II* (Columbia: University of Missouri, 2003), 242; Ernie Pyle, *The Last Chapter* (New York: Holt, 1946), 95–96; Roger Willock, *Unaccustomed to Fear: A Biography of the Late General Roy S. Geiger* (Quantico, VA: Marine Corps Association, 1983), 290; CINCPOA COMMUNIQUE NO. 317, Navy Daily Reports, April 1, 1945, Subject File: O, United States Marine Corps Historical Division.

21. 6th Marine Division Special Action Report, Section 11—Military Government, 50; Operational Report on Military Government, OKINAWA, Phase I and II, May 1, 1945, 1; Daniel D. Karasik, "Okinawa: A Problem in Administration

and Reconstruction," *Far Eastern Quarterly* 7, no. 3 (1948): 254–67; Roger V. Dingman, "Language at War: U.S. Marine Corps Japanese Language Officers in the Pacific War," *Journal of Military History* 68, no. 3 (July 2004): 876; Comments on Military Government, July 6, 1945, 1st Marine Division, 5, 7; Tsubota Collection, Veterans History Project. Immediately upon landing in Okinawa, Tsubota linked up with his unit and received his orders. He never received the training and briefings that soldiers received on board.

22. Major Hector Charles Prud'homme Jr., Record (Personnel Files), January 1946, 000019042, NPRC, 1; "Military Government School: Its Alumni Face a Big Test in the Marshalls," *Bureau of Naval Personnel Training Bulletin*, March 15, 1944, WWII Collection, 1933–1956, Box 48, Folder 4, Rare Book and Manuscript Library, Columbia University, New York, 1–9; Major Garnelle G. Wheeler, Activities of the Marine Corps in Civil Affairs in World War II, critical study of, March 1946, Montgomery Papers, 2. One of Prud'homme's hobbies was pistol shooting.

23. Memorandum, March 10, 1945, BG Silverthorn; Pyle, *The Last Chapter*, 96.

24. Comments on Military Government, July 6, 1945, 1st Marine Division, 5–7, Proclamations, February 13, 1945, 1st Marine Division.

25. Comments on Military Government, July 6, 1945, 1st Marine Division, 1.

26. Corps General Order Number 33, February 27, 1945, III Amphibious Corps, 1–2.

27. "United Nations" refers to the twenty-six Allied countries that signed the Atlantic Charter on January 1, 1942, to show their support for the war. The term was first used by President Franklin D. Roosevelt. The official UN charter was signed on June 26, 1945.

28. Pyle, *The Last Chapter*, 107; Executive Officer's Memorandum No. 94-45, March 21, 1945, Major General Roy S. Geiger Papers.

29. Hatfield, *Heartland Heroes*, 245.

30. Hatfield, *Heartland Heroes*, 245; Pyle, *The Last Chapter*, 96.

31. Hatfield, *Heartland Heroes*, 255.

32. Pyle, *The Last Chapter*, 98–99; Johnston, *The Long Road of War*, 124.

33. Captain's Message to All Hands, USS *Panamint*, March 31, 1945, Major General Roy S. Geiger Papers.

5. Having a Say: Okinawan Constructions of Identity

1. Haru Maeda, in *An Oral History of the Battle of Okinawa, Survivor's Testimonies* (Okinawa: Relief Section, Welfare Department, Okinawa Prefectural Government, 1985), 29.

2. *An Oral History of the Battle of Okinawa*, 28; Thomas M. Huber, *Japan's Battle of Okinawa, April–June 1945* (Honolulu: University Press of the Pacific, 2005), 112–18.

3. Miyagi Kikuko, "Student Nurses of the 'Lily Corps,'" in Haruko Taya Cook and Theodore F. Cook, *Japan at War: An Oral History* (New York: The New Press,

1992), 355; Kinjo Shigeaki, "Now They Call It 'Group Suicide,'" in Cook and Cook, *Japan at War*, 364.

4. Yokoyama Ryuichi, "Cartoons for the War," in Cook and Cook, *Japan at War*, 96; Nogi Harumichi, "I Wanted to Build Greater East Asia," in Cook and Cook, *Japan at War*, 55.

5. Kikuko, "Student Nurses of the 'Lily Corps,'" 355.

6. Diary, April 3–8, 1945, Detachment B-5, 27; Tomiko Higa, *The Girl with the White Flag: A Spellbinding Account of Love and Courage in Wartime Okinawa* (Tokyo: Kodansha International, 1989), 41–46; Japanese Imperial Army Statistics, Japanese Naval Underground Museum, Document Exhibit Room; Kikuko, "Student Nurses of the 'Lily Corps,'" 358; E. B. Sledge, *With the Old Breed at Peleliu and Okinawa* (Annapolis, MD: Naval Institute Press, 1996), 192; Bill Sloan, *The Ultimate Battle: Okinawa 1945—The Last Epic Struggle of World War II* (New York: Simon and Schuster, 2007), photos 25–27; Hamamatsu Shigeru, letter, *Ryukyu Shimpo*, in Mark Ealey and Alastair McLauchlan, trans., *Descent into Hell: Civilian Memories of the Battle of Okinawa* (Portland: Merwin Asia, 2014), 296; Kyoko Uehara, in *An Oral History of the Battle of Okinawa*, 18.

7. Diary, April 3–8, 1945, Detachment B-5, 23; LTC John Stevens and MSG James M. Burns, Okinawa Diary, April 30, 1945, RG 407, Box 2441, NARA; XXIV Corps After Action Review #125, RG 407, File 224-12, NARA; 27th Infantry Division letter to Commanding General, RG 389 Box 704, NARA; History of Military Government Operations on Okinawa, 1 April–30 April 1945 [L Day to L+29] by BG William E. Crist, May 10, 1945, RG 407, Box 2487, File 110-5.0, NARA, 17; XXIV Corps Military Government Daily Operations Log, RG 407, File 224-12, NARA; Masamichi S. Inoue, *Okinawa and the U.S. Military: Identity Making in the Age of Globalization* (New York: Columbia University Press, 2007), 59; Benis M. Frank, *Okinawa: Touchstone to Victory* (New York: Ballantine, 1970), 19; *An Oral History of the Battle of Okinawa*, 4; POW Interrogation Report Number 52, June 25, 1945, Nishiyama Sakae, 1; Major General Lemuel C. Shepard, 6th Marine Division, Military account, June 8, 1945, Subject File: O, Box 7, Folder 10/7, United States Marine Corps Historical Division, Quantico, VA, 4.

8. As quoted in Colonel Hiromachi Yahara, *The Battle of Okinawa: A Japanese Officer's Account of the Last Great Campaign* (New York: John Wiley and Sons, 1995); Masahide Ota, *The Battle of Okinawa: The Typhoon of Steel and Bombs* (Tokyo: Kume, 1984), 196.

9. Teruya Masako, newspaper interview, *Ryukyu Shimpo*, in Ealey and McLauchlan, *Descent into Hell*, 295.

10. Higa, *The Girl with the White Flag*, 42.

11. Norma Field, *In the Realm of a Dying Emperor: Japan at Century's End* (New York: Vintage, 1992), 101.

12. Yahara, *The Battle of Okinawa*, 211; Huber, *Japan's Battle of Okinawa*, 27–29.

13. *An Oral History of the Battle of Okinawa*, 4; Inoue, *Okinawa and the U.S.*

Military, 59; Frank, *Okinawa*, 19; XXIV Corps After Action Review #122, RG 407, File 224-12, NARA; Higa, *The Girl with the White Flag*, 94, 96, 110; Masahide Ota, "Straggler," in Cook and Cook, *Japan at War*, 371; Testimony 10, Oral History Collection manuscript room, Prefectural Peace Memorial Museum, English Book 1; Testimony 16, Oral History Collection manuscript room, Prefectural Peace Memorial Museum, English Book 1.

14. POW Interrogation Report Number 52, June 25, 1945, Nishiyama Sakae, 1; Tokimasa Yokota, in *An Oral History of the Battle of Okinawa*, 25.

15. Yukoh Tamaki, in *An Oral History of the Battle of Okinawa*, 21; Ota, "Straggler," 371.

16. Tamaki, Oral History Collection, 21; Higa, *The Girl with the White Flag*, 74.

17. Yokota, Oral History Collection, 25; Shigeaki, "Now They Call It 'Group Suicide,'" 364.

18. Japanese military instructions, translated, June 21, 1945, 1–4; Shigeaki, "Now They Call It 'Group Suicide,'" 364.

19. Cook and Cook, *Japan at War*, 363.

20. Kikuko, "Student Nurses of the 'Lily Corps,'" 354–55, 358; Setsuko Inafuku, speech, July 16, 2007; *Okinawan Documentary 6 14 0470*, Masayuki Hayashi, dir., June 14, 2003, Naha City Historical Association Archives, Naha City.

21. Kikuko, "Student Nurses of the 'Lily Corps,'" 355.

22. The training the student nurses received was rudimentary. They were taught to wrap bandages and give medicine and water. Kikuko, "Student Nurses of the 'Lily Corps,'" 355, 359.

23. Higa, *The Girl with the White Flag*, 49, 52, 60, 73–74, 92, 94; Oto Nagamine, in *An Oral History of the Battle of Okinawa*, 32; Jim Lea, "Okinawa Remembers When War Passed Its Way," *Stars and Stripes*, June 26, 1985, 14. Before combat operations, interactions between Japanese troops and Okinawans were relatively peaceful. Okinawans fulfilled their civil defense roles, and Japanese troops accepted their services with few incidents of abuse.

24. Mitsutoshi Nakajo, in *An Oral History of the Battle of Okinawa*, 27; Higa, *The Girl with the White Flag*, 42; Nagamine, Oral History Collection, 32; Kiyo Matayoshi, in *An Oral History of the Battle of Okinawa*, 19; Field, *In the Realm of a Dying Emperor*, 64.

25. Diary, May 1–31, 1945, Detachment B-5, 48; Shitsuko Oshiro, in *An Oral History of the Battle of Okinawa*, 12–13; Koei Kinjo, in *An Oral History of the Battle of Okinawa*, 15; Higa, *The Girl with the White Flag*, 73, 92; Nakajo, oral history, 27.

26. Higa, *The Girl with the White Flag*, 92–93.

27. Masako "Iha" Sunabe, interview by Lisa Tourtelot, Chatan, Okinawa, *Stars and Stripes*, February 11, 2014; Shitsuko Oshiro, Oral History Collection, 12–13; Nakajo, Oral History Collection, 27; Toyo Gima, in *An Oral History of the Battle of Okinawa*, 23; Nagamine, Oral History Collection, 32; Testimony 10, Oral History Collection manuscript room; Testimony 16, Oral History Collection manuscript room; Shigeaki, "Now They Call It 'Group Suicide,'" 366; Ota, "Straggler," 367;

Maeda, Oral History Collection, 25; Field, *In the Realm of a Dying Emperor*, 64;
Lea, "Okinawa Remembers When War Passed Its Way," 14.

28. John David Jackson Collection (AFC/2001/001/38452), Veterans History
Project, American Folklife Center, Library of Congress, 2; Japanese military
instructions, translated, June 21, 1945, 1–2; Shigeaki, "Now They Call It 'Group
Suicide,'" 364–366; Higa, *The Girl with the White Flag*, 73–74; Gima, Oral
History Collection, 23; Uehara Jintaro, interview, *Ryukyu Shimpo*, in Ealey and
McLauchlan, *Descent into Hell*, 423–25.

29. The Japanese used the same formula of indoctrination they had used for
years on the Okinawans as reasoning to support the call for suicide. The call for
suicide, however, appeared after the battle began. *An Oral History of the Battle of
Okinawa*, 4, 48; Site Map, Maya Cave, Oral History Collection manuscript room,
Prefectural Peace Memorial Museum; Nagamine, Oral History Collection, 32;
Edward Drea, *In Service of the Emperor: Essays on the Imperial Japanese Army*
(Lincoln: University of Nebraska, 2003), 57–58; Japanese military instructions,
translated, June 21, 1945, 1–4; Ota, "Straggler," 367–72; Shigeaki, "Now They Call
It "Group Suicide," 364.

30. Higa, *The Girl with the White Flag*, 94; Kikuko, "Student Nurses of the 'Lily
Corps,'" 357, 359, 361; *Okinawan Documentary 6 14 0470*.

31. Nakajo, Oral History Collection, 27; Higa, *The Girl with the White Flag*,
73–74.

32. This is consistent with the trauma theory of Dori Laub, a psychoanalyst
and trauma researcher. The dissonance the children experienced between what
they now witnessed and what they had known previously of the soldiers caused
them to doubt the traumatic violence they encountered; they struggled to process
and fully comprehend the violence. With confidence in their interpretations
shaken, the children noted the self-assured conviction of the Japanese soldiers
and assessed that the soldiers' assessment of the event must be more accurate.
In addition to the comfort and stability of the indoctrinated values, the children
adopted the reasoning of the soldiers for why the violence occurred. Higa, *The
Girl with the White Flag*, 92–94. Laub's theories are discussed in Cathy Caruth,
*Listening to Trauma: Conversations with Leaders in the Theory and Treatment of
Catastrophic Experiences* (Baltimore, MD: John Hopkins University Press, 2014),
52–53.

33. The Okinawans practiced gratitude when they ate in the same tradition
as the Japanese; Okinawans would say "Itadakimasu," which meant "I gratefully
partake." Higa, *The Girl with the White Flag*, 55–56, 60, 73, 94; Kikuko, "Student
Nurses of the 'Lily Corps,'" 361; Shigeaki, "Now They Call It 'Group Suicide,'"
363, 365.

34. Kikuko, "Student Nurses of the 'Lily Corps,'" 359; Shigeaki, "Now They
Call It 'Group Suicide,'" 364.

35. Higa, *The Girl with the White Flag*, 40. In rare instances, some Japanese
soldiers responded to the amicable manners of the devoted young Okinawans

with benevolence; they ignored groups of civilians, allowed privacy during mourning rituals, or hesitated when ordered to kill the people. Higa, *The Girl with the White Flag*, 52; Maeda, Oral History Collection, 29. Such infrequent instances of compassion served as further justification for Okinawans to retain their Japanese identity through the beginning of the battle.

36. The Japanese considered themselves pure and the Americans as demonic. Junko Isa, "Junko Isa," in Ruth Ann Keyso, *Women of Okinawa: Nine Voices from a Garrison Island* (Ithaca, NY: Cornell University Press, 2000), 6; "Fumiko Nakamura," in Ruth Ann Keyso, *Women of Okinawa: Nine Voices from a Garrison Island* (Ithaca, NY: Cornell University Press, 2000), 37; Ota, *The Battle of Okinawa*, 223; History of Military Government Operations on Okinawa, May 10, 1945, BG William E. Crist, 19; Captain Roy E. Appleman, notes, RG 407, File 224-12, NARA, 2; Okinawa Diary, April 30, 1945, LTC John Stevens and MSG James M. Burns; Nakajo, Oral History Collection, 27; John W. Dower, *War without Mercy: Race and Power in the Pacific War* (New York: Pantheon, 1986), 191, 196, 250; Nagamine, Oral History Collection, 32; Higa, *The Girl with the White Flag*, 110; Kikuko, "Student Nurses of the 'Lily Corps,'" 361; Shigeaki, "Now They Call It 'Group Suicide,'" 365; Takejiro Nakamura, interview in James Brooke, "Okinawa Suicides and Japan's Army: Burying the Truth?," *New York Times*, June 21, 2005.

37. Field, *In the Realm of a Dying Emperor*, 101.

38. Shigeaki, "Now They Call It 'Group Suicide,'" 365; Memorandum for Major General Pedro del Valle, 1st Marine Division, Original Records, Subject File: O, United States Marine Corps Historical Division, Quantico, VA, 4.

39. Higa, *The Girl with the White Flag*, 73; Nakajo, Oral History Collection, 27.

40. Kikuko, "Student Nurses of the 'Lily Corps,'" 361, 363.

41. Nakajo, Oral History Collection, 27; Field, *In the Realm of a Dying Emperor*, 64.

42. Kinjo, Oral History Collection, 15; Shitsuko Oshiro, Oral History Collection; 12–13; Shigeaki, "Now They Call It 'Group Suicide,'" 365; Higa, *The Girl with the White Flag*, 73, 93.

43. Shigeaki, "Now They Call It 'Group Suicide,'" 365–66; Japanese military instructions, translated, June 21, 1945, 1–4.

44. Kikuko, "Student Nurses of the 'Lily Corps,'" 361; *Okinawan Documentary 6 14 0470*.

45. *An Oral History of the Battle of Okinawa*, 4; Shigeaki, "Now They Call It 'Group Suicide,'" 366. Higa, *The Girl with the White Flag*, 70, 73, 80.

46. Higa, *The Girl with the White Flag*, 60.

47. Nakajo, Oral History Collection, 27; Kikuko, "Student Nurses of the 'Lily Corps,'" 359.

48. Shigeaki, "Now They Call It 'Group Suicide,'" 364; Higa, *The Girl with the White Flag*, 56. The Ryukyuan teachings they received in their homes from their parents and grandparents before the war provided them with a foundation upon which to find their Okinawan identity.

49. Field, *In the Realm of a Dying Emperor*, 101; Inafuku, speech; Diary,

April 30, 1945, Detachment, 30; Testimony 5, Oral History collection manuscript room, Prefectural Peace Memorial Museum, English Book 1; Isa, "Junko Isa," 7; Testimony 3, Oral History Collection manuscript room, Prefectural Peace Memorial Museum, English Book 1.

50. The severe conditions of war tainted the Japanese opinion of Okinawan women as mothers. In contrast to the prime minister's letters before the battle urging Okinawan women to procreate as a part of their duty to the empire, the Japanese now found the dirty, lice-ridden, and starving women repulsive and saw their childrearing practices as crude, vulgar, and immodest. Japanese soldiers reported with distaste that Okinawan women breast fed publicly and squirted their older children in the face with breast milk. Military government report, James Watkins papers, Folder 5, Local Materials Reading Room, Ryukyu University Library, Okinawa, Japan; Japanese letter, translated, Active 7(7-2-C), Archives: J, Folder: Japanese, Kadena Airbase Archives, Kadena, Okinawa, Japan; Japanese diary, translated, Active 7(7-2-C), Archives: J, Folder: Japanese, Kadena Airbase Archives, Kadena, Okinawa, Japan. Isa, "Junko Isa," 7.

51. Nagamine, Oral History Collection, 32; Site Map, Maya Cave, Oral History Collection manuscript room; Testimony 16, Oral History Collection manuscript room; Shige Ginoza, in *An Oral History of the Battle of Okinawa*, 34; Diary, May 1–31, 1945, Detachment B-5, 48; Gima, Oral History Collection, 23; Higa, *The Girl with the White Flag*, 92–93; Sunabe, interview, *Stars and Stripes*.

52. Diary, May 1–31, 1945, Detachment B-5, 48.

53. Shitsuko Oshiro, Oral History Collection, 12–13; Japanese military instructions, translated, June 21, 1945, 1–2; Higa, *The Girl with the White Flag*, 55; Shigeaki, "Now They Call It 'Group Suicide,'" 364; *An Oral History of the Battle of Okinawa*, 4.

54. Nagamine, Oral History Collection, 32; Site Map, Maya Cave, Oral History Collection manuscript room; Testimony 16, Oral History Collection manuscript room; Ginoza, Oral History Collection, 34; Diary, May 1–31, 1945, Detachment B-5, 48; Gima, Oral History Collection, 23; Higa, *The Girl with the White Flag*, 92–93; Sunabe, interview, *Stars and Stripes*.

55. Marine report, "Government," Subject File: O, United States Marine Corps Historical Division, Quantico, VA, 3.

56. Study of the Ryukyu Islands, Island Command, July 20, 1945, RG 407, Entry 427, NARA, 2.

57. Eishun Higa, in *An Oral History of the Battle of Okinawa*, 17; Nagamine, Oral History Collection, 32.

6. Policy into Action: The US Army Hits the Shore

1. CPL Robert L. Hostetler, interview by author, KAB, Koza, Okinawa, Japan, December 27, 2007.

2. Figure 23: Disposition of Corps and Division Military Government Detachments, RG 407, File 224-12, NARA.

3. Diary, April 1–April 3, 1945, Detachment B-5, 19.

4. Diary, April 1–April 3, 1945, Detachment B-5, 20; Hamamatsu Shigeru, letter, *Ryukyu Shimpo*, in Mark Ealey and Alastair McLauchlan, trans., *Descent into Hell: Civilian Memories of the Battle of Okinawa* (Portland, OR: Merwin Asia, 2014), 295.

5. Report of Psychological Warfare Activities Okinawa Operation, September 15, 1945, RG 407, Box 2502, File 110-39, NARA, 10; CINCPAC-CINCPOA Bulletin #161-44, November 15, 1944, 1; Nicolas Evan Sarantakes, ed., *Seven Stars: The Okinawa Battle Diaries of Simon Bolivar Buckner Jr. and Joseph Stilwell* (College Station: Texas A&M University Press, 2004), 61, 74; LTC Luker, Army Air Corps, C-54 pilot, head of Air Transport Command out of Yomitan, speech, June 23, 1995, Active 7(7-2-C) archives K-L, "Kadena Base History," Kadena Air Base, Kadena Air Base Archives; E. B. Sledge, *With the Old Breed at Peleliu and Okinawa* (Annapolis, MD: Naval Institute Press, 1996), 248–49; Bill Sloan, *The Ultimate Battle: Okinawa 1945—The Last Epic Struggle of World War II* (New York: Simon and Schuster, 2007), photos 25–27.

6. The Okinawa Prefectural Peace Memorial Museum cites the Okinawan civilian losses at 100,000. This number, however, is controversial because it does not make clear whether it includes Okinawans who fought in military units. Therefore, an estimated range of Okinawan civilian casualties would be from 70,000 to 100,000. Kyoko Uehara, in *An Oral History of the Battle of Okinawa, Survivor's Testimonies* (Okinawa: Relief Section, Welfare Department, Okinawa Prefectural Government, 1985), 18; Report of Psychological Warfare Activities Okinawa Operation, September 15, 1945, RG 407, Box 2502, File 110-39, NARA, 10; CINCPAC-CINCPOA Bulletin #161-44, November 15, 1944, 1; Japanese Imperial Army Statistics, Japanese Naval Underground Museum, Document Exhibit Room; *An Oral History of the Battle of Okinawa*, 4; Sloan, *The Ultimate Battle*, photos 25–27; Shigeru, letter, *Ryukyu Shimpo*, in Ealey and McLauchlan, *Descent into Hell*, 296.

7. Masahide Ota, *The Battle of Okinawa: The Typhoon of Steel and Bombs* (Tokyo: Kume, 1984), x; Diary, April 30, 1945, May 31, 1945, Detachment B-5, 27, 34, 54; War Department, *Yank* [magazine], November 30, 1945.

8. XXIV Corps Military Government Daily Operations Log, RG 407, File 224-12, NARA; Diary, April 3, 1945, Detachment B-5, 22–23, 28.

9. XXIV Corps Military Government Daily Operations Log, RG 407, File 224-12, NARA; Technical Bulletin, Military Government, February 25, 1945, RG 407, File 224-12, NARA; Annex 15, Tentative Operations Plan No. 1-45, January 6, 1945, RG 407, Box 2487, File 110-5.5, NARA; Detachment Daily Report, RG 407, File 224-12, NARA; Division report to XXIV Corps, RG 407, File 224-12, NARA; Status of Civilians Report, RG 407, File 224-12, NARA; Report to Tenth Army, RG 407, File 224-12, NARA.

10. Detachment Daily Report, RG 407, File 224-12, NARA; Division report to XXIV Corps, RG 407, File 224-12, NARA; Status of Civilians Report, RG 407, File 224-12, NARA; XXIV Corps Military Government Daily Operations Log, RG

407, File 224-12, NARA; Diary, April 3,1945, Detachment B-5, 22, 48; 7th division, speech transcript, Inclosure 2, Civil Affairs, RG 407, File 224-12, NARA, 2.

11. Detachment Daily Report, RG 407, File 224-12, NARA; Status of Civilians Report, RG 407, File 224-12, NARA.

12. Sarantakes, ed., *Seven Stars*, 34; Diary, 1944–1945, Detachment B-5, 23, 27; Hostetler, interview; Sledge, *With the Old Breed*, 192; History of Military Government Operations on Okinawa, May 10, 1945, BG William E. Crist, 17–18.

13. History of Military Government Operations on Okinawa, May 10, 1945, BG William E. Crist, 17; Okinawa Diary, April 11, 1945, LTC John Stevens and MSG James M. Burns; Sledge, *With the Old Breed*, 192; Diary, April 3–April 8, 1945, Detachment B-5, 23, 27.

14. The Americans were aware that separating the Okinawans from the Japanese by visual cues such as demeanor and clothing had its flaws. Propaganda leaflets distributed to the Okinawans warned them against wearing Japanese military clothing for warmth because the Americans would classify them as enemy soldiers. The content of the leaflets demonstrated that the Americans felt apprehension toward all non-Americans and could not identify cultural differences between the two groups; their reliance on superficial means of separation, therefore, was heavy. Leaflet 531, 563, Active 7(7-2-C) archive P, Kadena Air Base, KAB Archives.

15. History of Military Government Operations on Okinawa, May 10, 1945, BG William E. Crist, 19–20.

16. 7th division, speech transcript, Inclosure 2, Civil Affairs, RG 407, File 224-12, NARA, 3.

17. *The Ryukyu Handbook*, 1994, Department of the Army, VII.

18. History of Military Government Operations on Okinawa, May 10, 1945, BG William E. Crist, 20.

19. Diary, April 1–30, 1945, Detachment B-5, 37.

20. Diary, April 1–30, 1945, Detachment B-5, 23; XXIV Corps After Action Review, RG 407, File 224-12, NARA; Captain Roy E. Appleman, notes, RG 407, File 224-12, NARA.

21. XXIV Corps After Action Review #125, RG 407, File 224-12, NARA; Ealey and McLauchlan, *Descent into Hell*, 151.

22. Captain Roy E. Appleman, notes, RG 407, File 224-12, NARA, 3.

23. Diary, April 3–8, 1945, Detachment B-5, 27.

24. Leaflet X-7, RG 407, Box 2502, NARA.

25. Hostetler, interview.

26. Tenth Army Pamphlet—Information on Military Government, February 13, 1945; Okinawa Diary, April 11, 1945, LTC John Stevens and MSG James M. Burns; CINCPAC-CINCPOA Bulletin #161-44, November 15, 1944, 10.

27. Diary, April 3–8, 1945, Detachment B-5, 27.

28. Diary, April 3–8, 1945, Detachment B-5, 31. Although it did happen, giving Okinawans US military uniforms for warmth was against official policy.

Operational Directive #7, January 6, 1945, Commanding General, Tenth Army, 7; Hostetler interview.

29. Diary, December 28, 1944–May 31,1945, Detachment B-5; 7th division, speech transcript, Inclosure 2, Civil Affairs, RG 407, File 224-12, NARA; XXIV Corps Military Government Preliminary Planning, RG 407, File 224-12, NARA; XXIV Corps Military Government Daily Operations Log, RG 407, File 224-12, NARA.

30. XXIV Corps After Action Review, RG 407, File 224-12, NARA; XXIV Corps Military Government Preliminary Planning, RG 407, File 224-12, NARA.

31. Hostetler, interview.

32. The priority of survival remained a consistent theme with all soldiers. As one noncommissioned officer expressed it, "We were just happy it was them and not us . . . hey, that's the breaks. You live, you die. You couldn't let it get to you very much." He offered a similar response to American dead as well as Japanese dead. He described a fellow American's dead body in terms of his own survival. "I remember this one dude," he said, "but as bad as this was to look at all night, our big concern was that we were being silhouetted." Gerald A. Meehl and Rex Alan Smith, *Pacific War Stories: In the Words of Those Who Survived* (New York: Abbeville, 2004), 142.

33. XXIV Corps Military Government Daily Operations Log, RG 407, File 224-12, NARA; Masamichi S. Inoue, *Okinawa and the U.S. Military: Identity Making in the Age of Globalization* (New York: Columbia University Press, 2007), 61; Benis M. Frank, *Okinawa: Touchstone to Victory* (New York: Ballantine, 1970), 19; *An Oral History of the Battle of Okinawa*, 4–5; XXIV Corps After Action Review, RG 407, File 224-12, NARA; George H. Kerr, *Okinawa: The History of an Island People* (Tokyo: Tuttle, 2000); Walter LeFeber, *The Clash: U.S.–Japanese Relations through History* (New York: Norton, 1997); Ruth Ann Keyso, *Women of Okinawa: Nine Voices from a Garrison Island* (Ithaca, NY: Cornell University Press, 2000); Testimony 5, Kama Matsumura, testimony 10, Oral History Collection manuscript room, Prefectural Peace Memorial Museum, English book 1; Testimony 16, Oral History Collection manuscript room, Prefectural Peace Memorial Museum, English book 1; Site Map, Maya Cave, Prefectural Peace Memorial Museum; Shitsuko Oshiro, Oral History Collection, Prefectural Peace Memorial Museum; Oto Nagamine, Oral History Collection, Prefectural Peace Memorial Museum; Setsuko Inafuku, speech, July 16, 2007. While isolated, the military government camps did experience infiltration from Japanese soldiers as well as acts of conspiracy by Okinawan civilians. Outside a camp in Shimabuku, one Japanese soldier wearing civilian clothes was shot on April 15, 1945; another was shot in the same area the following day. On April 18, 1945, a Japanese sniper was shot and held for questioning by military government personnel from Shimabuku. In the camps Shimabaru and Tobaru-Maebaru, civilians were caught speaking with a Japanese soldier on April 20, 1945, and held for questioning.

34. Diary, April 3–8, 1945, Detachment B-5, 23; Okinawa Diary, April 11, 1945,

LTC John Stevens and MSG James M. Burns; XXIV Corps After Action Review #125, RG 407, File 224-12, NARA; 27th Infantry Division letter to Commanding General, RG 389, Box 704, NARA; History of Military Government Operations on Okinawa, May 10, 1945, BG William E. Crist, 17.

35. XXIV Corps Military Government Daily Operations Log, RG 407, File 224-12, NARA.

36. XXIV Corps After Action Review #122, RG 407, File 224-12, NARA.

37. XXIV Corps After Action Review #122; CINCPAC-CINCPOA Bulletin #161-44, November 15, 1944, 12–13; Strategic Estimate of the Enemy Situation: Iceberg, March 4, 1945, RG 407, Box 2455, File 110-2.15, NARA.

38. One soldier explained it this way: "When we got over here it was just, get 'em! Anybody gets in your way . . ." Hostetler, interview; 1LT Jesse C. Rogers Jr., Infantry, Psychological Warfare on Okinawa, RG 407, Box 2502, File 110-39, NARA, 2–3.

39. Diary, April 1–30, 1945, Detachment B-5, 31; 7th division, speech transcript, Inclosure 2, Civil Affairs, RG 407, File 224-12, NARA, 1; Control of Civilians, XXIV Corps letter, April 24, 1945, RG 407, File 224-12, NARA, XXIV Corps After Action Review #125, RG 407, File 224-12, NARA; XXIV Corps Military Government Daily Operations Log, RG 407, File 224-12, NARA; Wiley S. Iscom, *Diary of a Wardog Platoon* (Tennessee: Bible and Literature Missionary Foundation, 1997).

40. Diary, April 1–30, 1945, Detachment B-5, 31.

41. Diary, April 1–30, 1945, Detachment B-5, 36, 51; Military Government Action Report, 1 April–30 June 1945, XXIV Corps, RG 407, Box 2153, NARA.

42. XXIV Corps Military Government Daily Operations Log, RG 407, File 224-12, NARA; Diary, 1944–1945, Detachment B-5, 31.

43. Diary, April 3–8, 1945, Detachment B-5, 23.

44. Diary, April 3–8, 1945, Detachment B-5, 33.

45. Diary, April 3–8, 1945, Detachment B-5, 23, 31; History of Military Government Operations, May 10, 1945, BG William E. Crist, 20; Leaflet X-7, RG 407, Box 2502, NARA; Ealey and McLauchlan, *Descent into Hell*, 409.

46. Diary, April 3–8, 1945, Detachment B-5, 31–32; XXIV Corps Military Government Daily Operations Log, RG 407, File 224-12, NARA.

47. Diary, April 1–30, 1945, Detachment B-5, 31.

48. Diary, April 1–30, 1945, Detachment B-5, 32.

49. Diary, April 1–30, 1945, Detachment B-5, 32; Leaflet Survey Civilians, XXIV Corps letter, April 13, 1945, RG 407, File 224-12, NARA.

50. CINCPAC-CINCPOA Bulletin #161-44, November 15, 1944, 10; History of Military Government Operations on Okinawa, May 10, 1945, BG William E. Crist; *The Ryukyu Handbook*, 1944, Department of the Army, VII.

51. CINCPAC-CINCPOA Bulletin #161-44, November 15, 1944, 10.

52. XXIV Corps Military Government Daily Operations Log, RG 407, File 224-12, NARA; Diary, April 1–30, 1945, Detachment B-5, 31.

53. Sarantakes, ed., *Seven Stars*, 41; Okinawa Diary, April 17, 1945, LTC John Stevens and MSG James M. Burns; Arnold Fisch, *Military Government in the Ryukyu Islands, 1945–1950* (Washington, DC: Center of Military History, US Army, 1988), 45.

54. XXIV Corps Military Government Daily Operations Log, April 18, 1945, April 26, 1945, RG 407, File 224-12, NARA.

55. XXIV Corps Military Government Daily Operations Log, April 18, 1945, April 26, 1945, RG 407, File 224-12, NARA.

56. Surrender of the Ryukyus, Active 7(7-2-C) Archives A-D, Kadena Air Base, KAB Archives, XXIV Corps Military Government Daily Operations Log, RG 407, File 224-12, NARA; Diary, December 28, 1944–May 31, 1945, Detachment B-5.

57. Keyso, *Women of Okinawa*, 37, told by Fumiko Nakamura; Ota, *The Battle of Okinawa*, 223; History of Military Government Operations on Okinawa, May 10, 1945, BG William E. Crist, 19; Captain Roy E. Appleman, notes, RG 407, File 224-12, NARA, 2.

58. Diary, April 1–30, 1945, Detachment B-5, 31–33; XXIV Corps Military Government Daily Operations Log, RG 407, File 224-12, NARA.

59. Diary, April 1–30, 1945, Detachment B-5, 27, 32. Camp Sunabe recorded that the civilians participated freely. Camps Heinza and Tsumia also had men in labor battalions exercising initiative and offering to assume positions of local leadership by May 13, 1945. XXIV Corps Military Government Daily Operations Log, RG 407, File 224-12, NARA; 27th Infantry Division memorandum to Commanding General, RG 389, Box 704, NARA; History of Military Government Operations on Okinawa, May 10, 1945, BG William E. Crist, 17–19.

60. Okinawa Diary, April 30, 1945, LTC John Stevens and MSG James M. Burns.

61. Diary, May 1–31, 1945, Detachment B-5, 48. Okinawans "display almost none of the Japanese fanaticism." History of Military Government Operations on Okinawa, May 10, 1945, BG William E. Crist, 18.

62. Sarantakes, ed., *Seven Stars*, 35, 90.

63. "The general attitude of [Okinawan] men were largely similar to the give and take common sense approach to situations which one would expect of American village leaders." Diary, May 1–31, 1945, Detachment B-5, 48.

64. Diary, May 1–31, 1945, Detachment B-5, 41. Roughly 7 to 10 percent of Okinawan camp residents had associations with America. Out of those, the American connections varied greatly, ranging from a basic knowledge of the country and the English language to having lived in places along the Pacific Ocean like San Francisco, Hawaii, and Los Angeles, sometimes for as long as twenty-five years.

65. Diary, May 1–31, 1945, Detachment B-5, 41; Captain Roy E. Appleman, notes, RG 407, File 224-12, NARA, 2. "They exhibit no animosity toward Americans [and] declare their gratitude. They do not exhibit any noticeable

resentment against the American soldier." History of Military Government Operations on Okinawa, May 10, 1945, BG William E. Crist, 19.

66. Diary, May 1–31, 1945, Detachment B-5, 48.

67. Okinawa Diary, April 30, 1945, LTC John Stevens and MSG James M. Burns; Sarantakes, ed., *Seven Stars*, 34; Diary, 1944–1945, Detachment B-5, 48; XXIV Corps Military Government Daily Operations Log, RG 407, File 224-12, NARA.

68. Diary, May 1–31, 1945, Detachment B-5, 47.

69. Every military government camp, in varying degrees, relaxed their strict guidelines around the end of April/early May. Diary, April 1–May 31, 1945, Detachment B-5, 40–55; XXIV Corps Military Government Daily Operations Log, RG 407, File 224-12, NARA; History of Military Government Operations on Okinawa, May 10, 1945, BG William E. Crist, 17–20.

70. This exercise of authority was consistent with the guidance in the GOPER. General Buckner encouraged his subordinate leaders to make decisions at their level based on the circumstances they encountered. The GOPER also stated that the civilians could earn back their freedom by behaving favorably. Even though the camp commanders lacked an explicit order from XXIV Corps or the Tenth Army directing the shift in policy, their adjustment of policy based on perceived changes in the Okinawans' behavior fell within the general parameters laid out in the GOPER. Operational Directive #7, January 6, 1945, Commanding General, Tenth Army, 2.

71. Diary, May 1–31, 1945, Detachment B-5, 47.

72. Diary, April 1–30, 1945, Detachment B-5, 32. "The people call themselves Okinawans rather than Japanese." History of Military Government Operations on Okinawa, May 10, 1945, BG William E. Crist, 18.

73. For more examples of lesser punishments for similar crimes, see XXIV Corps Military Government Daily Operations Log, RG 407, File 224-12, NARA. On April 20 at Maebaru, two civilians seen with a Japanese soldier were only arrested by the military police. (The Japanese soldier was shot.) A similar incident occurring earlier in the month may have resulted in the shootings of the civilians as well.

74. The barbed-wire stockades still existed as punishment, but their use was far less frequent. One camp, for example, only used them four days out of the entire month of May. The offenders had roamed into off-limits areas and refused to answer questions linked to espionage. Similar crimes had warranted the death penalty a month earlier. Diary, May 1–31, 1945, Detachment B-5, 47.

75. Okinawa Diary, April 30, 1945, LTC John Stevens and MSG James M. Burns. The change in military government policy based on Okinawan cooperation and obedience and the American perception that the Okinawans were not Japanese and had loyalty and kinship toward the United States did not erase all security measures. Inbound civilians still underwent a screening process, living

quarters for Americans and Okinawans remained separate, and rule infractions still warranted punishment (although infrequently and on a less severe scale). Diary, May 1–31, 1945, Detachment B-5, 45–47; XXIV Corps Military Government Daily Operations Log, RG 407, File 224-12, NARA.

76. Interview Sheet for Prospective Local Leaders, Appendix to Military Government Operations Report—Ryukyus, August 2, 1945, RG 407 Box 2487, File 110-5, NARA.

77. Diary, April 1–May 31, 1945, Detachment B-5, 36, 41, 48; Eikichi Shiroma, in *An Oral History of the Battle of Okinawa*, 9; Okinawa Diary, April 30, 1945, LTC John Stevens and MSG James M. Burns; 27th Infantry Division memorandum to the Commanding General, RG 389, Box 704, NARA.

78. History of Military Government Operations on Okinawa, May 10, 1945, BG William E. Crist, May 10, 1945, 18. No local leaders had the authority to prosecute or punish rule breakers. In many ways, the power of the local leaders lay with easing cultural conflict and language translation. Diary, April 1–May 31, 1945, Detachment B-5, 42, 35.

79. Captain Roy E. Appleman, notes, RG 407, File 224-12, NARA, 2–3; Local Government Situation Report, Appendix, RG 398, Box 704, NARA; Diary, May 1–31, 1945, Detachment B-5, 47–48.

80. Local government at the initial stage of the occupation was considered a lofty goal and was not a priority for the planners. The GOPER laid out guidance for a hasty occupation under wartime conditions that corralled civilians and herded them away from hostile fire. Local government after the surrender carried greater importance as occupation goals transitioned toward economic stability and the reestablishment of villages. Operational Directive #7, January 6, 1945, Commanding General, Tenth Army, 9.

81. Military Government Action Report, 1 April–30 June 1945, XXIV Corps, RG 407, Box 2153, NARA, 5.

82. Diary, April 1–May 31, 1945, Detachment B-5, 40, 49; *An Oral History of the Battle of Okinawa*, 5.

83. Detachment Daily Report, RG 407, File 224-12, NARA; 7th division, speech transcript, Inclosure 2, Civil Affairs, RG 407, File 224-12, NARA, 2; XXIV Corps After Action Review #125, RG 407, File 224-12, NARA; Diary, 1944–1945, Detachment B-5, 22, 28, 31, 51; Inafuku, speech; XXIV Corps Military Government Preliminary Planning, RG 407, File 224-12, NARA; Mike Daly, "irei-no-hi: A Day of Remembrance," *Okinawa Living*, June 2007, 75; Hostetler, interview.

84. Diary, May 1–31, 1945, Detachment B-5, 52.

85. Diary, May 1–31, 1945, Detachment B-5, 33; Nako Yoshio, newspaper interview, *Ryukyu Shimpo*, in Ealey and McLauchlan, *Descent into Hell*, 410.

7. Benevolent Captors? Okinawans Encounter the Americans

1. Yasutaka Aza, in *An Oral History of the Battle of Okinawa, Survivor's Testimonies* (Okinawa: Relief Section, Welfare Department, Okinawa Prefectural Government, 1985), 35.

2. Thomas M. Huber, *Japan's Battle of Okinawa, April–June 1945* (Honolulu: University Press of the Pacific, 2005), 82–103; Bill Sloan, *The Ultimate Battle: Okinawa 1945—The Last Epic Struggle of World War II* (New York: Simon and Schuster, 2007), 179–94, 255–73.

3. Yokota, Oral History Collection, 25; Masahide Ota, "Straggler," in Haruko Taya Cook and Theodore F. Cook, *Japan at War: An Oral History* (New York: The New Press, 1992), 367–70; Huber, *Japan's Battle of Okinawa*, 105–18.

4. Gima, Oral History Collection, 23; Teruto Tsubota Collection (AFC/2001/001/30918), Veterans History Project, American Folklife Center, Library of Congress; Miyagi Kikuko, "Student Nurses of the 'Lily Corps,'" in Cook and Cook, *Japan at War*, 357, 360–62; *An Oral History of the Battle of Okinawa*, 25; Huber, *Japan's Battle of Okinawa*, 103–15; Nakajo, Oral History Collection; 27; Associated Press, Charles P. Gorry, 27th Infantry Division, photograph, May 16, 1945, No. 19380C, *New York World-Telegram* and the *Sun* Newspaper Photograph Collection, Library of Congress Prints and Photographs Division, Washington, DC; Ota, "Straggler," 367. An estimated four thousand civilians died by "bombardment or battle cause . . . starvation or asphyxiation in caves . . . the majority had died in caves." Diary, April 30, 1945, Detachment B-5, 30.

5. Kikuko, "Student Nurses of the 'Lily Corps,'" 360–62; Kinjo Shigeaki, "Now They Call It 'Group Suicide,'" in Cook and Cook, *Japan at War*, 365; Memorandum for Major General Pedro del Valle, 1st Marine Division, Original Records, Subject File: O, United States Marine Corps Historical Division, Quantico, VA, 4.

6. Memorandum for Major General Pedro del Valle, 1st Marine Division, 4, 8–9, 12.

7. Kikuko, "Student Nurses of the 'Lily Corps,'" 360; John W. Dower, *War without Mercy: Race and Power in the Pacific War* (New York: Pantheon, 1986), 191, 196, 250.

8. Kikuko, "Student Nurses of the 'Lily Corps,'" 360–61.

9. Tsubota Collection, Veterans History Project.

10. Kikuko, "Student Nurses of the 'Lily Corps,'" 361; Takejiro Nakamura, interview in James Brooke, "Okinawa Suicides and Japan's Army: Burying the Truth?" *New York Times*, June 21, 2005; Yasutaka Aza, in *An Oral History of the Battle of Okinawa*, 35; Memorandum for Major General Pedro del Valle, 1st Marine Division, 4, 7.

11. Kikuko, "Student Nurses of the 'Lily Corps,'" 362.

12. Kikuko, "Student Nurses of the 'Lily Corps,'" 359.

13. Study of the Ryukyu Islands, July 20, 1945, Island Command, 1; Norma Field, *In the Realm of a Dying Emperor: Japan at Century's End* (New York: Vintage, 1992), 101, 103; Takejiro Nakamura, interview.

14. Diary, April 3–8, 1945, Detachment B-5, 23.

15. Ginoza, Oral History Collection, 34; Memorandum for Major General Pedro del Valle, 1st Marine Division, 4; Jim Lea, "The War Is Not Over on Okinawa Isle," *Stars and Stripes*, April 22, 1972; Nagamine, Oral History Collection, 32; Kikuko, "Student Nurses of the 'Lily Corps,'" 360.

16. Memorandum for Major General Pedro del Valle, 1st Marine Division, 4; Lea, "The War Is Not Over on Okinawa Isle"; Nagamine, Oral History Collection, 32; Kikuko, "Student Nurses of the 'Lily Corps,'" 360, 365; Ginoza, Oral History Collection, 34; Sumie Oshiro, interview in James Brooke, "Okinawa Suicides and Japan's Army: Burying the Truth?" *New York Times*, June 21, 2005.

17. "Fumiko Nakamura," in Ruth Ann Keyso, *Women of Okinawa: Nine Voices from a Garrison Island* (Ithaca, NY: Cornell University Press, 2000), 37; Masahide Ota, *The Battle of Okinawa: The Typhoon of Steel and Bombs* (Tokyo: Kume, 1984), 223; History of Military Government Operations on Okinawa, May 10, 1945, BG William E. Crist, 19; Captain Roy E. Appleman, notes, RG 407, File 224-12, NARA, 2; Okinawa Diary, April 30, 1945, LTC John Stevens and MSG James M. Burns; Study of the Ryukyu?s? Islands, July 20, 1945, Island Command, 1; Nagamine, Oral History Collection, 32; Report of Military Government Activities for Period from 1 April 1945 to 1 July 1946, July 1, 1946, RG 200, Reel 2, Folder V1-3, NARA, 71; Lieutenant Commander John T. Caldwell, Memoir, Okinawa, 1945–46, 93085, 10.V, Hoover Institute Archives, 16; Edward L. Smith, 2d Comdr, Marine Corps, USNR, "The Navy Hospital Corspmen," *Hospital Corps Quarterly*, March 1946, 11; Diary, April 3–8, 1945, Detachment B-5, 23.

18. Smith, "The Navy Hospital Corspmen," 4–5, 11; Report of Military Government Activities, July 1, 1946, US Naval Military Government, 11, 71; Study of the Ryukyu Islands, July 20, 1945, Island Command, 1; Ginoza, Oral History Collection, 34; Diary, April 3–8, 1945, May 1–31, 1945, Detachment B-5, 23, 48; Ernie Pyle, *The Last Chapter* (New York: Holt, 1946), 125.

19. Jacquelien van Stekelenburg, "Collective Identity," in *The Wiley-Blackwell Encyclopedia of Social and Political Movements*, ed. David A. Snow, Donatella della Porta, Bert Klandermans, and Doug McAdam (Hoboken, NJ: Blackwell, 2013), 1:1–7; Leonie Huddy, "Group Identity and Political Cohesion," in *Oxford Handbook of Political Psychology*, ed. Leonie Huddy, David O. Sears, and Robert Jervis (Oxford: University of Oxford Press, 2003), 511–46.

20. Diary, April 1–30, 1945, Detachment B-5, 32; History of Military Government Operations on Okinawa, May 10, 1945, BG William E. Crist, 18.

21. Diary, May 1–31, 1945, Detachment B-5, 48.

22. Study of the Ryukyu Islands, July 20, 1945, Island Command, 1; Pyle, *The Last Chapter*, 125; Speech by Paul Skuse, American Legion, November 21, 1947, Paul Skuse Papers, Hoover Institute; Colonel Hiromachi Yahara, *The Battle of Okinawa: A Japanese Officer's Account of the Last Great Campaign* (New York: John Wiley and Sons, 1995), 207.

23. Nagamine, Oral History Collection, 32.

24. Tomiko Higa, *The Girl with the White Flag: A Spellbinding Account of Love and Courage in Wartime Okinawa* (Tokyo: Kodansha International, 1989), 107; Study of the Ryukyu Islands, July 20, 1945, Island Command, 4.

25. Nicolas Evan Sarantakes, ed., *Seven Stars: The Okinawa Battle Diaries of Simon Bolivar Buckner Jr. and Joseph Stilwell* (College Station: Texas A&M University Press, 2004), 88; Nicolas Evan Sarantakes, *Keystone: The American Occupation of Okinawa and U.S.–Japanese Relations* (College Station: Texas A&M University Press, 2000), 21.

26. Sarantakes, ed., *Seven Stars*, 89–96, 98–100, 102–3; Island Command, Unit Report No. 1, June 20, 1945, Fred C. Wallace papers, Box 1, Folder 7, US Army Heritage and Education Center, Carlisle, PA; Island Command, Unit Report No. 2, July 6, 1945, Fred C. Wallace papers, Box 1, Folder 7, US Army Heritage and Education Center, Carlisle, PA; Island Command, Unit Report No. 3, July 23, 1945, Fred C. Wallace papers, Box 1, Folder 7, US Army Heritage and Education Center, Carlisle, PA; Island Command, Unit Report No. 4, August 9, 1945, Fred C. Wallace papers, Box 1, Folder 7, US Army Heritage and Education Center, Carlisle, PA.

27. Ota, "Straggler," 368.

28. Yahara, *The Battle of Okinawa*, 153–56; Huber, *Japan's Battle of Okinawa*, 114–18.

29. Ota, "Straggler," 369–70; Yokota, Oral History Collection, 25.

30. Ota, "Straggler," 368–70; Laura Homan Lacey, *Stay Off the Skyline: The Sixth Marine Division on Okinawa* (Washington, DC: Potomac, 2005), 74, told by Marine Private Joe Drago.

31. One Okinawan soldier recalled that his devotion to Japan still held strong until late October, the time at which he finally found himself in a prisoner of war camp, his methods of evasion having failed. Ota, "Straggler," 372.

32. Japanese military instructions, translated, June 21, 1945, 2.

33. Ota, *Battle of Okinawa*, xi; Takejiro Nakamura, interview; *An Oral History of the Battle of Okinawa*, 4–5; Lea, "The War Is Not Over on Okinawa Isle"; Japanese military instructions, translated, June 21, 1945, 2; Jim Lea, "Okinawa Remembers When War Passed Its Way," *Stars and Stripes*, June 26, 1985, 14; Kikuko, "Student Nurses of the 'Lily Corps,'" 358; Yahara, *The Battle of Okinawa*, 216. Japanese soldiers speared a mentally ill woman found stumbling outside Shuri Castle when it served as the 32nd Army headquarters. The soldiers found her incoherent rants worrisome and killed her as a potential spy.

34. Ota, "Straggler," 371–72; Directive Number 33: Okinawan POWs— Reception and Processing of, United States Naval Military Government Headquarters, November 15, 1945, RG 407, File 224-12, NARA.

35. Yokota, Oral History Collection, 25.

36. Yokota, Oral History Collection, 25; Ota, "Straggler," 372.

37. Ota, "Straggler," 371.

38. Ota, "Straggler," 368; Aza, Oral History Collection, 35.

39. Ota, "Straggler," 370–71.

40. The group environment of the prisoner of war camps gave the Okinawan fighters the opportunity to shape an identity collectively through shared traumatic experience and group comparison. This process of collective identity building is called *consciousness.* Van Stekelenburg, "Collective Identity," 2; Huddy, "Group Identity and Political Cohesion," 511–46.

41. Ota, "Straggler," 372.

42. Ota, "Straggler," 372.

43. Touroko Oshiro, in *An Oral History of the Battle of Okinawa*, 37; Shigeaki, "Now They Call It 'Group Suicide,'" 363–64; Higa, *The Girl with the White Flag*, 116.

44. Rear Admiral Minoru Ota to Navy Vice Admiral, Telegram message 062016, Document Exhibit Room, Japanese Naval Underground Headquarters.

45. This is consistent with the sociological definition of collective identity: "the shared definition of a group that derives from members' common interests, experiences, and solidarity." Verta Taylor and Nancy E. Whittier, "Collective Identity in Social Movement Communities: Lesbian Feminist Mobilization," in *Frontiers in Social Movement Theory*, ed. Aldon D. Morris and Carol McClurg Mueller (New Haven, CT: Yale University Press, 1992), 104.

46. Taylor and Whittier, "Collective Identity in Social Movement Communities," 104.

8. No Initiative: Unbending Policy, Rigid US Marine Action

1. James W. Johnston, *The Long Road of War* (Lincoln: University of Nebraska Press, 1998), 131–32; George Lince, *Too Young the Heroes: A World War II Marine's Account of Facing a Veteran Enemy at Guadalcanal, the Solomons, and Okinawa* (Jefferson, NC: McFarland, 1997), 89–90.

2. Ernie Pyle, *The Last Chapter* (New York: Holt, 1946), 107–8, 130; Johnston, *The Long Road of War*, 126; Eugene B. Sledge, *With the Old Breed at Peleliu and Okinawa* (Annapolis, MD: Naval Institute Press, 1996), 192–93.

3. Comments on Military Government, July 6, 1945, 1st Marine Division, 6–9, 14; Teruto Tsubota Collection (AFC/2001/001/30918), Veterans History Project, American Folklife Center, Library of Congress; Comments on Military Government Operation, OKINAWA, 6th Marine Division Sector, 1 April to 29 June, 1945, July 6, 1945, RG 389, Box 704, NARA, 2, 5; XXIV Corps Military Government Daily Operations Log, RG 407, File 224-12, NARA; Laura Homan Lacey, *Stay off the Skyline: The Sixth Marine Division on Okinawa, an Oral History* (Washington, DC: Potomac, 2005), 68, 70, told by Private Thomas McKinney and Lance Corporal Tom Baird; Spot Promotion for Captain Wynne L. Van Schiak (014812), US Marine Corps Reserve, recommendation for, November 11, 1944, United States Marine Corps Personnel Records, St. Louis, MO; 6th Marine Division Special Action Report—Okinawa Operation, Phase III, Section 11—Military Government, RG 389, Box 879, NARA, 50; Operational Report on Military Government, OKINAWA, Phase I and II, May 1, 1945, RG 389, Box 704, NARA, 1–2, 4; Action Report Nansei Shoto Operation 1 April–30

June 45—1st Marine Division Military Government, RG 389, Box 879, NARA; Military Government Activities (From 011400 May to 020001 July), Detachment B-10, July 6, 1945, RG 389, Box 879, NARA, 10; Operation Report on Military Government, OKINAWA, Southern Phase, July 1, 1945, RG 389, Box 704, NARA, 4; Tony Fileff Collection (AFC/2001/001/3045), Veterans History Project, American Folklife Center, Library of Congress; Martin Kujala Collection (AFC/2001/001/5556), Veterans History Project, American Folklife Center, Library of Congress; John David Jackson Collection (AFC/2001/001/38452), Veterans History Project, American Folklife Center, Library of Congress.

4. Comments on Military Government, July 6, 1945, 1st Marine Division 4, 9; 6th Marine Division Special Action Report, 52.

5. Comments on Military Government, July 6, 1945, 1st Marine Division, 5, 14; Proclamations, February 13, 1945, 1st Marine Division; Military Government Plan, February 8, 1945, 6th Marine Division, 3.

6. Lacey, *Stay Off the Skyline*, 73–76, told by Marine Private Joe Drago.

7. Lacey, *Stay Off the Skyline*, 67, 69, 74–75; Military Government Activities, July 6, 1945, Detachment B-10, 3–4, 8; Comments on Military Government, July 6, 1945, 1st Marine Division, 10–11, 13; Tsubota Collection, Veterans History Project; Administrative Order Number 4-45, 1st Marine Division, April 11, 1945, RG 389, Box 704, NARA; Pyle, *The Last Chapter*, 108, Comments on Military Government, July 6, 1945, 6th Marine Division, 4; Fileff Collection, Veterans History Project; Ken Hatfield, *Heartland Heroes: Remembering World War II* (Columbia: University of Missouri, 2003), 253; Administrative Order Number 5-45, April 22, 1945, RG 389, Box 704, NARA; Memorandum 010923/1, May 1, 1945, RG 389, Box 704, NARA.

8. Operational Report on Military Government, OKINAWA, Phase I and II, May 1, 1945, 3.

9. Pyle, *The Last Chapter*, 104, 108, 124–25; Edward L. Smith, 2d Comdr, Marine Corps, USNR, "The Navy Hospital Corpsmen," *Hospital Corps Quarterly*, March 1946, 2.

10. Annex "Able" to Administrative Plan No. 1-45, January 16, 1945, RG 389, Box 704, NARA, 2–4; Propaganda for Use against the Japanese, December 29, 1944, 2nd Marine Division, December 29, 1944, 1, 3.

11. Comments on Military Government, July 6, 1945, 1st Marine Division, 7–8; Mark Ealey and Alastair McLauchlan, trans., *Descent into Hell: Civilian Memories of the Battle of Okinawa*, originally published in *Ryukyu Shimpo* (Portland, OR: Merwin Asia, 2014), 182.

12. Comments on Military Government, July 6, 1945, 1st Marine Division, 7.

13. CINCPOA COMMUNIQUE NO. 322, Navy Daily Reports, April 5, 1945, Subject File: O, United States Marine Corps Historical Division; Comments on Military Government, July 6, 1945, 1st Marine Division, 7–10.

14. Tsubota Collection, Veterans History Project.

15. Interview Sheet for Prospective Local Leaders, Appendix to Military

Government Operations Report—Ryukyus, August 2, 1945, RG 407, Box 2487, File 110-5, NARA; Comments on Military Government Operation, July 6, 1945, 1st Marine Division, 9; Lacey, *Stay Off the Skyline*, 68, told by Private Thomas McKinney; Comments on Military Government Operation, July 6, 1945, 6th Marine Division, 2, 5; XXIV Corps Military Government Daily Operations Log, RG 407, File 224-12, NARA.

16. Military Government Activities, July 6, 1945, Detachment B-10, 11; Appendix No. 3 to Annex "Able," January 16, 1945, 1; Appendix No. 1 to Annex "Able" to Administrative Plan No. 1-45, January 16, 1945, RG 389, Box 704, NARA; Appendix No. 2 to Annex "Able" to Administrative Plan No. 1-45, January 16, 1945, RG 389, Box 704, NARA. According to the prescribed composition, each detachment should have received one quarter-ton truck, one three-quarter-ton truck, two trailers, two 20 × 40 foot tarpaulins, and one small command post tent. The "C" detachments were also allocated an additional one-and-a-quarter-ton truck, nine more tarpaulins, and forty-five more tents.

17. Comments on Military Government Operation, July 6, 1945, 6th Marine Division, 2; Operational Report on Military Government, OKINAWA, Phase I and II, May 1, 1945, 4; Operation Report on Military Government, OKINAWA, Southern Phase, July 1, 1945, 2; Comments on Military Government Operation, July 6, 1945, 1st Marine Division, 3–4, 9.

18. The military government units severely lacked personnel; the few soldiers they did have lacked training and field experience. In addition to the enlisted soldiers, each civil affairs unit required nineteen majors for senior officer leadership; the units that landed had only seven captains and one lieutenant to lead and manage their enlisted formations. Some units were even smaller; one consisted of only one officer in addition to a few military police enlisted soldiers. Others had too few military police to control any type of perimeter on an encampment. Besides lacking trained specialists like interpreters, medics, and cooks, they lacked general soldiers who could assist with tasks such as controlling civilian movement, building structures, and serving food. Without such manpower, those tasks were unable to be completed. Comments on Military Government Operation, July 6, 1945, 6th Marine Division, 2, 5; Spot Promotion, November 11, 1944, Captain Wynne L. Van Schiak; Comments on Military Government Operation, July 6, 1945, 1st Marine Division, 6, 9, 14; 6th Marine Division Special Action Report, Section 11—Military Government, 50; Activities of the Marine Corps in Civil Affairs in World War II, critical study of, March 1946, Major Garnelle G. Wheeler, 1–2; Action Report Nansei Shoto Operation, June 30 1945, 1st Marine Division; Military Government Activities, July 6, 1945, Detachment B-10, 10; Operational Report on Military Government, OKINAWA, Phase I and II, May 1, 1945, 4; Operation Report on Military Government, OKINAWA, Southern Phase, July 1, 1945, 4.

19. Military Government Activities, July 6, 1945, Detachment B-10, 1–3; 6th Marine Division Special Action Report, Section 11—Military Government,

51; Comments on Military Government Operation, July 6, 1945, 1st Marine Division, 9.

20. Operation Report on Military Government, OKINAWA, Southern Phase, July 1, 1945, 2, 4.

21. Pyle, *The Last Chapter*, 126; Robert Lynn Maurer Collection (AFC/2001/001/10466), Veterans History Project, American Folklife Center, Library of Congress.

22. Johnston, *The Long Road of War*, 126.

23. Pyle, *The Last Chapter*, 130; Sledge, *With the Old Breed*, 192–93.

24. Jackson Collection, Veterans History Project oral history; Pyle, *The Last Chapter*, 107–8, 130; Fileff Collection, Veterans History Project.

25. Comments on Military Government Operation, July 6, 1945, 1st Marine Division, 9.

26. Lacey, *Stay Off the Skyline*, 70, told by Lance Corporal Tom Baird; Fileff Collection, Veterans History Project; Kujala Collection, Veterans History Project.

27. Pyle, *The Last Chapter*, 108.

28. Pyle, *The Last Chapter*, 125; Johnston, *The Long Road of War*, 131.

29. Comments on Military Government Operation, July 6, 1945, 1st Marine Division, 8; Pyle, *The Last Chapter*, 125.

30. Comments on Military Government Operation, July 6, 1945, 1st Marine Division, 8; Lacey, *Stay Off the Skyline*, 72, told by Private First Class Richard Whitaker.

31. Nicolas Evan Sarantakes, ed., *Seven Stars: The Okinawa Battle Diaries of Simon Bolivar Buckner Jr. and Joseph Stilwell* (College Station: Texas A&M University Press, 2004), 41.

32. Comments on Military Government Operation, July 6, 1945, 6th Marine Division, 4; 6th Marine Division Special Action Report, 52.

33. POW Interrogation Report Number 52, Nishiyama Sakae, June 25, 1945, Box 7, Folder 11, United States Marine Corps Historical Division, Quantico, VA, 1; Reservist and Civilian Conscription on OKINAWA ISLAND, 2nd Marine Division, June 9, 1945, Box 1, Folder 33/1, United States Marine Corps Archives and Special Collections, Alfred M. Gray Research Center, Quantico, VA; Major General Lemuel C. Shepard, 6th Marine Division, Military account, June 8, 1945, Subject File: O, Box 7, Folder 10/7, United States Marine Corps Historical Division, Quantico, VA, 4; Comments on Military Government Operation, July 6, 1945, 1st Marine Division, 9–10; Report of Japanese casualties, Office of Public Information, Navy Department, July 24, 1945, WWII: Okinawa: Original Records, Subject File: O, United States Marine Corps Historical Division, Quantico, VA; Patrick K. O'Donnell, *Into the Rising Sun: In Their Own Words, World War II's Pacific Veterans Reveal the Heart of Combat* (New York: Simon and Schuster, 2002), 266, told by Patrick Almond.

34. 6th Marine Division Special Action Report, 52; Comments on Military Government Operation, July 6, 1945, 6th Marine Division, 4.

35. Comments on Military Government Operation, July 6, 1945, 1st Marine

Division, 9; O'Donnell, *Into the Rising Sun*, 264, told by Joe McNamara and Elmer Mapes.

36. Tsubota Collection, Veterans History Project. Young Japanese men would grow beards to look old, harmless, and more like the dislocated Okinawan population.

37. Lacey, *Stay Off the Skyline*, 72, told by Private First Class Richard Whitaker; O'Donnell, *Into the Rising Sun*, 264, 266, told by Patrick Almond and Elmer Mapes.

38. Comments on Military Government Operation, July 6, 1945, 1st Marine Division, 9.

39. Comments on Military Government Operation, July 6, 1945, 1st Marine Division, 9; Comments on Military Government Operation, July 6, 1945, 6th Marine Division, 4; Military Government Activities, July 6, 1945, Detachment B-10, 4; Pyle, *The Last Chapter*, 108; Administrative Order Number 4-45, April 11, 1945, 1st Marine Division. The Japanese military employed school-aged children, sometimes as young as 13. Ealey and McLauchlan, *Descent into Hell*, 46.

40. Comments on Military Government Operation, July 6, 1945, 1st Marine Division, 9; Administrative Order Number 5-45, April 22, 1945, 1; Major General John Hodge to Major General Pedro del Valle, Authority for Okinawan Labor in XXIV Corps area, May 1, 1945, Box 704, RG 389, NARA; Military Government Activities, July 6, 1945, Detachment B-10, 3. Initially, the detachments issued a small number of passes that allowed some of the local population to enter and exit the camps freely. Within forty-eight hours, however, Okinawans with passes had traveled into combat areas and caused such confusion that the detachments stopped the use of the passes. XXIV Corps Military Government Daily Operations Log, RG 407, File 224-12, NARA, 1; Tenth Army to 1st Marine Division, Memorandum: Denying Passes to Civilians, Box 704, RG 389, NARA; Jim Lea, "The War Is Not Over on Okinawa Isle," *Stars and Stripes*, April 22, 1972, 2.

41. Tsubota Collection, Veterans History Project.

42. Military Government Activities, July 6, 1945, Detachment B-10, 2.

43. Tsubota Collection, Veterans History Project.

44. Pyle, *The Last Chapter*, 108, 125; Smith, "The Navy Hospital Corpsmen," 4–5, 11; Shige Ginoza, in *An Oral History of the Battle of Okinawa, Survivor's Testimonies* (Okinawa: Relief Section, Welfare Department, Okinawa Prefectural Government, 1985), 34; Eikichi Shiroma, in *An Oral History of the Battle of Okinawa*, 9; Roger V. Dingman, "Language at War: U.S. Marine Corps Japanese Language Officers in the Pacific War," *Journal of Military History* 68, no. 3 (July 2004): 853–83; Military Government Activities, July 6, 1945, Detachment B-10, 8.

45. Tsubota Collection, Veterans History Project; Lacey, *Stay Off the Skyline*, 75, told by Corporal William Pierce; O'Donnell, *Into the Rising Sun*, 264, told by Joe McNamara.

46. Lacey, *Stay Off the Skyline*, 73, told by Private Charles Miller.

47. Lacey, *Stay Off the Skyline*, 74–76, told by Corporal William Pierce and Private Joe Drago.

48. Tsubota Collection, Veterans History Project; Junko Isa, "Junko Isa," in Ruth Ann Keyso, *Women of Okinawa: Nine Voices from a Garrison Island* (Ithaca, NY: Cornell University Press, 2000), 6; Fumiko Nakamura, "Fumiko Nakamura," in Keyso, *Women of Okinawa*, 37; Masahide Ota, *The Battle of Okinawa: The Typhoon of Steel and Bombs* (Tokyo: Kume, 1984), 223; History of Military Government Operations on Okinawa, 1 April–30 April 1945 [L Day to L+29] by BG William E. Crist, May 10, 1945, RG 407, Box 2487, File 110-5.0, NARA, 19; Captain Roy E. Appleman, notes, RG 407, File 224-12, NARA, 2; LTC John Stevens and MSG James M. Burns, Okinawa Diary, April 30, 1945, RG 407, Box 2441, NARA; Mitsutoshi Nakajo, in *An Oral History of the Battle of Okinawa*, 27; John W. Dower, *War without Mercy: Race and Power in the Pacific War* (New York: Pantheon, 1986), 191, 196, 250; Nagamine, in *An Oral History of the Battle of Okinawa*, 32; Tomiko Higa, *The Girl with the White Flag: A Spellbinding Account of Love and Courage in Wartime Okinawa* (Tokyo: Kodansha International, 1989), 110; Miyagi Kikuko, "Student Nurses of the 'Lily Corps,'" in Haruko Taya Cook and Theodore F. Cook, *Japan at War: An Oral History* (New York: The New Press, 1992), 361; Kinjo Shigeaki, "Now They Call It 'Group Suicide,'" in Cook and Cook, *Japan at War*, 365; Takejiro Nakamura, interview in James Brooke, "Okinawa Suicides and Japan's Army: Burying the Truth?" *New York Times*, June 21, 2005.

49. Tsubota Collection, Veterans History Project; O'Donnell, *Into the Rising Sun*, 264, told to as Joe McNamara; Hamamatsu Shigeru, letter, in Ealey and McLauchlan, *Descent into Hell*, 296.

50. Okinawa Diary, April 30, 1945, LTC John Stevens and MSG James M. Burns; Nako Yoshi, interview, in Ealey and McLauchlan, *Descent into Hell*, 296.

51. Pyle, *The Last Chapter*, 109; O'Donnell, *Into the Rising Sun*, 280–81, told by Jerry Beau; Hisada Tamiko, interview, in Ealey and McLauchlan, *Descent into Hell*, 296.

52. Comments on Military Government Operation, July 6, 1945, 6th Marine Division, 4; Fileff Collection, Veterans History Project. Military Government Activities, July 6, 1945, Detachment B-10, 2–3, 8.

53. Comments on Military Government Operation, July 6, 1945, 1st Marine Division, 10–11, 13; Comments on Military Government Operations, July 6, 1945, 6th Marine Division, 4. Ninety percent of the inmates at the POW camp near Detachment A-1 were Okinawan civilians used for labor. Such practices by the provost marshal and military government were heavily supported and endorsed by the division.

54. Military Government Activities, July 6, 1945, Detachment B-10, 8.

55. Comments on Military Government Operation, July 6, 1945, 1st Marine Division, 9; Johnston, *The Long Road to War*, 131–32; Sergeant Frank Acosta, Marine Combat Correspondent, Comments on Marine Military Government, July 25, 1945, Box 844, RG 389, NARA.

56. Comments on Military Government Operation, July 6, 1945, 1st Marine Division, 9.

57. Lacey, *Stay Off the Skyline*, 69, 74–75, told by Private First Class James Chaisson, Lance Corporal Don Honis, Private Joe Drago, and Corporal William Pierce.

58. Lacey, *Stay Off the Skyline*, 67, 69, told by Private First Class James Chaisson, Lance Corporal Don Honis, and Private Norris Buchter; Fileff Collection, Veterans History Project.

59. Tsubota Collection, Veterans History Project; Hatfield, *Heartland Heroes*, 253; O'Donnell, *Into the Rising Sun*, 264, told by Joe McNamara.

60. Administrative Order Number 4-45, April 11, 1945, 1st Marine Division.

61. Corps Special Order 7-45, III Amphibious Corps, April 27, 1945, Box 704, RG 389, NARA.

62. Johnston, *The Long Road to War*, 134–35; Pyle, *The Last Chapter*, 116; Sarantakes, ed., *Seven Stars*, 40.

63. Major General Pedro del Valle, USMC, Oral History Transcript, Rare Book and Manuscript Library, Columbia University, New York, 185–87.

64. Lacey, *Stay Off the Skyline*, 69, 74–75, told by Private First Class James Chaisson, Lance Corporal Don Honis, Private Joe Drago, and Corporal William Pierce; Captain Roy E. Appleman, notes, 2–3. Civilians became pawns in tense disagreements about battlespace between the Army and the Marines. As the population roamed the island in search of family members and food, the services disregarded movement restrictions put in place by the other service. XXIV Corps Military Government Daily Operations Log, RG 407, File 224-12, NARA.

65. Comments on Military Government Operation, July 6, 1945, 1st Marine Division, 3, 6, 12–13; Comments on Military Government Operation, July 6, 1945, 6th Marine Division, 1; Memorandum to G-1: Status and Responsibilities of the MG within the Division, clarification of, June 1, 1945, Box 704, RG 389, NARA; Operational Report on Military Government, OKINAWA, Phase I and II, May 1, 1945, 2–4; Activities of the Marine Corps in Civil Affairs in World War II, critical study of, March 1946, Major Garnelle G. Wheeler, 2; Diary, February 28, 1945, Detachment B-5, 13–15.

66. Activities of the Marine Corps in Civil Affairs in World War II, critical study of, March 1946, Major Garnelle G. Wheeler, 2; US Marine Corps Civil Affairs Officers, Memorandum, April 13, 1944; Annex "Able," January 16, 1945, 4; 6th Marine Division Special Action Report, Section 11-Military Government, 50.

67. Operation Report on Military Government, OKINAWA, Southern Phase, July 1, 1945, 3, 4; Comments on Military Government Operation, July 6, 1945, 6th Marine Division, 5.

68. Comments on Military Government Operation, July 6, 1945, 1st Marine Division, 6, 12; Special Order 124-45, May 19, 1945, COL John C. McQueen; Performance of Temporary Duty, report on, case of Captain Wynne L. Van Schiak, July 2, 1945, 000014812.

69. Action Report Nansei Shoto Operation, June 30 1945, 1st Marine Division; Military Government Activities, July 6, 1945, Detachment B-10, 3, 5; 6th Marine Division Special Action Report, Section 11—Military Government, 52.

70. Military Government Activities, July 6, 1945, Detachment B-10, 3; Comments on Military Government Operation, July 6, 1945, 6th Marine Division, 3; "Okinawa," Culture report, WWII: Okinawa: Original Records: Subject File O, United States Marine Corps Archives and Special Collections, Alfred M. Gray Research Center, Quantico, VA, 2.

71. A small minority of Marines and attached military government soldiers felt kindly toward the Okinawans. They were criticized for such feelings. Pyle, *The Last Chapter*, 109, 129; O'Donnell, *Into the Rising Sun*, 280–81, told by Jerry Beau.

72. 6th Marine Division Special Action Report, Section 11—Military Government, 52; Comments on Military Government Operation, July 6, 1945, 6th Marine Division, 4.

73. Comments on Military Government Operation, July 6, 1945, 6th Marine Division, 4; Military Government Activities, July 6, 1945, Detachment B-10, 9.

74. Operation Report on Military Government, OKINAWA, Southern Phase, July 1, 1945, 4.

75. 6th Marine Division Special Action Report, Section 11—Military Government, 52.

76. William Baumgartner Collection, (AFC/2001/001/16149), Veterans History Project, American Folklife Center, Library of Congress; Comments on Military Government Operation, July 6, 1945, 1st Marine Division, 9–11.

77. Hatfield, *Heartland Heroes*, 254; Operation Report on Military Government, OKINAWA, Southern Phase, July 1, 1945, 4; Arnold Fisch, *Military Government in the Ryukyu Islands, 1945–1950* (Washington, DC: Center of Military History, US Army, 1988), 85; MSgt Daniel Wheaton message to Public Affairs, April 27, Kadena Air Base History, KAB Active 7(7-2-C), Archives K–L, Kadena Air Base Archives; Calvin Sims, "3 Dead Marines and a Secret of Wartime Okinawa," *New York Times International*, June 1, 2000, A8.

78. Sarantakes, ed., *Seven Stars*, 40; Operation Report on Military Government, OKINAWA, Southern Phase, July 1, 1945, 4.

79. Operational Directive #7 from the Commanding General of Tenth Army, January 6, 1945, RG 290, Box 2196, NARA; Sarantakes, ed., *Seven Stars*, 40, 45; Interview with MG John Hodge, Okinawa Diary, March 12, 1945, LTC John Stevens and MSG James M. Burns.

80. Operation Report on Military Government, OKINAWA, Southern Phase, July 1, 1945, 4.

81. Geiger to Jackson, letter, May 20, 1945, Geiger Papers. Shepherd also preached racism to his Marines as a command philosophy. He stated he "didn't always feel that way in Europe about some poor, German family man, but [he] felt with a Jap it was like killing rattlesnakes." MG Lemuel Shepherd, USMC, Oral

History Transcript, Headquarters, United States Marine Corps Historical Division, Quantico, VA.

82. Smith, "The Navy Hospital Corpsmen," 5, 7, 9.

83. Reservist and Civilian Conscription on OKINAWA ISLAND, June 9, 1945, 2nd Marine Division; Procedure for handling enemy nationals, May 2, 1945, 1st Marine Division, Detachment B-10; Military Government Activities, July 6, 1945, Detachment B-10. B-10 had six additional men assigned specifically for engineer duties—one officer and five Seabees—and extra salvage materials, yet no construction projects beyond shelter and camp boundaries were completed.

84. 6th Marine Division Special Action Report, 51.

85. "Okinawa," Culture report, 1, 5.

86. The GOPER, for example, stated that civilians would earn back their freedom through obedience and cooperation. Despite acknowledging this directive, the Marines never instituted it. Displays of obedience did not earn Okinawans in Marine military government camps any return of their freedoms. Even those few selected as informal leaders had similar limitations to the regular camp population and only enjoyed a slightly elevated degree of freedom when executing tasks related to their assigned duties. Operational Directive #7, January 6, 1945, Commanding General, Tenth Army, 1; War Department Field Manual 27-5, November 4, 1943, 4, 7, 10; Pyle, *The Last Chapter*, 138–39; Captain Roy E. Appleman, notes, 2–3.

9. The US Navy Period: Navigating the Transition to Peace

1. Memoir, Okinawa 1945–46, LCDR Caldwell, 9–10.

2. Nicolas Evan Sarantakes, ed., *Seven Stars: The Okinawa Battle Diaries of Simon Bolivar Buckner Jr. and Joseph Stilwell* (College Station: Texas A&M University Press, 2004), 88; Nicolas Evan Sarantakes, *Keystone: The American Occupation of Okinawa and U.S. Japanese Relations* (College Station: Texas A&M University Press, 2000), 21. Lieutenant General Simon Bolivar Buckner Jr. died on June 18, 1945, during the Battle of Okinawa. He was killed by a ricocheted bullet while visiting a Marine outpost. Buckner had identified Major General Geiger, commander of the III Amphibious Corps, as his successor, but his appointment was controversial because he was a Marine. Geiger held the position of Tenth Army commander for only four days and was replaced by General Joseph Stilwell on June 23, 1945. Sarantakes, ed., *Seven Stars*, 17, 19, 57, 75.

3. US forces on Okinawa transitioned to mopping-up operations following the end of the battle. The objective of mopping-up operations was to locate and destroy pockets of enemy resistance and enforce the surrender. Military Government Plan, 6th Marine Division, February 8, 1945, RG 389, Box 704, NARA.

4. Military Government Plan, 6th Marine Division, February 8, 1945, RG 389, Box 704, NARA; Sarantakes, ed., *Seven Stars*, 89–96, 98–100, 102–3; Island Command, Unit Report No. 1, June 20, 1945, Fred C. Wallace Papers, Box 1, Folder 7, US Army Heritage and Education Center, Carlisle, PA; Island Command,

Unit Report No. 2, July 6, 1945, Fred C. Wallace Papers, Box 1, Folder 7, US Army Heritage and Education Center, Carlisle, PA; Island Command, Unit Report No. 3, July 23, 1945, Fred C. Wallace papers, Box 1, Folder 7, US Army Heritage and Education Center, Carlisle, PA; Island Command, Unit Report No. 4, August 9, 1945, Fred C. Wallace Papers, Box 1, Folder 7, US Army Heritage and Education Center, Carlisle, PA.

5. John Dorfman Collection (AFC/2001/001/64154), Part I, Veterans History Project, American Folklife Center, Library of Congress; Report of Psychological Warfare Activities Okinawa Operation, September 15, 1945, RG 407, Box 2502, File 110-39, NARA, 10; CINCPAC-CINCPOA Bulletin #161-44, November 15, 1944, RG 407, Box 2502, NARA, 1; Japanese Naval Underground Museum, Document Exhibit Room, Japanese Imperial Army Statistics; *The Battle of Okinawa: Oral Histories* (Okinawa: Prefectural Peace Memorial Museum, 1990), 4; Sarantakes ed., *Seven Stars*, 61, 74, 89–90; LTC Luker, Army Air Corps, C-54 pilot, head of Air Transport Command out of Yomitan, speech, June 23, 1995, Active 7(7-2-C) archives K–L, "Kadena Base History," Kadena Air Base, Kadena Air Base Archives; E. B. Sledge, *With the Old Breed at Peleliu and Okinawa* (Annapolis, MD: Naval Institute Press, 1996), 248–49; Bill Sloan, *The Ultimate Battle: Okinawa 1945—The Last Epic Struggle of World War II* (New York: Simon and Schuster, 2007), photos 25–27.

6. Memorandum for Major General Pedro del Valle, 1st Marine Division, 4.

7. Diary, April 1–May 31, 1945, Detachment B-5, 23, 40–55; XXIV Corps Military Government Daily Operations Log, RG 407, File 224-12, NARA; History of Military Government Operations on Okinawa, May 10, 1945, BG William E. Crist, 17–20; Miyagi Kikuko, "Student Nurses of the 'Lily Corps,'" in Haruko Taya Cook and Theodore F. Cook, *Japan at War: An Oral History* (New York: The New Press, 1992), 362.

8. Report of Military Government Activities, July 1, 1946, US Naval Military Government, 5; Demobilization Planning—Assumptions for, July 28, 1945, RG 38, Box 170, NARA; Dorfman Collection, Part I, Veterans History Project; Memoir, Okinawa 1945–46, LCDR Caldwell, 5; Speech by Paul Skuse, American Legion, November 21, 1947, Paul Skuse Papers, Hoover Institute; Tomiko Higa, *The Girl with the White Flag: A Spellbinding Account of Love and Courage in Wartime Okinawa* (Tokyo: Kodansha International, 1989), 60.

9. Report of Military Government Activities, July 1, 1946, US Naval Military Government, 56.

10. Unit Report 1, June 20, 1945, Island Command; Unit Report 2, July 6, 1945, Island Command; Unit Report 3, July 23, 1945, Island Command; Unit Report 4, August 9, 1945, Island Command; Chas S. Nichols Jr. and Henry L. Shaw Jr., *Okinawa: Victory in the Pacific* (Washington, DC: Historical Branch, US Marine Corps, 1955), 266; Island Command, Action Report, Okinawa, 13 Dec 44–30 Jun 45, Fred C. Wallace Papers, Box 1, Folder 7, US Army Heritage and Education Center, Carlisle, PA; Major General Pedro del Valle, Rehabilitation

Area memorandum, June 21, 1945, Major General Roy S. Geiger Papers, Box 6, Folder 109, Alfred M. Gray Research Center, Quantico, VA, 1; Island Command Memorandum to James Watkins, Report on General Conduct of Military Government, July 14, 1945, Ryukyus Papers: Okinawan History: Tenth Army Phase, Box 3, Folder 5, US Army Heritage and Education Center, Carlisle, PA, 1; Island Command Military Government newsletter, July 30, 1945, Ryukyus Papers: Okinawan History: Tenth Army Phase, Box 3, Folder 5, US Army Heritage and Education Center, Carlisle, PA, 1; Sarantakes, ed., *Seven Stars*, 76, 89, 95–96.

11. Study of the Ryukyu Islands, Island Command, July 20, 1945, RG 407, Entry 427, NARA.

12. Memorandum for Admiral Nimitz, August 13, 1945, RG 38, Box 157, NARA. Operation Olympic was the first part of Operation Downfall, the plan to invade the home islands of Japan. Operation Olympic consisted of landings on the prefecture of Kyushu.

13. Memorandum for Admiral Nimitz, August 13, 1945, RG 38, Box 157, NARA; Report of Military Government Activities, July 1, 1946, US Naval Military Government, 56–57, 65; Special Proclamation 1, July 30, 1945, RG 407, File 224-12, NARA; Military Government Headquarters Memorandum Number 27, June 29, 1945, RG 407, File 224-12, NARA, 2; Appendix D, CINCAFPAC 230455, August 1945, RG 38, Box 157, NARA; United States Naval Military Government Special Proclamation Number 2, September 25, 1945, RG 200, Reel 8, Folder 2-VIII-2, NARA; Summary of Directives (Including Dispatches) and Proclamations Which Military Government, Okinawa, Is Now Being Exercised, January 15, 1946, RG 200, Reel 8, Folder 2-VIII-2, NARA; Appendix B, v73, July 18, 1945, RG 38, Box 157, NARA; Sarantakes, ed., *Seven Stars*, 106, 108; William Baumgartner Collection (AFC/2001/001/16149), Veterans History Project, American Folklife Center, Library of Congress.

14. Report of Military Government Activities, July 1, 1946, US Naval Military Government, 1. Arnold Fisch, *Military Government in the Ryukyu Islands, 1945–1950* (Washington, DC: Center of Military History, United States Army, 1988), 72–73; Report of Military Government Activities, July 1, 1946, US Naval Military Government, 1, 57; Special Proclamation 1, July 30, 1945, RG 407, File 224-12, NARA; Memorandum Number 27, June 29, 1945, Military Government Headquarters, 2.

15. Report of Military Government Activities, July 1, 1946, US Naval Military Government, 7; Dorfman Collection, Part I, Veterans History Project; Administrative and Economic Measures for Okinawa, ASCOM, September 19, 1945, Ryukyus Papers, Okinawan History: Tenth Army Phase, Box 3, Folder 5, US Heritage and Education Center, Carlisle, PA, 2; Rehabilitation Area memorandum, June 21, 1945, Major General Pedro del Valle, 1; Oto Nagamine, Oral History Collection, Prefectural Peace Memorial Museum.

16. Report of Military Government Activities, July 1, 1946, US Naval

Military Government, 7; Administrative and Economic Measures for Okinawa, September 19, 1945, ASCOM, 2.

17. Study of the Ryukyu Islands, July 20, 1945, Island Command, 1.

18. CINCAFPAC, Admin, Naval Dispatch Message CX 36856, August 26, 1945, RG 38, Box 170, NARA; John W. Dower, *Embracing Defeat: Japan in the Wake of World War II* (New York: Norton, 1999); Sarantakes, *Keystone*, 21; Sarantakes, ed., *Seven Stars*, 108, 114, 119–20; Edward Drea, *In Service of the Emperor: Essays on the Imperial Japanese Army* (Lincoln: University of Nebraska Press, 1998); Michael Schaller, *The Origins of the Cold War in Asia: The American Occupation of Japan* (Oxford: Oxford University Press, 1985); Naoko Shibusawa, *America's Geisha Ally: Reimaging the Japanese Enemy* (Cambridge, MA: Harvard University Press, 2006); Memorandum for F-1: Acceptance of the Surrender in the Ryukyus, United States Fleet, Headquarters of the Commander in Chief, Navy Department, August 26, 1945, RG 38, Box 170, NARA.

19. Rehabilitation Area memorandum, June 21, 1945, Major General Pedro del Valle, 2; SGT Oliphant, H.N., "The answer to the biggest question on any GI's mind is still iffy. YANK assembles here the best dope at the time of going to press on what the WD plans," *Yank* [magazine], September 7, 1945, File Y, Kadena Archives, Kadena AB; Demobilization planning, July 28, 1945, United States Fleet Headquarters, Commander in Chief, 1.

20. Demobilization planning, July 28, 1945, United States Fleet Headquarters, Commander in Chief, 2–3; Kujala Collection, Veterans History Project; SGT Oliphant, H.N., "The answer to the biggest question."

21. Martin Kujala Collection (AFC/2001/001/5556), Veterans History Project, American Folklife Center, Library of Congress; "Army Reveals Plans for Vast Reduction of Its Strength," *Hourglass* 2, no. 30 (August 30, 1945): 1–2, Fred C. Wallace Papers, Box 1, Folder 8, US Army Heritage Center, Carlisle Barracks, PA; Baumgartner Collection, Veterans History Project; SGT Oliphant, H.N., "The answer to the biggest question"; Rex H. Conley Collection, Veterans History Project, Jackson County Historical Society.

22. Postwar missions of Pacific Naval Bases, Group IV, Ryukus Area, RG 38, Box 170, NARA; Demobilization planning, July 28, 1945, United States Fleet Headquarters, Commander in Chief, 1; SGT Oliphant, H.N., "The answer to the biggest question"; Report of Military Government Activities, July 1, 1946, US Naval Military Government, 65.

23. A freeze order was put in place for military government personnel that prevented them from leaving the service and returning home. The order, however, was quickly rescinded and had little impact on the exodus of trained military government soldiers and sailors. Report of Military Government Activities, July 1, 1946, US Naval Military Government, 65; SGT Oliphant, H.N., "The answer to the biggest question."

24. Temporary duty, case of Lieutenant Colonel Donald T. Winder, July 13, 1945, Floor 3, Module 5, Row 44, NPRC; Legal Qualifications, First Endorsement

on LtCol. Donald T. Winder, December 11, 1950, Floor 3, Module 5, Row 44; Fisch, *Military Government in the Ryukyu Islands*, 69; Report of Military Government Activities, July 1, 1946, US Naval Military Government, 73; Major Hector Charles Prud'homme Jr., Record (Personnel Files), January 1946, 000019042, NPRC, 3; Organization of Division Civil Affairs Section and Provision of Civil Affairs Handbook of Reference and Indoctrination Material, Headquarters, Fleet Marine Force, July 17, 1945, RG 127, Box 13.

25. Memorandum Number 7, Dispatch, US Naval Military Government Unit, Okinawa, September 29, 1945, RG 200, Reel 8, Folder 2-VIII-2, NARA; Special Proclamation Number 2, September 25, 1945, United States Naval Military Government; Directive Number 129: Organization and Operating Procedure for Military Government, Ryukyus, United States Naval Military Government Headquarters, March 18, 1946, RG 200, Reel 8, Folder 2-VIII-2, NARA; Memorandum Number 27, June 29, 1945, Military Government Headquarters, 2; Memoir, Okinawa 1945–46, LCDR Caldwell, 3; Directive Number 11: Organization and Operating Procedure for Military Government, Okinawa, United States Naval Military Government Headquarters, September 29, 1945, RG 407, File 224-12, NARA; NOB Order No. 18-45: Military Personnel and Civilians—Unauthorized Circulation of, Office of the Commandant, Naval Operating Base, November 5, 1945, RG 407, File 224-12, NARA; Report of Military Government Activities, July 1, 1946, US Naval Military Government, 56, 64; CINCPAC/POA, Dispatch 212057 to MGHQ Okinawa and NOB, September 21, 1945, RG 200, Box 1, Folder 2-VIII-2, Reel 8, NARA. Because of the large expanse of Japan's empire, the Army's occupation duties stretched across numerous countries and islands. To fulfill the geographic requirements, the Army redistributed their civil affairs soldiers to Korea and the home islands of Japan. Appendix D, August 1945, CINCAFPAC 230455; Appendix B, v73, July 18, 1945; Memorandum for Admiral Nimitz, August 13, 1945; Fisch, *Military Government in the Ryukyu Islands*, 73–74; US Naval Summary of Directives, January 15, 1946; Memorandum for Rear Admiral McCrea, August 9, 1945.

26. Report of Military Government Activities, July 1, 1946, US Naval Military Government, 65; SGT Oliphant, H.N., "The answer to the biggest question"; Memoir, Okinawa 1945–46, LCDR Caldwell, 12.

27. Dorfman Collection, Part II, Veteran's History Project; Memoir, Okinawa 1945–46, LCDR Caldwell, 9–10, 12–13; Report of Military Government Activities, July 1, 1946, US Naval Military Government, 73.

28. Naval military government operations were run primarily by military government officers trained at the Civil Affairs schools. These men contributed as planners. Col. Murray found that he lacked lower-skilled ensigns to carry out daily duties. Memoir, Okinawa 1945–46, LCDR Caldwell, 9, 16.

29. Fisch, *Military Government in the Ryukyu Islands*, 73; The United States Navy on Okinawa, CDR Paul Skuse, December 31, 1959, Paul Skuse Papers, Hoover Institute; Directive Number 11, September 29, 1945, United States Naval Military

Government Headquarters, 1; Directive Number 7: Diversion of Native Resources to Non-Essential Purposes, United States Military Government Headquarters, September 26, 1945, RG 407, File 224-12, NARA; Administrative and Economic Measures for Okinawa, September 19, 1945, ASCOM, 2; History of Operations on Okinawa by 2LT P. J. Conti, historical officer, OBASCOM, November, 1945, RG 407, Entry 427, NARA, 8; Memoir, Okinawa 1945–46, LCDR Caldwell, 9, 16; Memorandum, Navy Subsidiary Demobilization Plan—Naval Governments, September 5, 1945, RG 38, Box 1, NARA; Report of Military Government Activities, July 1, 1946, US Naval Military Government, 65; Rex H. Conley Collection, Veterans History Project, Jackson County Historical Society.

30. History of Operations on Okinawa, November, 1945, 2LT P. J. Conti; History of Operations on Okinawa by 2LT P. J. Conti, historical officer, OBASCOM, January, 1946, RG 407, Entry 427, NARA; History of Operations on Okinawa by 2LT P. J. Conti, historical officer, OBASCOM, February, 1946, RG 407, Entry 427, NARA; Postwar missions of Pacific Naval Bases, Group IV, Ryukus Area; Permanent Bases in the Pacific, March 31, 1946, RG 38, Box 170; Directive Number 11, September 29, 1945, United States Naval Military Government Headquarters, 2.

31. Directive Number 11, September 29, 1945, United States Naval Military Government Headquarters, 2.

32. The other departments were Public Health, Public Works, and Supply. Directive Number 11, September 29, 1945, United States Naval Military Government Headquarters, 3–5. Report of Military Government Activities, July 1, 1946, US Naval Military Government, 59; Memoir, Okinawa 1945–46, LCDR Caldwell, 6; Directive Number 12: Military Government Districts— Establishments of, United States Military Government Headquarters, October 2, 1945, RG 407, File 224-12, NARA.

33. Directive Number 9, September 28, 1945, United States Military Government Headquarters; Directive Number 33, November 15, 1945, United States Naval Military Government Headquarters; Limits of Cognizance, January 15, 1946, United States Naval Military Government; Sarantakes, ed., *Seven Stars*, 89; Memorandum Number 27, June 29, 1945, Military Government Headquarters, 2; Special Proclamation No. 3, November 29, 1945, United States Naval Military Government; Special Proclamation No. 4, November 29, 1945, United States Naval Military Government; History of Operations on Okinawa, November, 1945, 2LT P. J. Conti, 8; Directive Number 47: Weapons and Ammunition, United States Naval Military Government Headquarters, November 15, 1945, RG 407, File 224-12, NARA; Report of Military Government Activities, July 1, 1946, US Naval Military Government, 56; History of Operations on Okinawa by 2LT Johnson, historical officer, OBASCOM, June, 1946, RG 407, Entry 427, NARA; Historical report, OBASCOM, July 1946, RG 407, Box 2, File 98-BC6-0.2, NARA, 2; Speech, November 21, 1947, Paul Skuse; Occupation timeline, June 8, 1979, Ed Freimuth.

34. Directive Number 11, September 29, 1945, United States Naval Military

Government Headquarters, 1; Directive Number 7: Diversion of Native Resources to Non-Essential Purposes, United States Military Government Headquarters, September 26, 1945, RG 407, File 224-12, NARA; Administrative and Economic Measures for Okinawa, September 19, 1945, ASCOM, 2.

35. Navy Military Government defined the time as a "new and fluid period of resettlement" with a proposed completion date of January 1, 1946. Directive Number 11, September 29, 1945, United States Naval Military Government Headquarters, 1, 4–5; Sarantakes, ed., *Seven Stars*, 31–32; Memoir, Okinawa 1945–46, LCDR Caldwell, 6; Report of Military Government Activities, July 1, 1946, US Naval Military Government, 2; Directive Number 29, October 23, 1945, United States Naval Military Government Headquarters, 1; Directive 28: Reuniting Families—Procedures for, United States Military Government Headquarters, October 20, 1945, RG 407, File 224-12, NARA; Directive 58: Township (Mura) Administration—Organization of, United States Naval Military Government Headquarters, December 4, 1945, RG 407, File 224-12, NARA, 1.

36. Directive Number 11, September 29, 1945, United States Naval Military Government Headquarters, 1.

37. Directive Number 11, September 29, 1945, United States Naval Military Government Headquarters, 1.

38. Memoir, Okinawa 1945–46, LCDR Caldwell, 6, 9. Emphasis in the original.

39. The headquarters required a mandatory weekly report, the FORM MG IND-1, every Monday morning. Report of Military Government Activities, July 1, 1946, US Naval Military Government, 74–75; Directive Number 5: Industrial Production Report—Submission of, United States Naval Military Government Headquarters, September 23, 1945, RG 407, File 224-12, NARA.

40. Memorandum, Post-War Plan for Civil Administration under Jurisdiction of the Navy, September 17, 1945, RG 38, Box 1, NARA; Fisch, *Military Government in the Ryukyu Islands*, 74–77.

41. Memorandum, Post-War Plan for Civil Administration under Jurisdiction of the Navy, September 17, 1945, 2.

42. Memorandum, Post-War Civil Government: Comments by CINCPAC, October 4, 1945, RG 38, Box 1, NARA, 2.

43. Memorandum, Post-War Civil Government: Comments by CINCPAC, October 4, 1945, RG 38, Box 1, NARA, 1–2.

44. Memorandum, Post-War Civil Government: Comments by CINCPAC, October 4, 1945, RG 38, Box 1, NARA, 1–2.

45. Although he was not particularly religious, Nimitz's daughter Mary became a Dominican nun. Brayton Harris, *Admiral Nimitz: The Commander of the Pacific Ocean Theater* (New York: St. Martin's, 2012), 219.

46. Memorandum, Post-War Civil Government: Comments by CINCPAC, October 4, 1945, 2.

47. Report of Military Government Activities, July 1, 1946, US Naval Military Government, 65; Memoir, Okinawa 1945–46, LCDR Caldwell, 9; Administrative

and Economic Measures for Okinawa, September 19, 1945, ASCOM; Fisch, *Military Government in the Ryukyu Islands*, 78; Sarantakes, *Keystone*, 33; Rex H. Conley Collection, Veterans History Project, Jackson County Historical Society.

48. Administrative and Economic Measures for Okinawa, September 19, 1945, ASCOM, 3; Island Command military government newsletter, Lieutenant Commander Watkins, May 9, 1945, Ryukyus Papers; Okinawan History: Tenth Army Phase, Box 3, Folder 5, US Heritage and Education Center, Carlisle, PA, 1; Technical Bulletin, Military Government, February 25, 1945, 48–49; Diary, May 1–31, 1945, Detachment B-5, 41; Interview Sheet for Prospective Local Leaders, Appendix to Military Government Operations Report—Ryukyus, August 2, 1945, RG 407, Box 2487, File 110-5, NARA; Comments on Military Government Operation, OKINAWA, 1st Marine Division, 1 April to 26 June, 1945, July 6, 1945, RG 389, Box 704, NARA, 9; Laura Homan Lacey, *Stay Off the Skyline: The Sixth Marine Division on Okinawa* (Washington, DC: Potomac, 2005), 68; Comments on Military Government Operation, OKINAWA, 6th Marine Division Sector, 1 April to 29 June, 1945, July 6, 1945, RG 389, Box 704, NARA, 2, 5; XXIV Corps Military Government Daily Operations Log, RG 407, File 224-12, NARA.

49. Memoir, Okinawa 1945–46, LCDR Caldwell, 3, 5; Fisch, *Military Government in the Ryukyus*, 105; Report of Military Government Activities, July 1, 1946, US Naval Military Government, 62; Administrative and Economic Measures for Okinawa, September 19, 1945, ASCOM, 3.

50. The Government Program for Okinawa, Colonel Charles I. Murray, January 15, 1946, RG 200, Reel 5, Folder 3-V-7, NARA, 2; Fisch, *Military Government in the Ryukyu Islands*, 105.

51. Naval military government officers like Caldwell witnessed the Okinawans' leadership and organizational skills. Later, Caldwell would use such demonstrations of ability to convince higher-level leaders to give more responsibility to the Okinawans. Memoir, Okinawa 1945–46, LCDR Caldwell, 7; A Political and Economic Plan for the Rehabilitation of Okinawa, Lieutenant John T. Caldwell, September 12, 1945, RG 200, Reel 8, Folder 2-VIII-2, NARA.

52. Memoir, Okinawa 1945–46, LCDR Caldwell, 3, 5; Fisch, *Military Government in the Ryukyus*, 105; Report of Military Government Activities, July 1, 1946, US Naval Military Government, 62; Administrative and Economic Measures for Okinawa, September 19, 1945, ASCOM, 3.

53. Administrative and Economic Measures for Okinawa, September 19, 1945, ASCOM, 2.

54. Directive Number 7, September 23, 1945, United States Military Government Headquarters; Directive 5, September 23, 1945, United States Naval Military Government Headquarters.

55. Directive Number 6: Former Residence of Civilians, United States Naval Military Government Headquarters, September 27, 1945, RG 407, File 224-12, NARA; Report of Military Government Activities, July 1, 1946, US Naval Military Government, 6–7, 44, 65; Memoir, Okinawa 1945–46, LCDR Caldwell,

9; Administrative and Economic Measures for Okinawa, September 19, 1945, ASCOM; Fisch, *Military Government in the Ryukyu Islands*, 78; Directive Number 129, March 18, 1946, United States Naval Military Government Headquarters; History of Operations on Okinawa, November, 1945, 2LT P. J. Conti, 5; Dorfman Collection, Part II, Veterans History Project.

56. Directive Number 29, October 23, 1945, United States Naval Military Government Headquarters, 1; Report of Military Government Activities, July 1, 1946, US Naval Military Government, 8.

57. Directive Number 9, September 28, 1945, United States Military Government Headquarters; Directive Number 6, September 27, 1945, United States Naval Military Government Headquarters; Directive Number 19, October 3, 1945, United States Naval Military Government Headquarters; Report of Military Government Activities, July 1, 1946, US Naval Military Government, 11.

58. Memoir, Okinawa 1945–46, LCDR Caldwell, 7; A Political and Economic Plan for the Rehabilitation of Okinawa, Lieutenant John T. Caldwell, September 12, 1945, RG 200, Reel 8, Folder 2-VIII-2, NARA.

59. Okinawa, despite American occupation, remained a part of Japan as a prefecture. Fisch, *Military Government in the Ryukyu Islands*, 89–120.

60. Memoir, Okinawa 1945–46, LCDR Caldwell, 7; A Political and Economic Plan for the Rehabilitation of Okinawa, September 12, 1945, Lieutenant Caldwell.

61. Memoir, Okinawa 1945–46, LCDR Caldwell, 7; A Political and Economic Plan for the Rehabilitation of Okinawa, September 12, 1945, Lieutenant Caldwell; Directive Number 11, September 29, 1945, United States Naval Military Government Headquarters.

62. Memoir, Okinawa 1945–46, LCDR Caldwell, 7.

63. Memoir, Okinawa 1945–46, LCDR Caldwell, 7; A Political and Economic Plan for the Rehabilitation of Okinawa, September 12, 1946, Lieutenant Caldwell.

64. Caldwell was not the only military government officer to submit a proposal for the operation of military government. Navy Lieutenant Fred Bartlett, a government officer, submitted a proposal to Government Officer Commander Murdock. It argued for the reestablishment of the prefecture but not for high levels of Okinawan responsibility. Bartlett's plan was better received by Murdock partly because the plan originated from Murdock's office. Memoir, Okinawa 1945–46, LCDR Caldwell, 8–9, 16; Fisch, *Military Government in the Ryukyu Islands*, 105; Directive Number 18: Memoranda on the Mission and Procedure of Military Government, Okinawa, United States Naval Military Government Headquarters, October 11, 1945, RG 407, File 224-12, NARA; Directive Number 11, September 29, 1945, United States Naval Military Government Headquarters.

65. Military Government Mission on Okinawa and Recommended Measures, October 18, 1945, Lieutenant Caldwell, 2–3.

10. New Visions, New Interpretations of Identity:
The Expansion of US Navy Military Government

1. Report of Government Section for April 1946, May 4, 1946, RG 200, Folder 3-V-7, Reel 5, NARA; Lieutenant Commander John T. Caldwell, Okinawa, 1945–46, 93085, 10.V, Hoover Institute Archives, 13–14; Arnold Fisch, *Military Government in the Ryukyu Islands, 1945–1950* (Washington, DC: Center of Military History, United States Army, 1988), 109; Edward G. Sward, Diary, April, 1946, personal collection; Report of Military Government Activities for Period from 1 April 1945 to 1 July 1946, July 1, 1946, RG 200, Reel 2, Folder V1-3, NARA, 63–64.

2. Directive Number 7, September 23, 1945, United States Military Government Headquarters; Dorfman Collection, Part II, Veterans History Project.

3. Dorfman Collection, Part III, Veterans History Project; Report of Military Government Activities, July 1, 1946, US Naval Military Government, 66, 71–73.

4. Directive Number 33: Okinawan POWs—Reception and Processing of, United States Naval Military Government Headquarters, November 15, 1945, RG 407, File 224-12, NARA; Limits of Cognizance and Relations with Army Commands, United States Naval Military Government, January 15, 1946, RG 200, Box 1, Folder 2-VII-2, Reel 3, NARA; Nicolas Evan Sarantakes, ed., *Seven Stars: The Okinawa Battle Diaries of Simon Bolivar Buckner Jr. and Joseph Stilwell* (College Station: Texas A&M University Press, 2004), 89; Memorandum Number 27, June 29, 1945, Military Government Headquarters, 2; Special Proclamation No. 3, November 29, 1945, RG 407, File 224-12, NARA; Special Proclamation No. 4, November 29, 1945, RG 407, File 224-12, NARA; History of Operations on Okinawa, November, 1945, 2LT P. J. Conti, 8; Directive Number 47: Weapons and Ammunition, United States Naval Military Government Headquarters, November 15, 1945, RG 407, File 224-12, NARA. OBASCOM was formerly known as ASCOM. Report of Military Government Activities, July 1, 1946, US Naval Military Government, 56; Occupation timeline, Ed Freimuth, June 8, 1979, Paul Skuse Papers, Hoover Institution.

5. Directive Number 29: Resettlement Plan and Policy, United States Naval Military Government Headquarters, October 23, 1945, RG 407, File 224-12, NARA, 3; Dorfman Collection, Part III, Veterans History Project.

6. Sarantakes, ed., *Seven Stars*, 116, 124; Fisch, *Military Government in the Ryukyu Islands*, 88; Report of Military Government Activities, July 1, 1946, US Naval Military Government, 56; Diary, April, 1946, Sward; Rex H. Conley Collection, Veterans History Project, Jackson County Historical Society.

7. Directive Number 19: Control of Civilian Movements, United States Naval Military Government Headquarters, October 23, 1945, RG 407, File 224-12, NARA; Fisch, *Military Government in the Ryukyu Islands*, 87–88. Military government food arrived by ship. Typhoon damage to ports delayed food distribution. Directive Number 9: Civilian Rations Issue, Reduction of, United States Naval Military Government Headquarters, September 28, 1945, RG 407, File 224-12,

NARA; Report of Military Government Activities, July 1, 1946, US Naval Military Government, 45; Dorfman Collection, Part II, Veterans History Project.

8. Directive Number 27: Available items for use of civilians, United States Naval Military Government Headquarters, October 18, 1945, RG 407, File 224-12, NARA; Dorfman Collection, Part II, Veterans History Project; Diary, April, 1946, Sward; Rex H. Conley Collection, Veterans History Project, Jackson County Historical Society. Calorie counts were reduced from 1,990 calories per day to 1,530 calories per day in August 1945. This was later reduced by half in late September 1945. Military government units were highly encouraged to salvage for food to make up for the lost calories. Report of Military Government Activities, July 1, 1946, US Naval Military Government, 45; Directive Number 9: Civilian Rations Issue, Reduction of, United States Naval Military Government Headquarters, September 28, 1945, RG 407, File 224-12, NARA.

9. Directive Number 29, October 23, 1945, United States Naval Military Government Headquarters, 3; Report of Military Government Activities, July 1, 1946, US Naval Military Government, 45; Dorfman Collection, Part II, Veterans History Project.

10. Dorfman Collection, Part II, Veterans History Project.

11. Directive Number 9, September 28, 1945, United States Naval Military Government Headquarters; Report of Military Government Activities, July 1, 1946, US Naval Military Government, 45.

12. Directive Number 19, October 23, 1945, United States Naval Military Government Headquarters; NOB Order No. 18-45, November 5, 1945, Office of the Commandant, Naval Operating Base; Memorandum Number 50: Off-Limits Areas, Okinawa Base Command, November 20, 1945 RG 407, File 224-12, NARA; Report of Military Government Activities, July 1, 1946, US Naval Military Government, 6–7, 72; Directive Number 13: Area Assignment; United States Naval Military Government Headquarters, October 2, 1945, RG 407, File 224-12, NARA; Directive Number 12, October 2, 1945, United States Military Government Headquarters.

13. Directive Number 19, October 23, 1945, United States Naval Military Government Headquarters; NOB Order No. 18-45, November 5, 1945, Office of the Commandant, Naval Operating Base; Memorandum Number 50, November 20, 1945, Okinawa Base Command; Report of Military Government Activities, July 1, 1946, US Naval Military Government, 72.

14. Directive Number 33, November 15, 1945, United States Military Government Headquarters.

15. Dorfman Collection, Part III, Veterans History Project; Diary, April, 1946, Sward.

16. Rex H. Conley Collection, Veterans History Project, Jackson County Historical Society.

17. Directive Number 9, September 28, 1945, United States Military Government Headquarters; Directive Number 33, November 15, 1945, United

States Naval Military Government Headquarters; Limits of Cognizance, January 15, 1946, United States Naval Military Government; Sarantakes, ed., *Seven Stars*, 89; Memorandum Number 27, June 29, 1945, Military Government Headquarters, 2; Special Proclamation No. 3, November 29, 1945, United States Naval Military Government; Special Proclamation No.4, November 29, 1945, United States Naval Military Government; History of Operations on Okinawa, November, 1945, 2LT P. J. Conti, 8; Directive Number 47: Weapons and Ammunition, United States Naval Military Government Headquarters, November 15, 1945, RG 407, File 224-12, NARA; Report of Military Government Activities, July 1, 1946, US Naval Military Government, 56; History of Operations on Okinawa by 2LT Johnson, Historical officer, OBASCOM, June, 1946, RG 407, Entry 427, NARA; Historical report, OBASCOM, July 1946, RG 407, Box 2, File 98-BC6-0.2, NARA, 2; Speech, November 21, 1947, Paul Skuse; Occupation timeline, June 8, 1979, Ed Freimuth; Rex H. Conley Collection, Veterans History Project, Jackson County Historical Society.

18. Samuel Eliot Morison, *History of United States Naval Operations in World War II: Victory in the Pacific, 1945* (New Jersey: Castle, 1960), 103; *United States Naval Administration in World War II*, vol. 149 (Washington, DC: Director of Naval History).

19. US Naval Military Government, Pacific Ocean Areas, Serial 52855, Admiral Raymond A. Spruance, CINCPAC, December 12, 1945, RG 407, File 224-12, NARA, 1; Sarantakes, ed., *Seven Stars*, 33; Fisch, *Military Government in the Ryukyu Islands*, 121–22; Memoir, Okinawa 1945–46, LCDR Caldwell, 9–13.

20. US Naval Military Government, Pacific Ocean Areas, Serial 52855, Admiral Raymond A. Spruance, CINCPAC, December 12, 1945, RG 407, File 224-12, NARA, 1; Fisch, *Military Government in the Ryukyu Islands*, 121–22; Memoir, Okinawa 1945–46, LCDR Caldwell, 9–13.

21. Serial 52855, December 12, 1945, CINCPAC, Admiral Raymond A. Spruance, 3–4; Report of Military Government Activities, July 1, 1946, US Naval Military Government, 62; LCDR James Watkins, Later Phases: Public Safety, RG 200, Reel 8, Folder 3-V-7, NARA, 13–14.

22. Serial 52855, December 12, 1945, CINCPAC, Admiral Raymond A. Spruance, 3–5; CINCPAC/POA Pearl, Dispatch 10196/NCR 2698 to NOB, April 12, 1946, RG 38, Box 170, NARA.

23. Memoir, Okinawa 1945–46, LCDR Caldwell, 9–13; Memorandum Number 154: US Naval Military Government, Pacific Ocean Areas, Deputy Commander for Military Government, December 12, 1945, RG 200, Box 1, Folder 2-VII-2, Reel 3, NARA.

24. Memoir, Okinawa 1945–46, LCDR Caldwell, 8.

25. By May 31, 1946, 138,000 Okinawans had arrived at close approximations of their home villages. Directive Number 58: Township (Mura) Administration—Organization of, United States Naval Military Government Headquarters, December 4, 1945, RG 407, File 224-12, NARA; Directive Number

84: Administrative Reorganization for Military Government, United States Naval Military Government, January 2, 1946, RG 407, File 224-12, NARA; Occupation timeline, June 8, 1979, Ed Freimuth, 4; Directive Number 129, March 18, 1946, United States Naval Military Government Headquarters, 9; Directive Number 96: Mura Administration—Control of, United States Naval Military Government Headquarters, January 12, 1946, RG 407, File 224-12, NARA; Memorandum Number 27, June 29, 1945, Military Government Headquarters, 2; Directive Number 24: Revision of Districts and District Boundaries United States Naval Military Government, October 21, 1945, RG 407, File 224-12, NARA; Report of Military Government Activities, July 1, 1946, US Naval Military Government, 8, 62; Memoir, Okinawa 1945–46, LCDR Caldwell, 13.

26. Military Government Directive 156, April 22, 1946 RG 407, File 227-12, NARA Report of Government Section for April 1946, May 4, 1946, US Naval Military Government, 1–2; Report of Military Government Activities, July 1, 1946, US Naval Military Government, 63–64; Memoir, Okinawa 1945–46, LCDR Caldwell, 11–14; Memorandum Number 27, June 29, 1945, Military Government Headquarters; Military Government Directive Number 2, April 30, 1946, RG 407, File 224-12, NARA; Directive Number 96, January 12, 1946, United States Naval Military Government Headquarters; Military Government Directive Number 5, May 4, 1946 RG 407, File 224-12, NARA; Fisch, *Military Government in the Ryukyu Islands*, 85, 109–10; Military Government Directive Number 3, May 3, 1946, RG 407, File 224-12, NARA.

27. Memoir, Okinawa 1945–46, LCDR Caldwell, 11–14; Diary, April, 1946, Sward; Report of Government Section for April 1946, May 4, 1946, US Naval Military Government, 1–2; Directive Number 58, December 4, 1945, United States Naval Military Government Headquarters; Directive Number 84, January 2, 1946, United States Naval Military Government; Report of Military Government Activities, July 1, 1946, US Naval Military Government, 63–64; Speech, November 21, 1947, Paul Skuse; Nicolas Evan Sarantakes, *Keystone: The American Occupation of Okinawa and U.S. Japanese Relations* (College Station: Texas A&M University Press, 2000), 34, 36; Military Government Directive Number 20, June 25, 1946, RG 407, File 224-12, NARA; Military Government Directive Number 11, May 22, 1946, RG 407, File 224-12, NARA; Memorandum Number 27, June 29, 1945, Military Government Headquarters, 5–6; Directive Number 129, March 18, 1946, United States Naval Military Government Headquarters, 6, 11; Speech by Koshin Shikiya, July 1, 1946, RG 200, Box 1, Folder 2-VIII-2, Reel 8, NARA; Koshin Shikiya letter to Paul Skuse, May 3, 1948, Paul Skuse Papers, Hoover Institute.

28. The Civilian Affairs Department was abolished and replaced with the General Affairs Department. Legal, Labor, Public Health, and Agricultural/Industry departments were also added. The new structure was complete by April 1946. Memoir, Okinawa 1945–46, LCDR Caldwell, 11, 13; Directive Number 95: Civilian Affairs Staff Functions—Reorganization of, United States Naval Military Government Headquarters, January 12, 1946, RG 407, File 224-12, NARA;

US Naval Military Government Administration in the Ryukyu Islands, Serial 0048, Admiral J. H. Towers, February 8, 1946, RG 38, Box 157, NARA; Report of Military Government Activities, July 1, 1946, US Naval Military Government, 11, 63; Directive Number 58, December 4, 1945, United States Naval Military Government Headquarters; Directive Number 84, January 2, 1946, United States Naval Military Government.

29. The Government Program for Okinawa, United States Naval Military Government, January 15, 1946, RG 200, Folder 3-V-7, Reel 5; The Mission of US Naval Military Government, Okinawa, United States Naval Military Government, January 15, 1946, RG 200, Box 1, Folder 2-VII-2, Reel 3; Directive Number 129, March 18, 1946, United States Naval Military Government Headquarters, 6–8; Directive Number 84, January 2, 1946, United States Naval Military Government; Serial 0048, February 8, 1946, Admiral J. H. Towers, 2–3; CINCPAC, Dispatch 110206/NCR 2590 to NOB, April 11, 1946, RG 38, Box 157, NARA.

30. Report of Military Government Activities, July 1, 1946, US Naval Military Government, 4, 8, 13, 49–50; Memoir, Okinawa 1945–46, LCDR Caldwell, 15–16; Later Phases: Public Safety, LCDR Watkins, 13–14; Fisch, *Military Government in the Ryukyu Islands*, 100; Directive Number 129, March 18, 1946, United States Naval Military Government Headquarters, 6–8; Military Government Headquarters Memorandum No. 23, June 22, 1946, RG 407, File 224-12, NARA.

31. Dorfman Collection, Part III, Veterans History Project; Directive 70: Officer-of-the-Day and Guard, United States Naval Military Government Headquarters, December 13, 1945, RG 407, File 224-12, NARA.

32. Dorfman Collection, Part III, Veterans History Project; Report of Military Government Activities, July 1, 1946, US Naval Military Government, 47, 73; History of Operations on Okinawa, March, 1946, 2LT P. J. Conti, 3, 6–7; Directive 70, December 13, 1945, United States Naval Military Government Headquarters, 2.

33. Dorfman Collection, Part III, Veterans History Project.

34. Directive Number 129, March 18, 1946, United States Naval Military Government Headquarters, 7–8; Report of Military Government Activities, July 1, 1946, US Naval Military Government, 4–5, 16–15, 75–76. The repatriated Okinawans were mostly conscripts and those transferred to the home islands because the Japanese government assessed them to have only a marginal ability to contribute to the war effort. CINCAFPAC, Dispatch 221255/NCR 4424 to CINCPAC, April 24, 1946, RG 38, Box 157, NARA; CINCPAC/CINCPOA Pearl, Dispatch 040316/NCR 8081 to NOB Okinawa, January 4, 1946, RG 38, Box 157, NARA; Fisch, *Military Government in the Ryukyu Islands*, 91.

35. Report of Military Government Activities, July 1, 1946, US Naval Military Government, 5; LCDR James Watkins Papers, RG 200, NARA; Rex H. Conley Collection, Veterans History Project, Jackson County Historical Society.

36. Directive Number 129, March 18, 1946, United States Naval Military Government Headquarters, 8, 11; Report of Military Government Activities, July 1, 1946, US Naval Military Government, 66, 71–73.

37. Directive Number 129, March 18, 1946, United States Naval Military Government Headquarters, 8,11; Report of Military Government Activities, July 1, 1946, US Naval Military Government, 66, 70–73; Memorandum Number 6: Transportation of Civilians, Army Service Command I, August 22, 1945, RG 407, File 224-12, NARA; Paul Skuse letter to Ed Freimuth, June 15, 1979, Paul Skuse Papers, Hoover Institute, 2; Paul Skuse, Memorandum, Domiciliary Search of Homes in Iribaru-ku, Yonagusuku-ku, Yongagusuku-son by MPs, March 23, 1949, Paul Skuse Papers, Hoover Institute.

38. Directive Number 129, March 18, 1946, United States Naval Military Government Headquarters, 8,11; Report of Military Government Activities, July 1, 1946, US Naval Military Government, 66, 70–73; Paul Skuse letter to Ed Freimuth, June 15, 1979, Paul Skuse Papers, Hoover Institute, 2.

39. Report of Military Government Activities, July 1, 1946, US Naval Military Government, 66, 70–73; Fisch, *Military Government in the Ryukyu Islands*, 85; MSgt Daniel Wheaton message to Public Affairs, April 27, Kadena Air Base History, KAB Active 7(7-2-C), Archives K–L, Kadena Air Base Archives; Calvin Sims, "3 Dead Marines and a Secret of Wartime Okinawa," *New York Times International*, June 1, 2000.

40. Memorandum Number 27, June 29, 1945, Military Government Headquarters; Memorandum Number 5, May 4, 1946, 2–3; Legal Administrative Order #2, April 15, 1946, Military Government Headquarters, RG 407, File 224-12, NARA; Directive Number 95, January 12, 1946, United States Naval Military Government Headquarters; Paul Skuse letter to Ed Freimuth, June 15, 1979, Paul Skuse Papers, Hoover Institute; Funakoshi Police Report No. 23: Death of a Policeman in the Line of Duty—Report of, Chinen Police Headquarters, November 1945, Paul Skuse Papers, Hoover Institute; Report of Military Government Activities, July 1, 1946, US Naval Military Government, 11, 71,73; Directive Number 129, March 18, 1946, United States Naval Military Government Headquarters, 7–9; Limits of Cognizance, January 15, 1946, United States Naval Military Government; Speech, November 21, 1947, Paul Skuse, 5; List of Police Stations and Number of Police Officers Assigned to Each Station on Okinawa, June 3, 1946, Paul Skuse Papers, Hoover Institute, 1.

41. Photo collection, 1946, Fred C. Wallace Papers, Box 1, Folder 7, US Army Heritage and Education Center, Carlisle, PA; Fisch, *Military Government in the Ryukyu Islands*, 138–39.

42. Speech, July 1, 1946, Koshin Shikiya; Historical report, July 1946, OBASCOM, 1; Serial 0048, February 8, 1946, Admiral J. H. Towers; History of Operations on Okinawa, June 1946, 2LT Johnson; Memorandum Number 27, June 29, 1945, Military Government Headquarters, 1; NOB Okinawa, Dispatch 010125Z/NCR 3217 to CINCPAC, July 2, 1946, RG 38, Box 157, NARA; CINCPFPAC, Dispatch 221255/NCR 4424 to CINCPAC, April 24, 1946, RG 38, Box 157, NARA; Memorandum to OBASCOM, June 1946, Deputy Commander for Military Government.

Conclusion

1. Carl von Clausewitz, *On War* (New York: Penguin, 1968), 109–10.

2. Eric Foner, *Reconstruction: America's Unfinished Revolution, 1863–1877* (New York: Harper and Row, 1988), 225.

3. Mary A. Renda, *Taking Haiti: Military Occupation and the Culture of U.S. Imperialism, 1915–1940* (Chapel Hill: University of North Carolina Press, 2001), 11, 15, 33–34.

4. Renda, *Taking Haiti*, 33–34.

5. Sheridan removed multiple governors and the New Orleans Board of Aldermen. Foner, *Reconstruction*, 307–8.

Bibliography

Primary

Unpublished

Battle of Okinawa Collection. Documentaries. Naha City Historical Association Archives. Naha, Okinawa.

Battle of Okinawa Collection. Early Occupation Papers. Documentaries. Naha City Historical Association Archives. Naha, Okinawa.

Columbia University Rare Books and Manuscript Library. New York, NY.
World War II Collection, 1933–1956.
Marine Corps Oral History Collection.

CPL Robert L. Hostetler, interview by author, KAB, Koza, Okinawa, Japan, December 27, 2007.

First Marine Division Papers. Camp Pendleton Archives. San Diego, CA.

General Douglas MacArthur Papers. MacArthur Memorial Library and Archives. Norfolk, VA.

General George C. Marshall Papers. George C. Marshall Foundation Archives, Library, and Museum. Lexington, VA.

General Joseph Stilwell Papers. United States Army Military History Institute. Carlisle Barracks, PA.

General Simon Bolivar Buckner Jr. Diary. Dwight D. Eisenhower Presidential Library. Abilene, KS.

General Simon Bolivar Buckner Jr. Papers. United States Army Military History Institute. Carlisle Barracks, PA.

Hostetler, Robert L., CPL, Papers. Private Collection.

Hostetler, Robert L., CPL, Photographs. Private Collection.

Japanese Collection. Manuscripts. Library of Congress. Washington, DC.

Japanese Naval Papers. Japanese Naval Underground Headquarters Archives. Tomishiro, Okinawa, Japan.

Japanese Occupation period. Microfiche. Modern Japanese Political Documents Division. National Diet Library. Tokyo, Japan.

John Caldwell Papers. Hoover Institute, Stanford University. Palo Alto, California.

Kadena Air Base Papers. Kadena Air Base Archives. Kadena, Okinawa, Japan.

Kowallis, Lieutenant Reinhart T. Photographs. Private Collection.

Marine Corps Oral History Collection. History and Museums Division, Headquarters, United States Marine Corps. Washington, DC.

Marine Corps Personnel Files. Archives. St. Louis, MO.

Montgomery, Gary, COL, Papers. Private Collection.

National Archives and Records Administration. College Park, MD.

Adjutant General Papers. Record Group 200. Microfilm WTKNS.

Civil Affairs Detachment Training Syllabuses. Record Group 496.

Civil Affairs Papers. Record Group 290.

Department of the Navy Papers, Record Group 80.

Naval Occupation Government Papers. Record Group 407.

Office of Naval Intelligence, Captured Japanese Documents. Record Group 38.

Provost Marshall Papers, Military Government Division. Record Group 389.

Records of the Office of the Chief of Naval Operations. Record Group 38.

Supreme Commander of the Allied Powers Papers. Record Group 331.

United States Civil Administration of the Ryukyu Islands. Record Group 260.

United States Marine Corps Papers, Record Group 127.

Watkins Papers. Record Group 407.

XXIV Corps Papers. Record Group 407.

Nisei Translators in the Occupation of Japan. Oral History Project, United States Army Center of Military History. Fort McNair, Washington, DC.

Occupation Collection. Folder 1950. Okinawa Prefecture Haebaru-Cho Archives. Okinawa, Japan.

Occupation Papers. 1950 Collection. Okinawa Prefectural Library. Naha, Okinawa.

Oral History Archive of World War II. Rutgers University. Newark, NJ.

Oral History Collection Manuscripts. Reading Room, Books 1 and 2, English. Okinawan Prefectural Peace Memorial Museum. Okinawa, Japan.

Paul Skuse Papers. Hoover Institute, Stanford University. Palo Alto, CA.

President Harry S. Truman Office Files, 1945–1960. Part 3: Subject File, Reel 32, Frame 0698. University of South Carolina, Columbia.

Rex Conley Interview. Veterans History Project, Jackson County Historical Society. Independence, MO.

Second Marine Division Papers. Camp LeJeune Archives. Jacksonville, NC.

Setsuko Inafuku, public presentation, KAB, Koza, Okinawa, Japan, July 16, 2007.

Spinks, James Rice. Papers. Institute on World War II and the Human Experience, Florida State University. Tallahassee, FL.

Sward, Anton. Diary. Worchester, MA. 1946.

United States Army Heritage and Education Center. Carlisle Barracks, PA.

Brigadier General Frederic Hayden Papers.

Carl B. Rauterburg Papers.

Major General Fred C. Wallace Papers.

Ryukyus Papers. Okinawa History: Tenth Army Phase.

United States Marine Corps Archives and Special Collections. Gray Research Center. Quantico, VA.
    Major General Roy S. Geiger Papers.
    Second Marine Division Papers.
    Sixth Marine Division Papers.
    World War II Marine Corps Papers.
United States Marine Corps Historical Division. Quantico, VA.
    Brigadier General Oliver P. Smith Papers.
    Okinawa Papers. World War II Collection.
Veterans Interviews. WWII. Marines. Army. Navy. Veterans History Project, Library of Congress, Washington, DC.
Wartime Translations of Seized Japanese Documents. ATIS Reports, 1942–1946. M-FICHE D767.2.W37. McKeldin Library, University of Maryland, College Park.
Watkins Collection. Local Materials Reading Room. Ryukyu University Library. Nishihara-Cho, Okinawa.
Western Historical Manuscript Collection. Collection Number: CO445, Folders 1–4. University of Missouri, Columbia.

Published

Air Corps Newsletter. 1944–1945. University of North Carolina–Chapel Hill.
"Armed Forces: The Sunday Punch." *Time*, November 24, 1952.
Bahr, Diana Meyers, ed. *The Unique Nisei: An Oral History of the Life of Sue Kunitomi Embrey.* New York: Palgrave MacMillan, 2007.
Berry, Henry. *Semper Fi, Mac: Living Memories of the U.S. Marines in World War II.* New York: Arbor House, 1982.
Boan, Jim. *Okinawa: A Memoir of the Sixth Marine Reconnaissance Company.* New York: ibooks, 2000.
Boardman, Eugene P., MAJ. "Surrender Propaganda." *Marine Corps Gazette*, January 1946, 44–46.
"Buck's Battle." *Time*, April 16, 1945.
Cohen, Theodore. *Remaking Japan: The American Occupation as New Deal.* New York: Free Press, 1987.
Cook, Haruko Taya, and Theodore F. Cook, eds. *Japan at War: An Oral History.* New York: New Press, 1992.
Donovan, J. A., MAJ. "The Occupation Marine." *Marine Corps Gazette*, April 1946, 19–21.
Dowling, Timothy C., ed. *Personal Perspectives: World War II.* Santa Barbara: ABC-CLIO, 2005.
Driver, Marjorie G., and Omaira Brunel-Perry. *Time of Agony: The War in the Pacific Saipan, the Personal Account of Sister Maria Angelica Salaberria.* Guam: University of Guam, 1994.

Ealey, Mark, and Alastair McLauchlan. *Descent into Hell: Civilian Memories of the Battle of Okinawa: Ryukyu Shimpo.* Translation. Portland: Merwin Asia, 2014.

Felsen, Henry G. "Yamachugi Welcomes the Troops." *Leatherneck*, March 1946, 24–25.

Fortune. April 1944.

Frank, Benis M., ed. *Marine Corps Oral History Collection Catalog.* Washington, DC: History and Museum Division, Headquarters, US Marine Corps, 1979.

Grantham, Homer H. *Thunder in the Morning: A World War II Memoir.* Fayetteville, IN: Phoenix International, 2003.

Green, Bob. *Okinawa Odyssey.* Albany, NY: Bright Sky, 2004.

Hatfield, Ken. *Heartland Heroes: Remembering World War II.* Columbia: University of Missouri, 2003.

Higa, Tomiko. *The Girl with the White Flag: A Spellbinding Account of Love and Courage in Wartime Okinawa. (Shirahata no shojo).* Tokyo: Kodansha International, 1989.

Hoyt, Edwin P. *Now Hear This: The Story of American Sailors in World War II.* New York: Paragon, 1993.

Huff, H. Stanley. *Unforgettable Journey: A World War II Memoir: A Teenage Soldier Writes Home Describing Training, Combat in Europe, and Occupation Duty in Japan.* Fort Wayne, IN: Bridgeford, 2001.

Isom, Wiley S. *Diary of a Wardog Platoon.* Tennessee: Bible and Literature Missionary Foundation, 1997.

Japan Times. 1944–1945. University of North Carolina–Chapel Hill.

Jenkins, William E. *Okinawa: Isle of Smiles. An Informal Photographic Study.* New York: Bookman Associates, 1951.

Johnston, James W. *The Long Road of War.* Lincoln: University of Nebraska Press, 1998.

Karasik, Daniel D. "Okinawa: A Problem in Administration and Reconstruction." *Far Eastern Quarterly* 7, no. 3 (1948): 254–67.

Keyso, Ruth Ann. *Women of Okinawa: Nine Voices from a Garrison Island.* Ithaca, NY: Cornell University Press, 2000.

Kluckhorn, Frank L. "Japan Occupation Problem to Allies: None of Our Troops Is Ashore on Foe's Mainland—Possibility of Treachery Also Studied." *New York Times*, August 15, 1945.

"Kyushu Diary." *Leatherneck* (February 1947): 34–39.

Lacey, Laura Homan. *Stay Off the Skyline: The Sixth Marine Division on Okinawa: An Oral History.* Washington, DC: Potomac, 2005.

Lattimore, E. "Pacific Ocean or American Lake?" *Far Eastern Survey* 14 (1945): 313–16.

Lince, George. *Too Young the Heroes: A World War II Marine's Account of Facing a Veteran Enemy at Guadalcanal, the Solomons, and Okinawa.* Jefferson, NC: McFarland, 1997.

Manchester, William. *Goodbye Darkness: A Memoir of the Pacific War*. Boston: Little, Brown, 1980.

Martin, Edwin M. *The Allied Occupation of Japan*. New York: Stanford University Press for the Institute of Pacific Relations, 1948.

Mason, John T. Jr., ed. *Pacific War Remembered: An Oral History Collection*. Annapolis, MD: Naval Institute Press, 1986.

Meehl, Gerald A., and Rex Alan Smith. *Pacific War Stories: In the Words of Those Who Survived*. New York: Abbeville, 2004.

"Mental Hazards to Peace with the Japanese." *Military Review* 4 (1946).

Morgan, Speer, and Greg Michalson, ed. *For Our Beloved Country: American War Diaries from the Revolution to the Persian Gulf*. Collingdale, PA: Diane, 1997.

Morison, Samuel Eliot. *Victory in the Pacific, 1945*. History of the United States Naval Operations 14. Boston: Little, Brown, 1964.

Nichols, David, ed. *Ernie's War: The Best of Ernie Pyle's World War II Dispatches*. New York: Random House, 1986.

"Occupation of Japan and Japanese Reaction." *Military Review* 6 (1946).

Ogawa, Dennis M., ed. *First among Nisei: The Life and Writings of Masaji Marumoto*. Honolulu: University of Hawai'i Press, 2007.

Osborn, Fairfield. *The Pacific World: Its Vast Distances, Its Lands and the Life upon Them, and Its People*. New York: Norton, 1944.

Polete, Harry. "Posts of the Corps: Yokosuka." *Leatherneck*, August 1947, 3–7.

Pyle, Ernie. *The Last Chapter*. New York: Holt, 1946.

Rath, Arthur J. *Soldiers Remember: World War II in the Pacific*. New York: Rath Organization, 1995.

Relief Section Welfare Department, Okinawa Prefecture. *An Oral History of the Battle of Okinawa: A Guide to Okinawa Prefectural Peace Memorial Museum*. Naha: Bunshin, 1985.

Sarantakes, Nicolas Evan, ed. *Seven Stars: The Okinawa Battle Diaries of Simon Bolivar Buckner Jr. and Joseph Stilwell*. College Station: Texas A&M University Press, 2004.

Sheeks, Robert B. "Civilians on Saipan." *Far Eastern Survey*, May 9, 1945, 109–13.

Sledge, E. B. *With the Old Breed at Peleliu and Okinawa*. Annapolis, MD: Naval Institute Press, 1996.

Sodei, Rinjiro. *Dear General MacArthur: Letters from the Japanese during the American Occupation*. Lanham, MD: Rowman and Littlefield, 2001.

Stars and Stripes. 1944–1945. University of North Carolina–Chapel Hill.

Takemoto, Paul Howard, ed. *Nisei Memories: My Parents Talk about the War Years*. Seattle: University of Washington Press, 2006.

Tatsuhiro, Oshiro, and Higashi Mineo. *Okinawa: Two Postwar Novellas*. Berkeley: Center for Japanese Studies, 1989.

Thacker, Joel D. "Year of Fulfillment." *Leatherneck*, November 1945, 15–19.

Triplet, William S. *In the Philippines and Okinawa: A Memoir, 1945–1948*. Columbia: University of Missouri Press, 2001.

Trussel, C. P. "Draft Opposition Rising in Congress." *New York Times,* August 14, 1945.

US Department of State, Office of Public Affairs. *In Quest of Peace and Security: Selected Documents on American Foreign Policy, 1941–1951.* Washington, DC: United States Government Printing Office, 1951.

US Government Printing Office. *Decade of American Foreign Policy 1941–49. Senate Document 123, 81st Congress, 1st Session.* Washington, DC: United States Government Printing Office, 1950.

Wallace, Robert F. *From Dam Neck to Okinawa: A Memoir of Anti-Aircraft Training in World War II.* Washington, DC: Naval Historical Center, Department of the Navy, 1999.

Watson, James. *My Brother's Letters.* Seattle: Twinview, 2013.

Weiss, Leonard. "U.S. Military Government on Okinawa." *Far Eastern Survey* 15 (1946): 234–38.

White, Theodore H., ed. *The Stilwell Papers.* Boston: Da Capo, 1975.

Wittles, David. *These Are the Generals.* New York: Knopf, 1943.

Yahara, Hiromachi, Colonel. *The Battle for Okinawa: A Japanese Officer's Eyewitness Account of the Last Great Campaign of World War II.* New York: John Wiley and Sons, 1995.

Secondary
Books

Alexander, Jeffrey C., Ron Eyerman, Bernard Giesen, Neil J. Smelser, and Piotr Sztompka, eds. *Cultural Trauma and Collective Identity.* Berkeley: University of California Press, 2004.

Alexander, Joseph H. *The Final Campaign: Marines in the Victory of Okinawa.* Washington, DC: History and Museums Division, Headquarters, United States Marine Corps, 1997.

Allen, Matthew. *Identity and Resistance in Okinawa.* Lanham, MD: Rowman and Littlefield, 2001.

Allison, Carolyn. *The Battle of Okinawa.* Washington, DC: Navy and Marine Corps WWII Commemorative Committee, Navy Office of Information, 1995.

Allport, Gordon. *ABC's of Scapegoating.* New York: Anti-Defamation League of B'nai B'rith, 1948.

———. *The Nature of Prejudice.* Massachusetts: Addison Wesley, 1979.

Alvah, Donna. *Unofficial Ambassadors: American Military Families Overseas and the Cold War, 1946–1965.* New York: New York University Press, 2007.

Anderson, Christopher J. *The Marines in World War II: From Pearl Harbor to Tokyo Bay.* London: Stackpole, 2006.

Appleman, Roy E., James M. Burns, Russell A. Gugeler, and John Stevens. *Okinawa: The Last Battle.* Washington, DC: Historical Division, Department of the Army, 1948.

Astor, Gerald. *Operation Iceberg: The Invasion and Conquest of Okinawa in World War II—An Oral History.* New York: Donald I. Fine, 1995.

Batchelor, John. *Ainu Life and Lore: Echoes of a Departing Race.* Tokyo: Kyobunkwan, 1927.

Bederman, Gail. *Manliness and Civilization: A Cultural History of Gender and Race in the United States, 1880–1917.* Chicago: University of Chicago Press, 1995.

Bennett, John W., and Iwao Ishino. *Paternalism in the Japanese Economy: Anthropological Studies of Oyabun-Kobun Patterns.* Minneapolis: University of Minnesota, 1963.

Bernstein, Gail Lee, ed. *Recreating Japanese Women, 1600–1945.* Berkeley: University of California Press, 1991.

Bethencourt, Francisco. *Racisms: From the Crusades to the Twentieth Century.* Princeton, NJ: Princeton University Press, 2013.

Bhowmik, Davinder L. *Writing Okinawa: Narrative Acts of Identity and Resistance.* London: Routledge, 2008.

Blackford, Mansel. *Pathways to the Present: US Development and Its Consequences in the Pacific.* Honolulu: University of Hawai'i Press, 2007.

Borton, Hugh. *American Prescreened Planning for Postwar Japan.* New York: The East Asian Institute, 1967.

Cameron, Craig M. *American Samurai: Myth, Imagination, and the Conduct of Battle in the First Marine Division, 1941–1951.* New York: Cambridge University Press, 1994.

Caprio, Mark E. *Japanese Assimilation Policies in Colonial Korea, 1910–1945.* Seattle: University of Washington Press, 2009.

Caruth, Cathy. *Listening to Trauma: Conversations with Leaders in the Theory and Treatment of Catastrophic Experience.* Baltimore, MD: John Hopkins University Press, 2014.

Cashin, Edward J. *Paternalism in a Southern City: Race, Religion, and Gender in Augusta, GA.* Athens: University of Georgia Press, 2001.

Clausewitz, Carl von. *On War.* New York: Penguin, 1968.

Coles, Harry L., and Albert K. Weinberg. *Civil Affairs: Soldiers Become Governors.* Washington, DC: Office of the Chief of Military History, 1964.

Dingman, Roger. *Deciphering the Rising Sun.* Annapolis, MD: Naval Institute Press, 2009.

Dower, John W. *Embracing Defeat: Japan in the Wake of World War II.* New York: Norton, 1999.

———. *War without Mercy: Race and Power in the Pacific War.* New York: Pantheon, 1986.

Drago, Edward L. *Initiative, Paternalism, and Race Relations: Charleston's Avery Normal Institute.* Athens: University of Georgia Press, 1990.

Drea, Edward J. *In the Service of the Emperor: Essays on the Imperial Japanese Army.* Lincoln: University of Nebraska Press, 1998.

Du Bois, W. E. B. *The Souls of Black Folks.* New York: Blue Heron, 1953.

Duus, Peter. *The Abacus and the Sword: Japanese Penetration of Korea, 1895–1910.* Berkeley: University of California Press, 1995.

Eiji, Takemae. *The Allied Occupation of Japan.* New York: Continuum, 2002.

Eldridge, Robert D. *The Origins of the Bilateral Okinawa Problem: Okinawa in Postwar U.S.–Japan relations, 1945–1952.* New York: Garland, 2001.

Feifer, George. *The Battle of Okinawa: The Blood and the Bomb.* Connecticut: Lyons, 2000.

Field, Norma. *In the Realm of a Dying Emperor.* New York: Vintage, 1991.

Fisch, Arnold. *Military Government in the Ryukyu Islands, 1945–1950.* Washington, DC: Center of Military History, United States Army, 1988.

Foster, Simon. *Okinawa 1945: Final Assault on the Empire.* New York: Sterling, 1996.

Frank, Benis M. *Okinawa: Touchstone to Victory.* New York: Ballantine, 1970.

Frank, Benis M., and Henry I. Shaw Jr. *Victory and Occupation: History of the US Marine Corps Operations in World War II, Volume V.* Washington, DC: Government Printing Office, 1968.

Frank, Richard B. *Downfall: The End of the Imperial Japanese Empire.* New York: Penguin, 1999.

Fujitani, T., Geoffrey M. White, and Lisa Yoneyama, eds. *Perilous Memories: The Asia-Pacific Wars.* Durham, NC: Duke University Press, 2001.

Garraty, John A., and Mark C. Carnes, eds. *American National Biography.* New York: Oxford University Press, 1999.

Genovese, Eugene. *Roll, Jordan, Roll: The World the Slaves Made.* New York: Vintage, 1976.

Gerstle, Gary. *American Crucible: Race and Nation in the Twentieth-Century.* Princeton, NJ: Princeton University Press, 2001.

Ginsburgh, Robert Neville. *Between War and Peace: An Administrative and Organizational Analysis of Selected Military Government Experiences of the United States Army during the Transition Phase.* Cambridge, MA: Harvard University, 1948.

Goldstein, Joshua S. *War and Gender.* New York: Cambridge University Press, 2001.

Gossett, Thomas. *Race: The History of an Idea in America.* Oxford: Oxford University Press, 1963.

Greitens, Eric. *The Heart and the Fist: The Education of a Humanitarian, the Making of a Navy SEAL.* Boston: Houghton Mifflin Harcourt, 2011.

Grimsley, Mark, and Clifford J. Rogers, eds. *Civilians in the Path of War.* Lincoln: University of Nebraska Press, 2002.

Harris, Brayton. *Admiral Nimitz: The Commander of the Pacific Ocean Theater.* New York: St. Martin's, 2012.

Hastings, Max. *Inferno: The World at War, 1939–1945.* New York: Vintage, 2012.

Hein, Laura, and Mark Selden. *Islands of Discontent: Okinawan Responses to Japanese and American Power.* Lanham, MD: Rowman and Littlefield, 2003.

Hicks, George. *Japan's War Memories: Amnesia or Concealment?* Aldershot: Ashgate, 1997.

Higa, Mikio. *Politics and Parties in Postwar Okinawa.* Vancouver: University of British Columbia Publications Centre, 1963.

Hook, Glenn D., and Richard Siddle, ed. *Japan and Okinawa: Structure and Subjectivity.* New York: Routledge, 2003.

Horsman, Reginald. *Race and Manifest Destiny: The Origins of American Racial Anglo-Saxonism.* Cambridge, MA: Harvard University Press, 1981.

Huber, Thomas M. *Japan's Battle of Okinawa, April–June 1945.* Fort Leavenworth, KS: Combat Studies Institute, 1990.

———. *Okinawa, 1945.* Havertown: Casemate, 2004.

Hull, Isabel V. *Absolute Destruction: Military Culture and the Practices of War in Imperial Germany.* Ithaca, NY: Cornell University Press, 2006.

Huntington, Samuel. *The Clash of Civilizations and the Remaking of World Order.* New York: Simon and Shuster, 1997.

Ikeda, Kyle. *Okinawan War Memory: Transgenerational Trauma and the War Fiction of Medoruma Shun.* New York: Routledge, 2013.

Inoue, Masamichi S. *Okinawa and the U.S. Military: Identity Making in the Age of Globalization.* New York: Columbia University Press, 2007.

Iriye, Akira. *Power and Culture: The Japanese-American War, 1941–1945.* Cambridge, MA: Harvard University Press, 1981.

Jarvis, Christina S. *The Male Body at War: American Masculinity during World War II.* DeKalb: Northern Illinois University Press, 2004.

Johnson, Chalmers, ed. *Okinawa: Cold War Islands.* Cardiff: Japan Policy Research Institute, 1999.

Kerr, George H. *Okinawa: The History of an Island People.* Tokyo: Tuttle, 2000.

Leckie, Robert. *Okinawa: The Last Battle of World War II.* New York: Viking, 1995.

Lefeber, Walter. *The Clash: U.S.–Japanese Relations through History.* New York: Norton, 1997.

Lie, John. *Multi-Ethnic Japan.* Cambridge, MA: Harvard University Press, 2001.

Linderman, Gerald. *The World within War: America's Combat Experience in World War II.* Cambridge, MA: Harvard University Press, 1999.

Lovejoy, Arthur O. *Primitivism and Related Ideas in Antiquity.* Baltimore, MD: John Hopkins University Press, 1935.

Lowie, Robert H. *Are We Civilized? Human Culture in Perspective.* New York: Harcourt, Brace, 1929.

Lynn, John A. *Battle: A History of Combat and Culture.* Boulder, CO: Westview, 2003.

Lyons, Michael J. *World War II: A Short History.* Cambridge, MA: Pearson, 2009.

MacGregor, Morris J. *Integration of the Armed Forces, 1940–1965.* Carlisle, PA: Center of Military History, 1981.

Matsumura, Wendy. *The Limits of Okinawa: Japanese Capitalism, Living Labor, and Theorizations of Community.* Durham, NC: Duke University Press, 2015.

McFerson, Hazel, ed. *Blacks and Asians: Crossings, Conflict, and Commonality.* Durham, NC: Carolina Academic Press, 2006.

McLaurin, Melton A. *The Marines of Montford Point: America's First Black Marines.* Chapel Hill: University of North Carolina Press, 2007.

McNaughton, James C. *Nisei Linguists: Japanese Americans in the Military Intelligence Service during World War II.* Washington, DC: Department of the Army, 2006.

Molasky, Michael. *The American Occupation of Japan and Okinawa: Literature and Memory.* New York: Routledge, 1999.

Murray, Williamson, and Allan R. Millett. *A War to Be Won: Fighting the Second World War.* Cambridge, MA: Belknap, 2000.

Myrdal, Gunnar. *An American Dilemma: The Negro Problem and Modern Democracy.* New York: Harper and Row, 1969.

Nelson, Christopher. *Dancing with the Dead: Memory, Performance, and Everyday Life in Postwar Okinawa.* Durham, NC: Duke University Press, 2008.

Nichols, Chas S. Jr., Major, and Henry I. Shaw. *Okinawa: Victory in the Pacific.* Washington, DC: United States Marine Corps Historical Branch, G-3 Division, 1955.

O'Donnell, Patrick K. *Into the Rising Sun: In Their Own Words, World War II's Pacific Veterans Reveal the Heart of Combat.* New York: Simon and Schuster, 2002.

Ota, Masahide. *The Battle of Okinawa: The Typhoon of Steel and Bombs.* Tokyo: Kume, 1984.

———. *Essays on Okinawa Problems.* Okinawa: Yui Shuppan, 2000.

Paret, Peter, Gordon A. Craig, and Felix Gilbert, eds., *Makers of Modern Strategy from Machiavelli to the Nuclear Age.* Princeton, NJ: Princeton University Press, 1986.

Pyle, Kenneth. *The Making of Modern Japan.* Massachusetts: D. C. Heath, 1996.

Renda, Mary. *Taking Haiti: Military Occupation and the Culture of U.S. Imperialism, 1915–1940.* Chapel Hill: University of North Carolina Press, 2001.

Roediger, David R. *Working towards Whiteness: How America's Immigrants Became White: The Strange Journey from Ellis Island to the Suburbs.* New York: Basic Books, 2005.

Samuels, Richard J. *Rich Nation, Strong Army.* Ithaca, NY: Cornell University Press, 1994.

Sarantakes, Nicolas Evan. *Keystone: The American Occupation of Okinawa and U.S. Japanese Relations.* College Station: Texas A&M University Press, 2000.

Schaller, Michael. *The Origins of the Cold War in Asia: The American Occupation of Japan.* Oxford: Oxford University Press, 1985.

Schrager, Adam. *The Principled Politician: Governor Ralph Carr and the Fight against Japanese American Internment.* Golden, CO: Fulcrum, 2008.

Shaara, Jeff. *The Final Storm: A Novel of the War in the Pacific.* New York: Ballantine, 2011.

Shibusawa, Naoko. *America's Geisha Ally: Reimagining the Japanese Enemy.* Cambridge, MA: Harvard University Press, 2006.

Shulman, Frank J., ed. *Doctoral Dissertations on Japan and on Korea, 1969–1979: An Annotated Bibliography of Studies in Western Languages.* Seattle: University of Washington Press, 1982.

———, ed. *Japan and Korea: An Annotated Bibliography of Doctoral Dissertations in Western Languages, 1877–1969.* Chicago: American Library Association, 1970.

Sloan, Bill. *The Ultimate Battle: Okinawa 1945—The Last Epic Struggle of World War II.* New York: Simon and Schuster, 2007.

Smith, Charles R. *Securing the Surrender: Marines in the Occupation of Japan.* Washington, DC: History and Museum Division, Headquarters, United States Marines Corps, 1997.

Smith, Mark M. *How Race Is Made: Slavery, Segregation, and the Senses.* Chapel Hill: University of North Carolina Press, 2006.

Smits, Gregory. *Visions of Ryukyu: Identity and Ideology in Early Modern Thought and Politics.* Honolulu: University of Hawai'i Press, 1991.

Sneider, Vern. *The Teahouse of the August Moon.* New York: G. P. Putnam's Sons, 1951.

Sollors, Werner, ed. *The Invention of Ethnicity.* New York: Oxford University Press, 1989.

Spector, Ronald H. *Eagle against the Sun: The American War with Japan.* New York: Free Press, 1985.

Swope, Kenneth M. *A Dragon's Head and a Serpent's Tail: Ming China and the First Great East Asian War, 1592–1598.* Norman: University of Oklahoma Press, 2009.

Takahashi, Jere. *Nisei/Sansei: Shifting Japanese-American Identities and Politics.* Philadelphia: Temple University Press, 2007.

Tanji, Miyume. *Myth, Protest, and Struggle in Okinawa.* New York: Routledge, 2006.

Tatsuhiro, Oshiro, and Higashi Mineo. *Okinawa: Two Postwar Novellas.* Berkeley, CA: Institute of East Asian Studies, 1989.

Thorseth, Mary. *Legitimate and Illegitimate Paternalism in Polyethnic Conflicts.* Sweden: Acta Universitatis Gothoburgensis, 1999.

Todorov, Tzvetan. *The Conquest of America: The Question of the Other.* Oklahoma City: University of Oklahoma Press, 1999.

Ward, Robert E., and Frank Joseph Shulman, eds. *The Allied Occupation of Japan, 1945–1952: An Annotated Bibliography of Western Language Materials.* American Library Association, 1974.

Weinberg, Gerhard L. *A World at Arms: A Global History of World War II.* Cambridge: Cambridge University Press, 2005.

Weiner, Michael, ed., *Japan's Minorities: The Illusion of Homogeneity.* London: Routledge, 2008.

Willock, Roger. *Unaccustomed to Fear: A Biography of the Late General Roy S. Geiger.* Princeton, NJ: Roger Willock, 1968.

Wu, Ellen D. *The Color of Success: Asian Americans and the Origins of the Model Minority.* Princeton, NJ: Princeton University Press, 2014.

Yoshida, Kensei. *Democracy Betrayed: Okinawa under United States Occupation.* Bellingham: Center for East Asian Studies, Western Washington University, 2001.

Yoshimura, Akira. *Typhoon of Steel: An Okinawan Schoolboy's Quest for Martyrdom in the Battle of Okinawa.* Portland, OR: Merwin Asia, 2009.

Zabilka, Gladys. *Customs and Culture of Okinawa.* Rutland, VT: Tuttle, 1959.

Articles/Other

Allen, David. "Prayer for the Past: Battle of Okinawa Remembered 62 Years Later." *Stars and Stripes* 66, no. 69 (2007): 4.

Berg, Manfred, Paul Schor, and Isabel Soto. "AHR Roundtable: The Weight of Words: Writing about Race in the United States and Europe." *American Historical Review* 119, no. 3 (June 2014): 800–8.

Brando, Marlon, and Glenn Ford. *The Teahouse of the August Moon.* DVD. Directed by Daniel Mann. Hollywood, CA: Warner Brothers, 1956.

Clarke, Hugh. "The Great Dialect Debate: The State and Language Policy in Okinawa." In *State and Society in Interwar Japan,* ed. Elise K. Tipton, 193–218. New York: Routledge, 1997.

Dingman, Roger V. "Language at War: U.S. Marine Corps Japanese Language Officers in the Pacific War." *Journal of Military History* 68 (2004): 853–83.

Fields, Barbara J. "Ideology and Race in American History." In *Region, Race, and Reconstruction: Essays in Honor of C. Vann Woodard,* ed. J. Morgan Kousser and James McPherson. New York: Oxford University Press, 1982.

Geiss, Thomas E., ed. *West Point Atlas for the Second World War Asia and the Pacific.* Garden City Park, NY: Square One, 2002.

Hall, Stuart. "Ethnicity: Identity and Difference." *Radical America* 23 (1989): 9–30.

Huddy, Leonie. "Group Identity and Political Cohesion." In *Oxford Handbook of Political Psychology,* ed. Leonie Huddy, David O. Sears and Robert Jervis. Oxford: University of Oxford Press, 2003.

Hughes, Matthew. "War without Mercy? American Armed Forces and the Deaths of Civilians during the Battle of Saipan, 1944." *Journal of Military History* 75 (2011): 93–123.

McPherson, Alan. "The Irony of Legal Pluralism in U.S. Occupations." *American Historical Review* 117, no. 4 (2012): 1149–72.

———. "Lid Sitters and Prestige Seekers: The U.S. Navy versus the State Department and the End of U.S. Occupations." *Journal of Military History* 78, no. 1 (2014): 73–99.

Santelli, James S. "A Brief History of the 4th Marines." Marine Corps Historical

Reference Pamphlet. Washington, DC: United States Marine Corps Historical Division, 1970.

Smith, Charles R. "Securing the Surrender: Marines in the Occupation of Japan." Marines in World War II Commemorative Series. Washington, DC: Marine Corps Historical Center, 1997.

Spector, R. "After Hiroshima: Allied Military Occupations and the Fate of Japan's Empire, 1945–1947." *Journal of Military History* 69 (2005): 1121–36.

Taylor, Verta, and Nancy E. Whittier. "Collective Identity in Social Movement Communities: Lesbian Feminist Mobilization." In *Frontiers in Social Movement Theory*, ed. Aldon D. Morris and Carol McClurg Mueller. New Haven, CT: Yale University Press, 1992.

Tourtelot, Lisa. "Bringing Back the Memories: Wife Fulfills Late Husband's Dream of Returning Sixty-Year-Old Album to Okinawan Family." *Stars and Stripes* 72, no. 220 (2014): 3–4.

van Stekelenburg, Jacquelien. "Collective Identity." In *The Wiley-Blackwell Encyclopedia of Social and Political Movements*, ed. David A. Snow, Donatella della Porta, Bert Klandermans, and Doug McAdam. Hoboken, NJ: Blackwell, 2013.

Wilson, Kirt H. "Towards a Discursive Theory of Racial Identity: *The Souls of Black Folk* as a Response to the Nineteenth-Century Biological Determinism." *Western Journal of Communication* 63 (1999): 193–215.

Index

Throughout the index, "US" refers to the joint forces of the US military. Military units are American unless otherwise stated.

1st Marine Division, 7, 8, 109–10, 111, 115–16, 118, 120, 129

III Amphibious Corps, 6, 176n23. *See also* Marine Corps; Marine Corps military government; *specific Marine divisions*

6th Marine Division, 7, 8, 40, 112, 120

7th Infantry Division, 7

XXIV Corps, 6, 7, 8. *See also* Army; Army military government; *specific infantry divisions*

24th Division (Japan), 59

27th Infantry Division, 6, 8

32nd Army (Japan), 8, 17, 21, 46, 62

77th Infantry Division, 8

96th Infantry Division, 7, 86

"A" detachments, 24, 26, 53, 54, 55, 75, 106, 109; A-1, 105, 109; A-3, 106, 118

ABDACOM (American-British-Dutch-Australian Command), 4

acceptance, 47, 49–50

accountability, 111, 113, 142, 144, 147

"Additional Instructions relating to Military Government," 57, 174n5

administration: camps and districts, 84, 135; government, 125, 145, 147–48, 158

administrative departments, 147, 148, 218n28

Administrative Plan 1-45, 35

adults, Okinawan, 49–50, 60, 70–73, 91–92, 95–97, 100. *See also* civilians

advantage seeking, 14, 15, 60, 91, 95–97, 101, 160

advisory groups, 135–36, 138, 147

airdropped pamphlets, 105

allegiances. *See* loyalty

altruism. *See* kindness

American-British-Dutch-Australian Command (ABDACOM), 4

American Samurai (Cameron), 13

analyses, cultural. *See* cultural analyses

Annex "Able," 14, 35, 37–39

Appleman, R. W., 79

Aragaki, 95

Army, 4, 5, 128, 158; Battle of Okinawa, 7–8; Civil Affairs, 23, 27, 28, 37, 170n8, 171n12; freedom of action, 30, 40; interservice conflict, 6–7, 36–37, 204n64; priorities, 25, 26, 32, 121; racism, 88–89. *See also* Army military government; *specific infantry divisions*

Army military government, 21–22, 30–31, 74–89, 121–23, 153; camps, 75–77, 87, 126; loosening of restrictions, 14, 85–88, 96, 126, 193nn69–70; policies, 14, 21–22, 30–31, 40, 85, 86; security measures, 74–75, 81, 96, 193n75; training, 51–55. *See also* Army

Army Service Command I. *See* ASCOM I

artworks, 150

ASCOM I (Army Service Command I; *formerly* IsCom, *later* OBASCOM), 128, 131, 132, 135

Asian Exclusion Act of 1924 (US), 3
Asians, US racism toward, 12–13, 16,
    17, 88–89, 143, 150, 173n42
associations to US, Okinawans with,
    42, 84–85, 87, 95, 114, 192nn64–65
attacks on US, 57–58, 103–4, 110, 112,
    114, 118
attitudes, Okinawan, 22, 27–29, 32–33,
    39, 42, 75, 78, 84, 132, 157, 159, 160,
    192nn61,63
Australia, 4
autonomy. See independence
Aza, Yasutaka, 90

"B" detachments, 24, 53, 54, 55, 75,
    106, 109, 118; B-1, 105, 109, 115; B-3,
    106, 118; B-5, 21, 81; B-10, 107, 119,
    206n83
bartering, 114
Bartlett, Fred, 214n64
base development, 127–28, 153
Battle (Lynn), 13
Battle of Okinawa, 2, 5–8, 18, 21, 92,
    97–99, 125–27; bombardments, 5–6,
    7, 21, 58, 61, 75; landings, 6, 7, 62,
    74–75, 102–3, 104–5
battlefield, removal of civilians from,
    11, 12, 24, 26, 38, 43, 65, 81, 93, 157
battlespace disagreements, 204n64
beaches, 102–3, 104–5, 106
beatings, 99, 151
behavior, civilian. See civilian behavior,
    and US responses to
belonging, 49
benevolence. See kindness
betrayal, Japanese, 59–61, 68–70, 98
bitterness, 11, 27, 29, 39, 47–48
Blood and Iron Corps (Tekketsu
    Kinnotai), 48, 97, 168n18. See also
    combatants: Okinawan
bodies, dead. See corpses
Boei Tai (Okinawan Home Guard), 62,
    63, 80, 168n18. See also combatants:
    Okinawan
bombardments, 5–6, 7, 21, 58, 61, 75
books about Japan, 27, 28
boys, Okinawan. See juveniles, Oki-
    nawan; student corps: military
brutality: Japanese, toward Okinawans,

59, 60–61, 64–68, 71, 72, 159; in
    Japanese-US combat, 12
Buckner, Simon Bolivar, Jr., 22–23,
    26–30, 36, 44, 157, 158, 170n5,
    206n2; interservice rivalry, 6–7, 37;
    on Okinawa and Okinawans, 75, 84,
    109–10, 120; racial beliefs, 16, 120,
    173n42; resource conservation,
    116–17. See also GOPER
building. See construction
buildings, 105, 119

"C" camp, 109
"C" detachments, 24, 75, 77, 106, 109,
    200n16
Caldwell, John Tyler, 124, 130, 133, 140,
    146, 213n51
calorie counts, cuts to, 142, 216n8
Cameron, Craig, 13
Camp Heinza, 192n59
camp leadership. See leadership,
    Okinawan
Camp Nodake, 21, 77, 81, 82, 84, 85, 86
Camp Sunabe, 76–77, 192n59
Camp Tobaru, 80, 82
Camp Tsumia, 192n59
camps, military government, 11–12,
    24; accountability, 111, 113; ad-
    ministration, 135, 136; attacks on,
    103–4, 110, 112, 114, 118; conditions,
    76–77, 90–91, 104, 111, 113–14, 158;
    construction, 87; establishment,
    75–76, 103–4, 108, 109, 111; interser-
    vice differences, 104, 116; Japanese
    infiltrations, 190n33; leaving, 81–82,
    83, 84; postwar, 126–29, 131, 135,
    136, 142, 143; security measures,
    81–83, 104, 110–11, 114–15, 118, 120.
    See also specific services' military
    government entries
capabilities, Okinawan, 16, 108, 135, 137,
    141, 144, 145–46, 153, 158, 213n51
casualties: civilian, 25, 76, 103, 110,
    179n4, 188n6; of crossfire, 92–93, 97,
    114. See also deaths; killings
categorizations of Okinawan identity,
    12, 13, 21–22, 33, 41, 121–23, 157;
    civilian POWs, 40; civilian pris-
    oners, 114; civilians, 132; different

from Japanese, 149, 153, 157; enemies, 17–18, 52–55, 86, 157, 158, 173n42; enemy aliens, 112; enemy civilians, 14–15, 17, 25, 32, 33, 40, 44, 52–55, 57–58, 79, 103, 104, 132; enemy combatants, 113, 122; enemy nationals, 40, 119, 121; inferior humans, 16, 78–79, 103, 108, 113, 114, 120; inmates, 40; Japanese, 14, 27, 32, 33, 40–43, 47, 52, 55, 58, 104, 108, 115, 118, 120–23, 158, 170n8, 181n7; Japanese civilian enemy, 108; Japanese civilians, 40, 52, 121; more American than Japanese, 75, 84, 121, 192n59; national loyalists, 40; natives, 144, 150; oriental, 150; people, the, 144; prisoners of war, 53; refugees, 40, 114; second-class, 11, 19, 27, 49; threats, 33, 52, 57, 174n5; war criminals, 53; weapons of war, 52. *See also* Okinawan identity
categorizations of Okinawans: Army, 14, 27–33, 40, 52–55, 75, 78–79, 86, 88, 104, 121–23, 159, 173n42; Marines, 14–15, 17, 19, 32–33, 39–44, 57–58, 103, 104, 108–9, 112–14, 119–23, 158, 159, 174n5; Navy, 15–16, 125, 132, 137, 141, 143, 144, 145, 148, 153, 158, 159
caution, 14, 40, 52, 55, 74, 80, 157
caves, 7, 26, 59, 65, 71–72, 75, 92–94, 115, 195n4
censorship, 30
Central Okinawan Administration, 147
charity. *See* kindness
Chatan camp, 82
Chibana, 109, 110, 115
Chihaya Unit (Japan), 98
chiji (Okinawan governor), 137–38, 140, 147
children, Okinawan. *See* juveniles, Okinawan
Chimu, 109
China, 3, 9, 13
Cho, Isamu, 97
CINCPAC-CINCPOA Bulletin #161-44, 23, 27, 28–29, 40, 52, 181n9
cities, 75

civil administration, 54, 132, 133, 138, 140–41, 147–48, 158
Civil Affairs, 23, 27, 28, 35, 37, 51–52, 56, 170n8, 171n12. *See also* military government
civil affairs officers, 35, 39
Civil Affairs schools, 14, 23, 27, 28, 37, 51, 56, 130, 210n28
"Civil Censorship Plan," 170n4
civil defense, 46–47, 50, 61, 63–64, 184n23
civil order, 148
Civilian Advisory Council (Okinawan Advisory Council), 135–36, 138, 147
Civilian Affairs Department, 131, 138, 218n28
civilian behavior, and US responses to, 30, 38, 40, 53, 74–75, 79, 84, 88, 104, 118–21, 128–29. *See also* cooperation
civilian shootings, 82–83, 92, 109, 114–15, 120
civilian welfare, 25–26, 38, 102, 107
civilians: during Battle of Okinawa, 8, 14, 15, 32, 59–73, 90, 102–3; US assessments of, 78–79, 95–96, 102–4, 108–9, 132, 157; US combatants and, 74, 90–97; US policies regarding, 25, 30, 38, 39, 43–44, 54, 104, 114, 115–18, 171n12, 174n5. *See also* civilian behavior, and US responses to; conduct toward civilians; control of civilians
clean-up effort, 76. *See also* mopping-up operations
close accommodations, 76–77, 83, 143
clothing, 79, 87, 107, 189n28
collective identity, 61, 91, 99–101, 186n48, 193n72, 198nn40,44. *See also* Okinawan identity
combat environment, 17–18
combat mission, 23–26, 34, 38–42, 51, 77, 102, 107, 142–43
combatants: Okinawan, 42, 48, 60–64, 80, 91–92, 97–100, 131, 143, 144, 168n18, 197n31, 198n40; US, 74, 90–97. *See also* Japanese military
committees, 137, 147
commonalities, 84–85, 88, 121
communication, 25, 30, 39, 82

community projects, 149
community reconstruction. *See* reconstruction: Okinawan society
compliance. *See* cooperation
conduct toward civilians, 38, 39, 43–44, 90–91, 94, 99, 104, 114–18, 174n5; Army, 21, 24, 26, 44, 55; Marines, 17, 32, 43–44, 102–4, 109, 112–21, 158, 174n5, 206n86; military police, 151
conflict, interservice. *See* interservice conflict
conflicts, civilian, 137, 152
confusion, over US plans, 53–56
Conical Hill, 90
consciousness, 101, 198n40
conscription, 11, 42, 45, 168n18. *See also* combatants: Okinawan
conservation of resources, 26–27, 38, 116–17
construction, 87, 107, 121, 126, 141, 152
contagious diseases, 25, 77
contradictions, in US orders, 53–54, 57, 175n5
contributions, Okinawan: administration, 135, 140; Japanese war effort, 45, 46, 62, 64, 80; military government camp life, 84–85, 126, 128, 192n59; outcome of own experiences, 14, 153, 160; postwar, 135–39, 144, 153, 158–59. *See also* leadership, Okinawan; Okinawan Advisory Council
control of civilians, 24, 30, 38, 39, 82–84, 102–7, 109–10, 112, 118–19
cooperation: Okinawan, 24, 32, 38, 74–75, 79, 84, 119, 128–29; Okinawan, US responses to, 14, 74–75, 79, 83–85, 95–96, 107–8, 119, 121–23, 193n75, 206n86
Corps General Order Number 33, 57, 174n5
corpses, 62, 76, 69, 190n32
Counter Intelligence Corps, 86
courtesies, 67, 185n33
courts, 152
cover-ups, of US misconduct, 151
crimes, military police, 151
Crist, William E., 11–12, 14, 23, 29, 30, 35, 40, 51, 53, 77, 157

crops, 76, 86, 141
crossfire casualties, 92–93, 97, 114
cruelty, Japanese, 15, 59, 60, 64–68, 71, 72, 95
cultural analyses, 11–16, 18–19, 21–22, 27–34, 39–44, 80, 121–23, 127–28, 156–57, 159–60. *See also* Okinawan responses to invasion, US predictions of
cultural continuity, 136–37, 138, 148, 153, 160
cultural differences, 11, 28–29
cultural disrespect, 151
culture: Japanese, 45, 52, 54; US, Okinawan interpretations of, 2
curfews, 43
customs, 11, 29, 45, 49, 50, 148, 171n12. *See also* traditions

"D" detachments, 24
daily reports, 39, 77
daily tasks, 86–87
dairy products, 116
data collection, 77
dead bodies. *See* corpses
death, for Japan, 48, 50, 61, 180n16
death penalty, 44, 82–83, 86, 115, 193nn73–74
deaths, 76, 188n6: children, 59, 65, 66, 68, 71, 94; civilians, 32, 59, 65–68, 82–83, 92–94, 97, 98, 112, 114–15, 195n4, 197n33; student corps, 64, 66
defeat, Japanese, 97–99
defensive lines, Japanese, 7–8, 90, 92, 97
dehydration, 62
del Valle, Pedro, 115–16, 118, 123, 129
demobilization, 124, 129–31, 153, 209n23
denial, of violence against civilians, 98–99
destruction, 16–17, 21, 32, 61–62, 75–76, 126, 127, 131–32, 141
detachments, military government, 24, 26, 53–54, 117–18, 131; A-1, 105, 109; A-3, 106, 118; B-1, 105, 109, 115; B-3, 106, 118; B-5, 21, 81; B-10, 107, 119, 206n83

devaluation, of Okinawa or Okinawans, 33, 57, 143–44, 159

differences, interservice. *See* interservice differences

differentiation, of Okinawans from Japanese, 52, 78, 79–81, 88, 103, 109, 110, 149, 189n14, 191n38

disassociation: by Okinawan combatants, from violence against civilians, 98–99; by Okinawans, from Japanese, 60, 61, 69, 85, 86, 91, 96, 100; of Okinawans from humanity, by Marines, 114

discipline, 44, 151

discretion. *See* freedom of action

discrimination. *See* subjugation

diseases, 25, 77

disguises, 102, 110, 202n36

disgust, at Okinawans' appearance, 78–79, 103, 108–9, 144

disobedience, 43, 81–84, 86, 115, 193nn73–75

displacement, 61–62, 64–65, 127, 147

disposition, Okinawan. *See* attitudes, Okinawan

disputes, civilian, 137, 152

disregard, of civilians, 92

distribution, 109–10, 111, 117, 142

districts, military government, 77, 131, 136, 138, 142, 143, 147

distrust: Marines of Okinawans, 104, 112, 113, 119, 122; Okinawans of Japanese, 68–69, 93, 100; Okinawans of US, 93

diversity, Japan's resistance to, 169n21

division military government officers, 118

doctors. *See* medical personnel

dog patrols, 81

Dorfman, John, 141, 149

Dower, John, 13

Drago, Joe, 32

Dutch East Indies, 4

economic structures, 136, 137, 145, 148

educational programs, 25, 145, 146

Edwards, Richard S., 133, 134

Eihan, Teruya, 62

elections, 151

enclosures. *See* stockades

enemies, Okinawans categorized as. *See under* categorizations of Okinawan identity

Enemy Situation Annex, 43

engineers, 75, 121, 126, 141, 206n83

English-speaking Okinawans, 42, 87, 112, 114

equipment shortages, 77, 81, 82, 106, 176n23

espionage. *See* spies

ethnic inferiority, 29, 150

ethnic tensions, 29, 30, 42

ethnicity: consideration of, 88–89, 156, 159, 161; malleability of, 15, 33, 61, 122, 160, 169n21; Okinawan, 11, 17, 169n21, 172n21; Okinawan, Japanese and 45, 47, 72, 148, 149; Okinawan, US assessments of, 12, 13, 16, 27, 28, 30, 33–34, 40, 52, 123, 134, 137, 141, 148, 149, 158, 181n9; US misconceptions about, 134

evacuations, 47, 104–5

evaluations based on experience, 88–89, 104

exclusion, 11, 45

excrement, human, 76, 78–79

Executive Officer's Memorandum No. 94-45, 57, 174n5

expansion, Japanese, 3, 9–10

experience, evaluations based on, 88–89, 104

families, Okinawan, 46, 70, 111, 142, 179n4

farming assets, 46

fears: Okinawan, of Japanese soldiers, 69, 71, 72, 100; Okinawan, of US troops, 67, 78, 79, 83, 90, 91, 93–94, 95; US, of civilian spies, 79, 83, 157

feces, human, 76, 78–79

fences, 75, 81, 111

firefights, 97–98

Firman (Commander), 124

fishermen, 42

flamethrowers, 26, 92

farm theft, 116–17

food, 46, 62, 69, 98, 107; shortages, 65, 75, 76, 142, 216n8; stolen by civilians, 82, 83; stolen from civilians, 67, 68, 69, 71, 116, 119. *See also* rations
foraging, 142, 216n8
Fort Ord, California, 51
Fortune magazine, 28
France, 3
fraternization, 30, 54, 88, 150–51
free movement, 43, 83, 102–3, 105, 106, 109, 202n40
freedom, Okinawans' earning back of, 24, 38, 193n70, 206n86
freedom of action, 24, 30, 33, 40, 43, 38, 53, 75, 85, 132, 157, 181n16, 193n70
Freeman, Douglas Southall, 173n42
friendship, 85, 87–88, 121, 143, 144
Futenma, 8

garrison, preparation of, 126–28
gas bombs, 92
Geiger, Roy S., 6, 7, 34–39, 44, 51, 120, 125, 206n2
generosity. *See* kindness
girls, Okinawan. *See* juveniles, Okinawan; student corps: nursing
Girls' Youth Organization, 48
glory of war, 47–48, 64
goods production, 136
GOPER ("Operational Directive #7 from the Commanding General of Tenth Army"), 14, 22–27, 29–30, 53, 54, 77, 169n24, 170nn4,8, 193n70, 194n80, 206n86
graves, mass, 76
Great Britain, 3, 4
Greater East Asia Co-Prosperity Sphere, 3
grenades, for Okinawan suicides, 63, 65, 72
Guam, 41

Haebaru Army Hospital, 61
Hagushi Beach, 6, 7
Haiti, 155
handicraft industry, 148
Hanna, Willard "Red," 148–49
hatred, of US, 67, 91, 94, 113

Hedo Point, 90
Heinza camp, 192n59
Hideyoshi. *See* Toyotomi Hideyoshi
Higa, Tomiko, 179n2
Himeyuri Student Corps (Lily Student Corps), 48, 61
Hodge, John, 6, 30
homelessness, 105, 112, 119
homes, 62, 65, 70, 71, 105, 119, 120
Horn, E. H., 52, 54
hospitals, 61, 64, 77, 92, 95, 152
Hostetler, Robert L., 74, 75, 181n8
hot weather, 97
household goods, 107
humane treatment, 44, 116
humanitarian needs, 25, 38, 44, 104, 132
hypocrisy, 98–99

identifying badges, 114
identity, Okinawan. *See* categorizations of Okinawan identity; Okinawan identity
identity rhetoric, 47
ideology, Japanese, 48, 70
Ieyasu. *See* Tokugawa Ieyasu
illegibility, of warning signs, 82
impacts on US mission, civilians', 12, 21–22, 26, 38, 39, 58, 102–3, 109, 142–43, 157
Imperial Diet, Japan, 28, 29
incendiary weapons, 26, 92, 94, 115
incentive program, US officers', 145, 146
independence, 9–10, 87, 146, 150, 153, 157
indiscriminate killing, 32, 102, 109, 114–15
indoctrination, Japanese, 15, 29, 45, 46–47, 50, 59–60, 66, 185nn29,32
industries, 136, 148, 151
inequality, 30–31, 45, 72
inexperience, US personnel's, 53, 56
inferiority, 13, 16, 17, 29, 42
infiltrations, military government camps, 190n33
information, lack of, 53, 55, 57, 175n5
"Information on Military Government," 52, 56, 175n5
ingratiation, 95–97, 100

initiative. *See* freedom of action

injuries, and student nurses, 64

intelligence estimates, 40, 43

intelligence summaries, 23, 27, 28–29, 38, 40–43, 52, 181n9

intermingling: Japanese with civilians, 12, 92–93, 95, 97, 109, 110; US with civilians, 142–43

interpreters, 56, 93–94, 107, 114, 130

interrogations, 111, 114

interservice conflict, 6–7, 36–37, 116, 117, 118, 122–23, 158, 204n64

interservice differences, 33, 41, 104, 116, 121–23, 145, 157

interservice meetings, 35

interservice rivalry. *See* interservice conflict

interviews, 86, 87

invasion of Okinawa, Japanese (1609), 9–10, 28, 49

involvement, Okinawan. *See* contributions, Okinawan

IsCom (Island Command), 127–29, 170n4, 171n10. *See also* ASCOM I; OBASCOM

island campaign, 4–5

Island Command. *See* IsCom

Itoman, 110

Jackson, John David, 108

Jackson, R. H., 120

Japan, 3–4, 9–10; Okinawa categorized as part of, 42, 108; US plan to defeat, 5, 22, 26, 46, 159, 208n12; US relations with, 12–13;

Japanese, US categorizations of, 27–29, 84, 149

Japanese, Yamato, 169n21

Japanese Americans, 12, 84

Japanese empire, 3

"Japanese Garden" (Karpen), 76

Japanese government, 3, 10, 11, 28, 39, 45, 85

Japanese military: Battle of Okinawa, 7–8, 21, 57–73, 80, 90, 92, 97–99, 125–26, 132, 202n39; cruelty, 15, 59, 60, 64–69, 71, 72, 95; differentiation from civilians, 78, 79–81; disguises, 102, 110, 202n36; Okinawans

and, 48–49, 64–70, 71, 86, 96, 100, 184n23, 185n35

Japanese-Okinawan relationship. *See* relationships: Okinawan-Japanese

Johnson, Andrew, 156

Johnson, Raymond, 55, 57

Johnston, James, 108

Joint Army-Navy Manual of Military Government and Civil Affairs, 37

joint operations, 36, 158

Joint US Strategic Committee, 5

junshi (suicide), 9

justice policies, 37

juveniles, Okinawan: Battle of Okinawa, 61, 62, 64–70, 72; identity realignment, 69–70; Japanese and, 46–50, 60, 64–70, 93, 185n32; suicide, 94, 180n16, 185n29; US and, 92–95. *See also* student corps

Kakazu Ridge, 8

Kamajo (civilian), 87

Kanto Army, 3

Karpen, A. G., 76

Katchin Peninsula, 111, 114, 119

Kerama Islands, 6

kidnappings, 112–13, 120

Kikuko, Miyagi, 48

killings: children, 59, 65, 66, 68, 71; civilians by Japanese, 59, 65–68, 98, 197n33; civilians by US, 26, 32, 44, 82–83, 92–94, 97, 112, 114–15; military personnel, 66, 151

kindness: Japanese, 48–49, 67, 185n35; US, 74–75, 94, 95, 96, 113, 143

kinship, 85, 87–88, 121, 143, 144

Korea, 3, 9

Koza field hospital, 77

Kuba, 8

L-Day, 51, 105, 175n7

labor, forced, 114, 119, 203n53

labor officers, 124

labor programs, 25, 77, 81, 86, 119, 132, 149

landings, 6, 7, 62, 74–75, 102–3, 104–5

landscape, 75

languages, 11, 28, 49, 52, 54, 56, 82, 146

Laub, Dori, 185n32

Lawrence, Henry, 148
leadership, Okinawan: military government camps, 15–16, 87, 106, 107, 112, 119, 125, 192n59, 194n78, 206n86; postwar, 136, 137, 140–41, 147–48
Leaflet 527, 30–31
Lee's Lieutenants (Freeman), 173n42
legal actions, 152
leprosy, 77
levelheadedness, 49–50, 71–73, 96
Leyte, 51
liaison officers, 35–36, 37, 53–54, 131
Lily Student Corps (Himeyuri Student Corps), 48
links to US, Okinawans with. *See* associations to US, Okinawans with
livestock, 116–17, 119
local leadership. *See* leadership, Okinawan
Loomis, F. B., 34–35, 37, 38
loyalty, 11–12; Army assessments of Okinawans', 14, 19, 22, 27–31, 40, 75, 88, 121–23, 157, 159; changes in Okinawans', 15, 18, 42, 60, 96–97, 100; Marines assessments of Okinawans', 14, 19, 32–34, 40–43, 58, 103–4, 107–8, 110, 112, 120–23, 157–58; Okinawans' to Japanese, 45, 50, 66–67, 91–92, 197n31
Luchuan dialect, 28, 49, 82
Lynn, John, 13

MacArthur, Douglas, 4, 7, 36, 51, 129
Machinato-Kakazu defensive line, 8
Maebaru camp, 82, 193n73
Maehira, killings in, 59
magazines about Japan, 27–28
mail service, 25, 30, 39, 149
management, 146–47, 148, 153
Manchuria, 3
manufacturing, 136
Marine Corps: Battle of Okinawa, 7, 8, 32, 34; Civil Affairs, 35, 171n12; disregard for Army, 114, 116–18, 122–23; freedom of action, 38; interservice conflict, 6, 37, 204n64; poor conduct, recent, 160; priorities, 32, 38, 43, 102, 121; racism, 17, 112, 205n81; on Saipan, 33, 41–42. *See*

also Marine Corps military government; *specific Marine divisions*
Marine Corps Air Station Futenma, 160
Marine Corps military government, 32–44, 102–23; camps, 102–4, 108–15, 118, 120, 126, 158; fixed assessment of Okinawan disposition, 17, 40–41, 43, 58, 103–4, 112, 114, 120–23, 205n71; personnel shortages, 106, 176n23, 200n18; plans, failures with, 35–36, 37, 105–7, 109, 175n5; policies, 14–15, 17, 33, 38–39, 40, 43–44, 56–57, 75, 122, 157–58, 174n5; restriction of civilians, 106–7, 110–11, 112, 206n86; training, 36, 37, 55–58, 174n5. *See also* Annex "Able"; Marine Corps
Marshall, George C., 23
mass graves, 76
materials shortages, 77, 81, 82, 106, 176n23
May, M. A., 118
mayors (*shicho*), 137
McQueen, John, 40
medical facilities, 25, 152
medical personnel: Okinawan, 25, 27, 95, 146, 151–52; US, 25, 144
medical policies, 25, 27
Meiji Restoration, 10
men, Okinawan, 46, 62, 80, 81, 86, 91–92, 111, 119. *See also* adults, Okinawan; civilians; combatants: Okinawan; Okinawan Advisory Council
military administration, 133
military fighting units. *See* combatants: Okinawan
military government: camps, 11–12, 24; mission, 23, 26, 88, 132, 158; plans, 11–12, 17, 21–27, 29–31, 33–40, 43–44, 123, 133; policies, 16, 17, 24–27, 29–31, 43, 44, 88–89, 146–47; reorganization, 117–18; training, 51–58; transitions, 130, 145, 152–53, 171n10; units, 23–24, 51. *See also* Annex "Able"; cultural analyses; GOPER; *specific services' military government entries*

military government detachments. *See*
  detachments, military government
Military Government Plan, 6th Marine
  Division, 40
military government schools. *See* Civil
  Affairs schools
military planning, 159. *See also* plans,
  US
military police, 56, 75, 81, 105, 107, 111–
  12, 118, 143, 151, 152
milk, 116
Miller, Charles, 112
mission, lack of information on, 53, 55,
  57, 175n5
mission success, 12, 16, 19, 22, 27, 38,
  145, 157, 159
mistrust. *See* distrust
Miyako, 45
mobilization: of Okinawans by
  Japanese, 46–47, 60, 80, 168n18; in
  United States, 5
mopping-up operations, 97–98, 125–29,
  131, 132, 142, 206n3
mortality, shared, 63, 69
Mosman, E. R., 55
Motobu Peninsula, 90
movement, civilian, 43, 83, 102–3, 105,
  106, 109, 111, 141–43, 202n40, 204n64
mud, 76, 97, 105
muras. *See* villages
Murdock (Government Officer Commander), 214n64
Murray, Charles I., 124, 130, 134, 136,
  138, 149

Nago, 7
Naha, 75, 76
Naha-Shuri-Yonabaru defensive line,
  7, 8
Nakagusuku Wan, 109
Nakamura, Fumiko, 48
Nakasone, Seizen, 76
National Mobilization Act of 1944
  (Japan), 46–47, 168n18
nationalism, 33, 40–41, 45–50, 59, 66,
  68–69
Nationalization Act of 1944 (Japan), 42
nationhood. *See* nationalism
Naval Affairs Committee, 133

Naval Operating Base, Okinawa (NOB),
  130, 131, 142
Naval School of Military Government
  and Administration, Columbia
  University, 37, 51, 56
Navy, 4, 6–7, 37, 117, 125, 129–31, 139,
  143–44, 150. *See also* Navy military
  government
Navy military government, 15–16, 124–
  25, 130–53, 158, 210n28, 214n64;
  camps, 131, 135, 136, 142, 143; Okinawans and, 15–16, 95–96, 145, 146,
  213n51; policies, 125, 141, 144–47.
  See also Navy
needs, civilians', 25, 38, 44, 92, 102, 104,
  106, 127, 132
Nei. *See* Sho Nei
Netherlands, 4
New Guinea, 41
news media, 36
Nimitz, Chester W., 4, 22, 23, 36, 133,
  134, 212n45
NOB (Naval Operating Base, Okinawa),
  130, 131, 142
Nodake camp, 21, 77, 81, 82, 84, 85, 86
noisy children silenced, 65, 68, 71, 72
noncombatants, Okinawan. *See*
  civilians
nurses, and US personnel, 88. *See also*
  medical personnel

OBASCOM (Okinawa Base Command;
  formerly IsCom *and* ASCOM), 141,
  142, 215n4
obedience. *See* cooperation
occupation. *See* military government
occupations, 4, 11, 18–19, 155–56,
  160–61
Office of Island Governments, 133
Okinawa, 9–11, 179n2; US categorizations of, 28, 42, 52, 108, 121, 150,
  172n30. *See also* Okinawa Prefecture
Okinawa, Battle of. *See* Battle of
  Okinawa
Okinawa Base Command (OBASCOM;
  formerly IsCom *and* ASCOM), 141,
  142, 215n4
Okinawa Prefectural Peace Memorial
  Museum, 188n6

Okinawa Prefecture, 9–11, 22, 27–29, 42, 45, 49, 60, 168n18, 172n33, 214n59
Okinawan Advisory Council (Civilian Advisory Council), 135–36, 138, 147
Okinawan Base, 141
Okinawan government: Japanese in, 29, 47, 172n33; postwar, 16, 25, 138, 140–41, 145–48, 151, 153, 158–59, 194n80; US categorizations of, 28–29, 145–46
Okinawan Home Guard (Boei Tai), 62, 63, 80, 168n18
Okinawan identity: before Battle of Okinawa, 48–50; changes to, 15, 60, 69–70, 86–87, 91, 95–96; during Battle of Okinawa, 69–73; collective, 61, 91, 99–101, 186n48, 193n72, 198nn40,44; conscious construction of, 15, 60, 73, 96, 101; Japanese associations, 11, 15, 27, 48–50, 60, 63, 66–67, 70–72, 86, 96, 186n35; present-day, 2; use of, for advantage, 14, 15, 60, 91, 95, 96, 101, 160. See also categorizations of Okinawan identity
Okinawan-Japanese relationship. See relationships: Okinawan-Japanese
Okinawan-Japanese rift, 85, 96–97
Okinawan Public Works, 149
Okinawan responses to invasion, US predictions of, 12, 14, 21–22, 27, 29–30, 33, 39–43, 52, 53, 58, 157
Okinawans, categorizations of. See categorizations of Okinawans
older Okinawans. See adults, Okinawan
Operation Downfall, 208n12
Operation Iceberg, 5–8, 25, 26, 34–36, 43, 123, 157. See also Battle of Okinawa
Operation Olympic, 128, 208n12
"Operational Directive #7 from the Commanding General of Tenth Army." See GOPER
Osborn, Fairfield, 28, 172n29
Ota, Minoru, 100
overcrowding, 114
oversight, 138, 148
ownership, 136, 137

Pacific War, 3–6, 11–13, 17, 22, 36, 45, 124
Pacific World, The (Osborn), 28, 172n29
pamphlet, Tenth Army. See "Information on Military Government"
pamphlets, airdropped, 105
participation, Okinawan. See contributions, Okinawan
passes, civilian, 202n40
paternalism, 78, 85, 121, 143, 159
patriotism. See nationalism
Pearl Harbor, Hawaii, 2–3, 53
personal relationships. See fraternization
personnel shortages, 81, 82, 106, 129–31, 134–35, 136, 138, 145, 146, 176n23, 200n18
philanthropy. See kindness
Philippines, 3, 41
physical characteristics, Okinawan, 149
placation squads, 99
"Plan for Post-War Civil Government," 133, 134
plans, US, 11–12, 17–19, 21–31, 33–44, 53–56, 125, 128–29, 131–32, 159–60, 212n35. See also Annex "Able"; cultural analyses; GOPER
points system, demobilization, 129–30
poison, 66, 68, 69, 94
police force, 18, 137, 143, 152
policies, US: civilians, 25, 30, 38, 39, 43–44, 54, 104, 114–18, 171n12, 174n5; combat, 40; justice, 37; medical, 25, 27; military government, 16, 17, 24–27, 29–31, 43, 44, 88–89, 146–47; occupation, 11–12, 133. See also specific services' military government entries
political reorganization, Japan (1870s), 10
political structures, 136, 137
population size, 12, 27, 39, 108, 156; Camp Nodake, 77, 81; doctors, 152; Katchin Peninsula, 111; police, 152; postwar, 127, 217n25; in US-occupied territory, 105, 109
pork, 116–17
Porky's III bar, 1–2
post-battle engagements, 97–98

postal service, 25, 30, 39, 149
preliminary instructions, to Okinawans, 105
preparations, US, 51–58
Price, John D., 130
Princeton University, Civil Affairs training school, 51
prisoner of war camps, 98–100, 198n40, 203n53
prisoners of war, 32, 43, 53, 80, 98–100, 106, 110, 112, 116, 198n40
proclamations of authority, 105
procreation, 46, 70, 187n50
propaganda, Japanese: actions contradictory to, 60, 68, 69, 88, 90–91, 94, 100; Okinawans and, 47–50, 95; of shared nationhood, 15, 45, 47, 48, 50, 64, 66, 70, 91, 100, 180n16; of US brutality, 67, 90, 93, 113
propaganda, US, 29, 30, 40, 80, 189n14
property and cultural objects, 16, 25, 57, 116–17, 119, 120, 127
Prud'homme, Hector C., Jr., 35, 36, 37, 182n22
punishments, 43, 81–84, 193nn73–75
Pyle, Ernie, 58

race: consideration of, 88–89, 156, 159, 161; malleability of, 15, 33, 61, 122, 160, 169n21; Okinawan, 12, 13, 18, 28, 29, 39, 42, 169n21
racial inferiority, 13, 16, 17
racial stereotypes, 13, 67, 83, 90–91, 93, 112
racial superiority, 3, 13, 17, 42, 46, 78, 143–44, 150
racism, 159; Army, 88–89; Buckner, 16, 120, 173n42; Marines, 17, 112, 205n81; Navy, 139, 143–44, 150; US, 12–13, 16, 17, 173n42. See also Asians, US racism toward
raids, 151
rapes, 44, 112–13, 120, 151
rationalizations, 66, 103, 113–15
rations, 25, 27, 38, 74, 75, 82, 84, 87, 105, 111, 142, 216n8
reassessment of conditions, 24, 33, 43, 38, 53, 74–75, 85, 158, 159
rebuilding, 126, 131

reconstruction, 155, 156; American South, 155–56; Okinawan society, 132, 136–37, 145–50, 152, 153, 159
recreation, 121, 152
redistribution, US personnel, 130, 158, 210n25
refugees, Okinawan, 70, 95, 127
registration, 75, 111
rehabilitation, 131, 132, 148, 152, 153
relatability. See commonalities
relationships: Okinawan-Japanese, 9–11, 15, 19, 39, 92, 96–97, 100–1, 172n33; Okinawan-Japanese, US understandings of, 12, 14, 27–29, 41–42, 53, 132, 159–60; US-Japanese, 12–13
religious practices, 29, 38–39
relocation. See resettlement
repatriations, 149, 219n34
reports of US misconduct, destruction of, 151
resentment, 11, 27, 29, 39, 47–48
resettlement, 128–29, 132, 137, 142, 143, 147, 212n35
resident populations, removal of, 133, 134
resistance: Japanese, 7–8, 92, 97, 125–26, 132; Okinawan, 29, 39, 42, 46–47, 58, 63–64, 93–94
resource conservation, 26–27, 38, 116–17. See also shortages; supplies
responses to invasion, US predictions of. See Okinawan responses to invasion, US predictions of
restoration. See reconstruction: Okinawan society
resupply, 25, 77
Richardson, Robert C., 23
rifle fire, 92, 93
rift, Okinawan-Japanese, 85, 96–97
rituals. See traditions
rivalry, interservice. See interservice conflict
romantic relationships. See fraternization
Ryukyu Handbook, 27, 28, 29, 40, 52, 78
Ryukyu Islands, 9–10, 128, 129
Ryukyu Kingdom, 8–10, 11, 29, 49, 169n21

Ryukyuan heritage, 11, 45, 49, 72, 73, 150, 186n48

Sabin, L. S., 133, 134
safety, US personnel. *See* security, US personnel
Saipan, 6, 27, 33, 41–42
salvage effort, 27, 38, 77, 82, 87, 107, 216n8
sanitation, 25, 76, 77, 78–79
sanshin (musical instrument), 49, 180n19
Satsuma clan, Japan, 9–10, 28, 49
scavenging, 67, 82, 142
school curriculum, 11, 47, 48, 149
screenings, 43, 81, 106, 111, 119, 193n75
secrets, US, 29, 38, 39, 43, 54, 110, 157
security, US personnel, 26, 29, 32, 38, 43, 53, 81, 110, 112, 157
security measures, US, 74–75, 81–83, 96, 104, 110–11, 114–15, 118, 120, 193n75
self-government, 135, 137, 145, 146
Sengoku ("Warring States") period, Japan, 9
Sennin-Go, 92
sense of self, Okinawan. *See* Okinawan identity
separations: civilians and US personnel, 54, 81, 106, 143, 193n75; military-age males and other civilians, 111
seppuku (death by disembowelment), 63
Shepherd, Lemuel, Jr., 118, 120, 123, 205n81
Sheridan, Philip, 156, 221n5
Sherman, Forrest P., 23
Shikiya, Koshin, 140, 147, 151
Shimabaru camp, 83, 86, 190n33
Shimabuku camp, 77, 83, 190n33
Shin. *See* Sho Shin
Sho Nei, 9, 10
Sho Shin, 9
Sho Tai, 10, 49
shootings, civilian, 82–83, 92, 109, 114–15, 120
shortages: food, 65, 67, 75, 76, 82, 142, 215n7, 216n8; materials, 77, 81, 82,

106, 176n23; US personnel, 81, 82, 106, 129–31, 134–36, 138, 145, 146, 176n23, 200n18; water, 62, 70, 77. *See also* salvage effort
Shuri Castle, 8, 9, 17, 21, 90
Shuri Line, 90
Silverthorn, M. H., 35
skilled personnel, shortage of, 129–30, 134, 145, 146
Skuse, Paul, 151
Sledge, E. B., 75
slogans, Japanese, 46, 47
Smith, Holland, 6
Smith, Oliver P., 36
Smith, Ralph, 6
Sobe, 105
Solomon Islands, 41
Southeast Asia, 3
Special Order 124-45, 6th Marine Division, 40
spies, 79, 85, 98, 157, 190n33, 193n73
Spruance, Raymond A., 22, 23, 140, 144–46, 158
stereotypes, racial, 13, 67, 83, 90–91, 93, 112
Stilwell, Joseph, 36, 84, 125–26, 128, 129, 141, 206n2
stockades, 81, 82, 84, 86, 111, 114, 119, 193n74
strategies, US, 5, 18, 22–23, 157, 159
student corps, 46, 48, 80; military, 61, 64; nursing, 48, 64, 66, 69, 92, 168n18, 184n22
studies, cultural. *See* cultural analyses
subjugation, 9, 10–11, 19, 27, 30–31, 72
success of mission, 12, 16, 19, 22, 27, 38, 145, 157, 159
Sugar Loaf Hill, 90
suicidal attack corps, 48
suicides: civilians, 65–66, 68, 69, 95, 180n16, 185n29; feudal Japanese (*junshi*), 9; Japanese commanders, 97; ritual (seppuku), 63; Saipan civilians, 33, 41
summer, 97
Sunabe camp, 76–77, 192n59
superiority, racial, 3, 13, 17, 42, 46, 78, 143–44, 150
supplies, 26–27, 32, 35, 97; clothing,

24–25, 27; food, 24, 25, 27, 38, 86, 116–17, 142, 215n7; shelter, 106, 200n16; sleeping cots, 106; tarpaulins, 106, 200n16; tents, 106, 200n16; transportation, 24–25, 27, 106, 200n16. *See also* resource conservation; salvage effort; shortages
surrenders: Japan to United States, 129; Japanese on Okinawa, 68–69, 97, 126, 131; Okinawan combatants, 98, 99
survival: civilians' efforts toward, 71, 82, 91, 95, 96; soldiers' priority, 190n32
suspicion, 33, 57, 79, 85, 112, 174n5

Tai. *See* Sho Tai
Taira, 110
Taiwan, 3
Task Force 58, Fifth Fleet, 6
tea ceremony, 21, 88
Tekketsu Kinnotai (Blood and Iron Corps), 48, 97, 168n18
temperament, Okinawan. *See* attitudes, Okinawan
Tennoist education, 47
"Tentative Military Government Plan for Phase II," 170n4
Tenth Army, 6; commanders, 6, 36, 125, 170n5; GOPER, 37; interservice rivalry, 6–7, 158; military government, 24; propaganda campaign, 30–31, 80; publicity, 36. *See also* Army; Marines Corps; Navy
Tenth Army pamphlet. *See* "Information on Military Government"
Tenth Army Technical Bulletin on Military Government, 40, 52, 56, 180n2, 181n7
terrorists, 161
theatre performers, 149–50
thefts, 67, 68, 69, 71, 116–17, 119, 151
Thousand People Cave, 92
Tobaru camp, 80, 82
Tobaru-Maebaru camp, 190n33
Tokugawa Ieyasu, 9
Tokugawa period, Japan, 9
torture, fear of, 67, 83, 91, 93, 95
Toyotomi Hideyoshi, 9

traditions: Okinawan, 9, 10; Ryukyuan, 49, 50, 180n19. *See also* cultural continuity; customs
training, US, 34, 37, 51–58, 157, 174n5, 182n21
translators. *See* interpreters
transport ships, training aboard, 51–58
transportation, 106, 107, 112
trauma theory, 185n32
travel, civilian, 62, 70, 102–3, 111
trust: Okinawans in Japanese, 66–67, 69, 93; US in civilians, 85–88
Tsubota, Teruto, 105–6, 110, 182n21
Tsumia camp, 192n59
Turner, Richmond Kelly, 22, 23
typhoons, 141–42

uncertainty, over US plans, 53–56
undetonated shells, 62
unequal treatment, between services, 36–37
uniforms, worn by civilians, 79, 87, 189n28
United Nations, 57, 182n27
United States Army School of Military Government, Charlottesville, Virginia, 37, 56
United States Naval Military Government, Okinawa. *See* Navy military government
University Study Center, 141
Unten, 45
urgency, Navy military government's lack of, 132–33
Uruma Shimpo, 147
US military forces: casualties, 126, 129; Japanese and, 13, 67, 83, 90–91, 93, 95, 186n36; Okinawans' views of, 47, 67, 78, 79, 90, 98, 99; ongoing presence on Okinawa, 18, 160; plans for Japan's defeat, 5, 22, 26, 46; postwar attrition, 15, 125, 130, 134–35, 158, 209n23; power, 4–5, 172n21; withdrawal from Okinawa, 145–46. *See also* Army; Marine Corps; Navy
US misconduct, destruction of reports about, 151
Urasoe-Mura defensive line, 7, 8
Ushijima, Mitsuru, 8, 97

Van Schiak, Wynne L., 35, 36, 37
vehicles, military, 106, 107, 112, 141,
    200n16
vigils, 160
villages (*muras*), 63–64, 106–7, 120, 147,
    152
volunteers, US, 130–31
visual cues, for ethnic differentiation,
    78, 79–80, 189n14

Wallace, Fred C., 127–28, 171n10
War Department (US), 129
war slogans, Japanese, 46
War without Mercy (Dower), 13
warnings, against disobedience, 81–82
wars, 155, 160
wartime occupation, Okinawan. *See*
    military government
wartime occupations. *See* occupations
Washington Conference, 3
water: flood, 141; shortages, 62, 70, 77;
    standing, 76, 97
Watkins, James, 148

Wavell, Archibald, 4
weather, shift in, 97
welfare, civilian, 25–26, 38, 102, 107
Winder, Donald, 35, 36, 37, 106, 107,
    120
women: Japanese, 84; Okinawan,
    46, 62, 70, 71, 84, 95, 112–13, 120,
    187n50 (*see also* adults, Okinawan;
    civilians)
World War I, 3
World War II, 2–3, 12–13, 22. *See also*
    Pacific War

xenophobia, 79. *See also* racism

Yahara, Ed, 32
Yahara, Hiromachi, 46, 62
young Okinawans. *See* juveniles,
    Okinawan
youth corps. *See* student corps
youth organizations. *See* student corps

Zahana, 110

Courtney A. Short holds a PhD in History from the University of North Carolina, Chapel Hill and specializes in military, American, and Japanese history, as well as race and identity studies. She previously served as Assistant Professor and Deputy Department Head of History at the United States Air Force Academy in Colorado Springs. She is a contributing author for the edited volume *The Worst Military Leaders in History* and won Honorable Mention for the 2017 Edward M. Coffman First-Manuscript Prize.

WORLD WAR II: THE GLOBAL, HUMAN, AND ETHICAL DIMENSION
G. Kurt Piehler, series editor

Lawrence Cane, David E. Cane, Judy Barrett Litoff, and David C. Smith, eds., *Fighting Fascism in Europe: The World War II Letters of an American Veteran of the Spanish Civil War*

Angelo M. Spinelli and Lewis H. Carlson, *Life behind Barbed Wire: The Secret World War II Photographs of Prisoner of War Angelo M. Spinelli*

Don Whitehead and John B. Romeiser, *"Beachhead Don": Reporting the War from the European Theater, 1942–1945*

Scott H. Bennett, ed., *Army GI, Pacifist CO: The World War II Letters of Frank and Albert Dietrich*

Alexander Jefferson with Lewis H. Carlson, *Red Tail Captured, Red Tail Free: Memoirs of a Tuskegee Airman and POW*

Jonathan G. Utley, *Going to War with Japan, 1937–1941*

Grant K. Goodman, *America's Japan: The First Year, 1945–1946*

Patricia Kollander with John O'Sullivan, *"I Must Be a Part of This War": One Man's Fight against Hitler and Nazism*

Judy Barrett Litoff, *An American Heroine in the French Resistance: The Diary and Memoir of Virginia d'Albert-Lake*

Thomas R. Christofferson and Michael S. Christofferson, *France during World War II: From Defeat to Liberation*

Don Whitehead, *Combat Reporter: Don Whitehead's World War II Diary and Memoirs,* edited by John B. Romeiser

James M. Gavin, *The General and His Daughter: The Wartime Letters of General James M. Gavin to His Daughter Barbara,* edited by Barbara Gavin Fauntleroy et al.

Carol Adele Kelly, ed., *Voices of My Comrades: America's Reserve Officers Remember World War II,* Foreword by Senators Ted Stevens and Daniel K. Inouye

John J. Toffey IV, *Jack Toffey's War: A Son's Memoir*

Lt. General James V. Edmundson, *Letters to Lee: From Pearl Harbor to the War's Final Mission,* edited by Dr. Celia Edmundson

John K. Stutterheim, *The Diary of Prisoner 17326: A Boy's Life in a Japanese Labor Camp,* Foreword by Mark Parillo

G. Kurt Piehler and Sidney Pash, eds., *The United States and the Second World War: New Perspectives on Diplomacy, War, and the Home Front*

Susan E. Wiant, *Between the Bylines: A Father's Legacy*, Foreword by Walter Cronkite

Deborah S. Cornelius, *Hungary in World War II: Caught in the Cauldron*

Gilya Gerda Schmidt, *Süssen Is Now Free of Jews: World War II, The Holocaust, and Rural Judaism*

Emanuel Rota, *A Pact with Vichy: Angelo Tasca from Italian Socialism to French Collaboration*

Panteleymon Anastasakis, *The Church of Greece under Axis Occupation*

Louise DeSalvo, *Chasing Ghosts: A Memoir of a Father, Gone to War*

Alexander Jefferson with Lewis H. Carlson, *Red Tail Captured, Red Tail Free: Memoirs of a Tuskegee Airman and POW, Revised Edition*

Kent Puckett, *War Pictures: Cinema, Violence, and Style in Britain, 1939–1945*

Marisa Escolar, *Allied Encounters: The Gendered Redemption of World War II Italy*

Courtney A. Short, *Uniquely Okinawan: Determining Identity During the U.S. Wartime Occupation*

Printed and bound by CPI Group (UK) Ltd, Croydon, CR0 4YY

09/06/2025

14685660-0002